THE OLYMPIC SPIRITS

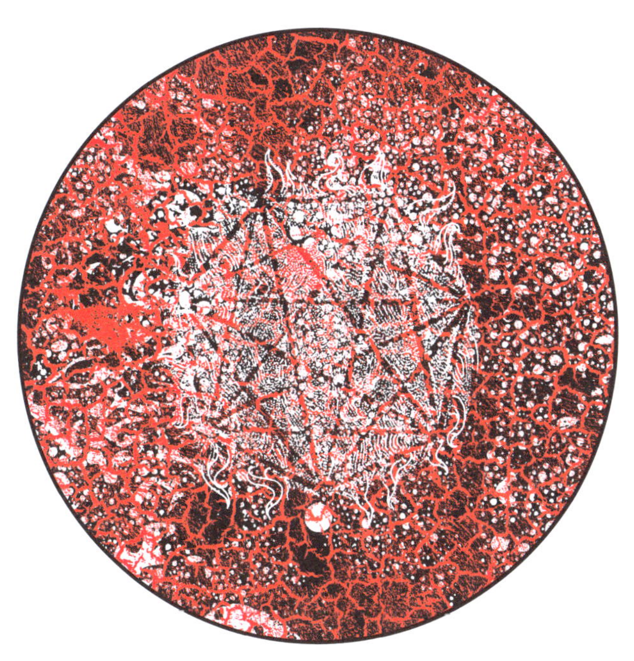

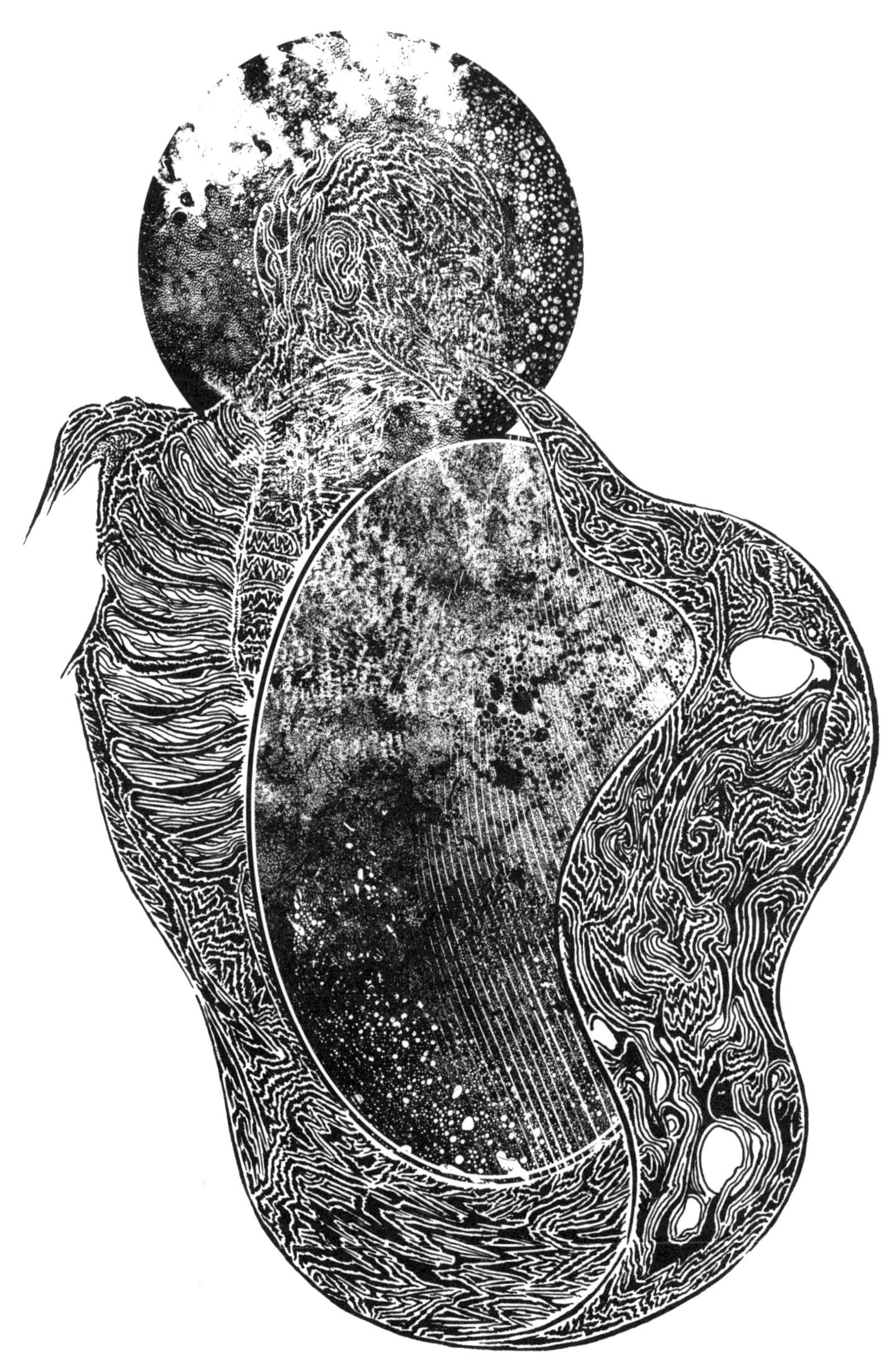

The OLYMPIC SPIRITS

Paracelsus' Practice of the Inner Stars

Frater Acher

with original images by

Joseph Uccello

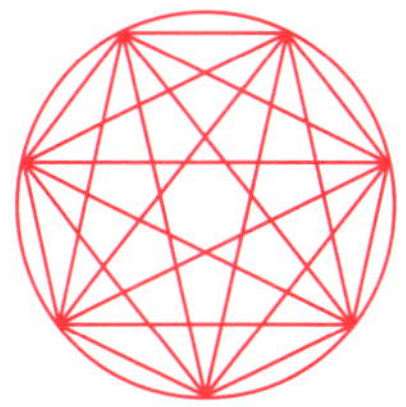

THREE HANDS PRESS
2025

Published by Three Hands Press 2026, San Francisco, CA.

Book Design by Joseph Uccello, Daniel A. Schulke,
and Frater Acher.
Typography, layout, and illustrations by Joseph Uccello.

Copyedited by Frater U∴D∴.

ISBN 978-1945147555 (HARDCOVER)

ISBN 978-1945147548 (SOFTCOVER)

In memoriam

PHILIPPUS AUREOLUS
THEOPHRASTUS BOMBASTUS
VON HOHENHEIM

also known as

Paracelsus

CONTENTS

Book 1

In this book we correct widespread misconceptions about the Olympic Spirits based on authentic source material. We trace the history of the emergence of these spirits from Paracelsus' biography as well as his mago-medical and little-known spiritual works. And we undertake a close examination of the legacy of the Olympic Spirits in the magical literature of the 17th century.

Book 2

Having based ourselves on a genuine understanding of the Olympic Spirits, we move on to develop their authentic practice. For this, we examine historical sources with a fresh view based on first-hand experience of the Olympic Spirits. By the end of Book 2, practitioners will be equipped and empowered to develop their own approach to consciously communing with the Olympic Spirits and making them an integral part of their own magical practice.

Appendices

For the first time in English language, we present four essential sourceworks of the Olympic Spirits' history. For the researcher and practitioner who would like to delve deeper into the genesis and intellectual milieu of the Olympic Spirits, these original documents open new doors of intimate understanding of these complex spiritual beings and their intricacies into an authentically European-animistic cosmos. They are best read in conjunction with the respective chapters in Book 1 where we introduce the authors and their spiritual world in more detail.

Introduction

Alterius non sit, qui suus esse potest.[1]
Rather stray than follow.[2]

THIS BOOK OFFERS access to a personal experience of the Olympic Spirits on a biographical, historical and practical level. The biographical level is oriented towards the person—and often larger-than-life personality—of Paracelsus i.e., Theophrastus Bombastus of Hohenheim (1493–1541) as the creator of the term Olympic Spirits and the radical new magical concept behind it.

The historical level refers to the tortuous path the Olympic Spirits have travelled in books and manuscripts over the last five centuries—and examines how they have constantly evolved and transformed into new forms and practices. The third and final level relates to your own lived experience of your Olympic Spirits—and all those daemons who wait beyond them—and offers practical guidance for your own magical work.

As we will see, neither of these levels stand well alone, but in coming together they form a powerful trinity, an equilibrium of understanding which might just give rise to the most meaningful of your magical work yet to come.

Certainly it is from such holistic understanding of the spirits which fill the human form that we are invited not only to live an *examined* life but also a *happy* one.

In the sequence of my own life, this book appeared after *Holy Daimon* (2018), *Black Abbot·White Magic* (2021), *Holy Heretics* (2022) and *Ingenium* (2022). I am looking back at these years as a time of intense focus and concentration. My life, my work and writing all revolved around the spheres of the Olympic Spirits in whose silent centre weaves our holy daimon. It is a personal joy for me to continue this cycle with the present work. *To make the serpent bite its tail*, as I like to put it, and with this book to lay out a path that can teach how

1 *Let them not be another's* [*servant*] *who can be their own* [*master*], Paracelsus.

2 Austin Osman Spare.

the work of our *daimon* is interwoven with the work of these wonderful celestial *daemones*.

I invite you to read this book in a decidedly *Paracelsian spirit*. In the initial two chapters we will be exploring the many things that this actually can mean. In the second part of the book, the practical sections, I will then encourage you to make your own choices. There is only one thing still more important than learning to read Paracelsus as the most important representative of a lived, Western Animism—and that is learning to live his spirit again. This book offers a path to reclaiming this way as your own.

At its heart, what a Paracelsian spirit means to me personally is to adopt a spirit of *Promethean freedom* as well as of *Pelagian accountability* in how I lead my life and practice magic. It means to insert the spark of my mind back into the living ecosystem of non-human persons who come together to form the world just as much as they form myself. It means not to accept any authority—not even that of the things I believe to be true—and instead to step out into life as a book that writes itself anew each day.

My hope is that this book will help to topple down the empty idols of the Olympic Spirits as they are known today in much of modern magic. In its place I am inviting us to build our own temple, from bricks of lived first-hand experience with the Olympic Spirits…As we will see, whoever succeeds in this work, has not accomplished the great work, but arrived at the possibly best position to begin it.

There are a lot of preachers here, but I don't see no saints.[3]

For he who is a *nectromanticus*, or *magus*, or *nigromanticus cœlestis*—he is a saint.[4]

LVX,

Frater Acher

Munich, November 2022

3 Petrol Girls, lyrics from song: *Preachers*, from album: *Baby*, June 2022.

4 Paracelsus, in: Sudhoff (ed.) 1929, Vol. XII, p. 405. Throughout the book, I am responsible for all translations from the original source languages into English, unless otherwise noted. In particular, the quotations from Paracelsus have been carefully modernized to facilitate access and understanding.

BOOK
1

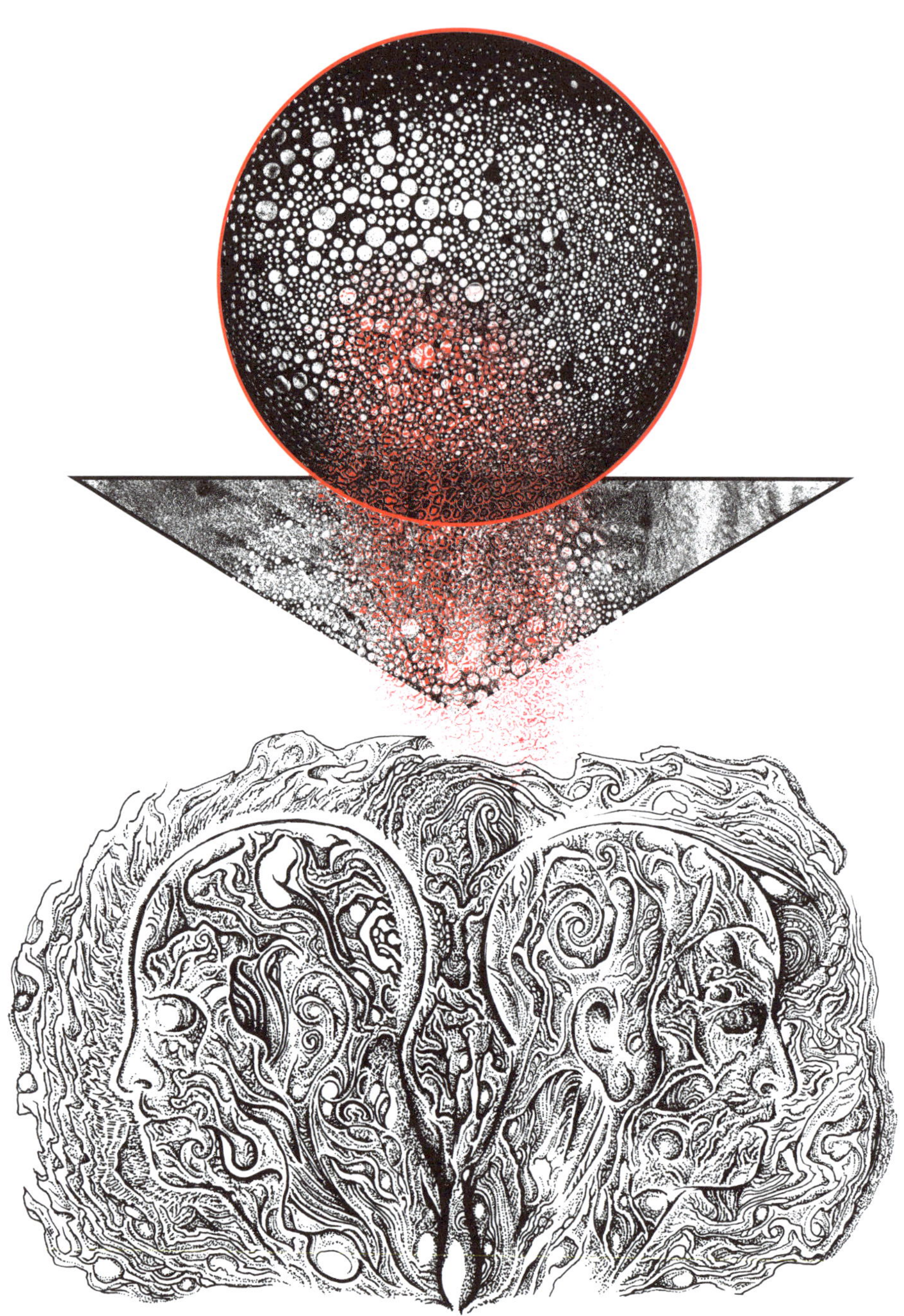

BOOK 1

CHAPTER I

PARACELSUS AND TRITHEMIUS

I

The Curtain Rises

ONCE UPON A TIME, in the now dark tail of the years 1510 to 1516, a young, short, half-bald hermaphrodite visited a man in his abbey St. Jakob at Würzburg whom they called the *Black Abbot*. There, the young man sat, almost still a boy in body, and yet the piercing bright light of a star pushing over the horizon line of his mind, completely absorbed in the process of *becoming*. Silently, he looked at the old man whom others had called "pansophiae splendor magus"[1] the mage shining with the light of pansophy, and drank from his words.

These were printed words on old manuscripts, revealed by Johann Trithemius (1462–1516) to the boy in the vernacular German, translated from Latin hands and Greek letters. Cryptic Greek authors again and again, for such was one of the many obsessions of the old man. But the boy did not read Greek, and so they sat among the books, and the old man told the hermaphrodite about the meandering pathways of forbidden knowledge running through time and marked by ink and paper.

And as he listened, the boy realised that this was not just a story about books, but about the Black Abbot himself, whose life had be-

1 Goldammer, 1955, p. 39.

come intricately intertwined with the relentless, wild hunt of forbidden knowledge—all of which he had sworn to find, grab and inhale.

Five hundred years have passed since these nights in the abbey of Würzburg. We still wonder what the hermaphrodite might have learned from the Black Abbot's life and the Black Abbot's books. This grizzled man, from whose heavy centre a pair of nimble eyes ceaselessly sought new aims, who seemed at once restless and broken. Broken in part by the storms of the world he had endured, and in part by his own vain hand.[2]

We dream back to these nights and wonder: What kind of lessons were these, that changed bodies here from hand to eye and mouth to ear? Of course, as is usually the case with dreams, our picture is blurred. What we do know for sure is this: soon after this encounter, the Black Abbot died and drowned in the shadows of history. Forgotten he was not by accident, but by design. His copious forgeries and fantasies had eroded the trust in his voice, nobody wanted to step onto the stones he had laid out to mark the narrow trail...A trickster, as the Black Abbot had been his entire life, was not entrusted with wisdom. Or so the people believed.[3]

The young man, the half-bald hermaphrodite, however, was about to embark on a journey the likes of which all of Europe had not seen before. His sharp, polemical voice—resounding in lecture halls, pubs,

2 *Forgery, of course, is partly about Schadenfreude: perhaps, then, Trithemius deserves his place in the gallery of once-great scholars whose worlds were turned upside down by their own failings and the zeal of their enemies. Nevertheless, it seems possible that Trithemius saw his creative efforts in a very different light. Nikolaus Staubach has offered a very suggestive reading of the episode, which tries to explain it using actors' categories. He points out that Trithemius took a passionate interest in the sort of knowledge that holy men and women obtained by revelation. Trithemius himself began his career with a vision about knowledge. [...] Trithemius himself suggests that this interpretation may be valid. He made clear that his two fields of activity—magic and scholarship—were linked. One kind of magic that Trithemius practiced and recommended supports the notion that his revelations came to him, in his view, from a supernatural source. He emphasized repeatedly that certain men could perform miracles, if they led a sufficiently austere and rigorous life and dedicated themselves intensively enough to contemplation—and, he admitted, so long as a good spirit aided them, since no human could attain knowledge except through the senses or through the help of a supernatural being.* Grafton, 2011, pp. 75–76.

3 Lehmann 1961, p. 4.

and crossroads all across the Old World—would change the face of medicine, of chemistry, and also of the forbidden arts forever. This now is the story of one such fingerprint this young boy, *Philippus Aureolus Theophrastus Bombastus von Hohenheim* (1493–1541), better known as *Paracelsus*, left behind for us. To begin this story, we have to begin to perceive this fingerprint, which, like all fingerprints, likes to go unnoticed, yet hides in plain sight, if only one knows how to look.

II

Enter the Black Abbott

AND SO WE return to St. Jakob in Würzburg, during the long nights when Paracelsus and Johannes Trithemius sat together and spoke. And we reconstruct some pieces of the puzzle that was likely to have come together and taken shape in the mind of Paracelsus at the time...

> *Quicquidem in mundo scibile est, scire semper cupiebam. Whatever in the world is knowable, I always desired to know.*[4]

> *Trithemius von Sponheim, who united in himself all the occult knowledge of his time, exerted a great influence as a teacher on the luminaries of the coming generation, even if he himself—apart from his steganography—was not active in the field of secret science in any other way than in the ecclesiastical polemic sense out of consideration for his position.*[5]

> *One has gone too far towards him, sometimes in terms of credulity, sometimes in doubt. Those who are willing and able will recognise from the case of Trithemius that the historian,*

4 Johannes Trithemius, *Nepiachus*, quoted after: Brann 1999, p. 93.
5 Kiesewetter 1977, p. 3.

> *in his striving for the actual historical truth, must never forget to respect the frequently improbable, but even then not invariably false lore.*[6]

Trithemius had erected his very own "Druid's harbourage,"[7] first in Sponheim, and later on, during the time of the visit(s) of Paracelsus in Würzburg. We also know he had been obsessed not only with knowing "whatever in the world is knowable", but, more specifically, with the Greek authors.

Let's read two reports from other visitors to Sponheim. The first one is retold by Klaus Arnold in his masterful biography from 1971. The second stems directly from a letter by the Dutch humanist Matheus Herbenus Traiectensis (1451–1538) to one Jodocus Beyselius from August 1495.

> *The enthusiasm of his friends for the Graecophile abbot sometimes took on strange forms: on a visit to Sponheim, Vigilius reports to Celtis that the abbot is Greek, the monks are Greek and so are the dogs, the stones and bushes are also Greek; the whole monastery seemed to be in the middle of Ionian country.*[8]

> *Where (in the monastery) walking around is allowed (which usually happens after the first friends meet and after the meal), the abbot shows me around and takes me to places in his admirable library where I look at a large number of Hebrew as well as Greek books. For the quantity of Latin [books] of every kind of art, science and ability was immense. I am therefore full of admiration for the care that a single man has taken in acquiring and setting up so many different documents, and am decidedly amazed, for I would not have believed that there could be such a quantity of foreign books in the whole of Germany. For I have found there books in five languages, which differ widely in style and character, in an-*

6 Lehmann 1910, p. 219.

7 *Druidenherberge*, Arnold 2003, p. 21.

8 Arnold 1971, p. 79.

cient codices, which Trithemius' attentive collecting zeal did not gather without much perspiration.

In this way, then, most learned Jodocus, I have found the Spanheim library crammed; for both itself and the walls of the entire abbot's residence, which is extensive, and the vaulted ceilings are, as I have seen, adorned with Greek, Hebrew and Latin verses and characters in quite the most elaborate manner. Therefore I ponder for myself whether there is a Hebrew or Greek Academy in our Germany. That is the monastery of Spanheim, where you can draw more learning from the walls than from the dusty libraries of many, empty of books. For what Germany can have in antiquity and learning in the form of books, the monastery of Spanheim possesses through the care of its abbot Trithemius. I stayed with our abbot for eleven days.[9]

Herbenus' letter makes it unmistakably clear: What the visitors found during their stay with the Black Abbot was not just a library, but an immersive experience. Entering Sponheim's chambers, one was immersed in a thoroughly sacred space dedicated to an ancient world of learning and revelation, the blending of past and present, and the co-creation of humans and angels. A world that was both spiritually genuine, and yet highly artificial and constructed in a mundane sense.

Just as Albertus Magnus in his *Speculum Astronomiae* had tried to build a literary bulwark against the destructive forces of his time—especially those within the Catholic Church—so Trithemius had built his own physical bulwarks first in Sponheim and later in St. Jakob in Würzburg. These were to withstand the changing times in the same sense that they were to provide refuge for the knowledge, voices, and secrets of the philosophers, historians, and magicians who had walked the narrow trail of mystical ascent and heresy over the last 1500 years.

At the beginning of the 16th century, the floodgate that allowed Arabic literary sources to stream into Western cur-

9 Lehmann 1961, pp. 23–24.

> *rents of learned magic already stood open wide and far.*[10] *For over two hundred years flowers of Greek, Syrian and Arabic knowledge had sprung up again in the West, often drawing their lifeforce from Egyptian and other ancient roots. In this continued process, Trithemius with his notorious libraries—the original larger one in Sponheim, and the second, still significant one in Würzburg—acted as a knowledge hub, aloof from academic oversight, which fed rivulets of Arabic, Greek and Syrian occult knowledge into the scholarly culture of Europe.*[11]

No complete record of Trithemius' libraries has come down to us. And even if that had been the case, the titles relevant for our exploration most likely would not have been listed in plain sight, given Trithemius' need to continuously disguise his alchemical and magical research as well as his practical work with angels.[12]

However, the paleographer and philologist Paul Lehmann (1884–1964) spent over fifty years tracing the now lost and scattered volumes that once made up Trithemius' treasures. While nowhere near to a complete index, his work from 1961 renders a thorough impression of the scope and breadth of the material collected by the Black Abbot. Next to a massive corpus of Medieval historic and ecclesiastical writings, Trithemius had collected philosophical, theological and scientific works by Aristotle (4th century BCE), Theon of Smyrna (1st century CE), Origen (3rd century CE), Tertullian (3rd century CE), John

10 These texts were brought to Europe as a result of the increased contact with Muslim Spain and Byzantium and were translated into Latin during the twelfth and thirteenth centuries. They contributed to European natural and occult philosophers a body of works containing philosophical notions of astral generation and causation that validateastrology and astral magic in non-supernatural terms, or without "Diabolicall Principles" as Lilly would say, thus contributing to the flourishing of European occult philosophy." Saif, Liana, *The Arabic Influences on Early Modern Occult Philosophy*, London: Palgrave Macmillian, 2015, p. 3. For its critical influence from the 13th century onwards Albertus Magnus's *Speculum Astronomiae* has to be mentioned, as well as Moritz Steinschneider's groundbreaking essays from the late 19th century (see Bibliography).

11 Lehmann, 1961, p. 23.

12 For a masterful summary and reading of the source material, see Anthony Grafton, *Worlds Made by Words—Scholarship and Community in the Modern West* (2011), pp. 56–78.

Chrysostom (4th century CE), as well as chronicles by Hegesippus (2nd century CE), Eusebius of Caesarea (4th century CE), Effrem Syri (4th century CE), Cassiodorus (6th century CE)—to name but a few.

Unfortunately, despite Lehmann's relentless effort, we know nothing about the historically recorded collection of "Chaldean, Arabic, Indian, Ruthenian, Tartar, Gallic and Bohemian"[13] books that would be of particular interest to us. Only one explicitly magical tome can still be traced down which unites an eclectic mix of Hebrew, Latin and German fragments on magical incantations and love spells, geomancy, technical tools for warfare, and astrologica—"a true picture of German unculture at the end of the 15th century", as the eminent scholar on Medieval grimoire history, Moritz Steinschneider (1816–1907) commented.[14]

Overall, Lehmann concludes, despite the slightly exaggerated praise his library garnered by some of Trithemius' friends, his collection did not necessarily stand out due to its quantity of books and manuscripts, but certainly due to their rarity, exquisiteness, and versatility.[15]

We can now see why Johann Trithemius has rightly been called "pansophiae splendor magus." And we shall move on to examine, why the young man who came to visit him in the early 1500s might have addressed him *quasi noster Pater Trithemius* ("as our father Trithemius") in a letter to a friend more than two decades later.[16]

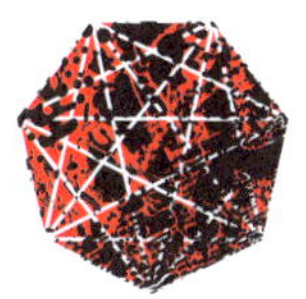

13 Lehmann, 1961, p. 18.

14 *In hebräischer, lateinischer, deutscher Sprache Beschwörungen, Geomantisches, Kriegstechnisches, Astrologica, Liebeszauber u.a., „ein wahres Bild deutscher Unkultur im Ende des 15. Jahrhunderts" (M. Steinschneider).* Lehmann, 1910, p. 212; also see: Lehmann, 1961, p. 33. Today, the volume is kept in the Bavarian National Library under the signature BSB Cod.hebr. 235 where it has been made available in digital form.

15 Lehmann, 1961, p. 20.

16 Sudhoff, 2000 (1894), p. 454.

III

Paracelsus Arrives

In the 16th century, his father sent him to the University of Basel. However, it is well established that Paracelsus, to whom the wisdom of the physicians of that time was an abomination from an early age, did not actually undertake any regular academic studies, which by the scholars of the four past centuries was very badly held against him, who would often pave his own way. Later, Paracelsus came to [...] Johann Trithemius von Sponheim, who probably mainly developed the occult disposition of the highly intelligent pupil. His love of the secret sciences, which had blossomed to great heights, then led him to the laboratory of the rich Sigismund Fugger at Schwatz in Tyrol, who, like Trithemius, was a famous alchemist and initiated his pupil into many secrets of the art of chemical analysis.[17]

WE KNOW VERY little about Paracelsus' youth, and—as we shall see—that is more likely to be by his own design than by accident. However, when Paracelsus died, he did so surrounded by chests and drawers full of manuscripts in his own hand. Most of his works were never published during his lifetime. Less than fifty years later, through the relentless effort by Johannes Huser (ca. 1545–1600/1601) a first "collected works" edition came into print. Despite the painstaking attention Huser paid to distinguish authentic from pseudo-Paracelsian manuscripts at the time, the results remained ambivalent.

17 Carl Kiesewetter, *Geschichte des Neueren Okkultismus*, New York: Georg Olms Verlag, 1977 (Leipzig, 1891).

REPORTED TRAVEL DESTINATIONS OF PARACELSUS

FROM APPROXIMATELY 1507 TO 1515

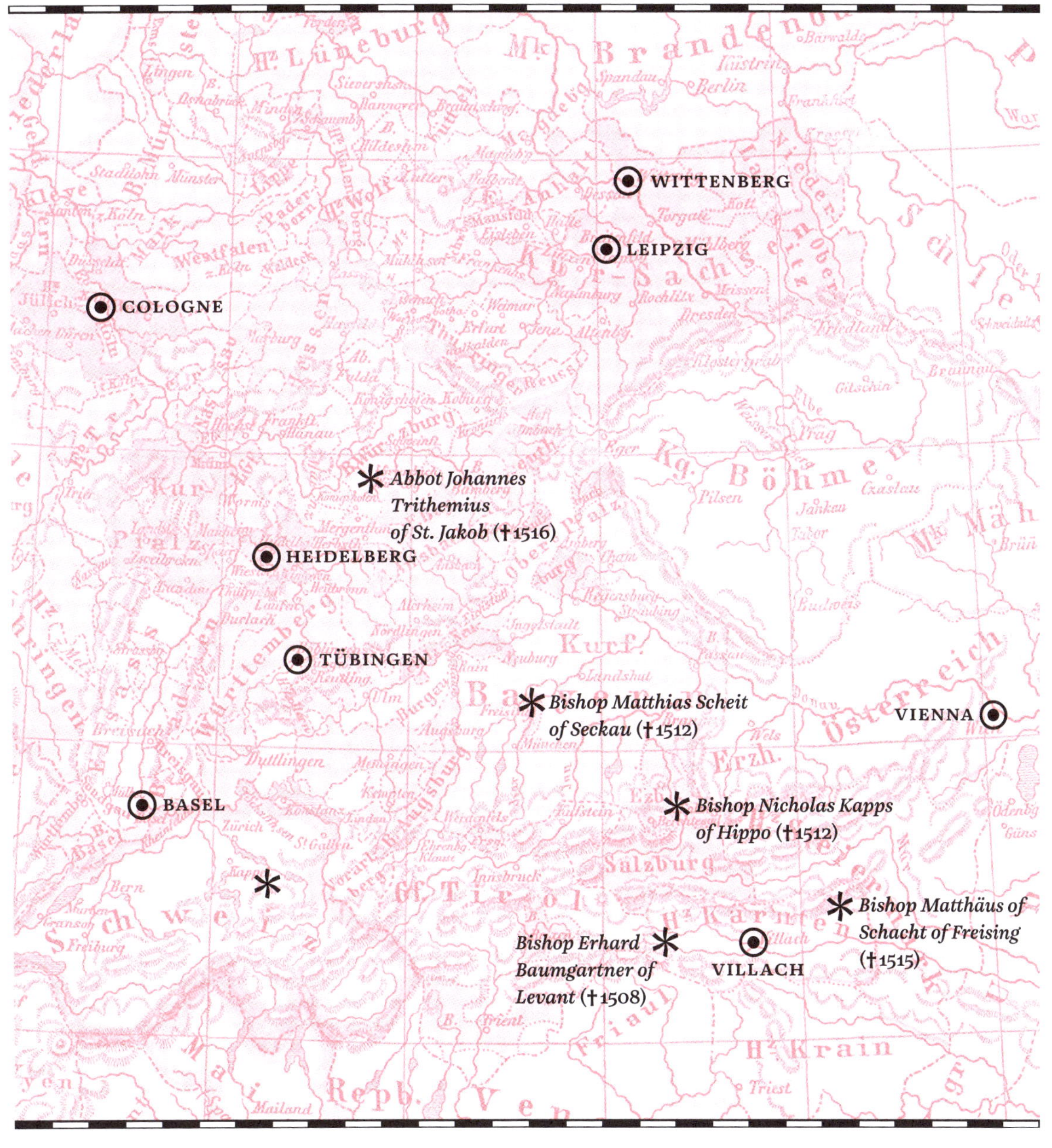

Thus, later Paracelsus scholars—preeminent amongst them Friedrich Mook (1844–1880), Karl Sudhoff (1853–1938), Will Erich Peuckert (1895–1969), and Kurt Goldammer (1916–1997)—continued to debate and often disagree on the alleged authenticity of many foundational Paracelsian texts.[18]

The current state of knowledge is further limited by the fact that most of this research has remained directed towards Paracelsus' medical and philosophical works.

In particular, Karl Sudhoff held a distinct anti-magical attitude towards all matters Paracelsian which strongly influenced his assessment of the genuineness of the earlier manuscripts and prints.[19] Sudhoff originally had planned to publish the theological writings in parallel to his new edition of Paracelsus' natural, philosophical and medical writings. However, that endeavour was stalled and only completed by Goldammer who carefully edited and published the spiritual, religious and socio-political texts of Paracelsus in seven large volumes between 1969 and 1971. Despite their significant volume, even these tomes only contain abbreviated versions (Kurzfassungen) of many of the original manuscripts, as Goldammer remarks in the sub-header of the books. Against this background, it does not seem surprising that the complex question of what influences shaped the mind and world of the young Paracelsus has remained controversial.

Will-Erich Peuckert, both in his *Pansophie* of 1935 and in his biography *Paracelsus*, published in 1941, avoids any direct statement regarding a possible pupil-teacher relationship with Trithemius. Instead, he emphasises that because of Paracelsus' young age, it would have been the years 1511 to 1516 when he might have been in contact with Trithemius. He also concludes that Paracelsus must have had

18 Many echoes of their debates as well as gems of their research we will encounter in the following two chapters.

19 See his Preamble to the 14th Volume of the Collected Works, in which appendix he grouped works that according to him were "Spuria Paracelsi". How he arrived at such a definitive assessment, Sudhoff did not share. The two main criteria seemed to have been that the original manuscripts by Paracelsus had been lost by the time these pieces were published in the second half of the 16th century (XII), and, secondly, that they treated topics which he pejoratively summarised as "occult stuff" (XXIX). Sudhoff's rigid subjectivity is summed up by his closing comment: *So the presumption remains. More must be left to future research. It will hardly be able to shake my point of view.* (XXXIII) See: Sudhoff, Vol. XIV, 1933, I–XXXIII.

access to Agrippa's *De Occulta Philosophia* in manuscript form, as Paracelsus refers to it long before the book appeared in print. The scenario that Paracelsus read Agrippa's original manuscript, which remained among Trithemius' possession until his death, therefore does not seem unlikely to Peuckert.[20]

The most detailed and objective assessment of the Paracelsus-Trithemius question was bequeathed to us by Goldammer in 1954. His essay *The Spiritual Teachers of Theophrastus Paracelsus*[21] spans more than thirty pages. It presents a carefully researched perspective on each one of the five theological teachers who were confirmed by Paracelsus himself in the second book of his *Great Miracle-Medicine (Grosse Wunderarznei)* of 1536.

> *[...] from childhood onwards I have pursued this work and learned from good teachers who were most profoundly grounded in the adepta philosophia and powerfully investigated the arts. First I was taught by Wilhelm von Hohenheim, my father, who never left me, and then by a large number, which cannot be named entirely, through many writings of the ancients and the moderns, by those who came here and made great efforts, as there were the bishop Scheit of Settgach, the bishop Erhart and his ancestors of the Lavanttal, the bishop Nicolaus of Hippo, the bishop Mattheus Schacht suffraganus Phreisingen and many abbots, like the one of Spanheim and the like more, and many among the other doctors and the like.*
>
> *I have also had great experience over a long period of time through many alchemists who have searched in such arts, namely through the noble and firm Sigmund Fugger of Schwaz together with a number of his laboratory assistants. Therefore, no one should be surprised that such corrections are now before their eyes [...]. Now if experience is available and the meaning and reason of the four philosophies together with the volcanic art and the physical, whether it would*

20 Peuckert (1941), p. 22; and Peuckert, 1956 (1935), pp. 208–209. For the possession of Agrippa's original manuscript, titled '*De magia*', with Trithemius see: Arnold, Klaus, Fuchs, Franz (eds.), *Johannes Trithemius (1462–1516)*, Würzburg: Königshausen & Neumann, 2019, p. 287.

21 Goldammer, 1954, pp. 7–41.

> *not be fair to make such corrections and to separate what is false and erroneous from what is good. At the same time, it is also proper to continue to search and to improve things and to change them.*[22]

With relieving freshness, Goldammer poses the central question "what would actually speak against the teacher Trithemius and the corresponding interpretation of the passage?" And he answers it himself: One "finds nothing."[23] Instead, he emphasizes the bias on Sudhoff's part in attempting to find an alternative interpretation. For the latter followed his own agenda, attempting to purify Paracelsus' apprenticeship years from the stain left by the association with the nefarious Black Abbot, in whom Sudhoff saw nothing but a "word-maker," a liar and forger of history.[24]

Goldammer continues to examine critical works of Trithemius and their possible influence on the young Paracelsus. In step with the other ecclesiastical dignitaries mentioned by Paracelsus, we begin to see Trithemius as a facilitator of Late Medieval theology, of Renaissance spirituality, of humanism and mysticism as well as romanticised historicism. Trithemius the polymath is likely to have contributed significantly to Paracelsus' own "comprehensive knowledge and his amazing expertise in all questions that moved the leading minds of the time."[25]

Of course, we cannot expect to find evidence on the side of Trithemius for his encounter(s) with Paracelsus. The latter would have been too young for this to be a meeting of equals. Correspondingly, he would have been too young for this to be a meeting of master and master student, as it took place with Agrippa of Nettesheim, who attracted Trithemius' hopes to have found the person who would carry on his torch.

Paracelsus himself has given us ample evidence. A single lead for those willing to follow the trail. As Goldammer concluded, there is sufficient indirect evidence to consider a personal relationship "between Paracelsus and Johann Trithemius as proven and secured."[26]

22 Sudhoff 1928, Vol. x, pp. 354–355.
23 Goldammer, 1955, p. 36.
24 Ibid., 36.
25 Ibid., 40.
26 Ibid, 49.

What remains a mystery is the specific nature of this personal acquaintance.

The Secret Conversation

LET'S RETURN TO the study of St. Jakob once more. The vaulted ceiling covered with Greek and Latin verses, the walls hidden behind leather-bound books, the night falling behind low windows. This is the place where we meet the Black Abbot and Paracelsus again. One of them tired of vainly trying to keep his life both in the up-draught of magic and worldly power. The other bright awake, barely no longer a child but not yet a grown-up man. So they sit surrounded by the end of one life, and the beginning of another. While united in place, they are lonely together. For all his life the old man felt alive only in the silence of his writings, and the young man in the embrace of open nature.

Out of respect for age and position, we have to imagine their gathering as a monologue. Paracelsus explicitly counts the Abbot of Sponheim amongst his teachers of *adepta philosophia*, which, in his idiosyncratic language steeped with vernacular and Latin neologisms, were the *occult arts*. It does not take a leap of imagination to consider that this was where Paracelsus first heard of the origin of alchemy:

OF a cosmos generated by the three living principles of mercury, sulphur and magnesia (i.e., salt) who set about their never-ending work in the four elements, generating the entire world as we encounter it.[27]

OF the premise that adeptic knowledge cannot be gained from books, but from an inner source of knowledge instead. Maybe Trithemius alluded to the *silver body*, the *mushaf as-suwar*, the occult teaching vessel that must be generated inside man. In his long monologue he might have quoted from memory: "Know that you can neither understand nor know the meaning of what the sages wrote in their books, except with the help of the vessel."[28]

AND Paracelsus might have heard of the idea of the transformation of metals being both an outer and an inner process. A spirit had to be

27 Zosimos 2016, pp. 84–5.
28 Ibid. 45, also see p. 223.

> acquired in the alchemist, through the purging forces of fire and light. Only then could the transformation of metals succeed, which was equally the transformation of the soul of the *adepti philosophiae*.[29]

Retracing the steps Paracelsus took in his youth does not at all diminish the extraordinary accomplishments this man achieved, despite all odds and against the publicly expressed will of academia across Europe. yet equally, we have to acknowledge that Paracelsus' *great work* lies in bringing this knowledge and work to brimming life again in the 16th century—in his very own and genuine form of expression. It does not lie, however, in inventing it from scratch. As he said himself, his work was one of correction, of advancement and of weaving arcane knowledge back into lived experience. He did this by releasing an iconoclastic storm against the institutions of learning of his time, and by keeping himself anchored, throughout his life, in the community of common people, in remote nature, and in the companionship of spirits. While Paracelsus wasn't yet the man he would eventually become when he encountered the Black Abbot, important seeds might have been sown during these nights. Ironically, some of these seeds indeed might have come from the occult manuscripts and books Trithemius gave him access to. Others, however, and possibly more important ones, would have come from the learnings Paracelsus took from the life of the Black Abbot himself.

In many ways, Paracelsus' biography and books represent an exact antithesis of Trithemius'. It is in this sense, first and foremost, that we suggest considering Paracelsus a *student* of the Black Abbot; as in *a subject that one studies*, so the young man might have studied Trithemius' life decisions and the price the latter paid for these.

Instead of learning to become *alike to him*, Paracelsus seems to

29 *And the metal bodies are also like that: They obtain a spirit when they are burnt over a gentle fire and are turned into spiritual ashes. In fact, they obtained that spirit from the fire and the air in the same way as human beings inhale the spirit from the air. Just as the bodies are burnt in the fire and the air, those bodies also obtain the spirits from the fire. As the created beings change and transform from one nature to another nature, this one dies and the other one lives. In the same way, the copper is burnt by the sulphur and changes from one nature to another, until God completes for you what you are seeking.* Zosimos, 2016.

have taken inspiration to follow his own genuine road of becoming, and to avoid the path the old man had taken.

Here are a few examples of the lessons Paracelsus might have taken from Trithemius' biography:[30]

NEVER to be constrained by institutions and orthodoxy. Trithemius' position in the Catholic Church was a critical enabler in establishing his life's work. yet, at the same time it was a cage from within which he had to operate and which constantly forced him to disguise and distort his alchemo-magical interest.

NEVER to pander to those in power. Trithemius had a weakness for being recognised and sought out by the powerful and mighty. His many historical forgeries can be interpreted equally as results of his mystical worldview, his biting sense of humour and as white lies for the mess his pandering to those in power had got him into. Trithemius liked to gamble high, and he mostly lost high as well.

NEVER to betray one's own values, whatever the consequence. Trithemius' most ghastly work, the *Antipalus maleficiorum* (1508), can be read as an attempt to ward off the suspicion of heresy and black magic into which he himself had fallen as a result of the Steganographia affair. Nothing could have more blatantly betrayed Trithemius' secret writings under the guise of the invented persona of Pelagius of Majorca than the opportunistic authorship of such a hate-spreading incendiary tome. Both Agrippa of Nettesheim and Paracelsus seem to have clearly recognised this major flaw in the Black Abbot's biography, and to have drawn their own conclusions from it.

NEVER to set one's heart on material possessions. Whether Trithemius tried to appeal to the mighty to gain the necessary means for his libraries, or whether the latter was an instrument to gain their personal attention, will always remain a mystery. Be that as it may, the attachment he held to the huge operation that the Abbey of Sponheim had become under his leadership must have been immediately obvious to Paracelsus. Similarly, the traumatic impact upon the man's life when he lost all of it in 1505.

30 For further detail on Trithemius' biography as well as magical program and work, see my book *Black Abbot · White Magic: Johannes Trithemius and the Angelic Mind* (Scarlet Imprint, 2021).

NEVER to pursue adepti philosophiae among books, but from nature and experience alone. Trithemius' lifelong magical program had been to scrutinise and purge the demonic magic of his ancestors from its stained telluric influences, and to reconstruct it as a pathway towards becoming alike to the angelic mind. The uncompromising pursuit of this program had led him into a labyrinth of books from which he never escaped again, with little impact in the material world of his own time.

NEVER to leave a bottle of wine unfinished in the hope of a better tomorrow. Trithemius' way of working was hasty, sloppy, downright fiery. In the end, it burned not only himself, but also the path he wanted to leave behind for others. His moral transgressions—whether in the form of literary forgeries or in the inflammatory writings of the witch craze—made his image a dark and degenerate one in the eyes of posterity. For what all this burning and driving forward, this delusion of truth, purity and eternity, Paracelsus might have wondered? A night out in the pub and the gutters makes an incredibly effective bridle for the intellectual mind which is only too happy to run wild with geniuses.

For anybody who read biographies of both Trithemius and Paracelsus, these brief enumerations portray a curious picture indeed: two sides of a coin, two snakes curling around a staff, two pathways into lives filled with magic which yet could not have been more different from each other. By rendering the antithesis of Trithemius' life—yet maintaining his intellectual brilliance, his fiery temper and the peripheral storms of the 16th century—we arrive at a most accurate outline of the man Paracelsus was destined to become.

As Isaac Newton famously said, we see further "by standing on the shoulders of giants." In the same manner, Paracelsus can be presumed to have stood on the shoulders of Trithemius. The latter's failings might have been the former's lessons. It is precisely not a lineage in the sense of an unbroken continuation that we find between these two men, but quite the opposite: the forces that eventually broke the older man were conquered with paradoxical wisdom by the younger.

Maybe Paracelsus wrote the above-mentioned letter, printed in 1606 and allegedly penned in 1532, or maybe he didn't. Either way we now might know how to read the term "quasi noster Pater, Trithemius" (as our Father, Trithemius). It marks the relationship of a spiritual student and a teacher, who both saw magic as Promethean fire—and yet whose pathways into and expressions of it could not have been more different.

Finally, we now also might know how to understand Paracelsus' rare autobiographical reflections a few years before his death (1537/1538), when he says:

> *Not that it is enough to attack me in several articles, but to claim that I am a strange head with a last, that is, confused answer, that I do not meet everyone according to their liking, that I do not answer everyone according to their intention in a humble way; that is what they regard and consider to be a great vice in me.*
>
> *But I myself esteem it a great virtue and would not have it be otherwise than it is. I like my way only too well. But in order that I may answer for how my strange wisdom is to be understood, notice therefore. By nature I am not subtly spun. Nor is it my country's way to gain anything by spinning silk. Nor are we brought up on figs, nor on mead, nor on wheat bread, but on cheese, milk and oat bread: all these do not make subtle journeymen. In addition, one is marked all one's life by what one received in youth [...]*[31]

AND HE HAD IN HIS RIGHT HAND SEVEN STARS: AND OUT OF HIS MOUTH WENT A SHARP TWO-EDGED SWORD: AND HIS COUNTENANCE WAS AS THE SUN SHINETH IN HIS STRENGTH.

REVELATION 1:16

31 Sudhoff Vol. XI, 1928, pp. 151–152.

AZOTH
THESE THINGS ARE DONE BY THE OLYMPIC SPIRIT, WHICH...
TEARS OFF THE SHA- DOW FROM ALL THE WORKS OF THE BODY
ALTERIUS NON SIT QUI SUUS ESSE POTEST · LET HIM NOT BELONG TO ANOTHER WHO IS ABLE TO POSSESS HIMSELF ·
§

BOOK 1

CHAPTER II

PARACELSUS' SPIRITUALITY

I

Paracelsus' Disappearance

FROM EARLY 1532 to mid 1533 we lose all trace of Paracelsus. For more than a year the man simply disappears.

Paracelsus is famous for having spent most of his life as an itinerant nomad. By the 1520s, wherever he arrives, furore is expected, and Paracelsus does not like to disappoint. Thus, we are quite well informed about his travels as an adult. Not only from his own writings, from his dedications to the few rulers who showed him goodwill, and from notes in his manuscripts as to which nobleman he had healed where and when. We also know of his frantic travels from his enemies, who regularly had to sweep up the shards when the short, stout man had left their city under cover of night.

But none of that from early 1532 to summer 1533. During these long months, when Paracelsus had been in the prime of his years, at the peak of his infamous fame, all we pick up is silence.

Most bibliographies of Paracelsus' works take printed editions as anchors for their timelines.[1] Logically, these are much easier to affirm

1 The most thorough and famous of which is Karl Sudhoff's *Bibliographia Paracelsica*, Berlin: Verlag Georg Reimer, 1894. In the following dates regarding Paracelsus' written or printed works we either refer to this volume, or to Sudhoff's careful introductions to the fourteen volumes of Paracelsus collected medical and philosophical works. See bibliography for further reference.

and pin down than the actual years when he wrote the original manuscripts. However, for most of his life Paracelsus had been prevented from publishing his already extant work. So the printing date tells us little about a work's appearance in Paracelsus' mind and own life.

The man's real seismic impact upon the domains of medicine, chemistry, theology and, of course, the occult arts only began to unfold posthumously i.e., from 1549 onwards. His first printed work that we know of—beside a pamphlet for his radically new methods of nature observation from his lectures in Basel from 1527—only appeared when he was already thirty-six years of age. And yet we do know that, during the time of his disappearance, he already carried with him, or held in safe deposit in Salzburg, the manuscripts of such important works as the Eleven Tracts, his *Opus Paramirum* and *On the Causes of the Invisible Diseases*. But nobody had seen or read them. And then he chose to vanish.

We also know it was during this time that Paracelsus turned away from medicine and focused solely on the *spiritual art*. When he returned from this interlude in the Appenzell mountains, he had written many of the manuscripts that would later on form his body of theological writings. In particular, a long vernacular exegesis of the Psalter of David, the book of psalms.

A few years later, in 1536, when he wrote the manuscript of his *Great Miracle-Medicine*, one of his significant medical works, he reflected on this critical period himself:

> *[...] and in all the ends and places [I have] searched diligently and assiduously. I have made inquiries about the certain, experienced, true arts of medicine. Not only amongst doctors, but also amongst shearers, barber-surgeons, learned physicians, women, black artists, if they cultivate this work, amongst alchemists, amongst monasteries, amongst the noble and the ignoble, amongst the bright and the simple.*
>
> *But I could not gain certainty in whatever disease it was. I thought about it a lot, that medicine is an uncertain art, which should not be used properly, because it is not fair to hit only with luck, to make one healthy and to spoil ten. This has given me cause [to inquire whether] it is a deception of*

> *spirits to thus deceive and belittle man. I left it [medicine] again, fell into other trades, but again returned to this art.*[2]

The period from 1532 to 1533 divides Paracelsus' biography in two halves: not equal in terms of count of years, but most equal in terms of the evolution of his thinking.

First, we have the longer period of his emergence as a medic and alchemist, as a student of first-hand experience of Europe's diverse cultures of knowledge, and as an iconoclast and rebel against ruling orthodoxy in the intertwined fields of 16th century spiritual and scientific teaching. At the end of this first period, Paracelsus is a man of forty years. Silently admired by many—especially the numerous nobles and commoners he had cured from seemingly incurable illnesses. But publicly despised and slandered by those he had attacked with vitriolic wrath in lecture halls, taverns and on street corners.

II

THE OLYMPIC SPIRIT

A First Glance

ONE OF THE most important sources on his ideas on the Olympic Spirits was possibly the last manuscript he wrote before his disappearance. It thus coincides with the autobiographically evidenced moment when he decided to pause his medical work, to disappear from the tempests and commotion of the mundane world, and to retreat to the mountainous regions of his homeland to study the spiritual arts.

It is in his manuscript of *De Causis Morborum Invisibilium* that he speaks of the unification of the Olympic Spirits (plural) into a single Olympic Spirit (singular), that he stresses such process's significance for the entire field of *Gabalia,*[3] and that he goes on to describe how these inner stars in man can be united.

2 Sudhoff (ed.) 1928, Vol x, p. 20, also See: Sudhoff, Vol. IX, 1925, p. 25.

3 A Paracelsian term that describes a particular "species" of magic, and which we will be exploring in more detail further on. (See Peuckert 1967, pp. 460–463).

> *In all things, know that in the creation of man, the invisible body was created like the visible. And both parts come out of the limbo.*[4] *For one part is earthly, and the other is heavenly: wherefore the heavenly hath its effect just as the earthly. But the earthly is commanded to build and to use the hands, therefore it is commanded more in consciousness than the invisible body. And what the outer body does, that is a whole work.*
>
> *But what the invisible body does is like the shadows of the body. For although the earthly body performs its works by imagination, it concerns only the corporeal: But what is done in that place, that also the imagination may cause to be done by the invisible body. [...] These things are done by the Olympic spirit, which tears off the shadow from all the works of the body. In the Olympic Spirit lies the art Gabalistica with its appendices, which art proves that to the imagination still much more is possible in those [human beings] in whom the joining of the Olympic Spirits has taken place. Then in the same way as the visible corpora can come together, so can the Olympic Spirits of creation, which are the heavenly bodies in man: These things are described in the books of the Gabalia.*[5]

Let's recapitulate what Paracelsus manages to condense in this important section.

Every material object exists twofold: in its inner and outer body. The former is invisible to the human eye, the latter physical and visible. In their natural state both bodies are *synchronised*, that is they are bound to each other like an object and its shadow.

This also applies to all humans who have both an outer, visible and an inner, invisible body. The behaviour of their physical body is determined by *imagination*, that is by an individually modulated

4 *Limus* or *limbus*, originally a term referring to the clay from which God created Adam (Genesis 2:7); in Paracelsian language, generally referring to the foundational substance (Urgrund) from which all physical or embodied matter emerged. (Goldammer (ed.), Vol. IV, 1955, p. 282).

5 Sudhoff (ed.) 1925, Vol. IX, pp. 297, 298.

combination of *human habit*, *will*, *belief*, and divinely inspired *ingenuity* (Latin: *ingenium*).

NOW the Olympic Spirit is a magical agent within man that holds the power to "tear off the shadow" from the body it was bound to. That is, the Olympic Spirit can separate visible and invisible bodies. Moreover, under guidance of the Olympic Spirit, the invisible body can then begin to operate by itself and perform works of equal effectiveness as the physical body.

THIS occult art, according to Paracelsus, is taught in that branch of magic which he calls *Gabalia*. From the above quote we can conclude that it is based on three central steps: the unification or awakening of the Olympic Spirit in man, the infusion of a human's imagination with their Olympic spirit, and the operative detachment of the inner body from the outer, so that the inner body can become the independent vessel of the mage's mind. *Gabalia*, thus, is the microcosmic alchemy to be performed within man.

LASTLY, Paracelsus suggests that the Olympic Spirits in their plural form—that is, in their state before they are united into one—are nothing else than the stars in the inner firmament of man.

These, and similar ones, were the thoughts that were on Paracelsus' mind before he went into exile for over a year. He pondered on the efficacy of human imagination, of how this inner agent held the capacity to become the single most important interface into the spirit-world, and what it might take for humans to conduct such work under conscious will. The healing of wounds, ulcers, syphilis, consumption etc. retreated to the background, as Paracelsus believed he was approaching the root cause of all diseases: the vexed application of free will in the tension field of divine fate patterns and an ecological cosmos, filled with independent spirits that infused and enlivened every grain of sand, leaf, twig, and drop of river water.

Paracelsus wrote the above elucidations on the Olympic Spirit from a medical perspective, as he was investigating the causes of the invisible or inner diseases. When he returned from his hiatus as a doctor, his theological writings in his luggage, he had expanded on the very same subject, but now from a spiritual perspective.

His research was aimed at determining the exact transition point at which man partly converged with the angelic realm, yet still formed a member of the material cosmos in flesh and blood. For Paracelsus that very transition point represented the *quintessentially human* in creation. Man shared his carnal body with animals, his participation in the four worlds of the elements with all creatures of this world; only this *fifth being* (literally: Latin *quint* or fifth, and *essentia* or being) seemed to actually distinguish man from the rest of creation. And just as this point, or gate, could become the entrance for undesirable spirit contacts and diseases, so it could also become the starting point for realisation of man in his divinely inspired form, yet still embodied in the flesh.[6]

The access medium through which humans could approach this gateway was the faculty of their *imagination*. Unfortunately, in the natural state of most men this medium remained dormant in its full capacity, as it was blocked by fantasies, confused and ruled by elemental desires and passions. Thus, *reason*, according to Paracelsus, becomes the perfected guide, the universal clearer of the path, the divine principle that God placed into our minds and into our hands so that we could begin to turn the human senses into tools of magic and medicine.

Essentially, what we witness here, is Paracelsus' radical reinterpretation of a Neoplatonic-Hermetic worldview. He upholds the polarity of matter and spirit, of the seven planetary spheres, the supralunar and sublunar realms, the four elemental worlds, and a living cosmos populated by an ecology of visible and invisible creatures across all of these domains. However, he departs in the conclusion that has to be drawn from it for human life, indeed for all life in creation. With Paracelsus, we do not find any notion of *theophany* through divine ascension; the path of mankind is not at all one *out of the material realm* and back into a sublime sanctuary shielded or relieved from chthonic chaos.

In fact, Paracelsus is radically anti-gnostic (i.e. positively not anti-cosmic) in his own cosmosophy because he advocates a path of *radical immanence*.

6 For an in-depth exploration of this fifth being within man, please see my book ***INGENIUM***, in particular Chapters IV and V (TaDehent, 2022).

III

The *Arte Gabalistica*

Senses Awakened by Reason

NOWHERE DO WE find his theology of immanence expressed more clearly than in the treatise *Of the Sense and its Tools.*

Just like the majority of Paracelsus' theological and social writings—many of them penned in a sermon-like style—this treatise first appeared in print in 1965. Thus, it eluded earlier biographers and researchers on Paracelsus' works and offers new pathways of understanding to the 21st century reader.

We are offering here a first translation of this text into English. Shorter sections unrelated to our study have been omitted, and the language has been carefully adapted with regard to semantics, syntax and grammar to become more accessible to contemporary reading culture.

De Sense Et Instrumenta

Of the Sense and Its Tools[7]

Man is more than cattle. He has in himself a fifth being; the same is man. And the same fifth being has a body in which and through which it works. And as the fifth being is sensitive, so it becomes sensitive only through this body. Just as no one sees the wind and no one can grasp it, and no one can do anything to it, so it is with the fifth being. But God wanted it to be sensitive. Therefore He gave it a body, so that the fifth being and the body are one, not two. And the body is conceived in the fifth being, and through the fifth being the body becomes sentient. For everything is one, like a body and its colour, as if the wind overtook a body and through the same body it becomes sensitive. For this reason the body cannot be separated from the quintessence, but [it] is eternally in it.

7 Goldammer (ed.), Vol. II, 1965, pp. 85.

Therefore, blood and flesh and the sun are one thing, indistinguishable, just as a colour and its body cannot be separated. For this reason, the sensus homo, et homo sensus [the senses are man, and man is his senses].

God does not want to have only heavenly creatures, like the angels, but also earthly ones, like man. And so it pleased God to forge another creature: the angels were the first, as we are the last at vitam perpetuam [for the life eternal]. [...]

Therefore not in blood and flesh is the whole man, but in the fifth being. Thus the body has bodily instruments through which the quintessence sees and exists and generates itself. These are the fifth being; wherefore it passes not away as the wind. Because what the body does, occurs through its actions, but the body does not cause it. And this is what it is. But if the wind passes away, or whatever the wind does, it does not harm the body, but it does harm the man. For man is bound with flesh and blood, and that same flesh and blood is the eternal soul.

From this it follows that to this quintessence it is a sin what the wind does. The wind harms [but leaves] itself without harm, because it has no soul; which would happen only if the wind were also corporeal. The sun has a quintessence, but the sun is without soul and without flesh. Therefore its action is without harm, just like that of the other celestial stars. For there is nothing eternal in them, or that which is destined to eternity. Therefore they oversee their office without sin, as one says.

Homo has in him the fifth being, all things elementary, the firmament etc. But he is a spiritual being, therefore the Ten Commandments are given to him. And if man says: But so is nature in me—he is not excused, because he shall be the master of nature. For homo is eternal, nature is not. Therefore he alone does wrong, other creatures do not. For others are deprived of the soul's quintessence. For this reason also man should be held to the eternal. For this reason he is made to have a pure heart toward God. What is a thing without its office, to which it is made? As a brain without wisdom, a heart without purity, eyes without sight etc. For if something should not be in man, it would not be constituted and he would not have it.

The soul of man is reason, which is thus above the quintessence. And that, which is above the quintessence, nevertheless guides the quintessence. So, if the ears are to hear, the soul is the judge of the hearing. And if an organ of the quintessence grows up in darkness [thus does not perform its office, as the eyes cannot do in darkness], it is dead.

Therefore men do not hear, therefore they do not see, they have no reason [because they grow up in darkness]. But everything that is in man is living and is sensitive life. Other things do their work, but without sensitivity. They are salty, sweet, pungent, but they themselves do not feel it in themselves. Therefore, man should seek and lead his soul to the same nature and bliss. For it is the reason, wisdom, sensuality of man. [...]

Our reason is the spirit. The spirit is the one that goes back to the master. Therefore, if the senses remain one with reason, they will be blessed together with reason. If not, then reason departs, and the senses come into the outer shadows together with the whole body [exteriores tenebras cum toto corpore], that is in hell [infernum].

Reason is an authority from God, because it is a spirit of God [spiritus domini[8]*], to which obedience must be shown in the place of God. And it is perfect in its action, not with thoughts, but with the knowledge of good and evil, and is one reason in all men, not different ones, with different laws, local customs, local liberties, as in the various peoples, where many sit together in council, and yet guess at nothing. Reason asks no one for advice, because it knows everything. Through it we must enter into eternal life [vitam aeternam]. [...]*

So I ask, why do your eyes see stone temples without feeling the abomination of God? Rather, look at His creatures and His work! Or if you do not want to see God rightly from

8 2 Cor 3:17, *Dominus autem Spiritus est ubi autem Spiritus Domini ibi libertas.* Now the Lord is the Spirit, and where the Spirit of the Lord is, there is freedom.

the created creature [natura creata], see the letters of His words and carry these letters in your hearts. Then you will also see God in the temple, which is the heart of man. Only there will you see God in His temple. But since we human beings are a temple, Christ must be in us. He himself comes into us through our obedience and love for God. That is why the authority of man [reason] did not command to craft temples of stone. That Solomon built a temple, he did so because of his earthly command for an earthly feast for the eyes. But we are of a new birth and see only spiritual and heavenly things. [...]

There is a great difference between the earthly and heavenly; that is the old birth and the new birth. Since we are in the new birth, we should also have no more respect for anything earthly, for nothing trivial, merely look at what is necessary in all things. For it is a well-known proverb: One should not give the dog everything after which he wags the tail. He who accustoms his tongue too much to licking, forgets the poor. The new creature has a food that is not earthly, that no one sees. It eats this food. But because it dwells on earth, it must also be fed earthly, just as Christ did on earth, from whose blood and flesh we were created.

So we say, I may do what also Solomon and David did—yet they were only earthly, and so they lived, being made of earth. But you are made of the blood and body of Christ. Therefore, do not do so [as Solomon and David did]. Let not our nose amuse itself with the scents of flowers and alabastric waters, but let it scent the sweat of the poor and take their sickness in the form of gashes, open sores, cancerous ulcers, fistulas etc. by the hand until the wounds of Lazarus are tended. So we should put the flowers to the poor, that they may smell them. Because they as sick ones need strength. [...]

The Ten Commandments are given to us for this reason, to guide the fifth being within us, all in God's will and none other. For God alone has given them to us, and His commandment is the bond of the quintessence, that it may be drawn, taught and bound as God wills. As He has commanded us to keep the Sabbath, and now we must not work all the days.

> *For if God commands us, we shall not lack anything in our labour and food. Yea, if He would have had us celebrate a whole week, He would have had us grow bread in the field. And with such a commandment we are also forbidden to be covetous of food. Therefore, although you do not see either the bond or the rope: the word of God is the bond. So you create the pride with the eyes, make yourself beautiful eyes in the mirror, with beautiful clothes, and adorn yourself with it, that you want to be something more in front of others. In this way, you make your eyes a wolf and a magnet, an agstone, that you devour what you see and snatch it to yourself. All this is not meant to be. For this purpose your eyes are not there. For the stomach eats on behalf of all our limbs, and the same is already satisfied with a little something.*
>
> *So it is no small thing to lead and direct the 5 beings [i.e., the senses] to God the Lord, because they are not ours, not made by us. For who wanted to claim that a man made himself to speak or to hear? We are created for good only insofar as God has ordered it through the authority [reason] within us, given and innate by God, to guide, teach, and comfort us, and to enlighten and judge us. This is our reason and conscience from above. But where we appropriate this in our free will, we steal from God what is His. But what will happen to those on the Last Day! For no one knows the scope and severity of God's judgment.*

So, let's recapitulate some of the ideas shared by Paracelsus in this treatise.

The most important tools of the magician are his senses which must be trained by the guiding light of *reason*. The way of the magician lies in transforming their senses from passive receptors to active sensors. This means that the magician's way is a constant effort to withdraw their own senses from the dominant influence of a particular element and from the constantly changing impressions of the outer and inner firmaments. The mage's senses have to become unattached agile *tools of exploration.*[9]

9 For further details on this process, please see my book *INGENIUM*, especially Chapter III (TaDehent, 2022).

Once such liberation and activation of the senses is achieved, the mage by no means follows the classical theurgist's path of withdrawal from material matter. Quite the contrary: it is only then that the adept's journey begins, namely that of purposefully sinking their senses back into the living body of creation.

However, now they are no longer bound by elemental, celestial or chthonic attachments, but they have become free. *The mage's senses have become awakened in the light of reason* to operate in the inner world of spirits as well as in the outer world of creation all at once.

To remain immanent to creation, to keep one's ear to the womb of the earth, one's eyes in the eye of the cosmos, one's lips to the mouth of the mundane world, with each passing day to throw oneself back into the struggle for sincerity, for healing, and balance, to solve the poison where it causes to perish and to bind it where it permits to prosper—that is the work of the mage according to Paracelsus.

The path Paracelsus advocates is to walk hand in hand with the (Platonic) demiurge. To urge each of us not to strive to escape chaos, but to take our own place in the round dance of the cosmos, in the death-bringing and birth-promising mystery we have all been thrown into. And yet Paracelsus' outlook is essentially saturnine and not at all imbued with Apollonian sweetness or drunkenness.

To Paracelsus, the entire world is a medicine cabinet. Pomp, frills, dance, charm, cheerfulness, pastime—all of these have to be cut back by the piercing light of reason. His demand towards himself and all of fellow humans is merciless. Because not a minute, not a moment's time must be lost while the poor remain poor and the sick remain sick. It is upon every one of us to get our act together and to intervene on their behalf.

Because all of Divinity is immanent, is embedded and present, shining through and forth from each object of creation, there are no temples, no shrines, no caves, no mysterious mountains a holy wo/man has to withdraw to. If at all, what sanctifies a human is how they chose to show up in the world, not how they withdraw from it.[10]

According to Paracelsus' cosmosophy, even God was not hiding

10 We see here echoes of the strong influence that Paracelsus' ideal of a mystical path—born not of any anti-cosmic Gnostic transcendentalism but of a commitment to radical divine immanence—had on later German mystics such as Valentin Weigel and Jakob Böhme.

from the world. S/he was plain and present everywhere around Paracelsus: standing in a field of beechnut, walking under the shadow of a larch, speaking to a village herbalist, or working alongside the nurses in a war-hospital—magic was immanent in all encounters he could possibly make. The work of the mage was not to chase and discover occult treasures or powers. Rather, it was to see the objects of the mundane world through an occulted light. Neither was it the work of the mage to find access to a new and ascended world. It was to rearrange their own inner constitution, their own embodied form as a divinely inspired agent. Humans had to train the faculties of their will and imagination, to sharpen their senses and beliefs in the merciless light of reason. That's how they acquired the tools to restore balance in a world that was spinning into chaos and collapse without human care-taking.

A mage was a medic to a world that could not heal itself. A mage was a gardener to a wilderness that would grow to suffocate itself. A mage was a knife, a phial of poison and a sharp eye, ready to make irreversible decisions, unbiased by personal attachments or desires. All in the pursuit of pulling man, spirits and nature away from the precipice they would otherwise tumble into. That was the kind of Christianity—deeply resonant with the Kabbalistic notion of *tikkune*—that Paracelsus believed himself to be an apostle of. Humans had a role to play in keeping this world intact. And they could only assume that role if each human for themselves undertook the hard work of becoming quintessentially human. That is, the *Arte Gabalistica*, to excavate and activate the fifth being in themselves.

> *But such a magical operation, as is the science called Gaballia or Gabalistica, does not spring from the spirits or from sorcery, but from the natural course of the subtle nature. For this is not the knowledge of man, who knows nothing out of themselves about the secrets, but this is the knowledge that man may be realised microcosmically, that is through both species, outer and magical, visible and invisible.*[11]

11 Sudhoff (ed.) 1929, Vol. I, p. 147.

IV

THE SCRIPTURE

An Animist's Handbook

IN THE FOLLOWING we will show how Paracelsus read the Bible, especially the New Testament, as the world's best and only necessary animist's handbook. He was Christian through and through, and yet entirely of his own kind.

To understand Paracelsus, we have to appreciate the historic context of Europe in the early 16th century. Within the geographic boundaries of mainland Christian Europe, the essential question was not *whether* one was a Christian, but *what kind* of Christian they chose to be. This again was where Paracelsus had his very own way of carving out a new path.

We have seen in the previous chapter how the *Arte Gabalistica* enabled the mage to awaken their senses in the light of reason and to begin to use their senses as the essential tools of learning from the cosmos. Or as Paracelsus might have put it: to read in the Book of Nature.

To a master of *Gabalia*, the entire macrocosm lay dormant in a single grain of sand. To such a practitioner this was not an intellectual theorem but a lived reality they held first-hand experience of. Every touch was full of voices reaching back to them. The world was speaking back to them in lived actuality. That was the Great Work according to Paracelsus: not the sublimation of matter, the shedding of the corpse and shell, but realising the full divine cosmos of life in the most mundane objects of inquiry. By awakening the choir of atavistic voices in any corpus the mage could become a co-creator, a conscious participant and—an initiate amongst their circles. A weaver of fate.

Medicine, chemistry, magic were united fields of practice in such a cosmology. For all of them had to begin with a tying into the animistic consciousness that enlivened the substance, organ or spirit in front of us. Such consciousness was not to be considered stable, but fluid and modular. It was made up itself of elemental cells of consciousness as well as celestial ones. And it was the work of the mage, the doctor or the *adeptus philosophiae* to shift, to tilt, to convey these consciousness-cells to rearrange themselves into a pattern that was more functional for human survival, prosperity and evolution. Magic was a matter of negotiation at a particle level of consciousness. It was psychoactive, in an entirely raw yet all-embracing sense of the word.

We should recall again that by the time Paracelsus began to write the majority of his own theological and exegetical works, he already was an accomplished medic and one entirely of his own making. In his early youth he had commenced his theological training with the clerics mentioned in the first chapter. Now he returned to the sources, both of his own education but, more importantly, of Christianity as such.

Paracelsus read the Bible like few others: *One palm closed around the axe to take down man-made orthodoxy, the other palm open, holding the hovering flame of divinity*. Merciless acuity and compassionate empathy alternate sharply in his theological explications; and neither of them are aimed at worldly or spiritual potentates, at academics or orthodox clergyman. Instead, his words are aimed at the common folk, at the people he encountered during his disappearance in the Appenzell region: mountain farmers, miners, innkeepers, folk-healers and wise-women. Throughout his life, Paracelsus was a master at breaking down the most complex concepts—from the vast fields of medicine, chemistry, magic, theology etc.—by exploiting the open quarry of the raw vernacular.

Thus, as we study some of Paracelsus' more stinging theological statements, we should keep in mind the enigmatic man who made these heretical comments. He used a most simple—sometimes profane—language to allude to highly sophisticated spiritual realities. And he wrote in an erratic manner, often dictating long passages to his servant in the middle of the night, pulling his wisdom from a *locus magicis* somewhere between his guts, his heart and the angels.[12]

While throughout his life he leveraged many of the same unique cosmic terminologies which he had coined early on in his career, we have no indication that he ever revisited his entire body of works to ensure coherence or consistency. Paradoxical entanglements and contradictions across his vast body of works were of no concern to this man, as long as the present paragraph at hand was genuine and

12 For further details see my book ***INGENIUM***, especially Chapter IV (TaDehent, 2022).

truthful. Thus, reading both cover to cover as well as across his texts and manuscripts is essential to understand Paracelsus. For each paragraph on a related topic, sometimes separated by most of the lifetime of this man, shines a new and different light on the same idea.

Challenging our own understanding to not become stagnant, but to remain fluid, tangential, and ever evolving, would have been something that would have greatly pleased the equally brilliant and choleric Swiss doctor.

Reading the Psalms with Paracelsus

I. READING PSALM 119:60 (*I am ready, and am not troubled: that I may keep thy commandments.*), Paracelsus offers most practical life advice:

> *Therefore David wants us to be ready, and not to push just up and away. He says "I am ready", that is, we are not to make preparations for our death, not to fast, not to pray, nothing like that, but to bring young and old into the same state, that is, to live with joy, not with sadness, and to walk in the Lord.*[13]

II. READING PSALM 90:5–6 (*They are like the new grass of the morning—in the morning it springs up new, but by evening it fades and withers.*), he sacks the admiration for an ancient past and classical authors. Unless insights can be drawn from (or verified by) first-hand experience in this very moment, they are not imbued with divine life, but made of the dead ashes of the past:

> *There Moses gives that parable. It says as much as: Why do we humans think so much of time? What is the morrow? Nothing! [...] What use are all the things that are gone, that are no more? So Moses gives us an example to understand. If the herb of yesterday is of no use to us, what use is the custom of yesterday, or of the day before yesterday, or of a thousand years ago? The old time is of no use to us. What is the use of*

13 Goldammer (ed.) 1959, Vol. VI, Part III, pp. 56–7.

Julius [Caesar]? Nothing! What of Augustus? Nothing! What harm does Nero do to us? Nothing! What harm Pharaoh? Nothing! What is the benefit of their laws to us? Nothing! Only God, who was at that time and still is, is useful to us, in whom we shall live. The others, the great Alexander, the great Pompey, the great Romulus's speech—they are all equal to yesterday's porridge which we eat and shit out again through the stomach. [...] Therefore all is nothing. What is nothing? What is built into time, into the past or the future; it all dries up and has no continuance. What dries up before God is nothing.[14]

III. READING PSALM 122:9 (*For the sake of the house of the Lord our God, I sought good things for you.*), Paracelsus emphasises the humble position of mankind in creation, that they live to serve Divinity and not to enslave the world for their own good:

And therefore David says that the earth does not belong to man, and that man is not its master, but God is the master here, and it is His house, where He keeps the people, accommodates them, as they are born from Adam. Such is what David recognises, and that also suits us fine, as we live in the house of God.[15]

IV. READING PSALM 122:1 (*I was glad when they said unto me, Let us go into the house of the Lord.*), he asserts the importance of leading a life that is genuine, independent and free of the dominion and judgement of other people.

So this is David's joy, that we are not under the righteousness or the will of man, but in God's will and in His power. And that we shall enter into the house of God without all the will of men, and above all the will of sorcerers and idols. Therefore notice that David here interprets the said Psalms in such a way that God protects us and no man, and that we will enter God's house and no man's house, and that man has

14 Goldammer (ed.), Vol. IV, Part I, pp. 216–7.
15 Goldammer (ed.), Vol. VI, Part III, p. 156.

> *nothing to give nor to take here. And that the house of God is our entrance after our death, when we go out of life; just as we came from heaven into the womb and enter into the house of God, which is the whole world.*[16]

V. READING PSALM 119:1 (*Blessed are they whose ways are blameless, who walk according to the law of the Lord.*), Paracelsus brings forth his most fundamental critique of the Church, the very argument that in his eyes deprives any man-made church of its raison d'être. God is always in the here and now, and reveals herself/himself to each one of us individually. Seeking out one's personal communion with the Divine is the work of man, and it cannot be eased or replaced by following well-trodden paths that others walked before us. We all need to accept the life-long struggle, the endless searching, knocking and entering of finding our own path.

> *David sets us here a psalm, in which he admonishes us and wants us to walk alone in the way of the Lord. And he forgets all the old fathers, the patriarchs, the kings, the priests, the Levites, the churches, the temples, the saints, and in summa all, and understands it quickly and says that those are blessed "'who walk in the way of the Lord". In this there is only one way to be understood, and none more, that is the way of the Lord, and none other, neither Moses, Abraham, Isaac, Jacob. […] So also in the New Testament we are not to walk in the teaching of the old fathers, of the religious patrons, of the saints, […] but to find these things all of ourselves, and to accept only the way of the Lord and to walk in the same, and not to leave or walk in any man's way.*[17]

VI. READING PSALM 119:11 (*I have hidden your word in my heart that I might not sin against you.*), we are reminded that we are not alone in finding our path in this world, but that the Holy Spirit was embedded as a seed in each one of us. However, learning to hear it speak from within us, is the responsibility of every grown adult, and cannot be accomplished on our behalf by others.

16 Ibid., 152.
17 Ibid., 1.

> *Know therein: From birth we bring two [ways of schooling]. One is baptism, which our father and mother give and send us, and its instructions. Baptism remains rightfully with us unto death; for it is administered in the name of God, of the Son, and of the Holy Spirit. Baptism may not be renewed nor changed, but it remains in its power as much as the same water was given power. And this same power shall never be renewed, for the baptism of the Holy Spirit follows after, when we come out of the children's mind and into the adult age. The Holy Spirit is to baptise us then, not water. Water baptism has happened and is enough, there is no need. The Holy Spirit is needed from now on. He comes not in the infant days, but in the grown-up days. So the children keep the righteousness [of water baptism], and the grown ones keep the righteousness [of the baptism of the Holy Spirit].*[18]

VII. READING PSALM 119:94 (*I am yours, save me! For I have sought according to your precepts.*), gives us a curious hint as to why man should seek out Divinity in all aspects of creation, both good and evil. In particular, it can be read as a exegetical permission for chthonic forms of magic and spirit-work. For as long as these respective spirits are not given the central space in our heart, reserved for the Holy Spirit, man should seek out contact to them, to understand how even they are contributing to upholding and extending God's work.

> *We have no lord but God. Therefore He has prepared the earth for us, gives us bread, the birds, the fishes, out of His great faithfulness. For we [all] are His. Now if we [creatures] are His, we also all serve Him, evil and good, even the devils as well as the angels. For if they were not God's own (as we all are)—who would prevent the devil from killing them all in a moment? But he is God's, therefore he must be obedient and stand bound in God's intercession. For God protects His own, even the devils from the angels and saints; for they would have no place if God did not protect them. Therefore He makes us secure, so that no enemy can harm us.*[19]

18 Goldammer (ed.), Vol. VI, Part III, p. 17.

19 Ibid., 77–8.

VIII. READING PSALM 119:101 (*I have kept my feet from every evil path so that I might obey your word.*) reaffirms the central role of reason and gnosis in Paracelsus cosmosophy. He exposes the prayer for forgiveness as a cowardly transgression, when man should ask for divine knowledge so that each one of us can make the right decision in their own responsibility and full awareness.

> *These are evil ways that [lead] away from the insight of divine knowledge: all begging for forgiveness and not for knowledge.*
>
> *Such praying is in the doctrine of man, the idol, who do nothing but spread out hypocrisy, but pray and give thanks. What is it that one gives thanks to God for their [own] good deed, and yet has no knowledge and insight of their own of the good deed? But the higher a man's knowledge, the higher should be their thanks. Therefore, this is the right way in all things: we should give thanks when we bear a thing of high understanding. We should not give thanks as a memory or as knowledge of a story, as men write and learn it, but from the light of the Holy Spirit that is in the heart, from the same we should know the things. [...]*
>
> *Such contemplation should proceed from the heart. Who knows how to give it but the Holy Spirit alone? Man does not know! [...] It is necessary for their hearts that they should be enlightened by God. But since they do not have this, they ask with their mouth, not with their heart.*
>
> *But in this way God does not hear them. For as they meditate in the yap, so David meditates in the heart. That is why they are false prophets.*[20]

IX. READING PSALM 119:114 (*You are my refuge and my shield; I have put my hope in your word*), Paracelsus shines an even brighter light on the way a Christian mage should interact with the spirits. He asserts the effective poisoning or healing powers contained in all natural beings, both visible and invisible. And yet neither of these should make man believe, hope on or even pray to them. The way to work with the spirits is to study them, to get to know their ways of being,

20 Ibid., 81.

their way of working and taking effect in the world, and yet to hold one's own heart reserved for the communion with the Holy Spirit. The Christian mage works with the beings and substances of the visible and invisible worlds, yet they do not venerate or idolise them.

Equally, Paracelsus clarifies that while all natural objects around us hold their specific agency and power, this is not true for humans. They are not one thing or object, but a microcosm in their own right and thus embody many spirits, faiths and forces.

> *Whereupon David says this much concerning such exaltation [of the saints or of nature], that all [their] laws are nothing. Whether they be just or unjust, right or wrong, we are not to hang our hope or faith on them. But: God, You are our helper and shield. [...]*
>
> *For you see marvellous powers in His works, with what great virtues they are endowed by God, which are so immeasurable before our eyes. So He can give this to the stones, to the herbs, and the like; so also has the heaven, as from the heaven many are made sick, and many miraculously whole, as [it also happens] from the powers of the creatures, the stones. So are the powers in the animals, in the birds, in the fishes, in worms; great wonders are in them. But all this has not the glory, God has the glory! So He has done His work and wants us to thank not the stones, not the herbs, but God. With this He shields us.*
>
> *But in man it is not so. For though we live on earth, we are good to nothing, and ought to nothing; [we are] not like a pebble, not like a piece of oak. Since then there is nothing in us [while we live] on earth, what then would be in us according to the nature of the earth? You shall look at it like this.*
>
> *Many spirits are there, many such effects, which concern us after our death, many kinds of faith, many kinds of idolatry with powers and the like, wonderful before our eyes. Although these things do our body favours, they make it healthy, help it and the like—so we should know that we should not let ourselves be seduced by them to believe because they help the body, they also help the soul, or to sanctify them because of their effect in the body. No! For the devil*

> *and his angels [sic!] also make well, make sick, afflict and help.*
>
> *These miraculous signs, which take place in the body, give no knowledge of God, but are his work, which may be good or evil. Therefore we should not exalt them ourselves, but remain in the word of God. For He is our helper, not what restores the body in all manner of sickness.*
>
> *Such power is also with the stones, in heaven, with the herbs, also God's saints have such power, the devil also. But we should not be moved by them, for they are little specks which the spirits put on our tongues, so that we may forget our faith in God by their signs.*[21]

X. READING PSALM 119:118 (*You reject all who stray from your decrees, for their deceitfulness is in vain.*), in Paracelsus' exegesis becomes a verdict on the inner experience of the mage. In the dialogue they hold with the spirits of the world, they need to learn to distinguish the voices of spirits, their own thoughts, and the divine ingenium.

Each of these form as thoughts in their mind, for this is how our mind, all spirits, as well as Divinity communicate with us. yet, it is the faculty of the mage to learn to distinguish these intuitions. While they learned to listen to all kinds of spirits, they follow few, and God above all.

> *Know also that God despises men who fall away from His righteousness. That is, He alone is our only hope and only our God. [...] For men all fall from God, and their thoughts are false and unrighteous. For see how a thought enters into the head, how no one sees it nor feels it, and yet it works in the people. Thus it is spoken of the spirits, that they are thus all false; for they and their thoughts are one thing, together they are one spirit. Now see for this the following example. You see what grows on earth, the spirits [of plants] that help us and those that kill us, those that wish us well and those that wish us ill—and so all grow in the garden.*
>
> *So then such variety grows in the garden, so it is also*

21 Ibid., 90–1.

> *among the spirits: many there are who want us well, many who want us evil; and but it is all poison, they may want what they want, but it is all poison and gall. From such good spirits comes that sometimes appearances happen, that one thereby learns something future e.g. the death of the lord, whether he dies or lives badly in the country, how expensive [it becomes] etc. Yet they shall not be worshipped.*[22]

XI. READING PSALM 119:127 *(For I love thy commandments more than gold and topaz.)*, we are reminded of the relationship we are to maintain with the spirits. Paracelsus, while confirming the pagan practice of embodying the spirits in statues, figurines, or spirit bottles, warns against offering "gold or topaz" to them. That is, it is a fine line for a magician to walk in order to work pragmatically with the spirits for healing purposes and yet not fall from the grace of their own God. For the Christian magician, so Paracelsus says, is not distinguished by the fact that they do not deal with spirits (for then they could not work with nature), but that they do so as a master of the art—leaving the realm of faith, hope of heart, and inner theology to Divinity alone.

> *That is why David says "Your law is dearer to me than gold and topaz." He is not referring here to gold [as a metal], but to the gods who must be fed with gold. Whose keys, spoons, garment, etc., must be golden, and who without [offering of] gold do not, nor can, accomplish their godliness. Likewise the Topaz: their sanctuary on the altar is adorned with precious stones, with pearls, that is their idolatry, and without such gold, silver, precious stones, the gods can neither speak nor whistle; they must be lubricated and studded with them, otherwise they do no good to anyone. Look at you faithful and faithful Christ—how far these walk from God!*[23]

XII. READING PSALM 119:129 *(Your statutes are wonderful; therefore I obey them.)*, Paracelsus expresses the above thought even more strongly. He emphasises further in which way a mage has to commune

22 Ibid., 94–5.
23 Goldammer (ed.), Vol. VI, Part III, p. 101.

and work with the spirits so that the mage's soul does not become entangled in the process but remains attached to Divinity.

> *As man lives, and whatever he does while he lives, he does by the power and force of his life; now the life is from God and is now his. So you see it in death: God takes it again, and the spirit, that is the spirit of life, goes again to the one from whom it came. So it is with the herbs, what they do, that does the Arcanum [the secret power] of the Godhead; so it is with the stars, and so it is with the spirits, and also with the devils. Now it should be natural for you to know: what man does, he does only by God's power; thus what the herbs do, they do by God's power; what heaven does, by God's power.*
>
> *So shall you also know: so shall ye also understand it of spirits and devils. Now, what is a spirit? A dead human being. What is a devil? An angel cast out from heaven. What is the soul? A condemned spirit. Now is to be spoken of the powers of the signs, which lend tongues to the false god of the earth. So know: the spirits possess the knowledge of all things, past, present, future, and [the knowledge of] all powers as they are in roots, stones, sky, sun and moon, and how these do service on the body of man, and also to his harm. This power, as it is in nature, so it is also in man. Likewise this power is in the devils.*
>
> *From such powers of the spirits and devils arises the strange art of the spirits, that this spirit performs this, and that one another. Now none of this is from God, but everything happens through the means of God. [...] So it happens through the means and not through God, but in the hand of God it remains. What is done by the means is not according to the faith that serves Christ, but it is according to the faith that serves the means. But to believe in the means [and not in God] is idolatry.*[24]

What we encounter here with Paracelsus is a Western shaman of the 16th century, speaking to us about his worldview and how to operate both from within Divinity and from within the spirit world. As always

24 Goldammer (ed.), Vol. VI, Part III, pp. 102–3.

in history, the common ground, the things taken for granted, did not need mentioning—only the unusual, the new and different needed to be pulled to the reader's attention.

Obviously, Paracelsus was not writing for a 21st century Western readership: nature-alienated, scientifically-educated, seemingly enlightened and yet deeply unsettled by their loss of identity. The lived reality of our ancestors five hundred years ago was an entirely different one.

In the 16th century, humans' vulnerability and blind exposure to the living powers of nature required no pointing out. Nor did the shape-shifting realm of spirits, the world of the immanently divine, and the grimaces of otherness that gaped at the farmer at the edge of his pasture from the steep mountain slopes.

What needed to be mentioned, what needed to be described instead, was how to assert one's humanity in such a wild and animistic world. Even more urgent: how to find one's place not only in human communion, but in communion with God, in the midst of the round dance of this untamed world. Paracelsus did not have to explain to anyone the reality of larvae, ghosts, mountain demons, wind spirits, or star intelligences. All of them were present in abundance.

Rather, what Paracelsus was trying to convey was how to stand in the gushing flow of encounters with all these beings and yet not to fall into the shadows of superstition, nor into the clutches of a gold- and soul-hungry church. How to stand upright by oneself, in the midst of a nature not only animated by spirits, but made possible by them in the first place—and to keep Divinity's flame burning in one's heart. Shielded from the distress of the world as well as one's fears, freed from fantasies, superstitions and longings. Illuminated only by the clear light of reason, and the infallible impressions of the human senses. That is the experience Paracelsus was aiming to share.

When he looked to the Scripture as an animistic handbook, it was because the Bible precisely *did not* speak of chthonic, elemental or celestial spirits in each chapter—but because it spoke of Divinity. To Paracelsus, it spoke about the *new* and the *different*, the thing men had to add, to excavate from their heart and light in the fire of their reason and experience. It spoke about Divinity as a relevant encounter for every one of us—and thus allowed each of us to hold on to the one thing humans lose the swiftest when hard pressed by their own cross and affliction.

The Bible, to Paracelsus, spoke about the *Quintessence*, the fifth-being within each human, and yet one of the rarest experiences of all: to focus one's joy, all of one's faith and hope on the divine flame within one's own heart-space, and on nothing else.

The simple people of the 16th century had to learn to use the clear light of reason in a world that was already deeply sensual and at the same time imbued with magic. We, the common people of the 21st century, must learn to regain our sense of touch, of smell and taste, in a world that has become static and sterile from five-hundred years under the light of allegedly *pure reason.* Healing the torn fabric between what we experience with our senses and think in our rational minds, is still the same exercise as Paracelsus ordered it centuries ago, only modern people approach it from the opposite end.

We recapitulate: reason is the tool of the mind, the senses are the tools of the body. Reason and senses, mind and body have to become integrated as well as purified from all ego-fuelled noise of fantasies and wishful thinking. Only then is reason ready to keep the senses on their path, and the senses became the tools of travel. Faith, finally, acts as the guiding light that both leads and shields the mage. Such is the foundation: a human's position at the outset of their expedition into magic.

We now also see the radical difference between genuine Paracelsian magic, as we encounter it here in his original writings, and ritualistic approaches of the 17th or 18th century, as known, for example, from the later Solomonic magic. The latter reflect, at best, a truncated, an opportunistic and utilitarian approach to what was actually to become, according to Paracelsus, a *way of life.* The idea of switching on one's spirituality when e.g., one took up prayers and fasting for several weeks before an important magical ritual, would certainly not have attracted the kindest of the many phrases Paracelsus had ready for such occasions to decry what was, in his eyes, clear evidence of dilettantism.

Keeping one's reason and senses connected to the Divine was the foundation of all magico-medical work. From here onwards it was not about devotion or purely technical skills, but about learning from experience, from one's few good deeds, as well as from the many bad. Standing with one's face to Divinity was, to Paracelsus, certainly not a short preparatory stage before some important ritual. Magic was not reserved for the ritual experience, magic served *all* of life. It happened now, and here, and everywhere. It was a human's purpose. And the world was the ritual circle.

V

NECTROMANTIA

An Animist Epistemology

HOW WE CAN know anything, is the question posed by the discipline called *epistemology*. Paracelsus' answer to this question is both simple and complex. For he liked to respond to it on multiple levels. So we will start with the simple and then work our way slowly into the more complex layers of acquiring knowledge.

At the most basic level, Paracelsus held that all true knowledge comes from experience. But what is an experience? In the German language, we can break the term *experience* into two essential components: it holds one word for the actual momentary state of being immersed into a *lived experience* (*Erlebnis*) and another term for the resulting *knowledge* one gains from such an experience (*Erfahrung*). The witnessing of and the knowledge gained from an experience are essentially intertwined and should never be broken apart. One cannot be truthful without the other. A wo/man who experienced something but has not grown in experience from it, is a fool. A wo/man who has not experienced something but acts as if they had, is a deceiver.

According to Paracelsus, we can only know something once we have been immersed in it, witnessed it, walked with it, adventured out into it. That is why in Paracelsian terms, reading a book or listening to a lecture (nowadays: a podcast) does not generate genuine knowledge. Neither reading nor listening are relevant sources of knowledge if we aim to explore a Paracelsian epistemology. At best, reading and listening can generate *possibilities and frameworks for future experimenting*.

This is an important point to clarify. Imagine you rode a horse and had two saddle-bags behind you, one to the left, another one to the right. In the left you store notes on *things to try out*; in the right you store notes on *things you have tried out*. If you aim to ride a long way, it's good practice to distribute your *knowledge* evenly. you don't want the horse's left to outweigh its right side. Instead, the weight of the saddle-bags should level each other out, allowing the horse to walk an even line for a long time.

That's how we can think about the balance of things we have heard or read and things we have witnessed. Interestingly, the German term *Erlebnis*, the momentary state of being inside an experience, is also translated as *adventure* in English. For if we have not gone through things ourselves, we can hold no genuine knowledge of them. We may repeat what other people have said, which often is a good first step, but such indirect knowledge is quite different from proper Paracelsian epistemology.

Knowledge requires *experience* and experience requires *contact*. Sensual contact that is, which means contact mediated by one or all of our human senses. Knowledge thus is stored in all created forms and, like a flower opening upon the touch of sunlight, this knowledge can be released upon contact. The release of such knowledge is not a *handing over* at all: nothing gets divided or taken away from an object when we participate in intimate knowledge of them. Quite the opposite: these are moments of communion and partaking.

Remember the moment you first saw your lover naked. This moment did not take anything away from your lover. They were not less or more themselves with or without clothes. And yet, seeing them naked for the first time opened a new world of experience to you. It was all already there; you simply had not witnessed it and therefore up until that point you did not have *genuine knowledge* of it. Reading about this experience or listening to a retelling of it on tape would have not at all been the same as was actually being immanently there in that very moment with your lover.

Thus, the acquisition of genuine knowledge, according to Paracelsus, is per default an *erotic* experience: an experience of risk-taking which unlocks sensual doors of partaking and communing. Prior to each experience we might have been able to imagine its door (as others may haven spoken about it to us); but genuine knowledge can only be gained by unlocking and walking through it.

Paracelsian knowledge is adventure, it results from movement into the world, it is unleashed by contact, and it is irreversible in its touch.

> *This is a 'vision': so one sees a thing, and from the same can tell what is in it; as a physician in herbs, an astronomer in heaven, an ore-man in ore, a philosopher in nature. For in all things are secrets which have all meaning, to know man's need.*[25]
>
> *Thus the arts arose, of which there are four: Because the spirits are diviners, they cannot speak with men, nor are they visible to him and the like: Therefore they brought the arts into the imagination of men, so that they found Geomantiam, Pyromantiam, Hydromantiam and Necromantiam: not from human light or light of nature, but from the infusion of the spirits, which thus made the first ones inventors of these arts, from which other disciples learned thereafter.*
>
> *Know, then, that their inventors were possessed with the spirits, and thus invented and devised the arts from the same possession. Because many say, it was given by God, others say, it was given by angels.*[26]

Paracelsus here describes the shamanistic practice of working with the spirits of an herb and heaven, of an ore and art to gain the knowledge occulted in all objects of creation. The spirit and its physical object, the practitioner and his divinely inspired imagination are the four cornerstones of *reading* in the Book of Nature. His is an *animistic epistemology* that is nowhere more clearly expressed than in his chapters on the art of *Nectromantia* and the artist called *Nectromanticus*.

We find these as part of his opus magnum, *Philosophia Sagax*, where *Nectromantia* is listed as one of the nine members of the four types of astrology.[27] These fourfold and ninefold structures represent a Paracelsian arrangement of cosmological sources of first-hand knowledge as well as the related human arts to draw this knowledge out, to circumvent the related risks and pitfalls, and to successfully apply them to the world.

25 Goldammer (ed.), Vol. VII, p. 246.

26 Sudhoff (ed.), XIV, pp. 165–166.

27 For a detailed treatment of these four types of astrology according to Paracelsus see the chapter 'The Olympic Spirits' in my book *Holy Heretics* (Scarlet Imprint, 2022).

It would be tempting to read the term *Nectromantia* as a distorted variant of the Greek word *necromancy*. And yet, it presents itself as a deliberate neologism of Paracelsus, which appears more than seventy times in this form in the *Philosophia Sagax*. He specifically differentiates it from the other eight *membra* that constitute the four types of astrology, those being: *magia*, *nigromantia*, *astrologia*, *signatum*, *artes incertae*, *medicina adepta*, *philosophia adepta*, *mathematica adepta*.

For our current inquiry, the differentiation from *Nigromantia* is of special concern. Paracelsus sees the art of *Nectromantia* as sharply distinguished from the work of the "conjurers" who attempt to "force and coerce" spirits to follow their own human will.[28] While he deems their work possible, Paracelsus condemns it sharply for going against the grain of nature.

> *The conjurors want to force and coerce through incantations, so that the sidereal body must do what they want, so that their power rules the sidereal body. They dare themselves to this, which is nowhere possible, neither with the saints nor with nature.*
>
> *Therefore, such recklessness accomplishes such virtue that they incite Satan, who is otherwise on a chain. For it is us who tread over serpents and dragons, and it is us who are Satan's chains, it is us who bind him.*[29]

The importance of the differentiation of *Nigromantia* and *Nectromantia* cannot be overemphasised. Understanding the divergency in these approaches towards approaching the world of spirits, offers the key to Paracelsian magic.

In the most simplest of terms, it is this. The nigromantist uses spirits to attempt to bend the world towards their will. The nectromantist uses themselves as a spirit to learn to listen to the secrets of the world. The nigromantist follows the logic—and tragedy—of all conquerors. The nectromantist follows the logic of the botanist and ethologist. The former lives to materialise their own agenda at all cost, the latter expends all cost to understand the secret agendas

28 Sudhoff (ed.), Vol. XII, p. 146.
29 Ibid.

they are surrounded by. The former looks at themselves and sees the world as a giant mirror. The latter looks at the world, and sees themselves as a single strand in a giant weave.

Science and art, in such Paracelsian sense, are one and the same, and both are void without divine inspiration. They are human attempts to step over sleeping serpents and dragons and to approach the secrets they guard. Not for exploitation of *I*, *Me* and *Mine*, but for restoring the natural balance that is constantly pushed out of its equilibrium by human blindness.

Let's read the following excerpts from Paracelsus' opus magnum, the *Philosophia Sagax* or *Astronomia Magna* (1537/1538), in which he expends great effort to help us understand the outline of a divinely inspired form of animistic epistemology.

Before we do that, however, we are inserting an excerpt from another manuscript he penned during the same year, his *Nine Books on the Nature of Things* (*Die 9 Bücher De Natura Rerum*, Viallach, 1537).

Where the first of the following quotes provides essential grounding in Paracelsus' animistic cosmography, the second quote from the *Philosophia Sagax* speaks to the specific human art of gaining knowledge about the world by means of mediation of spirits.

De Vita Rerum Naturalium[30]

No one can deny that the air gives life to all corporeal and substantial things that grow on the earth and are born from it. But what and how the life of each thing is in particular, is to know that it is nothing but a spiritual being, an invisible and intangible thing and a spirit and a spiritual thing. Therefore, just as nothing corporeal exists unless it has a spirit in secret, so nothing corporeal exists unless it has a life hidden in it and lives. For what is life but a spiritual thing, as described.

Nor has life only that which moves and stirs, such as men, animals, the worms of the earth, the birds of the air, and the fish of the water, but also all corporeal and substantial things. For this we are to know: that at the beginning of the

30 From the fourth book of Paracelsus' *Die 9 Bücher De Natura Rerum.*

creation of all things, God did not create a single corpus without a spirit, which it carries with it in secret, for what would a corpus be without its spirit? Nothing. Therefore the spirit has the power and virtue and lies in the hidden, and not in the corpus, because in the corpus is death, it is but the subject of death and in it is neither to be looked for nor to be found anything other than death. For the corpus may be destroyed in many ways, but the spirit not. It always remains a spirit and alive, is also the subject of life, and keeps its own corpus alive. But in the destruction of the corpus the spirit is separated from it and leaves the corpus dead and goes back to the place from which it came. Namely into the air and into the chaos of the upper and also lower firmament. From this we see that there are many and various spirits, just as there are many corpora. For there are the heavenly spirits, infernal spirits, human spirits, brazen spirits, mineral spirits, saline spirits, crystal spirits, liquid spirits, aromatic spirits, herbal spirits, root spirits, wood spirits, flesh spirits, blood spirits, spirits of the bones, etc.[31]

Therefore you should also know that the spirit is actually the life and the balsam of all corporeal things. [...] Now the life of man is nothing else but an astral balsam,[32] *a balsamic impression, a heavenly, invisible fire, an enclosed air and a tinctured salt spirit. It cannot be named otherwise and more clearly.*[33]

On the Art of Nectromantia[34]

Christ says that nothing is so secret that it will not be revealed, and theologians refer this to the heart of man alone,

31 In the original, the enumeration reads: "*spiritus coelestes, spiritus infernales, spiritus hominis, spiritus metalli, spiritus of minerals, spiritus of salium, spiritus gemmarum, spiritus marcasiten, spiritus of arsenicalien, spiritus potabilium, spiritus aromatum, spiritus herbarum, spiritus radicum, spiritus lignorum, spiritus carni, spiritus sanguinis, spiritus of the bones etc.*"

32 *Balsam* as a Paracelsian term refers to the essential life-giving principle or force.

33 Sudhoff (ed.), Vol. XI, pp. 329–330.

34 From Paracelsus' magnum opus *Philosophia Sagax*.

yet the philosopher may also need to refer it to the Light of Nature. For look at the herbs whose powers are invisible, and yet they can be found within them. [...]

Therefore the saying of Christ is not only spoken of the secrecy of the human heart, but also of the natural work of God. Therefore it is necessary that man should be made manifest, and likewise it is necessary in all things that nature should be made manifest, and what is in it. For to what end would it be good or useful that so much virtue should be in one thing and no one should know it? [...]

If he is to know, he must learn it through the eyes. What cannot be done through the eyes must be done through the art. As God has ordained it, so it is, so it should be used, of which Nectromantia is also one. [...]

And although it is so that the theologians do not want such, it is due to their folly and coarse understanding that they attribute to the devil a thing that is nevertheless from God, an upright art. [...]

So that by its natural effect the natural powers are experienced. For nature has nothing so secretly hidden in her that it may be hidden from the ground of this art. So the arts shall be experienced, and what lies in the sea, in the mountains, in the rock, in man, in all corners, in the day or in the darkness. Therefore it is necessary that we have a knowledge of this art Nectromantiae and understand and recognise it well in its foundation, so that we learn and experience the miracles and wonders of God in the natural mysteries.

So that I can explain to you how to recognise Nectromantiam, that we should be able and learn it properly, as an art that reveals what is hidden, and such arts are the noblest of all arts. Know, then, that we have a mandate from Christ, according to which we must all be guided and turned. This mandate is not only the intentions and teachings of eternal service, but also [the teachings] of the Light of Nature. And this very mandate is thus: seek and you shall find. This is the art that man should know, seek, and so he finds. So now we are commanded to seek, for not-seeking will not experience secrecy. For whom does a roasted dove fly into the mouth? Or whom does the vine go after? One must go after it himself. Now seeking happens in many ways, as there are many kinds of food and other such things, so also with seeking there are many kinds. But that which is to be learned by the seeking itself is to be kept, and the same is to remain unchanged and not to be suppressed, as has been done by the theologians. […]

[It is] as if there was a treasure hidden. Now the same treasure has a spirit, the same must be the art and the reason of the art and without this nobody creates nothing, because the same [spirit] makes the art. From this it follows that nature gives us arts which we should seek and the same arts are not from man but from nature, which at the same time acts wisely.

So where there is a heart, there is also a mouth, there is also a voice, there is now the exploration of the heart. So where the treasure is, there is also a mouth, the same is the art.[35]

Now see what the art gives and in what it works. It proves in the Light of Nature that every creature, sensitive or insensitive, is endowed with a natural spirit. Not only the grown things, but also the lasting ones. So know this spirit's type and quality. Just as a corpus is recognised in its shadow, so where the shadow is, there must be a corpus. How therefore a corpus is recognised by the shadow in a likeness of approximately what the corresponding corpus may be, know then to understand that in the same way as no shadow may be without a corpus and no corpus without a shadow, so also it may not be that there was any corpus in the elements without such a shadow-spirit, that is [its] vision and is a shadow of the same, an appearance as in a mirror. So the spirits go out from the creatures which appear under our eyes, not that they are spirits, but according to the likeness of a shadow they are to be understood. So you should know what appears there and not assume otherwise. And such shadow and mirror-like figure is commanded to the art Nectromantia, which can bring it there, as an apothecary brings the herb into the tins. Or as this example proves: there goes a voice

35 Sudhoff (ed.), Vol. XII, pp. 148–152.

of a man, which is heard and yet his person is not seen, and by means of the voice is understood approximately what the corpus is, that is what kind of corpus that is, from which the voice comes. So the name spirit comes, as if the voice would be called a spirit and yet it is not a spirit, but a voice from the same corpus.

So no thing exists without such a spirit, as I have now told, that is no corpus is without a shadow or voice. And as the sun makes any shadow, so there is another sun that makes the shadow in the nectromantia and is called sol gaba nale.[36]

Now such spirit stems from the firmament and is naturally brought into beings during their birth and for such spirits we must look. In the same way as one who follows a voice, or as a hunter follows a track, for the track is also the spirit. Because with such things one finds the searching or track-reading in many ways.

Now such spirits are of many kinds, one to every man, another to every beast, another to the birds, another to the worms, another to the metals, another to the gems, another to the wood, another to the ore, another to the herbs. Whoever wants to be a Nectromanticus, he should and must know such spirits, because without them he will find nothing.

Now if there is an art, as is reported amongst the five kinds, which teaches to seek, it goes only to this spirit and from this spirit into the corpus, from which it proceeds. So one should search, that one knows the trace through the nectromantic art and the body through the trace: So it is found, as it is said and assumed. For this spirit appears in mirrors and beryls,[37] *it drives the divining rods and draws to itself*

36 read: *the sun that gives the spirit of one's birth.* For further reference see Pagel, p. 99.

37 Beryl, a crystal-clear, colourless, semi-precious stone or gemstone, which, however, may also appear (depending on the presence of certain substances) in a crystalline form of various colours. The term was also used to indicate a gemstone in general. To beryl is attributed the ability of optical magnification, reflection as well as the bundling of light.
Source: *Frühneuhochdeutsches Wörterbuch*, http://fwb-on-line.de/go/berille.h1.0m_1647531439.

> *like the magnet draws the iron, it drives the sieve around, it draws the flames away from the light, for it has an attractive power, so that they are drawn to the things that are sought, like the iron to the magnet. Therefore, let no one be surprised at such things, for they are to be considered after the magnetic kind.*[38]

It is astounding to what great length Paracelsus was willing to go to help us avoid the false associations the term *spirit* held during his time and still holds today. He knew about the misperceptions, about the power politics affecting this term, and about the instant condemnation attracted by any art that would centre itself upon animistic spirit-communion. And yet, he found the way to preserve the integrity of the magician's work, and to express it in entirely new terms.

Nectromantia is the art of drawing out the hidden voice in each object. Like a shadow is cast off any object by the sun, so this voice is cast off any object by its inborn spirit. The one who seeks to listen to it, activates it. Because it is of a "magnetic kind" and it is the act of seeking it out that activates this hidden voice. This voice is the track the nectromantist follows like a hunter follows their game. And a game it is that unfolds between the human seeker and the spirit's voice sought. For not-seeking will not reveal secrecy. But by the act of seeking it out, secrecy is stirred to life, to speak, to reveal itself to the seeker. The world reacts to the nectromantist's touch, to their call and presence.

When we breathe softly upon an insect in our hand, it might uncurl its feelers and open its presence to us. In such manner our seeking has to be sent out into the world, like a breath, like a quiet calling voice, waiting for the world to respond. Nectromantia, Paracelsian magic in its essence, is *the art of creating resonance*. In equal measures, it requires an intentional touch and the ability to stay silent and to become the echo-body sent into resonance by the world's response.

In such manner, all realms of creation can be awakened to speak back to us: the realm of the stars, the realm of the poisons, the realm of the natural constitution, the realm of the spirit and the realm of Divinity. Generating such a form of living resonance or dialogue is the

38 Sudhoff (ed.), Vol. XII, pp. 157–159.

art of Nectromantia. However, the "voices" speaking back to us are prone to error and deception because they speak based upon their own limited perceptions. That is why it is essential that the nectromantist places themselves into the Light of Divinity when they look out and listen to the world.

Here now lies the essential difference between the Western mystic and the Paracelsian magician. The former strives to take the position of the angels closest to the throne, standing before God, with their eyes fixed on the source of creation, assuming the shortest path of return to the origin.

The nectromantist or Paracelsian magician strives to stand in the same place, but facing the other way. Divinity behind them, the light of God shining over their back into the world, illuminating their gaze into the mesmerising cosmos of creation. The mystic is an expert in evolution, in stepping out of the cycle of creation. The Paracelsian magician is the exact opposite: in companionship with the spirits of the world, they turn themselves into a tool of Divine involution. According to Paracelsus, this was a path open to every man and woman. In an expressly Pelagian sense, he condemned the idea of an Apostolic time, and encouraged everyone to become an *apostle* in their own life.

> *So the authorities should also provide servants with services, because Christ did not want to do or did all things alone, such as healing bodies, but he also used apostles. Likewise the emperor, though he would want to do all things alone, yet shall he not do them. He should not take to himself governors, but those who have full authority. Who knows, those who live in the fear of God may be more gifted by God than the emperor himself; and this may be more blessedly due to the common man. For he who has been made well by St. Peter is probably as well as he who has been made well by Christ. The disciple is like the master. He who does not accept the disciple does not accept the Master. […]*
>
> *For all things are done through servants, in the same way that God sent the angel Gabriel to Mary. But God wants it that way, so what is it to us?*[39]

39 Goldammer (ed.) 1965, Vol. II, p. 56.

Thus, there was no longer any need for priests or for priestly mediated divine revelation. Christ i.e., God incarnate was constantly revealing Himself everywhere in creation to everyone who was willing to see, at every single moment. What was needed was not a brighter light to penetrate the mind of every lay person, but a calmer mind that knows how to listen to the revelatory spirit-voices surrounding us at every moment.

Psalm 99:6/7: They called on the Lord and he answered them. He spoke to them from the pillar of cloud.

> *In the New Testament we don't have it like that, there we have Christ personally; which is more than God coming to them in a cloud. 'They called upon God and he came to them. So we do too, and Christ comes to us. In the Old Testament it was like the previous verse says, in the New Testament we are all equal. Equal to Moses, equal to Aaron, equal to Samuel. Therefore, God no longer appears to us; for we no longer have priests, we no longer need them. So we also have no need of a Vision, for we have heard and seen Christ with clear eyes and with our ears.*[40]

All this theory, only to reveal that the actual practice of gaining knowledge from spirits is not at all complicated! In fact, to Paracelsus it is so natural, that most humans simply do not realise that they are doing it already.

Becoming a magician—or shall we say: a nectromantist—thus is much less a matter of ascending into occult realms than becoming aware of what we are already engaged in.

> *But now about the fact that we also have a spirit, which flies out of us and does not stay within us, because every mind is like a spirit. As I intend to experience heaven, my spirit is in heaven, to experience the herbs, my spirit is in the herbs. Now there are spirits in the sky, spirits in the herbs, likewise in the air, in the water. The same spirits and my spirit, they come together. Now my spirit also has a course, I direct it, as I lead it. Now heaven also has a course in its spirit, and my*

40 Goldammer (ed.), Vol. IV, p. 306.

> *spirit is in me as in a beast [i.e., natural], and the spirit of heaven is in the stars as in a beast [i.e., natural]. So it comes about that the two come together, and whichever part surpasses the other is the master and becomes one.*[41]

Our mind is our spirit, and it continuously commingles with the spirits of the world. Depending on the course and force of the encountering spirits, our mind gets momentarily unified with the spirit of greater power. This is especially true with regards to contact with celestial beings and the Olympic Spirits.[42] In these moments our mind becomes the spirit's mind, or at least it becomes coloured by it. Our inner voice becomes (coloured by) the spirit's voice. Without even knowing it, we are in constant spirit communion.

Such unagitated, simple factual realisation rests at the foundation of every animistic worldview. And so it does with Paracelsus: human-to-spirit contact is not an exception, rather it is the norm. Becoming consciously aware of it, however, was already the exception for most Western humans at the time Paracelsus composed his manuscripts.

That is why he needed to invent so many new terms, why he had to take us—his readers—by the hand and lead us out of the forest of spirit-contact which we had become too blind to see. So that eventually we could turn around on the plain of phenomenological experience and, in its clear light, see the marvels and *magnalia* of our everyday lives.

41 Sudhoff (ed.), Vol. XIV, pp. 58–59.
42 Ibid., 59.

BOOK 1

CHAPTER III

THE BIRTH OF THE OLYMPIC SPIRITS

The Paracelsian tradition [...] was an initiatory tradition.[1]

IN WHAT FOLLOWS, we will examine the emergence of the idea of the Olympic Spirit(s) in the work of Paracelsus. By tracing their appearance, their development and continuous shaping through the complete works of Paracelsus we aim to gain a holistic perspective of what these entities were to him and how he encouraged his readers to think about and work with them.

Finally, at the end of this chapter, in possibly the most important section of this book, we will arrive at a faithful reconstruction of core elements of (Pseudo-) Paracelsus' *Astronomia Olympi Novi*,[2] the lost third book of his *Philosophia Sagax* (1537). This book specifically was intended to reveal the mysteries and practical ways of operating amongst these ancient and yet deeply personal entities. We will trace the development of the Olympic Spirit(s) chronologically. This means follow their appearance not according to when Paracelsus' works first appeared in print (most of them, as pointed out before, posthumously), but according to when he may have composed the original manuscripts. For the dating of the latter we rely on the meticulous work of Karl Sudhoff in his edition of Paracelsus' medical and philo-

1 Paola Zambelli, *White Magic, Black Magic in the European Renaissance*, 2007, p. 207.

2 As Carlos Gilly showed, the relevant chapters in this book were most likely written by Adam Haslmayr, yet in a decidedly genuine Paracelsian spirit. Equally, Haslmayr might have used material from the unpublished manuscripts of Paracelsus he had access to.

sophical works[3] as well as in his *Bibliographia Paracelsica*.[4]

For several reasons this present study cannot claim to be a concluding one. First, most of Paracelsus genuine works remained in manuscript form long after his death. While the research and curation undertaken by Sudhoff has been masterful in multiple ways, it has also proven to be biased by a clearly anti-magical attitude towards Paracelsus' oeuvre. Thus, as we will see in a later chapter, further material might need to be considered in the analysis of the emergence of the Olympic Spirit(s). yet, as these materials were classified by Sudhoff and others as spurious, later additions by the hand of early *Paracelsians*, they do not appear in their original timeline for Paracelsus' manuscripts.

Second, within the works of Paracelsus the term *Olympic Spirit(s)* is in no way sharply separated but rather intricately connected to several other related terms he coined such as the *inner firmament, the astral body, the inner stars,* etc.[5] To understand these terms in the proper context of Paracelsus' entire cosmography, the prior chapter has established essential foundations. Reading it in advance of this section is highly recommended.

Furthermore, we will discover the root-term *Olymp* is sometimes used in the classical sense of the word, meaning the high or supralunar realm of *heaven*, and sometimes as a generalised term to indicate something as *superior* or *ruling*. These applications of the root-term have to be distinguished from the expressed idea of the *Olympic Spirit(s)*, as the latter refers exclusively to the forces within the inner firmament and the celestially defined constitution of man.

In a following chapter we will investigate how Paracelsus' original and highly complex concept of the Olympic Spirit(s) continued to evolve —often experienced a sharp truncation— in the manuscripts and books of early Paracelsianism until the end of the 17th century.

For readers new to the subject, the obvious has to be pointed out right at the outset: within Paracelsus' original works the Olympic Spirit(s) are never called by titles or offices but plainly addressed in their totality by this overall term. The commonly known seven identi-

3 Karl Sudhoff, ed. *Theophrast von Hohenheim, gen. Paracelsus*, Sämtliche Werke, Vol. I–XIV, München, Berlin: R. Oldenbourg, 1922–1933.

4 Sudhoff, *Bibliographia Paracelsica*, Berlin: Verlag Georg Reimer, 1894 (Reprint by Martino Publishing, 2000).

5 See Pagel 1984, p. 99.

ties of *Aratron*, *Bethor*, *Och*, *Phaleg*, *Hagith*, *Ophiel* and *Phul* are additions that were only introduced with the Arbatel in 1575, more than thirty years after Paracelsus' death.

> *For that you bring it correctly into knowledge, then notice that heaven and earth are two, visible and invisible, and are both the limbus,*[6] *therefore man also [is] both. That is why the world is not too large for [human] imagination; one can imagine over [a range of] a thousand miles and make an impression a thousand miles [away]; one can also imagine as far as heaven and impress in heaven. And in the same way that the stars poison us on earth, so that we die, often without our [giving them] cause, so we can poison them, just as well as they poison us. For our speculation in imagining goes up, just as much as theirs comes down. If we enter into imagining in this way, our curses become true, but their poisoning is [likewise] our disease.*[7]

1520

A Philosopher First and a Medic Last

WE FIRST COME across the term *Olympus* in Paracelsus' unique kind of astro-medical elucidations of the *Eleven Treatises* which he wrote around 1520 and which were first printed in 1564 in Cologne.[8] Here the term appears in juxtaposition to the classical doctrine of the humours (hot, cold, moist, dry, and mixed). As most doctors would focus on these, their therapies would have to label many diseases as incurable because they could not be sufficiently affected by "purging and treating" the humours alone. The doctors who operate in this manner, "fire the arrow without its head".[9] According to Paracelsus,

6 *limus*, also *limbus*, originally meaning *clay*, *mud*, referring to the earth from which God created man in Gen 2:7. Paracelsus used the word broadly to indicate the raw foundation of all physical substance and being. See Goldammer 1955, p. 282.
7 Sudhoff (ed.), Vol. XIV, p. 316.
8 Sudhoff (ed.) 1928, Vol. I, XXXVIII.
9 Ibid., p. 18.

the true impact will only be made once the doctor begins to understand and address the astrological influences, because "the most is that which is above that [the humours] and that is *olympus* and the *celestial virtues (virtutes coelestes).*"[10] In fact, the doctor has to become alike to the *Olympus*, that is, heaven has to be in their hand, then the stars become their arcanum.

> *For the medic is also created like Olympus; that is the medic who knows heaven and knows to hold it in their hand, to whom belong the secrets of the stars.*[11]

Paracelsus returns to this idea later on in the treatise when he explains more explicitly how the doctor needs to be able to change and even replace specific celestial influences within their patient, in order to effectively address certain diseases.[12] He emphasises again, "this is the reason why God has created the medic: it is not their person alone, but the heaven in their hand, that makes the medic."[13]

He further stresses that some operations require the medic to be an "astronomus olympi superioris" i.e., to work with the stars in their influences in the firmament high above man in the sky. yet, other operations require them to be "astronomus olympi inferioris" i.e., to work with the stars and their influences within man, or in the lower firmament. Both approaches, though, require them to be a philosophus first and a medicus last.

> *This is the reason why God has created the medic: it is not their person alone, but the heaven in their hand, that makes the medic. [...] The first [kind of healing] needs an astronomus olympi inferioris, the other an astronomus olympi superioris, and each should be in his profession a philosophus first and a medic last.*[14]

10 Ibid.
11 Ibid., 30.
12 See for example: "Thus antimony is a cure of the ethics, because it transplants the star of Saturn into the star of Venus. This is the art of medicine." Sudhoff (ed.) 1928, Vol. I, p. 41.
13 Sudhoff 1928, Vol. I, p. 41.
14 Ibid. We should take specific note of Paracelsus' early advice to embrace and learn the art of "astronomia olympi inferioris." This relates to the realm of

In this early work we do not yet find the concept of the inner firmament in its full articulation. Instead, we encounter Paracelsus at a stage of his life where he was developing all of its components, often in juxtaposition to classical cures, and in his own unique interpretation of the doctrine of emanation according to Classical Astrology and Neoplatonism.

For Paracelsus, *emanation* indicated a hierarchy of influences. These *hierarchies* or *emanations* offered him the key to understanding which being or substance held an office above another one. What it did *not* indicate was a hierarchy or sequencing of chronological evolution or spatial distance.

As we saw in the previous chapter, for Paracelsus everything was present right now, pulsating, mixing, congealing, in the flesh of the ulcer, in the kidney-stones of the patient right in front of him. The stars were not distant, removed intelligences that required intricate conjurations to be pulled down into the sublunar realm. Rather, they were right here, right now, already held in the hand of the medic, in the spirit of the cure, in the body of the patient. The stars did not require conjuration, they required active mediation and careful intervention to be brought into a favourable *composition*.

1525–1526

Spirits Poured into Bodies

DURING THE NEXT eleven years, we have evidence for only two more authentic works by Paracelsus that make use of the term *olympic*. However, neither of them brings the word into context of the *Olympic Spirit(s)*. Sudhoff wasn't able to determine the exact year when Paracelsus penned the *Liber Meteororum*. Most likely it occurred between 1525 and 1526.[15] As the title of the book indicates, it is focused on weather patterns and their celestial causes. Thus, Paracelsus speaks of the *Olympus* as the heavenly origin of lightning and meteorites. He also infers that some beings are born within the heaven,

chthonic spirits and their "infernal pharmacy" as he later calls it. We will return later to this in his opus magnum, the *Philosophia Sagax* from 1537.

15 Sudhoff Vol. XIII, IV.

without seed or semen, just as some animals emerge from the ocean or how the salamander is born from fire.[16]

Equally without an exact date but attributed to the same period of 1525–1526, we discover *The Nine Books of the Natural Things* (*Die 9 Bücher De Natura rerum*).[17] Stemming from the creative career of the circa thirty-year-old Paracelsus, we encounter many critical thoughts of his later work in these early manuscripts. Or as Sudhoff put it:

> *Envisioned in his youth, matured and developed in the height of his life.*[18]

Together with his *Herbarius*, these fragmentary treatises contain insights Paracelsus collected during his long wanderings, focused on the local therapeutic material in the realms of flora, minerals and healing springs.

These nine treatises were only published from 1567 onwards and appeared disparately in various collections, as well as combined in a single book from 1570 onwards. They seem to have garnered considerable interest among early Paracelsians.[19]

Now, the first book of the *De Natura rerum* deals with the magico-medical qualities of *turpentine*. For Paracelsus this term specifically referred to the distillation of resin harvested from European larch trees. He compared it to the olibanum tree in the Southern region and called it the most wondrous of all trees in the German land. To him, the healing powers and versatility of its resin was comparable only to the milk offered by cattle to man.

Already in this early creative period, Paracelsus emphasises that the healing qualities of turpentine do not stem from the material substance as such, but from the "anima and animus with which the same is shielded".[20] Just like for all other natural objects, it is these spirits that imprint their *virtues* into the elementary composition of any substance.

16 Ibid.
17 Sudhoff (ed.)1930, Vol. II, p. VII.
18 Ibid., V.
19 Ibid., XIII.
20 Ibid., 64.

> *Furthermore, turpentine has a medicinal effect, which comes to it innately from the creation. For you should know that the medicine in natural things, which is an invisible spirit, is poured into the same corpus, as the spirit of man is poured into man. The turpentine is put into so many virtues, as first into the corpus elementarum, second into the heavenly impressiones, third into an olympic vulcanum, fourth into complexiones chaos, fifth into spiritum creatum.*[21]

The enumeration in this quote is Paracelsus' way of emphasising the positive qualities of turpentine in its full scope of its magico-medical application: from its impact on the substance of physical bodies (corpus elementarum), on altering astrological influences (celestial impressiones), to changing the heavenly governed chemistry in natural objects (olympic vulcanum[22]), to its ability to affect the properties of air and gasses (complexionem chaos), as well as its effect on the inborn spirits to all things created (spiritum creatum). Accordingly, it is the art of the medic to apply such powerful substances at the right time, in the right manner and to the right *realm of impact*.

1530–1532

A Union of Celestial Spirits

IN THE FOLLOWING years, leading up to the moment of his disappearance, Paracelsus worked on a series of interconnected manuscripts which he himself called his *Paramiric Works*.[23]

They deal with the origin of diseases according to his three essential principles (*sulphur, mercury, salt*), with the broad range of illnesses caused by accretion and concretion (i.e., *tartaric* illnesses), and with ailments related to the female body and sexual organs.

In these works the mentioning of the term *Olympus* is tangential again: Paracelsus explains that through the respective astral influ-

21 Ibid., pp. 67–8.

22 In Paracelsus, *vulcanus* refers to the chemically effective principle in natural objects as the counterpart to archaeus, which indicates the chemically effective principle in man (Goldammer 1955, pp. 279–287).

23 Sudhoff Vol. IX, p. 5.

ences stones can be generated anywhere in the organs of the body, for they are an *Olympus*.

> *Now the prima materia in man are all spirit and all heavenly bodies, and the time is their course. [...] The whole body gives the generation of this stone, because it is an olympus. Thus, the stone is generated olympi, since it must be taken all together.*[24]

What we observe in this section, is the often-implicit twofold connotation of the term *olympus* in his work. It refers to both a *superior* influence related to the inner stars of man, as well as to an effect that takes place when all these influences coalesce in one point.

Olympus, especially in its singular form, thus indicates the coming-together, a union of the celestial spirits within man in a single point of focus and concentration: *a concentration of spirits both in time and organic location.*

Directly following his Paramiric works, Paracelsus wrote his book *Of the Invisible Diseases* (*De Causis Morborum Invisibilium*). More so than in previous alchemo-medical manuscripts, we find evidence in it of Paracelsus' growing theological and spiritual interest. Karl Sudhoff considered the book an incomplete and at least partially failed attempt to provide a 16th century "psychogenic pathogenesis", as only its first book "was truly medical."[25] His assessment, though, speaks more to his own bias, that is the liberty he took to judge Paracelsus' works against what he wanted them to be, rather than what they were.

Following Paracelsus' remark in the prior book, that *olympus* indicates a unification of the inner celestial spirits, in *De Causis Morborum Invisibilium* we now come across the earlier quoted section of critical importance:

> *In all things, know that in the creation of man, the invisible body was created like the visible. And both parts come out of the limbo.*[26] *For one part is earthly, and the other is heav-*

24 Ibid., 172.
25 Ibid., 15.
26 As mentioned in a prior footnote, *limus* or *limbus*, originally referred to the

> *enly: wherefore the heavenly has his effect just as the earthly. But the earthly is commanded to build and to use the hands, therefore it is commanded more in consciousness than the invisible body. And what the outer body does, that is a whole work. But what the invisible body does is like the shadows of the body. For although the earthly body performs its works by imagination, it concerns only the corporeal. But what is done in that place, that also the imagination may cause to be done by the invisible body. […]*
>
> *These things are done by the Olympic spirit, which tears off the shadow from all the works of the body. In the Olympic Spirit lies the art Gabalistica with its appendices, which art proves that to the imagination still much more is possible in those [human beings] in whom the joining of the Olympic Spirits has taken place. Then in the same way as the visible corpora can come together, so can the Olympic Spirits of creation, which are the heavenly bodies in man: these things are described in the books of the Gabalia.*[27]

With this proclamation of the *Gabalistic Art* and its central tool, the *Olympic Spirit*, Paracelsus takes leave for seclusion in the Appenzell Alps—only to return to from it with a firework of elucidations on the exact design and functioning of this art, which he ignites with ink and pen and paper in the following years from 1532 to 1538. Through the analysis of *Nectromantia* in the previous chapter, however, we can make a critical deduction from the above quote. As we have seen, in his *Philosophia Sagax* (1537/1538) Paracelsus goes to great lengths to explain the nature of working with spirits in vision. It is there that he concentrates on the metaphor of the *shadow* of a corpus as its inborn spirit. He even goes so far to call them "shadow-spirits"[28] to underline the firmness of the bond and communion of these beings with the elementary corpus they are attached to. In the above quote from his treatise *Of the Invisible Diseases*, Paracelsus' revealed that it is the Olympic Spirit who "tears off the shadow from all the works

clay from which God created Adam (Genesis 2:7); in Paracelsian language, it indicates the foundational substance (*Urgrund*) from which all physical or embodied matter emerged. (Goldammer Vol. IV, Teil I, p. 282).

27 Sudhoff Vol. IX, pp. 297–298.

28 Sudhoff 1929 Vol. XII, pp. 157–159.

of the body".[29] Not only do we thus know that the Olympic Spirit is a concentration and unification of spirits within man. It is also of a different kind of nature than the spirits inborn into all objects of creation as it holds the power to separate the former from the latter.

1534
The Magic of the Microcosm

EMERGING FROM HIS hermitage in the mountains, we meet Paracelsus again in Innsbruck, and not in the best economical situation, as he puts it mildly himself. We find the remarks on his dire finances in the afterword of his *Three Books on the Plague*, which in 1534 he dedicated to the neighbouring city of Vipiteno/Sterzing in South Tyrol.[30] This book is an ideal object to trace the public appearance of the physician and magician Paracelsus.

By this time, he told us earlier, he had learned at the hands and mouths of *shearers, barber-surgeons, physicians, nigromancers, alchemists, the rich and the poor, the noble and the ignoble, the clever and the simple.*[31]

When he returned from his spiritual hiatus to work as a doctor again (possibly not merely for ethical reasons but also due to financial ones), he had come to the conclusion that, in order to heal the body, it was necessary to work both with the substances of the elemental bodies as well as with their spirits.

As we shall see from the following longer quotation, Paracelsus had arrived at several critical insights which we already find in a seminal state in his earlier works and which now began to evolve into mature shape.

He is working within the Hermetic tradition when he affirms that man indeed is a microcosm. However, to Paracelsus that meant significantly more than the conceit that man was composed of all components of creation. It also meant that man held inner points of connection to all interfaces and components of the cosmos. It was a

29 Sudhoff Vol. IX, p. 298.
30 Ibid., 26.
31 Sudhoff Vol. X, p. 20, see also Sudhoff Vol. IX, p. 25.

statement of man's relatedness to the entire cosmos of creation at once. Man was a *place of many bridges*, a travelling hub for consciousness, from where the spirit of the human mind could travel literally *anywhere*. For Paracelsus, this was a uniquely human feature in the cosmos.

In addition, man also was the only being in the created world who could *reverse the usual operating order of creation*. This is a crucial and often overlooked aspect of Paracelsus' cosmosophy. Let's explore it in more detail.

According to a Neoplatonic foundation, the usual mode of operation in the cosmos was from outside to inside, and from the greater power to the smaller power. If we imagine the cosmos as a sphere, with the solid earth at its centre, then this way of operating could be considered *centripetal* i.e., forcing gravitation from the outside towards its centre. To Paracelsus this was not only a cosmological but also a medical principle. In the natural way of the cosmos, something external always gave impetus to something internal, something stronger formed or imprinted itself into something weaker. In this manner, the outer stars acted as force locks that impacted on the elements which in turn affected the state of spirits, fluids and tissues in mineral, plant and animal bodies.

This was also true for the human condition, but it was not what made humans uniquely *human*. For, according to Paracelsus, what made humans *human* were two aspects that were lacking in all mineral, plant and animal bodies:

MAN AS A MICROCOSM was not merely a medium of all powers of creation, but these powers were actually *embodied* within humans themselves. The cosmos did not only imprint itself into man, it was ontologically present *within him*. Such is the concept of *radical immanence*, as explored earlier.[32]

32 See Jevons (1964), p. 140. And an additional observation may be helpful here: Today we are familiar with the hypothetical idea that one day it will be possible to bring an extinct creature back to life from its surviving cells. If one pursues the idea of the human microcosm in its ontological consequence in Paracelsus to the end, one could create not only a new, living human being from the cells of a dead human being, but *the entire world*. All creatures of the mineral, vegetable, animal and spiritual world are spiritually implanted or rooted in a single human cell. It is worth meditating on this thought in relation to one's magical praxis.

THE SECOND ASPECT that made humans human was of particular Pelagian origin: it was the triad of free will, reason and imagination. Where sulphur, mercury and salt constituted the omnipresent matrix of all things created, will, reason and imagination were the opposite side of the coin. In Paracelsus' cosmosophy, they were the triumvirate of forces reserved for the human species alone.

Now, as we will see in the following quote, it was by uniting one's *will, reason* and *imagination* that man could *reverse the normal centripetal force flow of creation into a centrifugal one.* Rather than *being merely a passive medium* of higher forces of creation, man could turn all things created into *a medium of her/his own agency*. The way a human achieved this reversal of processes was by first uniting their *Olympic Spirit* and imprinting it into the spirit of the object they had chosen as a medium. For as we have seen, meditating upon an object was the act of allowing the object's spirit and one's own meet each other. In such encounter the stronger spirit would begin to colour the weaker one.[33] On top of this, the Olympic Spirit possessed the quality of releasing and separating out the spirit of any object from its corporeal body. We now begin to perceive the technical outlines of Paracelsian magic in practice.

As we read the next longer quotation, it becomes apparent why we dedicated the previous chapter to immersing ourselves into some of Paracelsus' spiritual texts and into his cosmosophy of immanence in particular. For a correct interpretation of his works from 1533 onwards always has to take both sides into account: Paracelsus the alchemical medic, as well as Paracelsus the animistic mage. For Paracelsus it was never either/or, but always one within the other, and both intertwined: Animism within Psychology within Animism, Magic within Medicine within Magic, Astrology within Chemistry within Astrology. The Ouroboros of faculties. The Ouroboros of life.

Let's now peruse Paracelsus' original words from 1534:

> *In order that you may further understand the reason of the plague, as its origin is, take an example from this: You know that the incantations of faith [incantatoria fides] can paralyse, kill, sicken a man, but also make him healthy, strengthen him etc. Now this effect is not of faith alone, but is an im-*

33 Sudhoff Vol. XIV, pp. 58–59.

pression, just as heaven impresses itself upon us: [In] one [man] this way and another that way, one [heaven] strikes today, another tomorrow, then it kills this one and then that one, and so on: all this is heavenly influence, this is impression. These [impressions] do not force anyone, but those who are willing to follow, they drive them to such behaviour.

Now man is a heaven of Olympus [coelum Olympi], that means he is provided with such a nature and such an [inner] firmament, like a microcosm of the [outer] firmament, that [means] in him is the same force, quality and power. Thus it also happens that man olympically influences his fellow men, that is, that his imagination becomes an impression and accomplishes the corresponding will in the weaker men.

Now there must be a means by which such happens. For all things must have a means, and without means nothing happens. Now the human being is the beginning of such an incantation, he is what initiates it, but the beginning may not complete it. Still, the heavenly body in him is governed by him, that means he poisons [i.e., willingly manipulates] his own constellation, so that his will, his poison enters into it. So [once] the poison is in the constellation, it becomes the means; and it is from the constellation's power that everything may become equal and united.

The other, to whom it is intended, also has a heaven of Olympus [coelum Olympi]. In the same measure as the stars are subjected to the imagination, so these two fight with each other. But the stronger one wins, and yet also the winner must eat the poison himself, although he overcomes the other. These are the ways of the stars and the imagination, and how they come into being. The star is the means in man, otherwise it may not happen but through the means.

From this it follows that an image can enchant a man, not through the powers of [magical] characters or the like, by virgin wax. But it is the imagination that overcomes its own constellation and thus becomes the means to accomplish the will of their heaven, that is [the will] of their man.

In this, it must be understood that the stars have reason, wisdom, cunning, quarrels, war, weapons etc., just as we humans do. This is based on the fact that they are our par-

ents. Therefore, we have received such reason, wisdom, cunning, quarrels etc. from them. But because we have received them from them, it follows that they also have them, with the only difference that we act bodily and materially, but they act spiritually and invisibly. This no one must misunderstand, that such reason, wisdom etc., as the stars governs in us, would be from God, but they come from the great creature [the macrocosm]. For the wisdom which we have from God overcomes all heavens and stars: but here I speak of the earthly powers.[34]

1536

The Medium is the Message

IN HIS *Great Miracle Medicine* from 1536 we find Paracelsus again stressing that the true medic needs to consider the outer as well as the inner stars or firmament of man. The latter here are differentiated by the neologisms of the "Aether Olympii" as well as the "Sidus Physici corporis".[35]

Later on in the same work, the term "olympus" is used in combination with "firmament" and all of "nature" to highlight that a particular poison can be found anywhere in nature.[36] This emphasis is honed further when Paracelsus describes the "basiliscus Olympi" as the most dangerous of the basilisks, born from two different semens, and greatly poisoning anyone upon whom their gaze falls upon from heaven i.e., from "Olympus".[37] Then in the same year, we come across "A Mantic Draft. Given at Munich" that includes an early version of Paracelsus' approach towards the "Explanation of all Astronomy".[38] This chapter can be read as an early draft of material for Paracelsus' *Astronomia Magna*. In a further evolved version, yet largely maintaining the same descriptions, we find these elucidations repeated

34 Sudhoff Vol. IX, pp. 577–578.
35 Sudhoff 1928, Vol. X, p. 331.
36 Ibid., 440.
37 Ibid., 444.
38 Ibid., 647–8.

again in 1537/1538 in a stand-alone manuscript of the same title.[39]

In the following we are quoting the relevant section from the earliest version of this chapter. Paracelsus emphasises the essential role taken by the stars in acting as *mediums of creation.* However, his use of the word *star* does not only refer to the heavenly bodies in the outer firmament, but equally to their interwoven resonance organs all throughout creation.

Thus, the same *astrum* exists in the firmament, in man, in the animals, and in the elements. Like members of a family, these variations of the same star should be thought of as both united by kin as well as independent in their ability to generate impact and action upon their own determination.

> *Now is to speak of the medium that mediates between the highest stars and the body, and this in the following manner. There is a star which governs everything: in man the animal mind, in the animal its senses, in the elements their effects.*
>
> *That heavenly body is the highest creature in the created cosmos and is in the Olympo [i.e., in the elevation], that means, it has all things under itself.*
>
> *Now it should work in man, it should work in the elements, it should work in the cattle and direct and turn their mind and spirit. If it is to do this, it needs a means. But there has to be a medium and this is also an astrum, and lies in those [substances] in which the upper star takes effect. Now it is through that very medium that the effect takes place in the substance and in the body.*
>
> *As an example: If Mars should operate in a man, he may not do it, unless he has a medium which is his martial star. And from this it follows that Mars works through this medium. So if the upper star is to work in a parakeet, then an astrum must lie in the parakeet, as the means through which the upper star acts.*
>
> *Thus it follows that there is a star in man, and a star in birds, and in all animals, and all that they do, they do from the upper influence, that they receive through their constellation, decreed into such a same concordance.*

39 Sudhoff Vol. XII, pp. 447–477.

In such way now there is an astrum in the elements as well as in the earth and [it is] powerful. The same astrum ignites the impressions from the upper star and then works by itself in the earth, so that what is in the earth must come from it. So it is also in the element water and in the others.

Therefore there is first one astrologer from the [study] of the highest stars, another astrologer from the stars of the people, one astrologer from the stars of the elements, one astrologer from the stars of the animals. So there are four astrologers from the elements, two from the stars of men and animals, that is six, and one astrologer from the highest stars, which makes seven. But one more astrologer is present, arising from [the study of] the imagination of men, this one is above all the others, and is the eighth.

Astrology has been forgotten and omitted, also other [sciences] more by the astrologers.

But he who wants to be an astrologer, he should be experienced in all eight, knowing and wise. Although those who are experienced in the individual [astrological] sciences are not to be despised, they cannot act universally.

However, the heavenly body is divided into eight parts, one is powerful, six are subjects, the eighth is also powerful and equal to the first and is more than the first in some points, as will be explained later about the new heaven and firmament.

But it is only right that an Olympic Astrologer [astrologus olympi] must know the other [sciences], how the mediums of the stars operate, generate and realise. This prevents one from following the upper [read: outer] stars, if their influence does not want to be completed by the lower [read: inner] stars; but if the latter want it differently, better, more evil etc.[40]

40 Sudhoff Vol. x, pp. 644–5.

1537–1538

Applying the Methridatum Olympi

PARACELSUS' OUTER AND inner life remained too turbulent throughout his biography that he could have left us a perfect synthesis of his worldview. However, his "Astronomia magna, or the complete Philosophia sagax[41] of the great and the small World"[42] comes closest to a matured illumination of his overall view of the animate world and the myriad creative forces in macrocosm and microcosm.

As Sudhoff observed, it is his *Astronomia magna*, "which gives us insight into a special circle of Hohenheim's thinking, directed to the comprehension of the relationality of the world, as he believed to recognise it in the cosmos and in man, coloured by his Old Testament-Christian mind, and influenced by Neoplatonic undercurrents."[43]

On more than 440 pages in print Paracelsus sets out to lift the veil of the Light of Nature and to introduce his readers to the mysteries of the cosmos. Or as the full tile of the original edition explains:

> *ASTRONOMIA MAGNA: Or The complete Philosophia Sagax of the Great and Small World, by the highly enlightened, experienced, and proven German philosopher and medic, Philippi Theophrasti Bombast, called Paracelsi magni. In it he teaches all the natural Light's abilities and inabilities, also all the philosophical and astronomical secrets of the great and the small world, and their right use and abuse. Secondly, the mysteries of the celestial Light. Thirdly, the faculty of faith. And fourth, what the spirits work through man etc.* [44]

41 The Latin word *sagax* stems from the Indo-European root *sag-, to seek, track, trail.* It is also found in the Latin word *sagire, to perceive, to seek to know.* As an adjective *sāgax, sāgacis* thus refers to someone or something of keen perception and is also found in the English *sagacious.*

42 Paracelsus, *Astronomie magna, oder Die ganze Philosophia Saga der grossen und kleinen Welt*, Frankfurt am Main: Martin Lechler, 1571. For further details see: Sudhoff, *Bibliographia Paracelsica*, pp. 219–221.

43 Sudhoff Vol. XII, V.

44 Sudhoff, *Bibliographia Paracelsica*, p. 219.

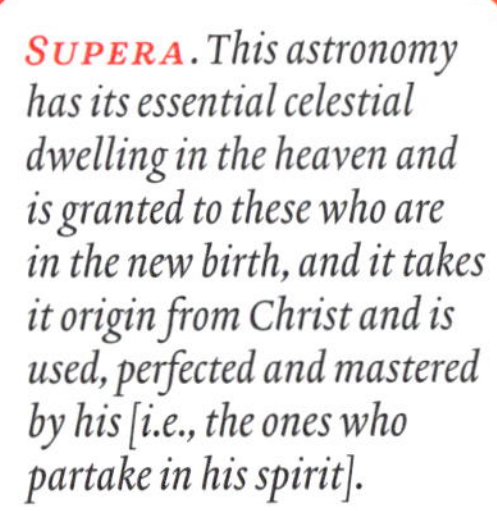

Astronomiæ. The astronomies are four, separated into four orders, none like the other. Yet, as their operations are similar, they are known to influence each other. How these four influences come together, unite, imprint and operate themselves within man, each one according to its nature, we shall explain in this figure.

Supera. *This astronomy has its essential celestial dwelling in the heaven and is granted to these who are in the new birth, and it takes it origin from Christ and is used, perfected and mastered by his [i.e., the ones who partake in his spirit].*

Naturalis Astronomia. *This astronomy comes from the firmament, and was essentially created within it by God the Father, and it is decreed to be a science and joined and passed on to the microcosm, as the one created from the 'limo terræ'.*

Olympi Novi. *This astronomy originates from faith, which means whatever the natural heaven is capable of, so can astronomy create it through faith; and it is used and given to the faithful and is perfect and opened through these.*

Inferorum. *This astronomy takes its origin from the natural realm of the firmament, and is only used by the infernal spirit; however, as these species also are natural astronomers, they can best be opened through themselves or through humans.*

This fourfold structure is indeed what we find in the *Astronomia Magna*; only with the usual caveat for Paracelsus that he had relatively little interest in the movement of the actual stars. Instead "the 'astrological' terminology hides a system of natural explanation by virtues or forces largely immanent in earthly objects."[45]

As alluded to in the subtitle of the book, he differentiates astronomia into four strands which all remain interrelated: natural, celestial[46], infernal[47], and astronomia *olympi novi*.[48] Thus, the *Philosophia Sagax* presents us with a most detailed exegesis of these four strands of astronomy, the divisions and sub-parts they each are made up of, and the respective magical arts and sciences the aspiring student had to explore and ultimately master. Unfortunately, the critical third book on the *Olympi novi seu fidei* was missing from Paracelsus' autographs; or at least it never made it into the first collected works edition (1589 to 1591) by Johan Huser (1545–1601).

Whether the missing book presents a deliberate omission on Paracelsus' side or whether it was owing to the disorganised state of his voluminous manuscripts at the time of his death, we do not know. Huser suspected it was deliberately hidden. As we will see from the following exploration of its indicated content, such scenario seems likely in light of Zambelli's viewpoint quoted above, considering Paracelsus' writings as an initiatory tradition.[49]

Paracelsus himself emphasised that the book of the *new firmament* (olympi novi) *originates from faith* and is only *given to the faithful.*[50] And despite the fact that this third book is missing from the *Philosophia Sagax*, the magnum is still giving us plenty of valuable leads on the secrets contained in the *Olympic art*.

45 Jevons, 1964, p. 139.
46 here titled by him as *supera*.
47 also titled by him as *satanistae*.
48 Sudhoff Vol. XII, p. 77.
49 Zambelli 2007, p. 207.
50 Peuckert 1967, p. 108. We have examined the treatise that decades after Paracelsus' death appeared under the same name in *Holy Heretics* (Acher, 2023).

EXCURSUS

Reconstructing the *Astronomia Olympi Novi*

THE TITLE OF the fourfold division of astronomia itself provides a critical hint.

At this late stage of his creative output we see Paracelsus' use of the term "olympic" has fully moved on from its classical association with the Greek mountain Olympus as the seat of the ancient gods and its related meaning of heavenly. The actual category of astronomy related to heavenly or celestial matters he labels as *supera*. Instead, the *astronomia olympi novi* refers to the processes that arise from and are perfected by *faith*.

Faith, for Paracelsus, had nothing to do with fanciful fantasies or wishful thinking. Instead, he used the term to refer to a foundational capability within man, described as the ability to unite one's faith and imagination, and to bring them jointly into exaltation and work with them according to one's free will. Faith as such was, for Paracelsus, the foundation of all genuine magic.[51]

> *If the medic [...] anchors themselves in faith, then the faith splits itself into two: one faith in God, the other in Satan. If he believes truthfully, according to the Gospel, a mountain will sink itself into the depth of the ocean; and even much easier than that he will be able to heal a sick man. Such remedy does not need any help but faith in Divinity. Yet when his faith does not stand in God but in the infernal ones [inferos], it follows that such faith takes effect through the infernal*

51 *For know this of faith, that faith can do this, whether I use it wrongly or not, yet it works signs.* [...] *For it is faith that does it, it creates outcome, it bears its fruit, according to how you believe. Therefore, that you do not abuse it, the commandment is given, because it comes true.* [...] *So it is with the faith: the same has force. If I believe wrongly, it goes out; if I believe righteously, it goes out.* Paracelsus, *Liber de superstitionibus et ceremoniis*, in: Sudhoff Vol. XIV, pp. 367–369.

forces, which hold a pharmacy that contains all mysteries of nature that are administered by them.[52]

As we can see from the quote, Paracelsus in his Astronomia Magna is very explicit that man should attach their faith to Divinity but in principle is free to *attach it to anything*. In fact, if man was to attach it to the "infernal ones" what is waiting for them is not the usual threat of eternal damnation but rather an entire telluric pharmacy presided over by the chthonic spirits. So according to Paracelsus, it is the application of man's free will to their capacity to have faith that opens the doors of spirit contact and enables daemonic access and affiliation.

Paracelsus actually expresses a very straightforward idea: like breathing, like standing on a cliff and calling to the sea, like carefully tasting an unknown fruit, faith is an inherent skill embedded into each human. Unlike the physical senses and their external capabilities, however, faith resides on the inside, on the intersection between man's mind and soul. Therefore, faith as a capability is equally rooted in our heart as it is in our head.[53]

If we were to translate Paracelsus' explanations on faith in the above quotes and elsewhere into a 21st century position, we could render it as such: he defines the human capability of having faith in something as the ability to *flow into one*—whether this means becoming one with an idea, an object, or a person, may this be temporarily or permanently. For Paracelsus, faith is our capacity to flow and merge into full identification with something. To have faith in something means that relating to this particular idea, person or object we burn the bridges of "If and But" and resolve the boundaries of "I."

52 Will-Erich Peuckert (ed.), *Paracelsus—Gesammelte Schriften*, Vol. IV, Basel: Schwabe Verlag, 2009, pp. 294–295.

53 The magical method called *prayer* in such a context breaks free from any orthodox handcuffs. Equally distorted like the term faith through centuries of dominion of organised religion, prayer is not a liturgical text learned by heart and recited at the correct moment. In stark opposition, Paracelsus portrays it as the science and art of knowing how to "seek and knock". If done "in the appropriate way and with a pure and unconditional heart, all that we seek will be given to us to be found, and all that is otherwise occult and cast away from us, will be opened and unsealed." (Sudhoff Vol. XIV, p. 513).

Let's illustrate this in a mundane context and consider the person you love most in your life. The relationship you hold to them is special for many reasons. One critical reason for all of us, however, is the fact that in this person's presence we do not need *to guard ourselves.* Loving them, amongst many other things, means we are willing to lower all defence mechanisms in their presence, and openly hand ourselves over to them. That does not mean we do this in an egotistical or self-abandoning way, but in a way that blurs the lines between "I" and "Thou", a way that allows this other person to step up so close to us that in some moments rather than sensing two separate people we begin to experience a *unified field of us:* perceptions, words, emotions flow unconstrained between us. Like clouds temporarily assume one body, so we become one. In these moments, the threshold that normally separates us from the world has turned so low, so thin, that even with the tips of our fingers we cannot feel it anymore.

Like a magnetic field, activated by an electric current, *faith is the force that unites.* It is nothing in itself, but a field of potential that requires both careful activation and deliberate direction. A magnetic field requires at least two objects that react to it so it can take effect in the world. Faith also requires at least two objects between which it can work to close out distance and distinction. Faith, therefore, is a human's inherent capability to—consciously or unconsciously—create affiliation, alikeness, or, in magical terms, sympathy.

This is why Paracelsus pauses so often to explain the power and poison that can be the force of faith. In our magical operations, faith is a most essential and yet most often overlooked tool. In magic, unlike in a romantic relationship, we do not use it to lower the threshold between ourselves and another person. Instead, we deploy it to lower the threshold between the physical realm that contains our bodily self and the realm of the spirit. In magic, at its most essential level, faith is what at least temporarily pulls us out of our identification with our blood, bones, skin and hair, and allows us to step over the threshold of becoming fully one with our travelling spirit.

Now in the normal condition of humans, their faith is not at all a conscious, finely calibrated tool of creating alikeness. Rather, the *field of their faith* is aligned and guided by the influences of their inner firmament. Thus, the average human acts as a tool or fulfilment medium of their faith as directed by the stars. The sides of *ingenious artist* and *passive executor* are reversed from what it could be, if only man had learned how to master the art of *Astronomia Olympi Novi*.

The difference here lies in the active relation each man has created between the triad of their *free will*, *faith* and *imagination* as well as the Olympic Spirits that make up their inner firmament.

For the sake of brevity, these three critical human capabilities can be defined as follows:

FREE WILL is man's ability to decide against all natural inclinations.
FAITH is man's ability to unite themselves with any object of their faith.
IMAGINATION is man's ability to transform and travel in their mind's eye.

The Olympic Spirits are the inner planets or stars within man. If we combine these two components—the three human capabilities applied against their inner stars—we enter the realm of the *Astronomia Olympi Novi*. Paracelsus hints at a path of taking control of our natural inclinations. And rather than being the passive product and executive organ of their influence, to become the active composer or ingenious artist of the inner firmament that creates our self.

With this context we can return to his *Astronomia Magna* and read two critical sections that in his usual language, steeped in neologisms and metaphors, explain this process.

> *What the alchemist breaks, the same loses the firmamental power. If the firmamental power is to work, then no breaking must take place. Know further that the philosophia adepta has a special art of composition. So in the same way as one naturally mixes many different bodies together, so also the sidereal arcana may be composed.*
>
> *From this follow the names, as tyriaca coelestis, methridatum Olympi, suffuff, that is infusion, aethereum, etc. This means just as they are made in their earthly way, so they are combined firmamentally.*[54]

54 Sudhoff Vol. XII, p. 98. See also Peuckert 1967, p. 125.

The adjunct *methridatum*, used by Paracelsus above to qualify the term *Olympi*, refers to a famous Medieval antidote. Known as *Antidotum Mithridaticum* or simply *Mithridat* it is one of the oldest general remedies and has taken its name from king Mithridates the Great (120–63 BC), one of the most famous ancient rulers of northern Anatolia and successful foe to the Roman Empire in the Mithridatic Wars. Pliny the Elder (23–79 CE) in his *Natural History* provides a colourful account of the learned king who is lauded as "*a more attentive investigator of life's problems than any of those born before him*" (Pliny, quoted after Totelin, p. 3). Following Pliny, countless sources through the centuries credit Mithradates as an outstanding pharmacologist, a lifelong researcher who discovered several unique antidotes. Most notably though, he is introduced as the inventor of what today is referred to as *antitoxic therapy* (Fossel, p. 39): the process of turning oneself immune to poisons by imbibing small portions of it on a daily basis.

So the above quote from the *Philosophia Sagax* gives us a very specific lead. With the neologism *methridatum Olympi* Paracelsus points us to the particular approach we have to take in order to begin to actively compose our own inner firmament.

What is required is an antitoxic therapy that we have to apply upon ourselves, just like the mythical king Mithridates did. The *special art of composition*, referred to by Paracelsus, in its initial step means nothing other than helping our mind become aware of the celestial firmament it is created from. It refers to the process of becoming able to see the actual planetary influences we are made up of, and which—in case they are not recognised for what they are and unconsciously acted out—form the very poison that binds us to our bestial nature. Paracelsus' most renowned saying *it is the dose that makes the poison* gains new depth and meaning in light of the above. Maybe more specifically, in the context of the *methridatum Olympi* it should read: *It is one's ability to see the poison that makes its antitode.*

This leads us to another essential section in the *Astronomia Magna*. Here, Paracelsus describes the impact of the *Olympic wine* on man i.e., the intoxicating effect the inner stars have on man when they are not realised for what they are, but when man subsides to them passively. That is the default position of most humans when we act as our inner stars' unconscious fulfilling medium, rather than using them consciously as the most powerful celestial tools to create ourself.

> *It is a natural astronomia that fabricates itself in man, and it is the firmament microcosmi his sky, his cursus, his sphere, and his aether and olympus.*[55]

> *So that you may understand the example, notice thus. In wine comes together a composition of all qualities of the senses and becomes a single drink from it, so to understand. [...] So such qualities are in the heavenly bodies, for man is guided by the heavenly bodies as well as by the elements, for every part goes into his body and his being. Now the properties of the wine in the heavenly body are also and equally both a vinum olympi and vinum terrae, just as it is a panis firmamenti and panis agri. And as by one man is led, so also by the other. The one is visible, the other invisible.*
>
> *Now notice that at the beginning of this introduction I pointed out that man may or may not drink earthly wine, according to measure or above measure. So he has also here a free will to drink the olympic wine or not. For one may stab or not, may steal or not, may murder or not. But now there is the prohibition, you shall not steal, you shall not murder, you shall not kill etc. That breaks the free will. Further it is also forbidden to us that we should drink wine in which there is abundance. Now it follows from the commandment that we, as human beings, should live soberly and not comply with the evil that is upon us. Nothing bad happens to him who lives in this way, he walks well, but he who lives according to his desires becomes drunk in them and is never in the degree in which he should be. Therefore we may well leave the wine, take it or not, just like we take other things or not.*
>
> *So as the elemental is received by us through the air, so also the firmamental comes to us through the air. And as the wine does its thing, as it is then revealed, so does the firmament, if it is a mustum [new wine, still fermenting], and*

55 Sudhoff Vol. XII, p. 175.

more and more skilfully than the wine. For the cause is that the firmament is more subtle, more skilful, more pure, and more full of sense and thought.

Therefore, notice how the wine of the firmament fills them up, and man never speaks, but the wine speaks. [...] They sing, they jump, they run, they dance, they rejoice; not from human reason but from the firmament's wine, which thus chases them, like the wine in a drunken man. Such mode of action is needed to explain the cause, because there are many who do not know this mode of action and the nature of the olympic wine and mustum. And those who speak drunken from the same wine are taken for scholars, for respectable teachers, and yet theirs is nothing but fully drunken speech. They speak from the fullness of the wine, from the fullness of the mustum, they get excited in the same, as every drunken man does who likes his bottle.

So theologians, preachers, lawyers, shysters, medics, explorers, warriors, gamblers etc., and in all things each one has a special way about them, the one for devotion, the one for weeping, the one for sighing, the one for laughing, the one for celebrating, the one for proclaiming, and so each one is taught by himself and not by God. For only those are taught by God who are filled with the wine of the Holy Spirit.

The other two wines are nothing but flying heads, distorted senses, deceivers and screamers, wanting to know all things for themselves, having no books, no counsel, no help, and persuading themselves. If the stones will speak, they are still stones. And if a scripture is full of their drunken speech, their drunken speech is still to be rejected.

Many have been such kind of drunken sidereal people ever, but they have not had the courage to determine their own end, their own kind of drunkenness. As in my times it has broken out once uncleanly and every one has let his wine speak, what therein nature has given him in her wine. So the hearts of men were revealed, and every man's wine did what it could do; their desire was there, and the wine led them to it.

And just as normal drunkenness is ought for nothing, for it comes from flesh and blood, so also this was not meant to be anything. And as a drunkard full of wine abides and re-

mains in their head and in their drunkenness, so also these full, olympic wine-preachers, wine-lawyers, wine-councillors abide. And I have considered it good to distribute the donum naturae inebriecatum,[56] *only so much is to tell here and out of need, so that one sees what these same noblemen, rulers, and their successors have for a reason, from which they speak. And their works, their signs, their doing and leaving indicate drunkenness or sobriety to us. And that they speak from drunkenness, not from sobriety, and from the fullness which has no inherent meaning at all.*

Therefore let each one judge the difference between the doctrine of drunken works and the doctrine of sober works, between the drunkenness of the wine of the Holy Spirit and the drunkenness of the wine of olympi and terrae.

For from the fruits,[57] *from the works they shall all be known. So you may understand this introduction of the sidereal wine in the way that these [latter two] wines fill and pervert the senses, and they speak, and the man speaks nothing. And like a drunkard who persuades himself, so also they are persuaded by these wines. They appear as something, which they are far from being.*[58]

In the previous chapter we learned about what Paracelsus had to say about each one of us holding the power to become an apostle. Not to deify Christ but to follow Christ and to deify the world around us. Here we return to this very idea, specifically in his emphasis that each man holds the "free will to drink the olympic wine or not", as well as to bolster up "the courage to determine their own end, their own kind

56 Read: *the gift of the drunken nature* i.e., the teaching of his that the terrestrial and celestial wines induce a state of drunkenness in the human mind, similar to a poison whose antidote can only be found through the *methridatum Olympi*.

57 Matthew 7:15–20: *Beware of false prophets, who come to you in sheep's clothing, but inwardly they are ravenous wolves. You will know them by their fruits. Do men gather grapes from thorn-bushes or figs from thistles? Even so, every good tree bears good fruit, but a bad tree bears bad fruit. A good tree cannot bear bad fruit, nor can a bad tree bear good fruit. Every tree that does not bear good fruit is cut down and thrown into the fire. Therefore by their fruits you will know them.*

58 Sudhoff Vol. XII, pp. 221–5.

of drunkenness." Paracelsus invites us to accept the essential challenge of any magical neophyte: just as Christ transformed water into wine, so Paracelsus dares us to transform *the wine of our Olympic Spirits.*[59]

By directing our will, faith and imagination towards the Holy Spirit, a spark can be brought forth from within us which holds the power to cease the wild hunt of the Olympic Spirits that silences the chorus of their passion-ridden voices tugging at us in all directions. We can choose to grow this spark through practice and exertion, through embedding ourselves into the right environment, through educating ourselves towards it—and thus grow this spark into a flame.

A flame that holds the promise to illuminate our new self in the light of the *olympi novi*, the newborn *Olympic spirit.*[60] Then this spirit can begin to colour our mind, and our mind in return becomes the candle to the flame of the Holy Spirit. We become the creators of ourselves. Not in an egotistical vacuum of divine self-empowerment, but in humble co-creation with the forces of nature around us, within us, guided by the Holy Spirit. We do as nature does. We resume our position in the cosmos without distorting or destroying it. That is the *Astronomia Olympi Novi.*

While the essential third book is missing from his *Philosophia Sagax*, Paracelsus has left us many leads to complete the puzzle.

The trick is to read his elucidations about the Olympic Spirit, about nature and its creative forces, and to constantly contemplate on the implicit meaning this has for man's position within the cosmos.

> *Now look at an example. If nature is to make a fool, it must first put itself into a foolish form, into such a being as that is to become as it wishes to create. As an example: a sculptor wants to carve a fool, he must first put his ingenium into a fool; if he wants to make a hare, he must put his ingenium into a hare. So also nature must do; so fools make fools, in each case the one [makes] the other.*[61]

59 Notice the plural, *Olympic Spirits.*
60 Notice the singular, *Olympic Spirit.*
61 Sudhoff 1929, Vol. XII, p. 263.

In the same way we hold the promise of turning ourselves into something we are not yet. The promise of taking the role of the conductor and to compose the cacophony of our Olympic Spirits into the symphony of the Olympic Spirit, in praise of the Holy Spirit.

The key to this process, as shown in the quote above, is to learn to consciously use our ingenium at will. I have written a separate book about the mystery of our ingenium.[62]

The key ingredients to activating this process, however, can be found in the three simple components of our *free will, faith* and *imagination*. They are stifled or nourished, atrophied or trained, addled or educated not through magical ritual (alone), but mostly through the environment we participate in, through the life we choose to lead amongst all our fellow everyday people, human and otherwise.

The subtlety of such process should not create any illusion about its radical impact. Composing the Olympic Spirit within ourselves is the key operation of the philosophia adepta. When successfully carried out, its effect is very straightforward and simple: it frees the human mind from the chatter of the Olympic Spirits, to be illuminated by the divine light.

> *And the final and fourteenth [kind of nectromantia coelestis] is that which nature has given as artem literatam, namely, that she leads the ingenium and lets it write. Thus if God leads the pen and lets it write, that is literata ars coelestis, in which there is no error.*[63]

Conclusions

> *For the medic is also created like Olympus; that is the medic who knows heaven and knows to hold it in their hand, to whom belong the secrets of the stars.*[64]

HOLDING IN OUR right hand the seven stars of our own mind, speaking truthfully, carefully, with the voice of sun: what a wonderful and

62 Acher, *INGENIUM*, (2022).
63 Sudhoff Vol. XII, p. 339.
64 Sudhoff Vol. I, p. 30.

deeply magical image of the one who perfected the Paracelsian art of the *Astronomia Olympi Novi.*

Throughout his life Paracelsus advocated for the ideal of turning the pages of the Book of Nature with one's feet. Enabling others to gather first-hand experience and lived reality of the mysteries of the cosmos was his paramount goal. Such magico-mystical aspiration was woven thoroughly through the mountain of unprinted manuscripts he left behind in 1541: Dictated as well as handwritten in his German vernacular, often oozing with ranting sarcasm, there was a mesmerising amount of method to his madness.

In his magico-medical and philosophical writings Paracelsus uses variations of the root word "olymp" more than fifty times. All the works in which the word is mentioned were either banned from print during his lifetime or written so late that we only know of them in manuscript forms which were published posthumously. The one exception is Paracelsus' *Große Wundarznei* from 1536.

We have followed this trail of the Olympic Spirits throughout these works, or rather, we have followed their printed echoes, as they survive almost 500 years after his death. What we found is a most practical philosophy of teaching ourselves to dissolve from the unconscious grip of our inner firmament and then to rearrange, to *recompose* the Olympic Spirits within ourselves. It is a process of detachment, rearrangement and fusion into one, which, as Paracelsus points out, is not to be confused with the processes and methods of alchemy.

Towards the end of his life he termed this art the *Astronomia Olympi Novi.* However, either he himself or early Paracelsians decided to withhold this critical third book from his opus magnum, the *Philosophia Sagax.* Maybe they deemed the adumbrations given in the other three books as perfectly sufficient for the worthy aspirant to find their own ways. In which case, we hope that with this present book and chapter we have further lowered the bar to follow this occult trail. Stepping over the threshold of practice, of course, is left to each one of us.

Paracelsus was neither Catholic nor Protestant, neither Neoplatonist nor Pagan, and yet in his own peculiar way he was all of this and more. He openly advocated to resurrect the Apostolic way as a living, contemporary reality amongst his fellow people. And to him the art of retuning the chaos of our Olympic Spirits into the symphony of our Olympic Spirit was at the heart of such path.

For the one who dared to walk this path, exclusion and ostracism from his social environment was almost a given. yet, the promise was to accomplish something very few people ever dared to accomplish: *to become truly human.* To hold the seven stars of one's mind in one's right, to hold one's face in the realm of the sun, and to accept the burden of speaking with the sword of truth.

Such Great Work had to happen not in an occult ivory tower of learned privilege and nobility, but among peasants, in inns, on crossroads and in the centre of a most daring life.

What Paracelsus developed with his Olympic Spirits was an animistic cosmology of divine immanence. Jesus Christ was no longer needed as a middleman, and neither were Neoplatonic vertical realms of emanation. The work of spirits had become horizontal: a level playing field, where the worst and the best, the rich, the poor and the ugly of the spirit world could show up any moment, anywhere, for they all were immanent to the very essence of created matter. The practice ground to tame ourselves and to tune ourselves into an instrument of Divinity, was not the hermit's cave, and neither the scholar's library, but the mundane world of the travelling man.

The inner *astra* or stars, through an antitoxic therapy of applying the poison of the world to ourselves, are turned into the essential tools of practice. All duality is cancelled out in this work: body and soul, matter and spirit, world and man interrelated, interwoven; they become one. In a single grain of sand, in the shape of a single human everything was present all at once, permeating each other: the visible and the invisible, the ephemeral and the eternal. Dissolving such embodied reality meant death, not ascension or progress.

Largely unacknowledged by most modern scholars of Paracelsus, it was Martin Buber who held a deep appreciation for Paracelsus' work and, more importantly, also knew how to read it.

In his seminal book *I and Thou* we come across an ingenious single paragraph summary of the work of the *Astronomia Olympi Novi*. Buber speaks of it as *man's decisive moment*, one that determines all of one's destiny.

> *The [...] soul's becoming a unity [...] is not something that occurs between man and God, but something that occurs within man. The forces gather in the nucleus, everything that*

wants to pull them away is overcome, the being stands alone in itself and jubilates, as Paracelsus says, in its exaltation.

This is the decisive moment of man. Without it, he is not fit for the work of the spirit. With it: it is decided in his innermost whether this [experience] signifies a beginning or a satisfaction. Once gathered into unity, the human being can go out to meet mystery and salvation in an encounter that has only now become whole. But he can also savour the blessedness of the gathering [into union] and, without calling upon his highest duty, fall back into distraction.

Everything on our way is decision: intended, divined, occulted; this decision taken in our innermost being is the most primal decision man can take, charged with the mightiest consequences for our destiny.[65]

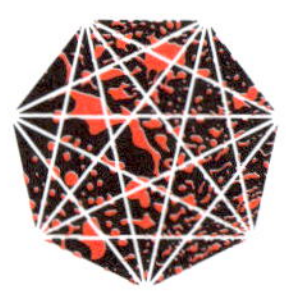

65 I also reproduce here the original of the quotation to do justice to Buber's masterful and complex use of the German language: *Das [...] Einswerden der Seele [...] ist nicht etwas, was sich zwischen dem Menschen und Gott, sondern etwas, was sich im Menschen ereignet. Die Kräfte sammeln sich in den Kern ein, alles, was sie abziehen will, wird einbewältigt, das Wesen steht allein in sich selbst und jubiliert, wie Paracelsus sagt, in seiner Exaltation. Das ist der entscheidende Augenblick des Menschen. Ohne ihn ist er zum Werk des Geistes nicht tauglich. Mit ihm: es entscheidet sich in einem Innersten, ob dies Rüste oder Genügen bedeutet. Der Mensch kann, zur Einheit eingesammelt, zur nun erst vollkommen geratenden Begegnung mit dem Geheimnis und Heil ausgehen. Er kann aber auch die Seligkeit der Sammlung auskosten und, one sich in die höchste Pflicht zu nehmen, in die Zerstreuung zurückkehren. Alles auf unserm Weg ist Entscheidung: gemeinte, geahnte, geheime; diese im Innersten ist die urgeheime und an Bestimmung mächtigste.* (Buber 1962, p. 136).

WHAT THE ALCHEMIST BREAKS, THE SAME LOSES THE FIRMAMENTAL POWER. IF THE FIRMAMENTAL POWER IS TO WORK, THEN NO BREAKING MUST TAKE PLACE. KNOW FURTHER THAT THE *PHILOSOPHIA ADEPTA* HAS A SPECIAL ART OF COMPOSITION. SO IN THE SAME WAY AS ONE NATURALLY MIXES MANY DIFFERENT BODIES TOGETHER, SO ALSO THE SIDEREAL ARCANA MAY BE COMPOSED.

FROM THIS FOLLOW THE NAMES, AS *TYRIACA CŒLESTIS*, *METHRIDATUM OLYMPI*, *SUFFUFF*, THAT IS INFUSION, *ÆTHEREUM*, ETC. THIS MEANS JUST AS THEY ARE MADE IN THEIR EARTHLY WAY, SO THEY ARE COMBINED FIRMAMENTALLY.

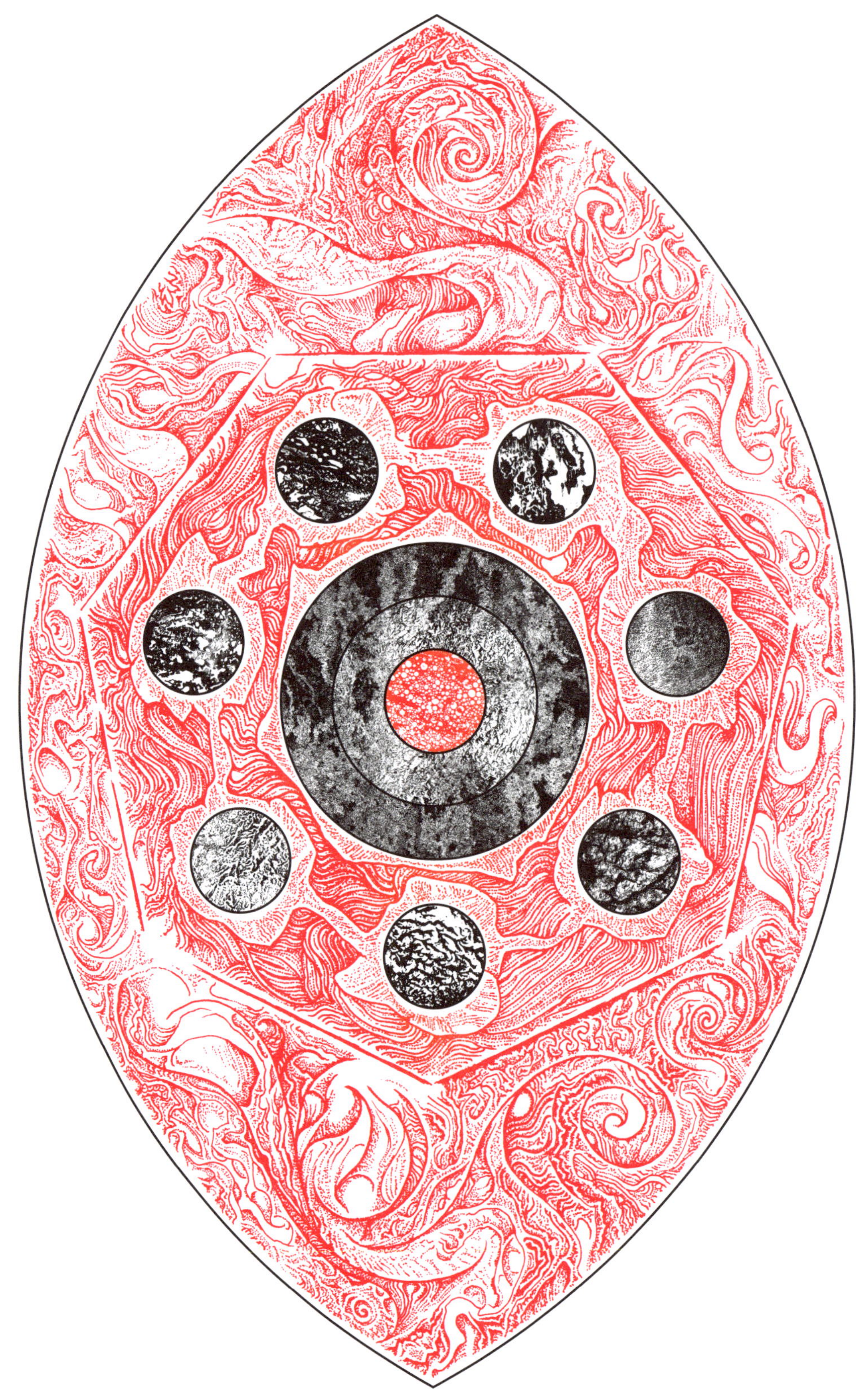

BOOK 1

CHAPTER IV

THE LEGACY OF THE OLYMPIC SPIRITS

Introduction

A COMPREHENSIVE history of the Olympic Spirits from the 16th century onward has yet to be written; and it will not be the present book that fills that gap. Rather, in this chapter we will examine selected milestones along the path left by the Olympic Spirits in occult literature from the mid-16th to the end of the 17th century. Attempting to discuss every single manuscript and book from this period that relates to the Olympic Spirits would result in an encyclopædic work—not in a chapter that, despite its length, aims to be read in its entirety to establish a conscious, informed, and purposeful foundation for one's own research and practice.

As mentioned in the Introduction, this book is best read from beginning to end, in the order in which the chapters are presented. The content of the previous chapters is therefore not repeated in the current study, but is expected as given knowledge.

This is important to highlight as the current chapter is focused on the literary evolution of the Olympic Spirits term. As such, younger sources are not necessarily more true or, simply put, better than older ones. However, in many cases the latter tend to be much more readily available today, or still hold a stronger influence over our current perception of the Olympic Spirits.

In fact, unsurprisingly, what we will witness—and discover to culminate in the work of Robert Fludd—is a continued deviation from the spiritual core tenets of the Olympic Spirits as developed by Paracelsus.

We encourage the reader not to attach any judgement to such historic evolution. Whether we resonate more or less with a particular contribution to the development of the Olympic Spirits is irrelevant. Understanding practical magic from its historic roots is not a matter of personal preferences. Instead, what the following chapter can help us realise is that each practitioner whom we will encounter on the following pages *had to make these spirits their own* in order to contribute their own elucidations on their nature and dynamics.

Trafficking with daemons,[1] *becoming sociable with spirits* is the very foundation of magic throughout history. In such a practice, historic consistency always comes second compared to personal relevancy. The idea of an "authentic" Olympic Spirit practice, therefore, by definition stands in tension to the idea of any kind of orthodoxy or fixed tradition. For each practitioner has to bring this work to life—and invite it to be marked by their contemporary time, their physical location and the spiritual position in the living cosmos we all participate in.

> *To the one who weaves threads, God connects the spirit with Olympus.*[2]

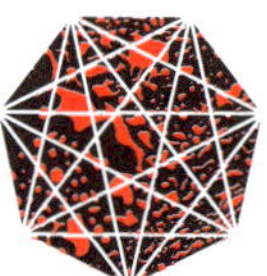

1 For further exploration of this notion see Martha Rampton, *Trafficking with Demons—Magic, Ritual and Gender from Late Antiquityto 1000*, London: Cornell University Press, 2021.

2 Anonymous, inscription on a 16th century French wall tapestry, showing a weaving crone with this purported saying by Charlemagne. A reference to the following chapter.

I
Anacrucis

BY THE EARLY 1600s, Paracelsianism[3] had spread like a wildfire across continental Europe. Not only were schools of scholars deeply split between traditionalists—i.e., supporters of Aristotle, Galen and other representatives of Medieval knowledge-orthodoxy—and early Paracelsians. But the latter group itself by no means stood united. It was made up by medics, (al)chemists, theologians, mystics and natural magicians—many of them operating in multiple of these fields at once. This scattered community of aspiring researchers who sought to break up, reshape, and reorient the encrusted knowledge society of the late sixteenth century quickly revealed itself to be deeply internally divided.

The deepest rift in this diverse community split its camps into one group that aimed to place the Paracelsian principles of natural observation, experimentation, and practical experience at the centre of their evolving skills. The other camp saw these practical pathways of empiricism as a mere validation strategy for a spiritual reality that had already been predetermined: they were searching for the divine light in the book of nature. And yet, whatever nature had to reveal, to them it was already clear that it could only be proof to the ontological reality of the Holy Scripture.[4]

3 For the definition of the term, we follow Walter Pagel's essays and books on the subject, in particular: *Paracelsianism has its established place in the history of science and of medicine. It is there presented as the exponent of innovating ideas. These lent the basis for an observational naturalism and medical practice which in radical confrontation threatened to overthrow the still ruling ancient tradition. However, Paracelsianism was more than a new ideology with practical consequences in academic pursuits. It was a movement of far-reaching influence in many different fields—moulding and transforming the view of the world and of man. It entered the scene with a religious fervour which it retained for two centuries and which even today finds its devotees. Its history has never been written although we are well acquainted with the life and work of Theophrastus Paracelsus (1493–1541) and his "chemiatric" followers.* Pagel, 1984, VIII.

4 As at any moment in history, so also at the beginning of the 17th century, the traces were scarce left behind by genuine "empirical mystics" such as Para-

Essentially both groups aimed at reconstituting and mending a world that to them was at risk of falling into radical fragmentation, meaninglessness and chaos. What they were aiming for beyond scientific or spiritual proof was to create a new universal system of knowledge, either based upon the methodology of scientific examination or upon inner divine inspiration. And, as we see so evidently in the early Rosicrucian manifests from the same time, their work held the equally as noble as naive aspiration to reform entire communities, nations, and even humankind itself.

> *The reasons for this continued interest in a universal chemical system are varied. Partially they may be ascribed to the uncertainty of proof in this period, but no less important was the chemists' strong call for reform in the understanding of nature. Here their emphasis on the use of observational evidence was consistently linked with their quest for truth in religion. They supported their plea with a medical trump card—the reputed cures effected by Paracelsus and his followers.*[5]

As we noted in the previous chapter, Paracelsus himself would have neither sympathised with pure empiricists nor with pure mystics; his path was not a straight line but a meandering interweaving of insights gained from divine divination, from moments spent in the presence of his *musa sagax*,[6] and the testing of this inspired knowledge in stained, burned and often messy practice.

Despite the reductionist trends both on the side of empiricists and mystics, the triumph of many Paracelsian ideas stands in stark contrast to the low volume of his publications Paracelsus witnessed before his death.[7] As discussed in the previous chapter, Paracelsus ex-

---

celsus himself, who saw their communion with the *musa sagax* as the first-hand source of mediation of knowledge about themselves and the world.

5 Debus 1977, Vol. 1, p. 206.

6 For an in-depth exploration of this term and Paracelsus' underlying ideas, please see my book *INGENIUM* (2022), and in particular the chapter titled Celestial Inclinations.

7 As a rough approximation we can consult the content section of Sudhoff's *Bibliographia Paracelsica*. The section of publications intra vitam Paracelsi covers less than 40 pages; the following section of original publications from his manuscripts subsequent to his death (1549–1588) covers more than

pected the adept to be an adeptus philosophia first and a medic only second.[8] In a similar vein he himself acted as an apostle of his new radical ideas first, and as a publishing academic second if not last.

From a viewpoint of early Paracelsianism, the anacrusis to such a grandiose as well as disruptive spiritual, social and scientific movement has to be sought for in the 1560s and 1570s.

At least since the 1530s, Paracelsus maintained a widespread network of followers and sympathisers if not to say disciples. They ensured his writings, even in manuscript form, circulated beneath the surface of orthodox catechisms and the formal culture of scholarship. This approach was not only pragmatic with regard to the open hostility between Paracelsus and traditional scholars of his time. It was also adequate with regards to the actual nature of his teaching. As Paola Zambelli so attentively observed, the Paracelsian tradition was from the beginning *an initiatory movement.*[9]

Thus, the diffusion of Paracelsianism had gained its own subcultural momentum by the early 1560s, when finally critical titles went to press—initially much ignited by the editorship of Adam von Bodenstein[10]—that further disseminated the concept of his Olympic Spirits into the official scholarly culture.[11]

First amongst these were his *De Peste Libri Tres cum Additionibus* from 1563, printed in Straubing, as well as his *De Causis Morborum Invisibilium*, printed in Cologne in 1565. Both books present critical sources of the Olympic tradition.

---

300 pages (Sudhoff, 1894, vii).

8 Sudhoff Vol. 1, p. 41.

9 Also compare Wels (2020), p. 182, translation by the author: *The actual genre of Paracelsus—this impression imposes itself on the reading of his writings—is the oral instruction, which in its digressions and excursions, its direct address of the listener and reader everywhere shines through the written form. From Paracelsus speaks not the professor, but the wandering physician and "miracle healer," the "master," who addresses the small circle of his students.*

10 Sudhoff 2000 (1894), p. 698.

11 *The determined and largely successful efforts of the conservative medical party to prevent the publication of the works of Paracelsus, was in some measure a tribute to their potential influence. That their fears* [...] *were entirely justified is shown by the great popularity of these books when they finally began to appear in print. This period of active publication of his works began about 1560 and extended for about a hundred years.* Stillman (1920), p. 167.

The first introduces the term "coelum olympi" as the inner firmament of man. As seen in the preceding chapter, it explains the interdependencies between the outer, celestial firmament's influence on man, and man's imagination and free will as the essential tools that influence their inner firmament. His book on the Invisible Diseases goes even one step further. Here we read of the essential process of uniting the Olympic Spirits into a singular spirit within man. This printed work also identifies the Olympic Spirits as the *stars of the inner man* i.e., the sidereal or astral spirits within man, referenced so often in many of his other works.[12]

Only two years later, 1568 Paris a book sees the light of day that gives a most comprehensive treatment of Paracelsus' work and ideas. It would have been impossible to write this tome at the time based on Paracelsus' hitherto printed books alone. Thus, its publication provides eloquent evidence of the vivid underground circulation of his materials in the late 16th century. This book is Jacques Gohory's—published under his pseudonym "Leone Suavio"—*Theophrastus Paracelsus' Compendium of both Philosophy and Medicine: From the Best of his Books; with Scholia in 4 books.*[13]

Gohory presents the earliest in-depth study of Paracelsus' cosmosophy, specifically focussing on his magical and alchemical works. He is placing it into the historic context of classical authors and puts a deliberate emphasis on its relations to Johannes Trithemius' *Steganographia.*[14]

Despite its significant volume of more than 370 pages, Gohory's book does neither reference the Olympic Spirits explicitly, nor does it generally make use of the term olympic in its broader Paracelsian sense as celestial. However, we do find emphasis of Paracelsus' approach of working with spirits through the mediation of one's own body and soul.

12 For further details and source quotes please refer to the previous chapter.

13 Jacques Gohory, [i.e., Leone Suavio], *Theophrasti Paracelsi Philosophiae Et Medicinae Utriusque Universae, Compendium: Ex optimis quibusque eius libris; Cum scholiis in libros IIII. eiusde[m] De Vita Longa, Plenos mysteriorum, parabolarum, aenigmatum*, Paris: Rovillius, 1567. For a good introduction to Jaques Gohory see Jeanice Brooks, "Music as Erotic Magic in a Renaissance Romance", in: *Renaissance Quarterly*, Vol. 60, Number 4, Winter 2007, pp. 1207–1256. I am grateful to Joseph Peterson for recommending this great article.

14 Bowen, p. 340.

The Paradox of the Olympic Spirits

EXAMPLES OF THE PARADOXICAL INTRODUCTION OF THE SEVEN OLYMPIAN SPIRITS IN THE *ARBATEL* (1575)

Names (Aphorism §15)	Relating to the concept of 7 planetary rulers...	...yet providing entirely unknown titles for these entitites.
Names (Aphorism §18)	Relating to the concept of the importance of spirit names and seals...	...yet only revealing the Olympic Spirit's titles, and encouraging the magician to find out their 'starry names' for themselves, which will only work if passed on personally to the magician by the spirits, and 'expire' after 140 years.
Rulership (Aphorism §16)	Relating to the concept of periodic rulership by planetary spirits...	...yet deviating from the rhythm of 354 years given in Trithemius' *De Septem Secundei*, and introducing a new rhythm of 490 years each.
Hierarchies (Aphorism §17)	Relating to the traditional concept of spirit hierarchies...	...yet giving seemingly random and inconsistent rulership over hierarchies for each Olympic Spirit (e.g., PHUL, OPHIEL and PHALEG have none, some others like ARATRON on the other hand, have eight different hierarchies to rule over).
Provinces (Aphorism §16)	Relating to a sequence of multiples of seven with regards to provinces ruled by each Olympic Spirit...	...yet breaking this pattern by giving a 'wrong' value for BETHOR in the original 1575 edition (PHUL 7, OPHIEL 14, HAGITH 21, OCH 28, PHALEG 35, BETHOR 32 instead of 42, ARATRON 49).
Practice (Aphorism §17/21/42)	Relating to classic grimoire techniques by instructing evocation through magic in the planetary hour and day, including invocation and departure prayers...	...yet emphasising that no one will be able to call these spirits successfully unless they are born a magician. Thus, not providing any technical details for the successful setting of communing with these spirits (no paraphernalia, no temple setting, no instructions on use of their seals, etc.)
Practice (Aphorism §25)	After careful exposition of the nature, titles, seals, rulership, hierarchies, provinces, and evocative process to conjure the Olympic Spirits...	...revealing a 'way to all secrets' that is unrelated to magic, but based upon 7 Biblical guiding principles, which if adopted consistently in one's own life, will attract the Holy Spirit and God's angels as direct teachers to the practitioner.

> *We dwell, not in the hells, but amongst the stars of heaven: the spirit that thrives in us will do it.*[15]

Shortly after, in 1571, Paracelsus' magnum opus, the *Astronomia Magna*, also known as *Philosophia Sagax*, is printed in Paris.

Here for the first time a broader audience is introduced to Paracelsus' metaphor of the olympic wine. In an unapologetically Pelagian turn, the metaphor is used to emphasise every human's personal responsibility to determine by themselves and according only to their free will how much of the influence of each Olympic Spirit they will allow to come through and affect themselves in their inner firmament.

Nevertheless, the Olympic Spirits in the *Astronomia Magna* remain a complex concept. They are alluded to be of spirit-nature, yet equally they take root both in the elements and in the mind of man. Thus, Paracelsus can speak of *elementary stars* as well as of *olympic stars* and still refer to the same concept. This means that the Olympic Spirits express themselves through the four elements as well as through the inner firmament of man.

As so often in a worldview that is deeply foreign to the clean dividing lines of the modern academic and much more familiar to the relational, organic ecosystem cognition of tribal societies, inside and outside, macro- and microcosm blur in Paracelsus writings and appear as deeply interwoven.[16]

II

The *Archidoxis Magica* and the *Arbatel*

THE *ARCHIDOXIS MAGICA* are a compilation of seven magical treatises whose earliest evidence is a manuscript from 1570 which is today kept in Nuremberg.[17] The book must not be confused with Paracelsus' *Archidoxae Philippi Theophrasti Paracelsi Magni*, which he wrote around 1526 when in Basel.[18]

15 Gohory (1567), p. 235.
16 Sudhoff Vol. XII, pp. 222–223.
17 Schneider, 1982, p. 9.
18 Sudhoff, 2000 (1894), pp. 170–174. A digital copy can be found under: https://www.digitale-sammlungen.de/en/view/bsb10151875?page=1

The word *archidoxis* is a Paracelsian neologism and is best translated as *foundational premises* or *Grundlehren* in German.[19] While both books belong to Paracelsus' works deeply rooted in Renaissance Hermetism, the *Archidoxis* spans over ten treatises and adopts a mystical-scientific approach. The *Archidoxis Magica*, on the other hand, contains seven treatises and, as its title suggests, is of decidedly magical nature.

> *The Archidoxis are [...] the great program of an adept's renaissance, a renaissance that begins with observation, with experience, with the work in the laboratory, from which, as it was once called, a philosophy of the workshops shall arise, a new system of medicine and a new world view. As strange as they seem to us, as much as they resemble an alchemical recipe book—it is not about the recipes, it is about a whole new structure. The Paracelsus of the semi-scholarly saga, the one who owned the lapis, who knew the arcana, to whom the tinctura belonged, in whose sword-butt Hirschvogel's engraving showed the Azoth hidden, the wise beyond all knowing—in the end he has his foundation in this work.*[20]

The seven treatises of the *Archidoxis Magica* now aspire to achieve the same programmatic relevance in the realm of natural magic.

Sudhoff already illustrated the fragmentary publishing history of the *Archidoxis Magica*: in 1570 Gerhard Dorn published a Latin translation from a German manuscript with the title *Libellus de Spiritibus Planetarum*. The same treatise appears in print again only one year later, but now in a German translation.[21]

The version of the *Archidoxis Magica* known today in the English-speaking world is a translation by Robert Turner from 1656 under the new title *Of the Supreme Mysteries of Nature*. His model was the *Archidoxis Magica* in the version of Johann Huser from 1570 who had

19 Peuckert, 2010 (1965), Vol. 1, p. 334.

20 Ibid., 335.

21 Sudhoff 2000 (1894), pp. 209 and 224. A digital copy of the German version can be found here: https://www.digitale-sammlungen.de/en/view/bsb10151878?page=,1. A digital copy of the Latin version is available here: https://www.e-rara.ch/bau_1/content/titleinfo/2478920.

recompiled the seven tracts from partly-printed, partly-handwritten originals.

Interestingly, while the publishing history of the *Archidoxis Magica* is many centuries long, it always travelled alongside Paracelsus' better-known works, and this despite its reputation as a spurious creation of one of the earliest Paracelsians. However, in 1982 one of the most respected authorities on Paracelsus, Wolfgang Schneider, presented new evidence why the majority of the treatises in the *Archidoxis Magica* should not be considered spurious but as an authentic work by Paracelsus.[22]

With this evidence in mind, we have to conclude that the *Archidoxis Magica* by far antedates the famous Arbatel from 1575—one of the most consequential links in the evolutionary chain of the Olympic Spirits tradition.[23]

This is of interest to our inquiry for two reasons. The *Archidoxis Magica* and the *Arbatel* represent two of our most explicitly magical source texts of early Paracelsianism. However, while Paracelsus' direct authorship of the former has been sufficiently proven, the *Archidoxis Magica* do not make mention of the Olympic Spirits and

22 In the following we quote Walter Pagel's succinct review of Wolfgang Schneider's 1982 publication *Paracelsus—Autor der Archidoxis Magica:* "The idea that Paracelsus was also a practising magus has been largely based on the *Archidoxis Magica.* This treatise had been regarded as spurious already in Huser's classical edition of the works, where it was relegated to the Appendix to the last volume. It is a richly illustrated corpus of magical signs and seals, mostly attached to amulets. The arrangement of the text varies in manuscript and printed versions. Inspired by the acquisition of a new manuscript, the author, the greatest living authority on Paracelsus' pharmacology and chemistry, now submits in the present book a detailed collation of all the versions available. The new arrangement of the text leaves the normally discredited genuineness of the treatise less unlikely than before on the strength of the higher age of the new manuscript. His conclusion is: the work as such is spurious, but the first four books of the treatise may very well be genuine. Tentatively, their date could be the same as that of the genuine *Archidoxis*, the fundamental chemical textbook of Paracelsus, namely 1526. As with all of Schneider's publications, the present book, which also contains a full facsimile of the new manuscript, is of great importance and interest." *Medical History*, 1983 July 27(3), Cambridge: British Society for the History of Medicine, 1983, p 331.

23 As the *Arbatel* and its unique place in the grimoire tradition has received in-depth attention by scholars over recent decades, we will not distract ourselves with a full repetition or even summary here. Notable contributions to call out are listed in the Bibliography.

neither do they use the term *olympic* in general. Their practical sections on celestial talismanology and planetary magic are rather traditional. The *Arbatel*, on the other hand, evidently was not written by Paracelsus but devotes an entire grimoire to the practice of working with the Olympic Spirits. We are faced with a seeming paradox here. Despite the consistent mentioning of the Olympic Spirits in Paracelsus magico-medical works over several decades, he chose to leave them out from his *Archidoxis Magica*. As we can exclude pure oversight as the reason, we have to presume that Paracelsus apparently did not consider the *Archidoxis Magica* the proper context for the Olympic Spirits. This could either be down to the nature of the alchemo-magical operations contained in the *Archidoxis Magica*, or it could have been a decision Paracelsus took in light of the intended audience of this book.

The *Arbatel*, on the other hand, places the Olympic Spirits at the heart of its operation. And yet again, scholars and practitioners have wondered for centuries why it fails to contain more in-depth and explicit ritual instructions for enabling communion and active work with the Olympic Spirits.

Instead, the *Arbatel* presents an innovative reworking of Paracelsus' Olympic Spirit concept with the function of the magician's faith at its centre. Its outer appearance is that of a traditional grimoire, according to Carlos Gilly even the first book of this genre ever to appear in print. However, the text leaves gaps and includes paradoxes that deliberately break the genre-expectation of a traditional grimoire. This is not an oversight or a fact caused by the disappearance of its later books. Instead, it is a critical feature for the *Arbatel*'s positioning in an authentic current of Paracelsian magic. Paracelsus himself had already polemicised against the use of classical grimoires such as the explicitly mentioned *Clavicula Salomonis*, and instead pointed to his elucidations on *faith* in magic as the gateway to successful practice.[24]

> *Arbatel is one of the most lucid books ever written on magic, but at the same time it's frustratingly terse. In fact it seems*

24 Sudhoff Vol. XIV, p. 514. For Paracelsus' elucidations on faith as the most essential magical tool, please refer to the previous chapter as well as my book *INGENIUM* (2022).

> *to have been intended as a syllabus for a private course of study in Renaissance magic, rather than a full explanation of any one topic.*[25]

> *The* Arbatel *is one of the most influential magical texts. Its many aphorisms are designed to guide us through a transition from an ordinary life to a magical life. […] The* Arbatel *can be approached in many ways—as an outline of magic techniques through the ages, as a step-by-step guide to communicating with angels, as a book of maxims for decent living, even as a Bible study guide. We can continue to find exciting possibilities to explore, following in the footsteps of many important mystics and philosophers who were beaconed by* Arbatel's *light, including John Dee, Böhme, Weigel, Khunrath, Fludd, Steiner, and generations of anonymous grimoire writers.*[26]

The most famous elements of the *Arbatel* are its original seven spirit names, seals and descriptions given in Aphorisms XV to XXI. To this day the origin of these names remain unknown. Attempts such as Dr. Skinner's to decipher them as derivates of original Greek terms have remained superficial at best. Furthermore, they invited the false conclusion that the appropriation of the Olympic Spirits by 17th and 18th century Solomonic grimoires could be read in reverse, and instead further suggest the Greek origins of this relatively young genre.[27]

Neither of these conclusions can be made from the original text of the *Arbatel*. The newly added names of the Olympic Spirits indeed might have been constructed by a learned 16th century scholar such as Gohory, leveraging Greek etymologies. Such thesis would require further investigation and evidence of source material that most likely has been lost. However, the rest of the text explicitly confirms a de-

25 Joseph Peterson, "Arbatel: Concerning the Magic of Ancients" *Watkins Review*, 2009, Aug 15.

26 Ibid.

27 Stephen Skinner and David Rankine, *The Veritable Key of Solomon—Sourceworks of Ceremonial Magic* Volume IV, (2008) p. 223, footnote 1. Also Stephen Skinner, *The Complete Magician's Tables*, (2006) pp. 213–214, tables M42–M50.

voted Paracelsian foundation and not at all a reference to Greek or even Graeco-Egyptian traditions.

At least until further evidence emerges, this means that all later uses of the names of the Olympic Spirits of *Arbatel* in books, grimoires, and works of art from the 17th century onward refer—knowingly or unknowingly—to an explicitly Paracelsian frame of reference.

The opposite table summarises some of the most often remarked upon seeming contradictions in the *Arbatel*.

For ritually-inclined readers of the last centuries, first among these paradoxes featured the explicit instruction not to use the names and seals highlighted so prominently in the text, but to ensure one receives these from the spirits themselves. Instead the *offices* of the spirits should be used to call upon them.

In a Paracelsian context, the term *office* should not be mistaken to simply mean a rank in the classical spirit hierarchies e.g., a *prince*, *governor* or *king*. Instead, the word refers to their actual function in the cosmos. I.e., one is advised to call upon the Olympic Spirits by calling upon the purpose and position they hold in the vast spirit ecology of Paracelsus' cosmography.

What we encounter here is an ancient lock and key system that applies to many ritual magical settings which do not follow the rubber-stamp recipe approach of the later 17th and 18th century grimoires. To unlock contact to a particular daemon the operator needs to show they have an authentic and comprehensive understanding of the spirit's nature *as it relates to the entire ecosystem of spirits to which both the conjured daemon as well as the operator belong.*

This is not at all an artificial device, but rather an organic operative principle of the cosmos we live in: conjuring a daemon means the outer man has to attune themselves to their presence in actions, movements, and the spoken word. The inner man equally needs to attune themselves to their office, by bringing themselves into resonance with the influx of this daemon.

Paracelsian magic, as we shall see in several examples further on, is essentially conducted through the operator's heart-space. The cognitive mind, however, plays an important role as well: Consider the heart-space of the resonance body through which communion is enabled; the images held and actions taken by the human imagination represent the hand that pulls the strings over this resonance body.[28] It is only together that they can make the rhythmic sound which amplifies the presence of the daemon. Because a daemon's very nature is rhythm.[29]

> *And in the fabric of the heavens [...] there is a great and very sweet sound that soothes the ears of the heavenly ones, which, composed of unequal intervals, is made by the impetus and movement of the spheres, which tempering high with low smoothly produces various concords.*[30]

> *For think that everything rejoices in its like, and even that everything is assisted externally by its like; especially since nature seeks nature, and, embracing its peer, refuses all contraries. Thus too, though not struck with fingers or plectrum, a string may be moved, as if it sounded in concordance with [other] strings to which it is tuned, so much power has the concord of things in everything.*[31]

28 This process takes place from both sides of the resonance body—from the side of the inner man as well as from the side of the spirits. Thus, our heart-space acts as a gate between material and spirit realm, and the goal in ritual is to harmonise the rhythms played from both ends.

29 We should call out that this technique is universal not because of elaborate historic transmissions across cultures and continents, but because it is *a principle embedded into nature.* That is, like water flows downstream and hot air rises, so daemons can be called through our heart-space, irrespective of our presence in time and space. Franz Bardon, for example, used the same method to call upon the many spirits enlisted in his books. However, unfortunately he then embroidered such essential approach in heavy garments of ritualistic settings and development curriculums for peripheral occult skills. For further reflections on the daemonic nature of rhythm see: Robert Müller-Sternberg, *Die Dämonen—Wesen und Wirkung eines Urphänomens*, Bremen: Carl Schünemann Verlag, 1964. For further information on the influence of celestial sounds on the human constitution see: Jeanice Brooks, *Music as Erotic Magic in a Renaissance Romance*, in: *Renaissance Quarterly*, Vol. 60, Number 4, Winter 2007, pp. 1207–1256.

30 Gohory (1571), quoted in Brooks (2007), p. 1215.

31 From Giovanni Aurelio Augurelli's (1456–1524) poem *Chrysopoeiaie libri III*, this particular section was explicitly referred to by Jacques Gohory in his writings, quoted in Brooks (2007), p. 1217.

What we tried to illustrate here is that by using the *offices* of the Olympic Spirits as the key to their conjuration, the practitioner has to show that they have observed the cosmos from close up, that they have fully immersed themselves into its ecosystem, that they have learned to distinguish the myriads of tones, rhythms and concords that fill its realms—and now are able to tune everything out, only to bring forth from their heart-space an intentional resonance with the daemon of their calling.

That is what constitutes the implicit Paracelsian theory of calling the Olympic Spirits; we shall see how we turn this into practice in the second part of this book. For now, though, we will return to our historic analysis of the evolution of the Olympic Spirits.

As we have seen, Paracelsus deliberately avoided introducing the Olympic Spirits in the context of his most explicitly magical manuscript, the *Archidoxis Magica*. This temptation now is what the anonymous author of the *Arbatel*—at least when read superficially—gives in to. He extends the narrative of the Olympic Spirits from a context of inner alchemy and astrological mysticism into the realm of operative ritual magic. Nonetheless, in doing so, the author still proves to be an adept of the original teachings of Paracelsus—by riddling its popular grimoire appearance with a lock and key system that only experienced Paracelsians would have been able to unlock.

> *As each person chooses to lead his life, so he will attract the kinds of spirits which have a similar nature and quality.*[32]

> *The human soul is the sole producer of wonder, to the extent that it is joined with the chosen spirit; once joined it will reveal what you desire.*[33]

The *Arbatel* is an instant success on the clandestine book market. Only four years after its release, 1579 in Basel, it is already included in the collected works edition of Agrippa of Nettesheim. What would

32 *Arbatel*, Aphorism 46

33 *Arbatel*, Aphorism 35.

become the infamous fourth book is here still called *De Caeremoniis Magicis liber*; the *Arbatel* is included on pages 705 to 740.[34]

III

Johann Huser's *Collected Works Edition*

FINALLY IN 1589 and 1591 Johannes Huser releases the essential collected works edition of Paracelsus in ten volumes. Following Adam von Bodenstein's efforts as a posthumous publisher of Paracelsus, Huser's edition quickly established itself as the most authoritative source for the broad dissemination of Paracelsus' cosmosophy and teachings.[35] What previously had circulated as individual releases as well as within an underground manuscript network, is assembled here for the first time into a complete printed edition.[36]

Until this time, most of the autographs by Paracelsus had been considered lost after his death. However, Huser managed to track down the scattered remains and to get access to them or what were considered direct copies thereof. The result was his monumental complete edition of Paracelsus' medical and natural-philosophical works.

Huser had taken great care to remain truthful to Paracelsus' complex autography and grammar and to change as little as possible. Thus, this edition has been referred to as authoritative ever since.[37]

> *This is absolutely the best [collected works] edition, far superior to all others. It must have gone well; for to all appearances, before the year 1600, the publisher began a reprint*

34 For a digital edition see, e.g. https://www.digitale-sammlungen.de/en/view/bsb11111983?page=763&q=arbatel

35 Gilly (1998), p. 165.

36 Johannes Huser (ed.), *Theil I–X Der Bücher und Schrifften, des Edlen, Hochgelehrten und Bewehrten Philosophi und Medici, Philippi Theophrasti Bombast von Hohenheim, Paracelsi genannt,* 1589 to 1591.

37 For reference, see the succinct introduction to the Huser edition at the excellent Paracelsus Project of the University of Zurich: https://www.paracelsus-project.org

> *of the out-of-print volumes in somewhat smaller and more compressed print […]*[38]

Luckily for us, in the final volume Huser decided to include an important section of texts of a magico-astrological character whose authenticity remained doubtful at the time.

Amongst several astrological prognostica we find the *Azoth*, *Save*, *De Ligno et Linea Vitae*, the already mentioned *Archidoxis Magica* as well as the interpretation of magical divination cards found at Nuremberg.[39]

Specifically with regards to the inclusion of the *Archidoxis Magica*, Huser added the following comment:

> *But it should not remain unreported that some doubt about these books Archidoxis Magicae, whether they are Theophrasti. […]*
>
> *However, because they are not inconsistent with Theophrasti's things, and are accepted and recognized by many as his books, they may stand for this time next to the others, until one becomes more certain of the author. […] the characteres and sigilla in the preceding 3 books are found unequal, perhaps for reasons that they were not copied and cut correctly (as often happens) due to lack of diligence. Because the autograph is not available, I have left them the same as found in the previous German edition. However, so that the reader does not miss anything, the deviating figures now follow, as Gerhard Dorn had them set in his Latin edition. Wherefrom he took their images, I do not know.*[40]

38 Sudhoff 2000 (1894), p. 693.
39 Ibid., 406.
40 Ibid., 407.

IV

Khunrath's *Amphitheatrum Sapientiæ Æternæ*

HEINRICH KHUNRATH'S (1560–1605) *Amphitheatrum Sapientiæ Æternæ Christiano-Kabalisticum* was first published in 1595.[41] The today rare, large-format and expensively produced first-edition of the book is followed by a smaller-format, extended version in 1609.[42]

It is the latter edition, published four years after Khunrath's untimely death and with unfinished commentary on the additional five engravings, that is most often referred to as a classic of Western occult book publishing.

Like so many of the milestones on the long and varied historical publication path of the Olympic Spirits, Khunrath's masterpiece deserves a book of its own with detailed reflections on his concept of magic. This notwithstanding, we commit ourselves here to brevity and conciseness to highlight only some important connections to Paracelsus' stars of the inner firmament.

Khunrath's aspiration was nothing less than a great synthesis of an idealised Christian Magical tradition in iconographic emblems. All of the latter he designed himself. And it was from his drawings that the images were executed with great skill and at great cost by Hans Vredemann de Vries, Johann Diricks van Campen and Paulus van der Doort.[43]

Due to the size and complexity of these emblems, the first edition of the *Amphitheatrum* only contained four of them, while Khunrath had created another five for the latter unfinished edition. As intended by author and artist, everything pales next to the splendour of these divinely-inspired illustrations. Which partly explains why, at least in the reception history of the book from the point of view of subsequent

41 Heinrich Khunrath, *Amphitheatrum Sapientiæ Æternæ*, s.l., 1595.

42 Khunrath, *Amphitheatrum Sapientiæ Aeternæ*, edited posthumously by Erasmus Wohlfahrt, Hanau, 1609.

43 Carlos Gilly, *Khunrath und das Entstehen der frühneuzeitlichen Theosophie*, in: Khunrath, 2014, pp. 9–10.

magicians, the 365 accompanying aphorisms[44] have so far been largely overlooked, and, unlike the graphic plates, have not found their way into the collective memory of modern magic.[45]

> *The text part of the Amphitheatrum includes 365 spiritual aphorisms from the biblical-apocryphal Book of Wisdom and the Sapientia Salomonis in two Latin versions: On the one hand they are taken from the Vulgate, on the other hand they are reproduced in the translation by Santes Pagnini (1470–1541). The engravings as well as their brief explanations and the compilation of the aphorisms seem to have been created largely independently of each other. The 365 aphorisms are individually annotated according to seven levels of spiritual perfection.*[46]

Khunrath was inspired by the ancient idea that *Wisdom* as such had existed in a primordial state of divine union before the cosmos had come into existence. Thus, man's ability to extract wisdom from the three realms of the macrocosm, the microcosm as well as the holy scripture, offered the most reliable Ariadne's thread in order to return into the original divine union.[47]

While Paracelsus was obsessed with the idea of healing, Khunrath was concerned with capturing wisdom—synthesized in a state of inner coherence and alignment, ideally perfected aesthetically in the visual form of a timeless engraving. As such, Khunrath's *Amphitheatrum* was not only hugely aspirational but presents one of the most stunning examples of *talismanic book publishing* in the Early Modern period.

We encountered Paracelsus' work as *initiatory* in nature. This means that he viewed the written word as a necessary evil to capture his cosmography and teachings. However, the actually initiating experience escaped the written medium's capabilities and had to be

44 306 in the first edition from 1595.

45 See Carlos Gilly's critical appraisal of the textual elements of the *Amphitheatrum* in: Carlos Gilly, *Khunrath und das Entstehen der frühneuzeitlichen Theosophie*, in: Khunrath (2014), pp. 10–11.

46 Schmidt-Biggemann, 2013, p. 9.

47 Ibid., 11; and, specifically, his elucidations on *Logostheology* in Khunrath's work.

sought out by each reader in following the path of their own experience. That is why Paracelsus, with great pleasure and ardent zeal, throughout his lifetime continued to lean against the conventions of the book as a *sacred* medium.

Khunrath on the other hand had deliberately chosen this medium to perfect its initiatory capabilities. He willingly depended on the written word and even more so on the visual depiction of his ideas. To him, the magical book was not a necessary evil but a *magical instrument* as such. To speak with a modern expression by Byung-Chul Han, Khunrath's engravings were meant to inspire *symbolic perception*:[48] that is to slow down time and to invite the viewer into a shared space of divine orientation, to present to them pearls of permanence in the gushing river of the ephemeral cosmos.

> *As a faithful lover of Theosophy, doctor of both medicines and follower of the spagyric art, as Khunrath calls himself in most of the figures, he felt himself capable not only of formulating the utterable, but also to artistically represent the inutterable, and one could vary for the Amphitheatrum the apt phrase coined by David Knight for alchemy: "Drawing the unspeakable: 'Theosophy' as visual art".*[49]

For both Paracelsus and Khunrath, man's ability to truly *see* carried the seed of wisdom. A major difference in their approach, however, was that Paracelsus was willing to work with the written word as a mere concession, only to encourage people to look back at themselves, the world and the scripture; whereas Khunrath believed the book itself could become the mirror in which the majesty of all three realms could be united.

Khunrath had been deeply influenced by Paracelsus, and his *Amphitheatrum* has often been read as a synthesis of the three main areas of Paracelsian philosophy: magic, alchemy and *gabalia*.[50] As

48 Byung-Chul Han, *The Disappearance of Rituals: A Topology of the Present*, 2019.

49 Carlos Gilly, *Khunrath und das Entstehen der frühneuzeitlichen Theosophie*, in: Khunrath 2014, p. 11.

50 Gilly 2014, pp. 9–14. With regards to the Paracelisan neologism *gabalia* as a term for the practice of divinely inspired natural magic, see the previous chapter.

such, the book presents a major milestone in the dissemination of *theosophy*: an old Greek term, already known from the works of Pseudo-Dionysius Areopagitas, first reinterpreted by Balthasar Flöter in reference to Paracelsus as a *theodidacto ac theosopho viro*, then introduced as a generic designation by the *Arbatel*, and now made available to a much wider audience by Khunrath's work.[51]

The spiritual movement indicated by this term from the 16th to the 18th century was very distinct and had little in common with the reinterpretation of the term in the 19th century. It described a path towards divine revelation that led *through* the depth and wisdom of the world, whether this was achieved in the form of early modern scientific research, of intimate personal experience mediated by the *musa sagax* or in the form of the congenial interpretation of the liberal and occult arts.[52]

Within such context, manual labour was no longer regarded as a useless yoke, but as an ever-present tool to attune oneself to the divine spirit woven into the world. According to theosophy, the difference of whether work was *divine* or *mundane* did no longer reside in the nature of the task itself but in the very approach man allowed themselves to pursue it.

Let's refresh our memory with Paracelsus' definition of the magical art of *gabalia* again:

51 Ibid., 12–13.

52 Ibid., 11: "From the middle of the 16th century until the 18th century, theosophy represents the attempt to follow the mundane path of knowledge of God, which theology has neglected: the path of the study of nature in order to reach the knowledge of God. At the same time, theosophy means the application of this knowledge in order to obtain a more intimate vision of reality and thus new knowledge about nature. The appropriation of this term by modern movements of the 19th and 20th centuries should not make us forget that since the appearance of Balthasar Flöter's edition of Paracelsus' *Philosophia magna* in 1567, the publication of the book *Arbatel* in 1575, and the emergence of Johann Arndt's De antiqua philosophia ca. 1580, 'Theosophy' (and not 'Pansophie,' 'Cosmosophy' and similar later names) was a most precise term to characterize the philosophical movement extending from Paracelsus through Weigel, Arndt, Sclei, Crollius, Haslmayr, Nollius, Hirsch, Fludd, Böhme, Franckenberg, van Helmont, Kozák, Comenius to Maul, Welling and Oetinger, one does not want to forget the 'Brüderschafft der Theosophen vom RosenCreutz,' as Adam Haslmayr calls them."

> *In the Olympic Spirit lies the art Gabalistica with its appendices, which art proves that to the imagination still much more is possible in those [human beings] in whom the joining of the Olympic Spirits has taken place. Then in the same way as the visible corpora can come together, so can the Olympic Spirits of creation, which are the heavenly bodies in man: These things are described in the books of the Gabalia.*[53]

Man had to create within themselves the conditions for faith, imagination and free will to unite, supported by the Olympic Spirit and without being disturbed by fragmentary planetary passions. The proper alignment of the inner man was the foundation for the mundane work of the outer man to be deified. And yet, it was not only in divine prayer aloof from the world, but specifically also in the cauldron of everyday experiences that such shape of the inner man was forged.

We will quote one of Khunrath's key reflections on this subject, and see how it brings us full circle both in our investigation on the Olympic Spirits, as well as to the essential tenets of Paracelsian spirituality.

> *Verse 181, Prov. 3:5 Trust in the Lord with all your heart, and do not rely on your prudence. Distrust thyself: forsake thyself, and leave thee and thy business and thy doings unto the Lord God. Cast thy care upon the Lord, and He shall feed thee. Ps. 55:23. He Himself will be your government. Let this be your motto, namely, My help is from the Lord, who made heaven and earth. Ps 121:2: He who hopes in the Lord will prosper in body, mind and soul, so that a healthy mind will be in a healthy body, macrocosmically and microcosmically, inwardly and outwardly. In sum: in all your actions and works let Jehovah be your beginning and end, the Alpha and Omega. […] Without inspiration, help and guidance of God, do not desire to know high things: All in God, who is All in All, thou canst do all things.*
>
> *Rely not on thy understanding: for he that trusteth arrogantly on his prudence, imagination, and foolish counsels and labours, with neglect of the law of Scripture, of nature,*

53 Sudhoff Vol. IX, p. 298.

and of his pure conscience, is a fool; and therefore walketh foolishly in all his ways.

The world heathenly believes that happiness is always a companion of our prudence, or depends on our prudence: hence comes the proverb: Every man is the maker of his own happiness. Therefore also Seneca says: Follow reason and bear the fate. And Juvenal says: where prudence is, there God is not far removed.

But our wise teaches the opposite, namely: That Jehovah the author of happiness gives happiness; and that he takes and gives prudence and good progress of our things. This is also to be observed in physico-chemical works; namely, that if we do not obtain the good will, the being and being able from the Lord through prayer, then we can neither learn nor accomplish anything in nature according to the straight line of truth.

Therefore, we Theosophists must be diligent in the chamber of prayer, that God may teach us rightly and prepare us, and ask Him cordially not to take away His Holy Spirit from us, but to bless us and our work: that He may preserve our minds, senses and reason, so that we may not be seduced by devilish folly and fancies; and that He may guide our hands and feet, so that we may not spoil the work. [...]

Therefore, our reason, or the audacity of our ingenium, should not appropriate or arrogate to itself any wisdom, nor should it persuade itself as if it were capable, without the special and particular blessing of God, of governing life, actions and work, or of procuring for itself happiness and the good progress of its affairs; or that it lies in its power to work and do something good: But let it[54] *Christianly place all things in the hand of the Almighty and merciful God, and, according to the wise counsel of our sage, trust in the Lord with all its heart, from the beginning of its ways even unto the end. That is, it should begin and end all its actions, in prayer and work with God, and in trust in God.*

Now the Theosophist is to consider this carefully, and not lack anything in it; much more than the Sophist in their

54 Note, "it" here refers to man's reason and ingenium.

> *labyrinth. The will of the Lord Jehovah is to us, who wander about in the great labyrinth of the unclean world and are like groping in the darkness, a much more certain thread of Ariadne, with which she delivered Theseus from the labyrinth. Therefore, you, disciple of the cabala, of magic and alchemy, obey and examine yourself by this touchstone: If your trust is in the Lord, you will draw from the Lord the salvation of the will, and everything will go happily for you; and you will be three times, even four times as blissful, as well in practice as in theory, and will not be disgraced in eternity, as the Holy Scriptures and experience testify. [...]*
>
> *The following verse also wants to say the same, which was inscribed in France in an old castle in an old carpet, in which was shown a woman, who pulled through a thread, of which the king in France Charlemagne is said to have often spoken the contemplation:*
>
> *Nenti fila Deus mentem conjungit Olympo.*
>
> *I.e. God promotes the work of the profession, and joins the thread of the spinner, and the help, which we should ask from him in our work, unites the mind with heaven. It makes us think and pray up to heaven. [...] Then therein lies hidden the secret of divine conjunction and union in its general physico-chemical stone, of which to speak more publicly is not advisable.*[55]

These instructions are deliberately given in a way that the superficial reader might skim over them, mistaking them for nothing but a general pious reminder to place one's spiritual work under the direct aegis of God. yet, as we have seen in the chapter on Paracelsus' unique spirituality, they draw to the foreground the very same ideas we had found to be central for Theophrastus' understanding of the art of *gabalia*.

The initial section of the quote is arguing against prudence, ratio and logic which are arrogantly rooted only within themselves and cut off from the balancing influx of Divinity. Khunrath is not at all advocating for blind faith, devout subservience or against an erudite cul-

55 Khunrath 2014, pp. 446–447, translation by author, Verse 150 in the 1595 edition, Verse 181 in the 1609 edition.

ture. Quite the opposite: the Church finds no mentioning in his elucidations, but a direct, fully responsible relationship with the Divine is advocated for. Man is made responsible to educate their heart just as much as their mind, and to keep both of them under the *special blessing* of God and in the presence of the Holy Spirit.

Khunrath calls on his fellow human beings not to strive to soar above creation, but to humbly take their divinely inspired place within the fabric of the world. As such, we hear an echo of Paracelsus' animistic worldview, in which all elements of creation meet on an equal footing—every stone, moment and star equally can be encountered as teacher or student to each other—and Divinity is the one great mediator amongst them all.

Curiously, we also see a human's *ingenium*—their inborn capability to spark new inventions and ideas—as the fulcrum of balancing between audacious arrogance and ecological integration. The difference being whether it acts under the spell of fragmented celestial passions, or illuminated by the light of the Holy Spirit.[56]

Of particular interest to our investigation, however, is the allegory mentioned at the end: the weaving crone depicted on a French wall tapestry, in relation to the purported saying by Charlemagne: *Nenti fila Deus mentem conjungit Olympo.*

This Latin sentence has often been incorrectly translated as *Every Calling hath a promise from God.* A much more precise rendition in English, however, is the following:

> *To the one who weaves threads, God connects the spirit with Olympus.*

Equally, when we compare the above translation from 2014 with the original German-Latin text, we realise the second sentence following this Latin quote was rendered incorrectly as well. An accurate translation into English from the original reads as following:

> ORIGINAL GERMAN-LATIN: *[…] conjungit mentem Olympo, heisst uns hinauff gehn Himel dencken und bethen.*

56 For further elucidations on the role of the human ingenium in magic, see my book ***INGENIUM*** (2022).

> CORRECT ENGLISH TRANS.: [...] Connecting your mind to Olympus means thinking and praying yourself into heaven.

So here we have it: Paracelsus had advised that the celestial spirits in man had to be united into one, to form the *Olympic Spirit*. This spirit was the centre of the magical art of *gabalia* and acted as a catalyst for the Holy Spirit to take residence in the mind of man.

Heinrich Khunrath, in his usual enigmatic tone, gives us a further hint as to the exact nature of this work: *To the one who weaves threads, God connects the spirit with Olympus.*

Once we learn to go about our everyday actions in the same manner as God is weaving creation in every moment—carefully pulling thread over thread, patiently forming patterns, stitching each action to its next, both as a response and address to the world we are woven inside ourselves—our thoughts and prayers and actions will all begin to become one, and lift us up to heaven. Working our days like a divine weave is the outer way of uniting the Olympic Spirits into one.

V

Adam Haslmayr's *Theophrastiæ Cabalisticæ Isagoge*

> *[Paracelsus'] explosive theological and natural philosophical manuscripts, which had been deposited in a safe place, proved to be dangerously charged sleepers, which in the generations to come threatened to blow up the religious monopoly of the confessional churches and the epistemic rules of conservative scientists.*[57]

By the early 1600s Paracelsus was considered a revolutionary medic, a heretic theologian, an atheist, a magus as well as a seer—all in paradoxical personal union.[58] The explosive force of his works had

57 Gilly 1998, p. 154

58 Ibid., pp. 156–7, 165.

proven impossible to be contained by authorities of spiritual and academic institutions. All at once, an "unstoppable flood of editions"[59] was released upon the book market, while his many theological works "were passed on from hand to hand and copied with a frequency which makes up for the loss of the Paracelsian autographs." [60]

Among the driving forces of early Paracelsianism, Adam Haslmayr (1562–1630) occupies a special position.

> *[...] Adam Haslmayr, a Tyrolean schoolmaster, musician and alchemist who had read the theological books of Paracelsus so intensively and had internalised them to such a degree, that he spoke only of the holy Theophrastia.*[61]

It was Carlos Gilly's liminal study from 1994 *Adam Haslmayer—Der erste Verkünder der Manifeste der Rosenkreuzer* which portrayed this fascinating figure in all its spiritual complexity as well as literary impact. After nearly ten years of research, Gilly uncovered the character and story of a man who so identified with Paracelsus that he did not hesitate to speak of him in the first person and spent five years in penal service on a galley in the Mediterranean as the price of his relentless dedication to broaden and publicise a decidedly Paracelsian spiritual movement.[62]

Haslmayr was an Austrian trained church-musician and appointed as Latin headmaster in Bolzano in 1588. In the following years he garnered some reputation mainly through his musical compositions and activities and was repeatedly able to gain financial support from the patricians of Bolzano. In 1593, he even received from the Archduke Ferdinand II of Tyrolia the right "to bear a coat of arms, namely, in reference to his name, a hazel grouse with a green branch in its beak."[63]

Nine years later, in 1602, we first hear of his suspicious alchemical endeavours. And already in the following year he was dismissed from school service —not as a "heretic", but as a "confused head".[64] Con-

59 Ibid., 155.
60 Ibid., 160.
61 Ibid., 166.
62 Ibid., 167.
63 Dörrer 1946, p. 44.
64 In the earliest known study on Haslmayr, Anton Dörrer points out that the

tinuing his alchemo-philosophical studies, he gained the support of the Archduke Maximilian of Tyrolia who became a patron of his work, which Haslmayr presented to him in the form of short treatises.

In the years from 1600 to 1612, Haslmayr now led a life that was as busy as it was unsteady. Whether he experienced the loss of his permanent and respectable position in Bolzano as disgrace or liberation, we do not know. However, at the end of these dozen years Haslmayr had established himself as an essential link in the network of the early Paracelsians. Amongst his personal acquaintances were Benedikt Figulus, Joachim Morsius and Carl Widemann.[65]

The price that Haslmayr paid for his relentless pursuit of reestablishing Paracelsianism as a spiritual pathway was tremendous. In 1612 he was condemned as a heretic and from 1613 to 1617 he was forced to perform service as a convict on a galley in the Mediterranean.

> *Archduke Maximilian the Teutonic Master, however, was too great a friend of serious music not to have taken care of the reprimanded. He provided Haslmair with a position as a chapel singer in the royal convent of Hall. At the same time Haslmair worked as a notary in the neighboring Heiligkreuz. Unfortunately, he got more and more involved in doctrinal disputes, wrote as a follower of Paracelsus combative diatribes against the student of Galen, Dr. Hippolyt Guarinoni and did not forego accusations even against the sovereign. [...] The Innsbruck court [...] threw him into the Kräuterturm on August 1, 1612. Haslmair was sentenced and brought to Genoa as a galley prisoner. Only after several years of being sent to high personalities, such as Prince*

circumstances of his appointments as Latin headmaster in Bozen in 1588 already indicate that Haslmayr was considered to have "an ideologically embattled personality in the intellectual life of Tyrolia" (Dörrer 1946, p. 43). Thus, we cannot presume that his Paracelsian and alchemical studies started only in 1602, but rather that they led to an untenable situation as principal only at that time.

65 Carl Widemann (1555–1637) was a German author, physician and collector of Paracelsica and occult manuscripts from Augsburg and secretary to the English alchemist Edward Kelley at the court of Emperor Rudolph II.

> *August von Anhalt, Haslmair regained his freedom and was able to return to Tyrolia.*[66]

Already in 1610 Haslmayr had read the handwritten version of the *Fama Fraternitatis*, to which he wrote an official response (printed in 1612 and later), in which he emphatically invited the original Rosicrucians to come to Tyrolia. Even during his years on the galley he maintained a lively correspondence and kept writing new occult treatises, imbued with Paracelsian spirit and assailed by salt water. After his death in 1630, Carl Widemann managed to save Haslmayr's extensive and unique library from the authorities.

For our current exploration, Haslmayr's legacy stands out for two reasons especially. First, despite the intense personal consequences he had to bear, Haslmayr continued to advocate for Paracelsianism as a decidedly *spiritual movement* aimed at restoring Christian faith from the degrading influence of the organised churches. Second, and even more importantly, Haslmayr had direct access to the theological writings of Paracelsus and was personally instructed by the last known medical assistant of Paracelsus, *Lorentz Lutz of Meran.*[67] Thus, rather than on speculation and rhapsody, his writings shine a genuine light on the occult foundations of the "Schola Paracelsica Christiana".[68]

In direct opposition to what Haslmayr called the *wall-church,*[69] he advocated for a community enlivened and constituted by divine spirit alone. Such a "School of Pentecost and of the Olympic languages" would be open "to all wise believers in Christ at any time".[70] One of the aphorisms he coined summarises this intention succinctly:

66 Dörrer 1946, p. 45.

67 Lorentz Lutz. Citizen and barber-surgeon in Algundt, a quarter of a mile from Meran in Etschland. Obijt. He knew Theophrastum himself, and Gabriel von Marwisen stayed with him, also Adam Haslmayr travelled with him. Has many writings Theophrastica, which are not yet common. (Carl Widemann, *Directory of some spagyric physicians and other artists*, translation by author, quoted after: Paulus, Julian, *Alchemie und Paracelsismus um 1600. Siebzig Porträts*, in: Telle, Joachim (ed.), *Analecta Paracelsica—Studien zum Nachleben Theophrast von Hohenheims im deutschen Kulturgebiet der frühen Neuzeit,* Stuttgart: Franz Steiner Verlag, 1994, p. 340; see also: Gilly, 1998, p. 168).

68 Gilly 1994, p. 193.

69 "Mauerkirche", see: Gilly 1994, p. 194.

70 Haslmayr, quoted in Gilly 1994, p. 194.

"The mind alone is the temple."[71] Neither outer ceremonies were required for this Paracelsian *school* to come to life, nor was this community bound by any place, city or people.

From the Christian orthodoxy's point of view, Haslmayr was on deeply heretical terrain with his explanations. The Church located his teachings of the "Sancta Theophrastica" far beyond an inner-Christian mystical current, but, rather, in the spirit-haunted wilderness of practical magic.

One of the crucial reasons for this is the emphasis Haslmayr placed on reconstructing a Christian spirituality that was free of pastoral or priestly mediation, placing every practitioner into direct contact with Divinity. As we saw in the chapter on Paracelsian spirituality, this was by no means an invention on Haslmayr's side but a direct continuation of the core theological ideas of his teacher's teacher.[72]

> *The books of the Christians are all creatures, they came on paper through the prophets, they are nothing else than memories and products, through which we humans are convinced and reminded of what is in us, from which we understand that the mind is not in the book, but in the spirit. But the spirit in the people, we must let it work in us freely, like all prophets and apostles, and listen with David, what God speaks in us [...].*
>
> *Therefore, the Illuminati and enlightened theosophists point you only to the One, to the centre and life of all things, which is hidden in all creatures, that is* VERBVM DEI. *Without which nothing can live (John. 1), for if the word would not be, we would worship the earth and believe the enthusiasts, who first want to bring in an alien life, and juggle in the mass in German and Latin. The only One is our Book of All, from which we can and should recognise all wise books and arts easily and without effort, ut supra, only through prayer. And this book is in me, in you, and in all men, great and small, learned and unlearned, young and old.*[73]

71 "Pura mens is der Tempel", Op. cit.

72 Goldammer Vol. II, 1965, p. 56.

73 Adam Haslmayr, in Gilly 1994, pp. 195–6.

In a direct line of transmission from Paracelsus, Haslmayr placed paramount emphasis on the importance of personally experiencing the divine word and letting it come alive in each practitioner. The Pentecostal spirit had to be made a personally lived experience and reality in every human being. Still, such divine experience was not meant to induce glorious rapture, but a gnostic consciousness that resulted in concise spiritual instructions.

The Olympic languages, as Haslmayr called them, were the key to unlocking this occult process, as they constitute the medium for spirit-inspired teaching, learning and education of the practitioner's heart and mind.

The very term actually provides a great examples to illustrate how closely Haslmayr's own writings were guided by Paracelsus' original works. Let's read another quote from a manuscript by Haslmayer first, followed by an excerpt of Paracelsus' Philosophia sagax. Between the two sections we will discover instructions on the use and functioning of the Olympic languages, given as clearly and concisely as might have been the case in the books of the time:

> *Your supposed high schools of the 7 sects or liberal arts shall give way to the Vulturnus [south-east wind], yes to the next breeze and be hung up in smoke. Before all the wise men of Christ, you shall be a fool's cap [...]*
>
> *Let your noble Latins know, who also through this [i.e., by the foolishness] promised heaven and built and erected her a school and collegia, that the Olympic linguae, yes the languages of the school of Pentecost, the teachers of the Holy Spirit, the Theophrastia, the eternal Sophia must flourish and be revealed, and they your Latins shall not be worthy to be dogsbodies of the wise.*[74]

> *What comes from God into that [i.e., into the world], that is also from God in man: namely, that each one works in a body that is similar to it, the elements in their body, as well as the sidereal spirit in its body, therefore also the divine in its divine [body]. Now there is a point to notice in man, which*

74 Adam Haslmayer in a manuscript from 1612, quoted in Gilly 1994, p. 200.

> *is that he has a mind outside of all of these, namely that he should ask, seek and knock, so he finds and it is granted to him, it is opened to him. So, through the angel, eternal nourishment is given to the one who has worked towards God, as through the natural spirit, it is given to the one who has worked towards the elements. Not only to the mind that is from God is given, but also to the other according to their schoolmasters, from whom they are descended, to learn and investigate from him in this and that into which they are born: That means, man is made from the elements and from them he must learn the natural [things]. The music [he must learn] from Venus, the warfare from Mars, the housekeeping from Saturn etc. etc. So he should also learn from God what is and belongs in the eternal. Now this point is making the following point: much asking, knocking and searching.*[75]

Here we find the pagan Olympic Spirits, not as dead symbols but as living custodians of the arts and crafts. Man, on the other hand, is uniquely gifted with a mind that could liberate itself from instinct and impulses, to consciously commune with the former in the spiritual act of *asking, seeking* and *knocking.*

With an even more magical tenor we find the same approach emphasised in the Pseudo-Paracelsian *De Natura Rerum*:

> *Therefore we should know what the ancients in the Old Testament, who were in the first generation, obtained and accomplished through their ceremonies and conjurations: this is what we Christians, who are in the second generation, the new ones in the New Testament, should obtain through prayer, that is, through asking, seeking and knocking in faith. In these three main points stands all our reason of the Magical and Caballistic Art, by which we may attain and bring about everything we desire and wish for, and nothing shall be impossible for us Christians: of which I have described to you further in the Libell de Visione, and in other books of the Caballia [...].*[76]

75 Sudhoff Vol. XII, p. 303.
76 Sudhoff Vol. XI, 1928, p. 394.

Subsequently, "the three cabalistic principles"[77] of *Asking*, *Seeking* and *Knocking* came to form the heart of the "Schola Paracelsica Christiana" as envisioned by Haslmayr.

In direct reference to Haslmayr's explanations, Benedictus Figulus summarized the most important principles of this Paracelsian school in a manuscript from 1609:

> *The first Cabala was uttered from the mouth of the Spagyrus Trismegistus I[esu] Christi, our Lord and Saviour: to* **ASK**, *to* **SEEK**, *to* **KNOCK**. *The three main points of the true Christendom as the unsurmountable Cabala are: (1) To love our enemies, (2) to depart from what is ours, (3) to patiently endure all disgrace suffered, (4) to raze all honour offered.*[78]

These weapons of self-conduct the *student* of this Paracelsian occult school had to acquire through divine prayer and by centering their life on this spiritual path. In the second phase, after the preparatory work in the oratory was completed, they had to walk out into the physical world, encounter challenge, love, loss and pain—in order to distinguish and master outer and inner forces of this *terra olympica* as Haslmayer called it. Only then, in the third and final phase, the student would be able to work in the laboratory of the art.

> *Is thus indicated by this clearly and in detail enough how and in which measure such parergon must take place at the beginning in the prayer, followed by Saturn in the search in Olympus, and finally by the help of Vulcan in the chemical laboratory.*[79]

In other words, the aspirant had to move from *withdrawal* to *exposure* to *active participation*. Likewise, he moved from *inner* to *out-*

77 Gilly 1994, p. 188.

78 CABALISTICA *prima Ex ore Spagyri Trismegisti I[esu] Christi Domini et Redemptoris nostri prolata:* PETERE, QUAERERE, PULSARE. *Die 4 Haupt Puncten Des Wahren Christenthumbs alß der unuberwindlichen* CABALAE: *1) Unsere Feindt alle lieben, 2) Aygens verlassen, 3) Angethane Schmach gedultig leyden, 4) Anerbottene Ehr allenthalben verniechten.* Gilly 1994, p. 199.

79 Gilly 1994, p. 189.

er work, to finally accomplishing *both at the same time*.

Finally, in addition to the three inner and four outer principles of the work, there was one last ingredient which we already encountered in our exploration of Heinrich Khunrath's work. Following the *Philosophia Sagax* of Paracelsus, Haslmayr also recognised Wisdom—in the sense of mystical self-knowledge—as the final key to attaining the "secret sacrament of nature". Only through the understanding of the three spirits inherent in man—the animal, the sidereal and the divine—was man able to prepare themselves to become fully *human*.

Let's recapitulate. The Olympic Spirits stand below Divinity and yet it is through their mediation that the elements and the animalistic spirit in nature are enlivened. Man is endowed with all three spirits: animal, celestial and divine. However, in their normal state most humans resemble animals much more than celestial spirits, let alone vessels of Divinity. The celestial spirits—acting as intermediate beings between the world of creation and the Creator—thus offer a dual key: by exploring them with practical wisdom in the Light of Nature man can begin to understand the dynamics of all elements of creation. And equally, by not giving in to their celestial promises one by one, but by uniting them all together into one Olympic Spirit within the human body, they become the compound medium through which man is able to experience undivided Divinity within themselves again.

Olympi terrae in Haslmayr's terminology was another word for the mundane world, in which the mysteries of the celestial spirits were both hidden and yet constantly at work. We will examine it in greater detail further on. *Olympic linguae* on the other hand was the direct experience of these forces within the practitioner once their mind had been prepared as *the only temple*.

With this in mind, Adam Haslmayr's own explanation of the cabalistic key which he used to illustrate many of his manuscripts suddenly shift from reading arcane and occult, to a direct address to the reader to unite the Olympic Spirits into one within themselves. For what emerges from this synthesis are no longer seven celestial spirits but *one star* hovering above the seven, and all of them within man.

> *Therefore, the Chymical Art teaches not to make gold, but to recognise God and ourselves and to despise gold as much as it remains gold and money. And it is not a fraudulent art,*

but a gift of the Holy Spirit, a fulgor[80] *of angelic wisdom and the most excellent work of the royal wedding [...] and is the best part of philosophy, as it teaches us to separate body, soul and spirit from each other, to calcify and reunite them into a nobler body, and to prove miracles.*

For the star, which is mentioned in this paragraph, is a special stone and key to dispel many diseases in people and metals, for which reason it is not called in vain by the wise: a golden stone. And it is one star.

This star hovers above all seven spirits of the firmament, revealed as Apocalypsis Hermetis, and it passes through all solids: of the vegetable, the animal and the mineral monarchy it leads in itself, and is of the element water and the sacrament and secret of the word, that is, of the floating spirit over the water its subject [...].[81]

With such a key we are well equipped to delve into a fully restored manuscript by Adam Haslmayr as given in the appendix to this book: *Extract from the Introduction to the Theophrastic Cabala. Being the introduction of the sacred, secret art and wisdom of the prophets. Without which art and grace no one can understand or thoroughly explain the Holy Scriptures.*[82]

Announcing in the first sentence that the "Cabala is the Olympic Spirit", Haslmayr proceeds to give a detailed exposition of the core tenets and the magico-mystical approach taken by the living Paracelsian collegium he so ardently was focussed on maintaining during his lifetime.

While Ms.Q.286/20 in the *Herzogin Anna Amalia Bibliothek* in Kassel today is the only known extant version of this manuscript, one has to presume copies of it circulated within the illicit occult network to which Haslmayr belonged. In true Paracelsian spirit, it

80 i.e., a splendour, a dazzling brightness.

81 Adam Haslmayr, *Amphitheatrum Chimicum Sacrum*, quoted in Gilly 1994, p. 16.

82 Haslmayr, *Extractus et Theophrastiae cabalisticae Isagogen, Daß ist, Die einlaittung der Heiligen geheimen Khunst vnd Weisheit der Propheten. Ohn welche Khunst vnnd gnaden kheiner die heilig Schrjft verstehen noch gründtlich erkhleren khan.* Weimar: Herzogin Anna Amalia Bibliothek, Ms. Q. 286/20.

is written not only in German but often in the direct spoken dialect by Haslmayr. The transcription therefore turned out to be quite laborious and the translation into English was carefully adapted for the modern reader.[83] The version in the appendix also contains detailed notes on the most important points which are meant to facilitate both understanding as well as possible implementation in one's own magical practice and everyday life.

VI

Benedictus Figulus: the Olympic Compiler

> *Much beloved hearts, charitable patrons and friends, just as the deer in Psalm 41 cries out for fresh springs of water, so now all this time since I have won your clientele, with all lovers and adherents of the dear Celestial Philosophy and Alchemy, I have been urged to drink with you from the fountain of truth, not only what the natural light but also the light of the Holy Spirit from its own Celestial Source reveals in the Holy Scriptures.*[84]

Directly interwoven with the story of Adam Haslmayr is that of Benedictus Figulus (1567–missing after 1617), with the essential difference that an in-depth biographical and work-related study of Figulus is still lacking.

Accordingly, in many books that refer to his works we find speculation and adoption of unverified facts from earlier authors instead of actual source analysis. A significant exception was presented by Joachim Telle in 1987,[85] following which we can provide a rough outline of his life.

83 I am deeply grateful for the painstaking transcription by Anne Hila. This book would not have been possible without her talent and dedication.

84 Benedictus Figulus, *Rosarivm Novvm Olympicvm Et Benedictvm*, 1608, p. a ii.

85 Joachim Telle, *Benedictus Figulus: Zu Leben und Werk eines deutschen Paracelsisten, in: Medizinhistorisches Journal,* Bd. 22, H. 4 (1987), pp. 303–326.

Figulus was born on December 29th, 1567 in Uttenhofen, Franconia. He grew up in relatively poor circumstances. According to his own statements, he first came across the works of Paracelsus at the age of twenty around 1587/88. During this time he worked on his doctoral studies which he eventually had to abandon due to adverse circumstances. Whether these were due to financial hardship or his early heretical activities, Figulus does not specify in the short biographical accounts which we find inserted into the prefaces of two of his books from 1608.[86]

From 1600 he attracted attention as a preacher.[87] And from 1601 onwards, he entered the period of his life that lasted until his disappearance, which latter he romanticised and called his *pilgrimage* in reference to Paracelsus' own biography: a restless, lifelong itinerant existence.

On his many journeys Figulus often came into conflict with the authorities, not only because of his alchemical interests or his heretical teachings, but also because of his illegitimate partnership with his servant, or as he called her, his "beloved Sponsa" and their two children. From 1604 he professed himself openly as a "Discipulum Paracelsi."

Looking back today at the scanty facts of his life as well as the many collected writings that bear his name as an editor, two characteristic features stand out above all: at the height of early Paracelsianism and the emergence of the first Rosicrucian writings, Figulus was an extremely well-travelled and well-connected heretical vagabond.[88] He was in direct contact with Adam Haslmayr and Carl Widemann, and was personally acquainted with Johan Valentin Andreae. Whether he was even one of the central sources of inspiration for Andreae's first drafts of the Rosicrucian manifestoes is open to conjecture, but it remains undecided which of the two men had the stronger effect on the other. What is certain is that Figulus' copies and collections of unprinted early Paracelsica were essential for the spreading of the "Schola Theophrastica,"[89] that is, the spreading not

86 Peuckert, 1956, p. 486.

87 His own words were "concionator" and "verbi divini minister". See Telle 1987, p. 305.

88 Johann Valentin Andreae himself described him as an orbis circumcellio. See: Telle, 1987, p. 308.

89 Figulus according to Peuckert, 1956, p. 361.

only of the medical writings of the Hohenheimer, but above all of his magico-mystical works.

Accordingly, it is not surprising that Figulus and Haslmayr knew each other at least since 1607.[90] But beyond mere acquaintance Figulus was personally affected by the arrest of Haslmayr in 1612, as the latter's conviction to the galley also led to the issuance of a personal arrest warrant against Figulus himself. From 1617 onwards his trace is lost and the exact date of his death is still unknown. An overview of his works can be found in Telle's essay from 1987.

> *This, however, is what makes Figulus important for us above all others: he is the barometer of the times. A history of Figulus—it would be good to have it—would not report on any genius or creative thought, but we would recognize the climate of the time by it and its development.*[91]
>
> *He was not an independently productive specialist writer who participated in the professional development of the Paracelsian or alchemical heritage. But his Alchemica editions secure him the rank of a capable editor […].*[92]

True to his main capacity as a copyist, editor and disseminator, we find a remarkable milestone of the evolution of the Olympic Spirits right at the beginning of his famous *Thesaurinella Olympica aurea tripartita. This is: A heavenly golden treasure chamber, equipped with many exquisite gems* from 1608.

In his dedication to Rudolph II, Figulus chose to put his name below a most unique year specification. The last three lines read:

> *Hagenau, the 3rd October, in the year of the restored redemption cIↄ. Iↄcvii. Under the regiment of the Olympic governor, Angel HAGITH, in the year 197.*[93]

90 Edighoffer, "Adam Haslmayr", in: Hanegraaff (ed.), *Dictionary of Gnosis & Western Esotericism*, 2006, pp. 459–461.

91 Peuckert, 1956, p. 362.

92 Telle, 1987, p. 319

93 In the original: *Hagenau den 3. Octobris, Anno reparatæ salutis cIↄ.Iↄcvii. sub regimine verò Gubernatoris Olympici, Angeli HAGITH, anno centesimo xcviic*

Figulus here overtly emphasises the Olympic Spirit of Venus, Hagith, whose influence, according to the *Arbatel*, had become predominant since 1410. The related paragraph in the *Arbatel* reads:

> *But here we want to show how these princes and powers can be engaged IN CONVERSATION. ARATRON appears on the Sabbath and the first hour of that day, and gives truthful answers about his provinces and provincials. Similarly, the other are also ordered in their days and hours. Each one them PRESIDES for 490 years. The first cycle started sixty years before the birth of Christ, when the administration of prince BETHOR began; this lasted until the year 430. He was followed by PHALEG up to the year 920, then OCH until the year 1410, and then HAGITH reigns up to 1900.*[94]

Apparently written in 1607 and first published in 1608, *Thesaurinella Olympica aurea tripartita* thus deliberately places itself in the direct line of transmission from Paracelsus to the Arbatel and onwards into the early 17th century. This spiritual lineage is of such importance to Figulus that he acknowledges the chronology of the Olympic Spirit in the dedication to Rudolph II. Of course, this symbolic reference to place one's own work directly under the tutelage of the Olympic spirit of one's own time did not go unnoticed. Some 350 years later, Will-Erich Peuckert still referenced Figulus's dedication by signing his own introduction to his liminal GABALIA with the seal of Hagith.

Where the Thesaurinella is referencing the Olympic Spirits in the conclusion of its preface, Figulus' most well-known work, the *Rosarium Novum Olympicum Et Benedictum* does this even more overtly right on its title page. Before we take a look at the title emblem, however, let's familiarise ourselves with the book as such. The *Rosarium Novum Olympicum* presents a miscellany of various Paracelsus-related manuscripts, with partially unclear authorship by Figulus himself, as well as Paracelsus, Johannes Trithemius and Alexander von Suchten (1520–1575).

Part of this compendium is a treatise titled "A truly substantiated theory of the Cabalistic writings of Theophrasti, extracted by us from the origin and polish of the Quintia Essentia called Olympus Terræ:

94 *Arbatel*, Aphorism §16, in: Peterson 2009, p. 31

Which is the only genuine Prima Materia, the tinging key and concerns the clear salt, spirit, soul, spirit [sic], corpus, aqua and ignis."[95]

Here we find note of the original man as described by Moses in the Book of Genesis, who "was extracted from a salty Quintia Essentia and entirely enclosed in the Terra Olympi"[96]; yet such knowledge is positioned as a secret too high to be disclosed in the treatise itself. However, the text does mention that regaining such state of divine proximity can be achieved in two different ways: by means of a natural path of *manual labour* or through a philosophical path of *the art*. The prima materia of either way, however, is the *Terra Olympi*. yet in the same breath Figulus also mentions that these secrets are far beyond the comprehension of a simple God worker, and are therefore best left shrouded in silence.

> *The same man He [God] built and drew out of the Salian Quinta Essentia, which was locked into the Terra Olympi, beautiful, sheer, pure and clear: If now this Terra has been called a salt spirit, in which such great secrets are hidden, then now in these things it is not necessary to inquire higher, also to inquire for more clarity is not advisable, nor to judge of it, because it would be much too difficult for a godly worker, therefore want to let go of such woolgathering in these Arcanis, not to brood higher in it, so that no one takes the wrong route: therefore I want to speak of the matters naturally known to us, [and] let such high secrets rest, furthermore explain me.*[97]
>
> *This should not be forgotten now, because in this lies all art and mastery. Here the speech is about the philosophical work which is brought from the earthly and from the matter into a clear revelation. Now for this there are two different ways, one happens naturally by much manual labour, but is equal in nature. The other way is worked philosophically artificially: yet both [ways] are alike to each other, like a pure spirit and fixed salt spirit together with its spiritual earths,*

95 Benedictus Figulus, *Rosarivm Novvm Olympicvm Et Benedictvm*, Basel: in verlegung des Autoris, 1608, pp. 32–47.

96 Figulus 1608, p. 33.

97 Ibid., 33.

> *therein the whole work is conceived. From the Terra Olympi it is drawn, heavenly cooked, mixed together into one. The other is of such nature as the finite astrum, which is supernaturally revealed and made known by God alone.*[98]

As we might see, at this point a more in-depth foray into the critical term *terra olympi* seems called for.

VII

Terra Olympi

The Nexus of Heaven and Earth

THE TERM *TERRA OLYMPI* does not appear in the surviving works of Paracelsus. In the analysis here, however, we encountered it earlier in an allusion in the writings of Adam Haslmayr from the early 16th century, which were specifically aimed at the continuation of the spiritual current of Paracelsianism.

> *Is thus indicated by this clearly and in detail enough how and in which measure such parergon must take place at the beginning in the prayer, followed by Saturn in the search in Olympus, and finally by the help of Vulcan in the chemical laboratory.*[99]

Haslmayr described the journey of the mage relating to three domains: the time spent in divine prayer, the time spent exploring the terra olympi, and finally the time spent in the laboratory of the art.

Thus, the *terra olympi* occupied the vast living territory between *oratorio* and *laboratory*. The middle stage of the work, when the mage strides out into the world of creation deciphering, learning, assembling and strengthening their own practice of Paracelsian *Gabalia*. No longer is the practitioner constraining themselves in inner divine retreat but deliberately exposing themselves to the world of

98 Ibid., 35–36.
99 Gilly 1994, p. 189.

creation. Still, their practice has not yet arrived at the stage where the work could be guided in a deliberate and structured way, as an experiment in a laboratory would.

Later on in the 17th century we find a sanitised version of this idea in the famous *Raphael oder Artzt-Engel* (1676), by Abraham von Franckenberg (1593–1652), disciple and early biographer of Jakob Boehme. Here, Franckenberg provides a table that neatly divides the three domains of *Kabala*, *Magia* and *Chymia* into their respective loci of practices: *Oratorium*, *Auditorium*, and *Laboratorium*.[100]

As Peter J. Forshaw observed, such artificial division and categorisation would have considerably violated the much more ecological and interdependent understanding of these domains by the early Paracelsists:

> *This association of esoteric sciences and spaces is undoubtedly inspired by the Paracelsian doctor Heinrich Khunrath of Leipzig (1560–1605), whose De Igne magorum (1608) insists on the vital necessity of working alchemy, magic and cabala in conjunction. These three arts combine in Khunrath's Christian-Cabalist, Divinely-Magical, and Physico-Chemical magnum opus the Amphitheatrum sapientiae aeternae (1595/1609), finding their most profound expression in his image of the Lab-Oratorium, probably one of the best-known images of early modern esotericism.*

The idea of the tripartite division of the spiritual path is certainly not new. yet, following the Paracelsian premise of *Asking, Seeking, Knocking*, his early hagiographers re-envisioned it in the following three domains:

> ¶ *Divine prayer, or asking for angelic guidance in the oratory,*
> ¶ *Saturnian exploration of the terra olympi, or seeking wisdom in the vast auditorium*[101] *of the world,*
> ¶ *Putting the Vulcanic art to work, or knocking on the doors of specific substances and spirits in the laboratory.*

100 Forshaw 2010, p. 170.

101 Auditorium literally translates as a "place where something is heard".

Such interpretation of the *terra olympi* as the auditorium of the world—or more specifically: the time spent seeking wisdom in the world of creation—can be derived from the published works of Heinrich Khunrath, Adam Haslmayr and Benedictus Figulus respectively.[102]

However, this only constitutes the outer or exoteric localisation of the *terra olympi*. As we shall see, there is a much more esoteric meaning of the term which we do not find in the printed works of the early Paracelsists. The fact that this mystical reading of the term escaped later authors is quite excusable—after all, they had neither access to direct disciples of Paracelsus such as Haslmayr, nor the privilege to see the private correspondence of the early Paracelsists, at least in part, as we have today. Thus, already in the *Nodus Sophicus enodatus* of 1639 we find *terra olympi* translated as a plain alchemical synonym for *earth*.[103] The exoteric tradition of the term continues until the 19th century, where for example we encounter the term again in Johann Friedrich John's German *Handbook of General Chemistry*, who explains that the earthen parts of a substance "were called Terra Olympi by the alchemists."[104]

In order to uncover the mystical significance of the terra olympi it is worthwhile returning to its root and to inquire about the origin of the term itself. As it wasn't taken from Paracelsus' works, it might be worthwhile considering where Adam Haslmayr—or possibly another early Paracelsist from whom he would have borrowed the neologism—took inspiration to create the term. A possible hint at the esoteric meaning of the expression could have been taken by Haslmayr or others from an ecclesiastical publication in 1546 which provides a surprisingly precise backdrop for a Paracelsian interpretation of

102 A tempting and rich detour at this point would be a closer iconographic examination of Frederico Gonzaga's (1500–1540) emblem of Mount Olympos and his accompanying motto: Fides Olympus. A visit to his Renaissance Palazzo Te and Palazzo Ducale in Mantua make for a most magical excursion and are highly recommended. One will find ample material for further meditation on the nature of terra olympi in ancient pagan ritual as well as the Neoplatonic ascent of the soul towards Divinity. I am fondly recalling my own synchronistic visit together with José Gabriel Alegría Sabogal in 2022 during the weeks of writing this chapter.

103 Anonymous, *Nodus Sophicus enodatus, d.i. Erläuterung etlicher vornehmer Philosophen Schrifften vom Stein der Weisen*, s.l.: Friedrich Gruner seel. Erben, 1639, p. 37.

104 Johann Friedrich John, *Handwörterbuch der allgemeinen Chemie*, 4,2: T–Z, Leipzig [u.a.]: Brockhaus, 1819, p. 323.

the term: this is Luigi Lippomano's *La Catena in Genesim* (Paris, C. Guillard, 1546), a collection of commentaries written by about sixty Greek and Latin authors, dedicated to Pope Paul III.

Ironically, Luigi Lippomano (1496–1559) was an Italian bishop, hagiographer and conservative anti-reformer. Thus, his book by no means was meant to inspire a mysto-magical cosmosophy of deeply heretical nature such as the spiritual worldview of the early Paracelsians.

Still, in his commentary on Genesis 7:20 Lippomano references Saint Augustine's exegesis of the first book of the bible:

> *AUGUSTINE IN QUESTIONS ABOUT GENESIS. If the earth of Mount Olympus (as history conveys) could enter the space of tranquil air, where, as it is said, neither clouds can be seen nor wind be felt, but inasmuch as the earth is the heavier and lower element, why [should it not be possible] also for water, which is lighter and higher, to swell, and that at least for a short time?*[105]

In an alchemical reading, here the term *terra Olympi montis* is used to suggest that a kind of earth exists that indeed is a cosmological hermaphrodite: it is still part of the chthonic realm and yet at the same time elevated to partake in celestial qualities. The image of the *earth of Mount Olympus* i.e., the chthonic matter hosting the celestial dwelling of the classical pagan gods of the Greek, is the ideal symbol to illustrate such a hybrid substance.

Contracted to *terra olympi*, such term would have worked for Haslmayr and others to both provide ancient orthodox lineage to their novel interpretation as well as, in a much more occulted sense, to allude to the essential concept of Paracelsian spiritualism: the actual Olympic Spirits. For *terra olympi* would have signified the corporeal immanence of the Olympic Spirits in actual matter. Hence, the image of the *earth of Mount Olympus* was meaningful in a dual sense: both as the location in classical history where the pagan gods once dwelled, as well as in a Paracelsian sense as *earth enlivened*

105 *AVGVSTINVS IN QUAESTIONIBVS SUPER GENESIM. Si terra Olympi montis (ut tradit hiftoria) potuit invadere spatium tranquilli aeris, ubi dicitur nec nubes videri, nec ventus sentiri, qua tamen terra grauius et inferius est elementum, cur non et aqua crescendo, quae levior ac superior est, idque ad tempus saltem exiguum?* Lippomano, 1546, fol. 140.

by the actual Olympic Spirits. Now we begin to see the significance associated with this term from the viewpoint of mystical Paracelsianism: The *terra olympi* was a codeword to describe the mechanism within all of creation that allowed matter and spirit to interlock. Understanding the mystery of the *terra olympi* meant apprehending how the celestial spirits inseminated themselves into creation. It was the mystery that revealed the substantiation of spirit into the vessel of elementary or chthonic matter. Equally, this mystery held the key to reversing such process of Neoplatonic involution i.e., to reestablish direct communion with Divinity beyond the boundaries of the mortal flesh. For the same pathway that nature chose to imbue matter with spirit could be chosen by alchemists and mystics alike to transubstantiate matter again and engage with the spirits directly. In other words, *terra olympi* is the circuit board of creation within which the currents of spirits could be found and maintained by gross matter. It is the thin interface where mortality and divinity interlock into one.

In light of such elucidations, Benedictus Figulus' cryptic reference in his *Rosarivm Novvm Olympicvm Et Benedictvm* gains new perspective:

> *From the Terra Olympi it is drawn, heavenly cooked, mixed together into one.*[106]

And even the title of the treatise itself takes on programmatic meaning as describing a theory of Paracelsian cabala that guides the reader to discover the actual prima materia of their work, the spirit-imbued *terra olympi*:

> *A truly substantiated theory of the Cabalistic writings of Theophrasti, extracted by us from the origin and polish of the Quintia Essentia called Olympus Terrœ: Which is the only genuine Prima Materia, the tinging key and concerns the clear salt, spirit, soul, spirit [sic], corpus, aqua and ignis*[107]

Finally, what Figulus referred to carefully in his writings, he dared to display as a blazing emblem on the front of his *Rosarivm Novvm*

106 Figulus 1608, p. 33.
107 Ibid., 32–47.

Olympicvm Et Benedictvm: here we see the tree of the seven Olympic Spirits in full glory, crowned by the sun, and rooted in the titular *terra olympi*.[108]

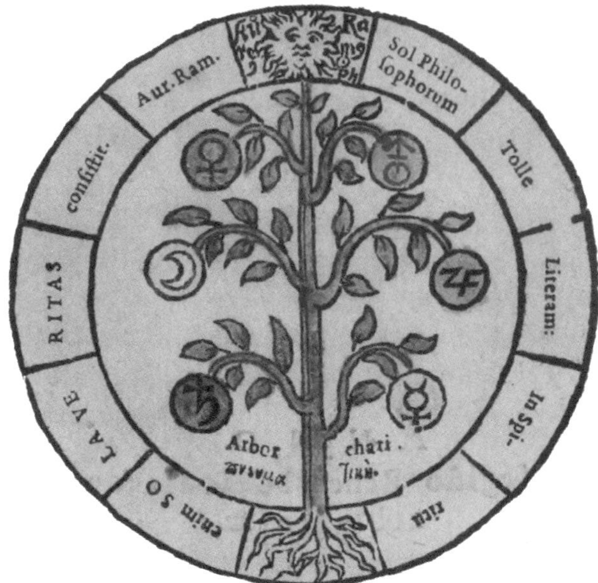

A close observer would have spotted that through the ring enclosing the drawing, a direct path leads upwards on both sides from the chthonic roots of the tree back to its solar crown: a reference to the fact that the *terra olympi* is both elemental as well as celestial in nature. The symbolic meaning is further emphasised by the Latin sentence contained in the twelve sections[109] making up the circle around the tree:

> *Sun of the philosophers, remove the letter, for in the spirit alone there is truth. Aur. Ram.*
> [possibly: *Aureus Ramus* = Golden Branch][110]

108 *See* the emblem from Figulus' *Rosarivm Novvm Olympicvm et Benedictvm* (this page).

109 The twelve-part structure could be an allusion to the astrological houses.

110 In the original: *Sol philosophorum Tolle literam: in Spiritu enim* SOLA VERITAS *consistit. Aur. Ram.*

But our journey leads us further into the mystery of the *terra olympi*, for it is the nature of the chthonic realm to offer circles of descent into past and meaning. So far, we have mainly drawn upon printed material from Heinrich Khunrath as well as Benedictus Figulus. As referenced earlier, however, we also hold the privilege of having access to some of the private correspondence of the ever-prolific Adam Haslmayr. Luckily, one of his letters to landgrave Moritz von Hessen-Kassel (1572–1632) can still be found in the vast archive of *Chemical Correspondences by* the latter.[111] Specifically, our attention is drawn to volume 19, part 5, page 116 recto.

The image on the cover of *Rosarivm Novvm Olympicvm Et Benedictvm* depicts the process of the Olympic Spirits *taking root* in matter in a vertical cross-section. In a plain circular diagram the gaze of the observer descends from the sun via the planetary branches of the tree to the place of their unification in matter in the roots. What is left in darkness here is how this insemination of the Olympic Spirits in the *terra olympi* actually takes place. And this is the mystery Adam Haslmayr made great efforts to reveal in the above letter to Moritz von Hessen-Kassel, one of the most prominent patrons of mystics and alchemist of his time.[112]

In the above-mentioned private letter, Haslmayr included the most explicit and detailed version of a magico-alchemical glyph which—in a simpler form—he liked to use in many of his manuscripts intended for broader circulation.[113] We are providing the original together with a modern render of it on the following pages.[114] What we see is a complex diagram made up of three sections: a circular diagram at the top, a triangular diagram at the bottom and another, larger circular drawing taking the largest part of the page in its middle.

111 Various, *Chemische Korrespondenz des Landgrafen Moritz*, 2° Ms. chem. 19[5], Kassel, 1604–1631.

112 Moran, Bruce T., *Moritz von Hessen und die Alchemie*, in: Borggrefe, Heiner (et al.), *Moritz der Gelehrte—ein Renaissancefürst in Europa*, Eurasberg: Minerva, 1997, pp. 357–360.

113 My thanks go again to Carlos Gilly, for the pioneering research and publications he has done on the subject of the early Paracelsists and Rosicrucians. see: Gilly, 1994, Chapter XII.

114 Referring to image above: Adam Haslmayr in: Moritz, Hessen-Kassel, 1604–1631, Chemische Korrespondenz des Landgrafen Moritz, Universität Kassel, 2° Ms. chem. 19[5], online source: https://orka.bibliothek.uni-kassel.de/viewer/image/1380890069017/1/.

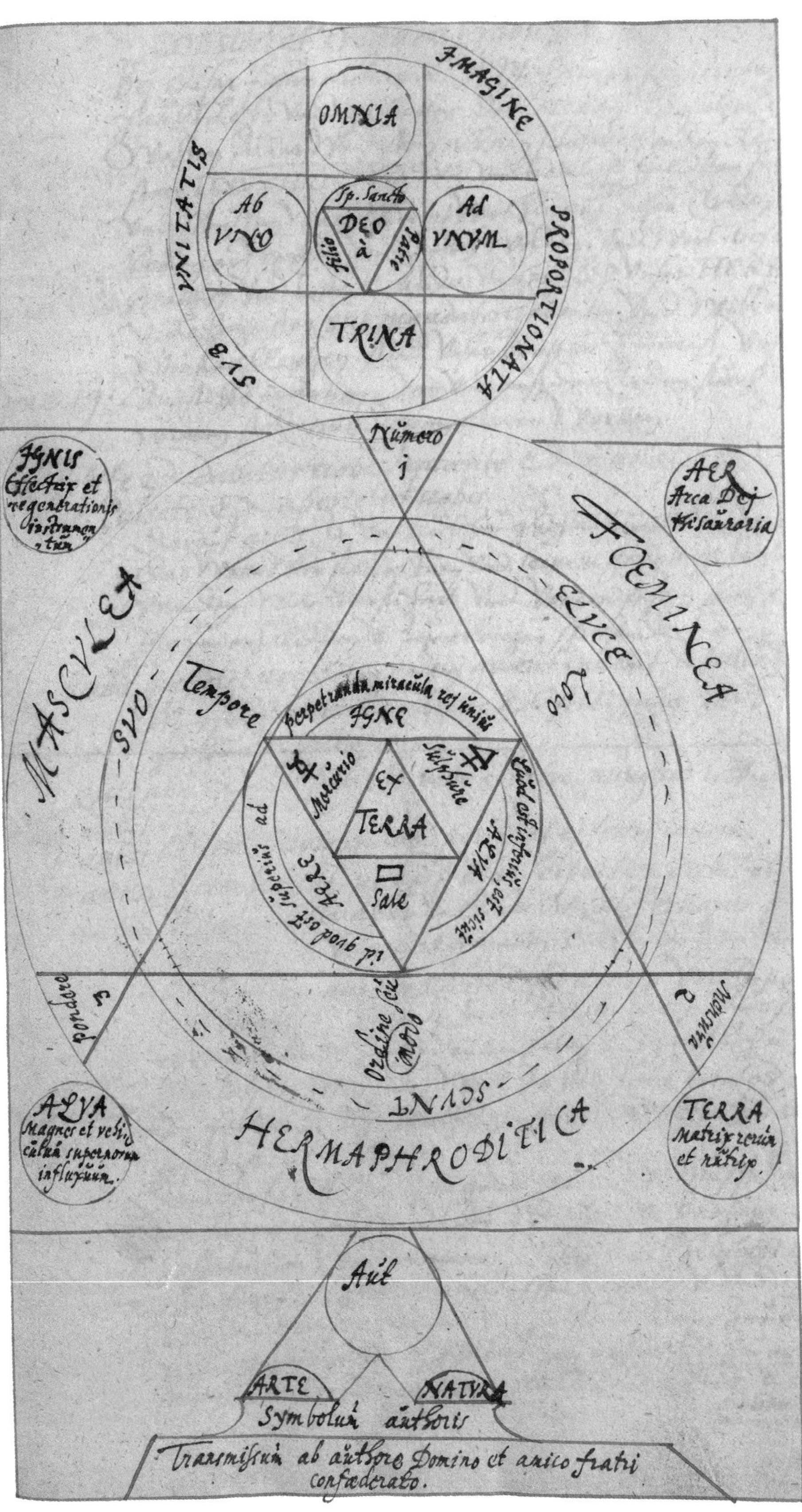
IMAGINE PROPORTIONATA SUB UNITATIS
OMNIA
Ab UNO
Sp. Sancto
DEO à
Filio
Patre
Ad UNUM
TRINA
Numero j
IGNIS Effectrix et regenerationis instrumentum
AER Arca Dei Thesauraria
MASCULEA
FOEMINEA
SUO
E LUCE
Tempore
Loco
perpetranda miracula rei unius
IGNE
Mercurio
Sulphure
Ex TERRA
Sale
AQUA
AERE
id quod est superius ad
Quod est inferius, est sicut
pondere
Mensura
Ordine
SUNT
ALUA Magnes et vehiculum supernorum influxuum.
TERRA Matrix rerum et nutrix.
HERMAPHRODITICA
Aul
ARTE
NATURA
Symbolum authoris
Transmissum ab authore Domino et amico fratri confoederato.

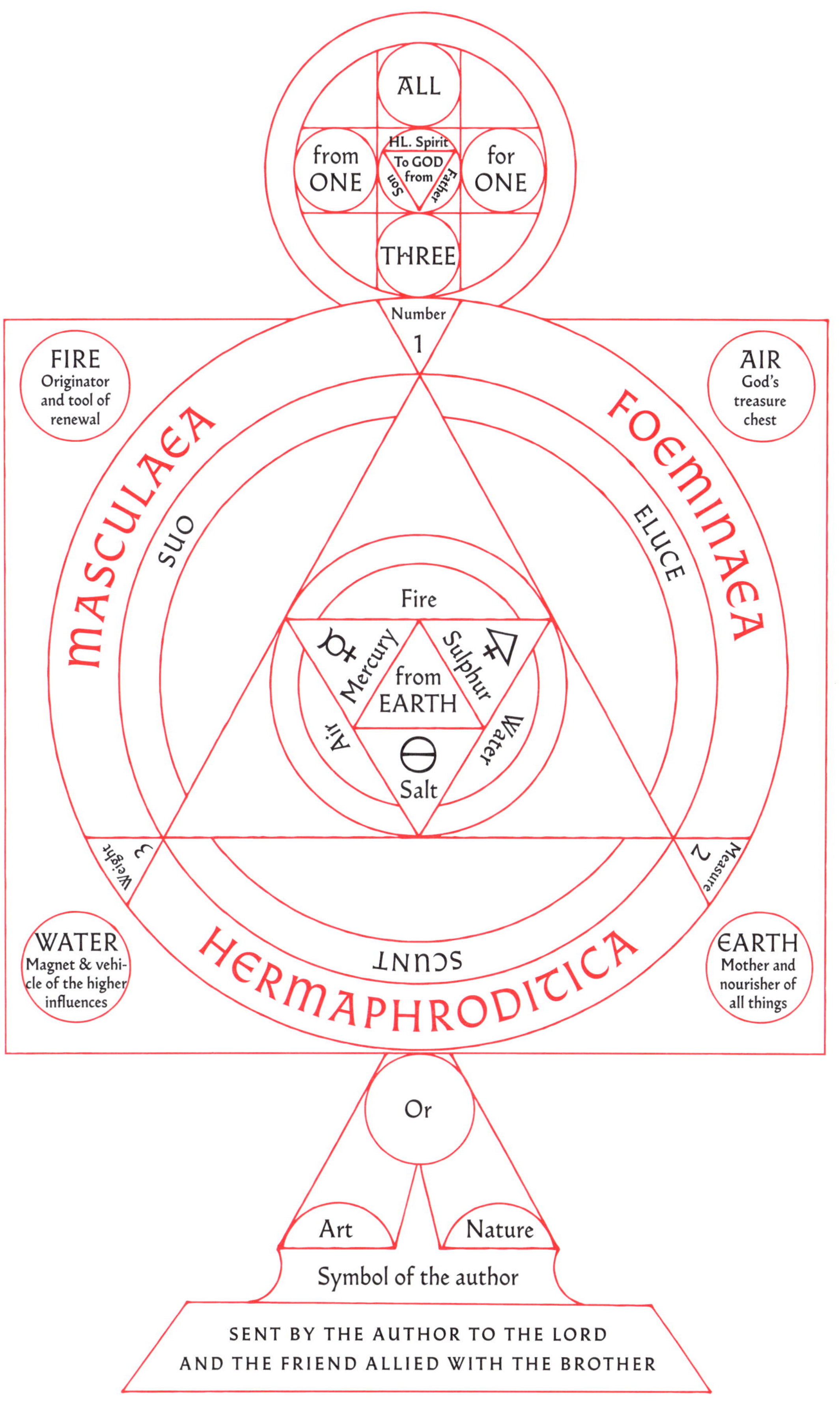
ALL
from ONE
HL. Spirit
To GOD
from
Son
Father
for ONE
THREE
Number
1
FIRE
Originator and tool of renewal
AIR
God's treasure chest
MASCULAEA
SUO
FOEMINAEA
ELUCE
Fire
Mercury
Sulphur
from EARTH
Air
Water
Salt
3
Weight
2
Measure
WATER
Magnet & vehicle of the higher influences
EARTH
Mother and nourisher of all things
SCUNT
HERMAPHRODITICA
Or
Art
Nature
Symbol of the author
SENT BY THE AUTHOR TO THE LORD
AND THE FRIEND ALLIED WITH THE BROTHER

In essence these three sections can be read to depict the three stages of the work identified above: the anchoring of the practitioner in divinity and angelic guidance (top), the exploration of the *terra olympi* (middle) and the perfection of wisdom in the sophisticated balance between artificial and natural processes (bottom). However, what makes reading this visual cypher rather complex is that Haslmayr is changing the visual perspective between the outer two diagrams and the middle one: the top and bottom sections give the impression of a vertical cross-section; almost as if we were looking at a liturgical *monstrance*.[115] However, as we will see, the central section of the diagram has to be read as a horizontal cross-section. Haslmayr invites us in this central section to take a glimpse at the area which remains only hinted at in Figulus' cover emblem of the *roots* of the Olympic tree.

In the following we are walking through each section of the diagram and provide a brief interpretation of each segment.

The top section is the easiest to decipher. Aligned into a cross-pattern we see five spheres, all contained within a sixth sphere. The central one reads *To God, from the Holy Spirit, Father and Son.*[116] The surrounding four spheres read *All for One, Three from One.*[117] And the final sphere includes the words *Images in proportion under unity.*[118]

With these references a program is outlined that the practitioner had to master in the oratory before they were ready to journey out into the art. It was about God in the three realms of the *Father* (transcended divinity), *Son* (human incarnation) and *Holy Spirit* (angelic mediation), and about the practitioner's ability to create conscious communion in each one of these. Equally—just as in any Late Medieval magical ritual—this phase would have ensured the practitioner does not work through selfish motivation, but as a divine medium. For the *images* they would bring forth had to stand in balanced proportion to divine unity.

115 A monstrance, also known as an *ostensorium*, is a vessel used in Roman Catholic service as a reliquary for the display of holy relics. The word monstrance comes from the Latin word *monstrare*, meaning "to show".

116 *DEO à Sp. Santo, Patre, filio.*

117 *OMNIA ad UNUM. TRINA ab UNO.*

118 *IMAGINE PROPORTIONATA SUB UNITATIS.*

Now, the central section places our *Earth* at its centre, surrounded by a triangle of the Paracelsian generative forces *Mercury*, *Sulphur* and *Salt*, followed by the other three elements in the sections of a circle (Fire, Water, Air). In the outer section of this circle we read an essential quote from the Tabula Smaragdina: *that which is below is like that which is above to perform the miracles of one thing.*[119] As such, this innermost section is clearly identified as the core or original seed of the microcosm. It is into this raw kernel of elementary and generative forces that the Olympic Spirits inseminate their celestial presence.

As we have pointed out before, this central section is depicted in *horizontal view*. Imagine you are looking at a cross-section of the *terra olympi* under a microscope: This means that what we see is the microcosmic seed of the substance into which the Olympic Spirits descend from above; the spirits themselves are not depicted in this image.

This inner core is now enclosed in a triangle that fans out into the three sections of a circle denominated as *time*, *place* and *order without movement.*[120] The inscription around this circle reads ELUCE-SCUNT SUO, that is, *they shine forth by themselves.* This circle is intersected by the arms of the central triangle, opening another three circular sections inscribed with *Masculine*, *Feminine* and *Hermaphrodite*. Next to these we see the three endpoints of the large triangle as *Number 1*, *Measure 2*, and *Weight 3*.[121]

Here now we perceive the microcosm becoming embedded into the macrocosm: cosmic principles such as time, place and order immediately begin to condition the emergence of the individual microcosmic being. They inevitably guide and shape the way each seed begins to express itself as it expands outwardly into the world.

This process is described as the seed beginning to *shine forth by itself*, which means that the seed naturally begins to express itself in the language and forces of the cosmos it has come alive in. At the same time, the seed cannot remain a seed either. Evolution out into the world is a natural law. Thus, the seed must clothe itself with the

119 *quod est inferius, est sicut id quod est superius ad perpetranda miracula rei unius.*
120 *Tempore. Loco. Ordine seu movo*
121 *Numero 1. Mensura 2. Pondare 3.*

mentioned material constraints that sequentially begin to condition its gender, variety, measure and weight.

What the reader is guided to understand here, is how the small world and the large world are beginning to weave themselves into each other. While they are separated, they are one equally. As the practitioner would have learned from the prior phase, each image—that is, each microcosmic seed—needs to come to stand in proportion under unity. *Everything for One, Three from One.*

This central diagram is flanked by four smaller circles in the corners of a square, which contain the names as well as short explanations of the mystical effects of the four classical elements: *Fire* as the instrument of regeneration, *Water* as the magnet of higher influences, *Air* as the medium of divine treasures, and *Earth* as the matrix of all things.

IGNIS *Effectrix et regenerationis instrumentum.*
FIRE *Originator and tool of renewal.*

AER *Arca dei thesauraria.*
AIR *God's treasure chest.*

TERRA *Matrix rerum et nutrix.*
EARTH *Mother and nourisher of [all] things.*

AQUA *Magnes et vehiculum superorum influxuum.*
WATER *Magnet and vehicle of the higher influences.*

More so than most modern elucidations on the Western elements, these succinct summaries provide ample source for meditation of their place and effect in the alchemical process described before. *Fire* as the element of generation ignites and renews, *Air* as the element of utterance is a medium of spiritual treasures, *Earth* as the element of patterns nourishes and sustains, and *Water* as the element of solution attracts and integrates new influences.

These are the raw tools of the art. However, as deceptively simple as they might appear, each one of these takes on a threefold as well as a sevenfold expression, depending on whether their living force is placed under the agency of *Mercury*, *Sulphur* or *Salt* and/ or any of the seven Olympic Spirits. In total this leads us to 84 (= 4 elements × 3 generative forces × 7 Olympic Spirits).

What we see in this central part of the diagram is the genius mind of a late 16th century Paracelsian hard at work to codify and encrypt the very mechanics according to which the Olympic Spirits interlock into substance. In stark contrast to magical grimoires or classic alchemical formulas, however, Haslmayr's emblem is not encoding a simple recipe. Instead it is outlining a full cosmosophy.[122]

The centre of the diagram thus shows the actual *generative code* of the *terra olympi*: it represents all creative cosmic forces which have their unique function to play in the shaping of each created being across the mineral, plant and human realms.

Thus, the spectator is guided to understand that *all created beings are terra olympi*. The mysterious prime matter of the Great Work is *everything and everywhere*. What seals its secrets is by no means its remoteness or scarcity, but the angelically mediated wisdom of being able to see what creates and conditions each aspect of it. Adam Haslmayr is portraying the full ecology of spirits coming together to condition matter into an individual being. In doing so, he offers a map and travel guide to the alchemists who attempted to interfere with this organic process of nature, and to *refine* it through their art.

Finally, the bottom part of the diagram is formed like the foot of a monstrance. Here at the base is where we arrive last. In large letters we read *Art Or Nature*. The words *Art* and *Nature* each occupy a semicircle, indicating that they need to come together in order to complete the work. The *Or* between them, however, occupies a full circle, which indicates the essential choice made by the alchemist in the laboratory, to either apply their art, or to allow nature to take over itself at each stage of the Great Work.

122 Due to its importance we wish to summarise this central section one more time in its most condensed form: at its heart we encounter the microcosm consisting of the three Paracelsian forces of creation in combination with the four elements. This seed of matter, imbued by the Olympic Spirits, is then moulded by the three conditional forces of creation, that is, the *time*, *location* and *order* of its inception. From here, the seed is expanding into the next sphere of creation, which means it will be dressed in either male, female or hermaphrodite gender. Finally, it will assume its unique number, measure and weight, to come into full embodiment and shape.

The last two lines can be read in a dual sense. In a magico-alchemical sense, the *symbolum authoris,* placed directly under the semicircles of art and nature, indicates that each practitioner is the *author* of their work and the result they produce is the *symbol* that represents themselves. Art and artist thus become one, mutually refer to and involve each other. In this way, the phrase would have emphasised the accountability of the practitioner and the critical choices they make as they attempt to take nature beyond herself in the laboratory of their art.

The final line then says *Sent by the author to the Lord and the friend allied with the brother.*[123] Which, in the above reading, would have brought the diagram full circle: where it began at the top with the practitioner in the oratory, anchoring themselves in divine presence, the last line presents the accomplished work as a service offering to the Lord i.e., to God, who is addressed as *friend* allied with the brothers of this divine art. It was for Divinity alone to assess whether the artist had succeeded in a creation in proportion Alternatively, these last two lines can also be read in a mundane manner. In this case, they would have allowed Haslmayr to emphasise that this diagram is his personal symbol and that he dedicated it here to this patron and allied friend. As we are dealing with a private correspondence between Haslmayr and Moritz von Kassel-Hessen, however, such pragmatic reading begs the question why the actual author didn't indicate his or his patron's name at least with initials. It seems that both interpretations were deliberately invited for.

In Haslmayr's original letter the glyph appears without any introductory title on the same folio. However, he included both three pages of *Considerations on the Figure of the Ergon and Parergon*; as well as a dedicated succinct treatise in ten points titled *Ergon et Parergon Fratrum R. C. et est Cabalistica deductio de Olimpo Terrœ, quo Natura eiusque Magisterium praccipue in Terra latet et ad Creatorem suum referatur tingens et transmutans Metalla.*[124]

Interestingly this latter treatise was put into print in 1624 and included in the posthumous publication of Michal Maier's *Ulysses.*[125]

123 *Transmissum ab authore Domino et amico fratri confaederato.*

124 For a full translation of both works, see Appendix I & II in this book.

125 Michael Maier, *Tractatus Posthumus, sive Ulysses; hoc est: Sapientia Seu Intelligentia, Tanquam Coelestis Scintilla beatitudinis, quod si in fortunae et corporis bonis naufragium faciat, ad portum meditationis et*

However, up until the 20th century it was considered an anonymous fragment and remained unidentified with regards to Haslmayr's authorship.[126]

VII

Oswald Croll

The Magician in the Basilica

THE LITTLE WE know about Oswald Croll's biography stands in stark contrast to the eruptive force with which his most famous book, the *Basilica Chymica* (1609) went on to shape not only the lively current of Paracelsianism, but most of Western Early Modern Medicine. It is often claimed that it was the Basilica specifically that had a leading influence on the inclusion of the emerging branch of chemistry in the faculty of Western medicine.[127]

Croll was born in 1560 in the village of Wetter (Hesse) as the son of the mayor. He first went to study in Marburg in 1576 and then continued on in Straßburg, Geneva, and Heidelberg, where he gained his medical promotion. Initially, he made his living as a tutor. It was a profession he learned to lament and ultimately gave up to become an itinerant "medical nomad". Foremost during the decade of 1593 to 1603, this allowed him to continue to travel across Europe and establish a network of broad scientific contacts, among them Johann Huser, the famous first editor of Paracelsus' collected works, and Giambattista della Porta (1535–1615) whom he visited repeatedly in Naples. After a sensational healing of Christian I of Anhalt-Bernburg, Croll was appointed as personal physician in 1598.[128]

Croll died suddenly in 1609, and his reputation and influence grew only after his death, especially with the publication of his *Basilica*

---

patientiae remigio feliciter se expediat, Frankfurt: Lucas Jennis, 1624, pp. 183–187.

126 Craven 1910, pp. 160–163.

127 Frietsch 2013, p. 104.

128 Kühlmann, Telle (ed.) 1996, pp. 6,17, and: Schröder 1957, p. 421. See also: Debus 1977, Vol. 1, 117–118.

Chymica which was reprinted in eighteen editions in three languages over the following fifty years.[129]

Croll's recipes were a bridge that led directly from the mystical elucidations of Paracelsus into the emerging field of critical scientific medicine. His only published work, the Basilica, "replaced the mystical and preparatively unclear Paracelsian prescriptions with precise working instructions, which he himself had tested by critical methods and his own experiments. In addition, Croll was able to give the controversial chemiatry an academic standing through his high reputation as a physician and scientist."[130]

The *Basilica* is an extensive work of more than 400 pages. It is divided into three sections: a comprehensive 110-page introduction entitled *Admonishing Preface to the Honest Reader*,[131] a 200-page main section containing the actual Paracelsian prescriptions, and a slender 80 page concluding section of a more compilatory nature, famously entitled *De signaturis internis rerum.*

Croll used his introduction to the Basilica to balance the detailed prescriptions in the main section with the Paracelsian philosophical foundations. His introduction, which took on a life of its own, provided the *ethos*, while the work was found in the main body.[132] Thus, philosophy and practice were deliberately placed side by side in his only book, jointly introducing the Paracelsian medicine as part of the ancient tradition of human *theiosis*. Because the aim of this art was by no means merely the obliteration of disease but the complete restoration of man to his divine state. Thus, Paracelsian medicine acquired the status of a critical factor within the overall historical course of human redemption.[133]

129 Ibid., p. 1

130 Schröder 1957, p. 421.

131 Praefatio ad monitoria ad lectorem candidum (Croll, 1609, p. 1).

132 The favourable reception of the *Basilica* was mainly based on the desire for information about alchemical medicines, which was powerfully incited by the controversy in medicine and natural history. In addition, the *Basilica* offered not only a lavish abundance of prescriptions for the preparation and application of chemical remedies, but also extensive explanations of the Hermetic philosophy of nature in the *Remembrance Preface*—thus standing out from competing works as a kind of summa of the *Paracelsian Alchemia medica*. Kühlmann, Telle (ed.), 1996, p. 9.

133 Kühlmann (ed.) 1996, p. 4.

According to Croll, man's position in the world was of essentially dialectic nature. Through the insights derived from the observation of the cosmos humans were changed, and through their behaviour towards the cosmos they changed the world in return. Knowledge from the world and behaviour towards the world formed a holistic whole — which is why no theory could ever realise itself without its integration into robust practice.[134]

Oswald Croll devotes a long and explicit section in his introduction to the Olympic Spirit which we have translated in full below.[135] Indeed, this section can be regarded a most elegant *summa* of the Paracelsian elucidations on the inner firmament as we encountered them before.

It illustrates why Croll should be considered a *magician in the basilica* in a dual sense: in an almost magical manner, his book subverted not only all defences of the Christian Church but equally those of Galenic medicine. With a bang of a book and a firework of translations and reprints, Croll opened the book of Paracelsian *Philosophiae* on the lectern of university teaching.

As we shall see in the next chapter, this event had significant implications not only for Western medicine, but also for Western Magic and the history of the Olympic Spirits specifically.

> *And just as this Hyle in the great world comprehends all the stars or celestial bodies in their peculiarities, so also the inner heaven or firmament of man, which is the Olympic Spirit, comprehends all the astras and celestial bodies in their peculiarities. And thus the invisible man is not only all the heavenly bodies, but also completely one with the spirit of the world, like the white with the snow. [...]*[136]
>
> *Before we proceed, however, the necessity of this place requires us to deal a little more extensively with the sidereal or invisible man, namely with his origin and power.*
>
> *This Olympic Spirit, if it had been taken into account by Aristotle and considered by Galen, would not have been introduced by the pagans as the teacher of misconception such*

134 Ibid., p. 6.
135 The English translation is based on the 1629 German edition.
136 Croll, 1629, p. 14.

great errors in philosophy and medicine, to say nothing of theology. The invisible man or Olympic Spirit is born to us in this manner: our first parents Adam and Eve were not born of parents, as we are their descendants, but sprang from a clod of earth or from the great world, as already mentioned, and this concerns the mortal body which is visible and invisible. Then the whole creation is assembled and collected into the small world, so that there is nothing in the entire world that cannot also be found in every man. The natural elemental, visible and comprehensible body they received from the earth: the invisible, impalpable and sidereal (which is the dwelling of the spirit and of life) from the stars or heavenly bodies of the firmament. And so Adam had two bodies, namely the visible elemental and the invisible sidereal. And so, through procreation, two men are always born, namely the corporeal, elemental, visible as an instrument of the invisible, and then the invisible, non-corporeal and sidereal, which moves man, governs and conducts all workings.

Once the stars are in the human being in this manner, then these two are produced all the time through the birth: the visible elemental body indeed from the four elements, from the flesh and blood in the mother's womb. The invisible sidereal [body], as is capable of the Philosophia adeptæ, from the stars of the firmament.

For this man, who is the small world, remains one in everything with his father, who is the great world. Just as, however, the great world is distinguished from the Angelic world by its bark [i.e., physical shell], so man as the small is distinguished by his skin from the great [world]. Therefore it follows that the sidereal, inner, Olympic and uncorporeal man or Gabal is one with the firmament of the Astrorum as hitherto openly reported, just as the redness is one with the wine, the white with the snow, or the sunshine with the air. And therefore the other part of man[137] *or the sidereal body*[138]

137 Original footnote: *The inner man, thus ascending the inner heaven, a strange constellation.*

138 Original footnote: *The consumption of the apple has brought the sidereal body into his body.*

of man is called genius or spirit, because it originates from the firmament. Or is also called Penatis, because it is born penes nos or with and by us, as a visible shadow of the body, a House of God, shadow-shaped body, a familiaris sophorum homunculus, a good apirit, or Paracelsian inner Adech, Spectrum, Light of Nature, Evestrum præsigiens, and Prophetic Spirit in man. Yeah it is also called an imagination or conceit, which comprehends all stars in itself, is all stars itself, and has an equal course, capacity and nature as the [outer] firmament.

Now the stars (I do not speak of the seven visible coals of heaven, the bodies, namely the Astrorum, but of the invisible and incomprehensible body of all things or the Astral Spirit)[139]*, are nothing but the powers of the angels. But the angels (so only from the sight of God are preserved and nourished) are a created wisdom of God. From this follows that whoever knows God, to him also the Astra are known. But to whom the stars are known, to him also the world cannot be unknown. And therefore also the son of the world, namely man. [...] Through the natural, innate faith, by which we become like the spirits, all magical transactions and miraculous works are performed, if imagination is added. [...] This is a part of the Gabalic art, which rests on three pillars: namely, the true prayer, which is performed in spirit and in truth, since in the most holy there is a union of God and the spirit of the creature, since God with the inner spirit is encountered not by force or recitation of words, but in a holy silence, without opening the mouth. On the other hand, [it rests] on the natural faith in or wisdom of the first creation of God the Heavenly Father of all men, as a hereditary property at the same time communicated and innate. Thirdly, [it rests] on the powerfully elevated imagination, how great and wonderful it is the light of nature [...] quite clearly presents and shows to us. [...] But enough of this. For such sharp contemplations and reflections, sought by the distant antiquity, will undoubtedly appear too pointed to the inexperienced. They are read by few and understood by still fewer. Accord-*

139 Original footnote: This spirit is the genuine *Astronomiæ Doctor*.

ingly; they require a more expansive narrative than can be performed here. Let us return, then, to our purpose.[140]

Condensed on a few pages and positioned as the philosophical underpinning to any practical medicine, Croll presents the reader with a succinct and overt summary of the deeply animistic Paracelsian cosmography. All bodies are enlivened by spirits, and knowledge of the world is gained by trafficking with spirits. Man is placed in a unique position within this cosmos for a dual reason:

¶ *As an embodied microcosm, man carries within himself material and spiritual ties to all the elements and beings of creation. These ties can be activated into conscious contact i.e., spirit communion, according to man's ability to actively use the threefold faculties of his faith, his imagination, and his prayer to turn themselves alike to the spirits of their communion. This innate human ability to establish spirit communion with all aspects of the macrocosm is what Croll terms the Olympic man or Gabal, which draws its powers from the Olympic Spirits within man.*[141]

¶ *Second, human beings are not only endowed from birth with spirit cells that weave their bodies and bring their minds into resonance with the vast ecology of the entire macrocosm. But by ascending this inner heaven, into this strange constellation, man can gain conscious communion with the angelic realm and realise themselves again within the House of God. Croll does not differentiate clearly between the Olympic Spirits, the angelic realm and even the encounter with Divinity.*[142] *Instead, twice in the section quoted*

140 Croll 1629, pp. 34–39.

141 See also: Han van Ruler, *The Crisis of Causality: Voetius and Descartes on God, Nature and* Change (1995), p. 295, footnote 105.

142 It is through the conscious knowledge of the Olympic Spirits—Croll says: *but to whom the stars are known, [...] in a holy silence, without opening the mouth*—that man can enter the *House of God*, and (re)connect with the angelic realm. The essential connection of this process to attaining communion with one's birth-genius or holy daimon finds reference in Croll's introduction, yet remains ambiguous and nothing more than a hint.

> *above he stresses that they are all interconnected: for the one who knows God, he says, also knows the stars and equally knows the world. Additionally, he provides a long list of mysterious spirit names associated with man's ability to gain angelic and even divine knowledge from within themselves.*

As we will see in the following chapter, it was no other than Robert Fludd (1574–1637) who picked up on this essential section in Croll's introduction and spotted both its potential and significance as well as its insufficient precision with regards to clearly differentiating the Olympic Spirits from one's birth-genius. Next to the *Arbatel* (1575), Oswald Croll's famous introduction to the *Basilica Chymica* presents the most widely-read source text of the literary tradition of the Olympic Spirits.

As we have seen, Paracelsus in his original works had placed all the keys for a deeper understanding of these spirits and their function within the microcosm of man. However, deliberately so, these keys remained scattered among his vast corpus of writings and invisible to most readers, interested in either his chemo-medical or more explicitly magical writings. Croll on the other hand provides much less depth of insight into the nature and dynamics of these spirits, yet he offers a most succinct summary of their functioning—presented on the first few pages, as a direct address to the readers of one of the most influential books in the early 17th century.

In our journey to trace the literary tradition of Olympic spirits, we cannot overemphasise the importance of this 1609 publication. It made the concept of the *Olympic Spirit* known and accessible to a large audience in the learned circles of Europe. But in its summary brevity and inadequate differentiation of the types of spirits, Croll's introduction—together with the *Arbatel*—is also responsible for the shortening and uprooting of the concept from the actual corpus of Paracelsian writings.

If previous source-works ensured the underground tradition of the Olympic Spirits remained intact and alive, Croll's *Basilica Chymica* was the literal rock plunged into the waters of 17th century public attention, creating huge surface ripples in place and time.

VIII

Robert Fludd

The Maker of a Lost Tradition

THE FIRST TWO decades of the 17th century can easily be rated the *golden age* of Paracelsus-inspired publications. In addition to the many books mentioned, we see the sweeping arrival of the Rosicrucian manifestos, an explosion of reactions and responses as well as the public formation of early modern *theosophy*, *pansophy*, and *chemistry*, the latter receiving its first academic professorship in Marburg in 1609.[143] Paracelsus' name was frequently invoked in these diverse yet interconnected disciplines, and usually in the spirit of rebellion against tradition and the call for a comprehensive reformation of the sciences, arts or all of society.

If we turn our gaze forward on the timeline of 1609, we observe how the scenery changes. From a few important plants in the garden of the legacy of the Olympic Spirits, we step out into the vastness of an open forest of publications. Many of the plants here are connected to each other by biographical paths, and yet most of them are offshoots, not originals. The eccentric, peculiar uniqueness of the Paracelsian writings is replaced by books that serve to preserve and convey concepts rather than lived experiences. The first imprint is replaced by its cast. Tradition in its elegant garb emerges and replaces the ragged nomad who originally instigated a revolution.

Examples of such publications are the expensively produced *Calendarium naturale magicum perpetuum* by Johann Baptist Großschedel von Aicha and executed by no other than Matthäus Merian the Elder,[144] the pseudo-Paracelsian *Philosophia Mystica* of 1618,[145] Caesare Longino's *Trinvm Magicvm, Sive Secretorvm*

143 Bruce T. Moran, *Moritz von Hessen und die Alchemie*, in: Borggrefe, Lüpkes, and Ottomeyer, Hans (eds.), *Moritz der Gelehrte—Ein Renaissancefürst in Europa* (1997), p. 369.

144 Matthäus Merian the Elder for Johann Baptist Großschedel von Aicha, *Calendarium naturale magicum perpetuum*. Oppenheim: Johann Theodor de Bry, 1614–1620(?).

145 Anonymous, *Philosophia Mystica: Darinn begriffen Eilff unterschidene*

Magicorvm Opvs, ET: Tractatus de Proprii cuiusque nati daemonis inquisitione from 1630,[146] the anonymous *Ars magica: sive magia naturalis et artificiosa* from 1631,[147] Robert Turner's English translation of pseudo-Agrippa's infamous *Fourth Book*, including the *Arbatel*,[148] the anonymous compilation *Philosophy Reformed & Improved in Four Profound Tractates*,[149] quoting the introduction to the Basilica by Oswald Croll, and of course the popular German edition of the *Arbatel* of 1686.[150] Finally, we should mention the essential *Clavicula Salomonis et Theosophica Pneumatica* of 1686,[151] popularised by Johann Scheible in the 19th century, which provides the most prominent example of the Olympic Spirits woven into the Early Modern garment of Solomonic magic.

Theologico-Philosophische, doch teutsche Tractätlein, zum theil auß Theophrasti Paracelsi, zum theil auch M. Valentini Weigelii, [...]. Newstadt: Lucas Jenes, 1618.

146 Caesar Longinus (ed.), *Trinvm Magicvm, Siue Secretorvm Magicorvm Opvs: Continens I. De Magia Naturali, Artificiosa & Superstitiosa Disquisitiones Axiomaticas. II. Theatrum Naturae praeter Curam Magneticam, & veterum Sophorum Sigilla & Imagines Magicas...III. Oracula Zoroastris, & Mysteria Mysticae Philosophiae, Hebraeorum, Chaldaeorum, Aegyptiorum [...] Accessere Nonnulla Secreta Secretorum, et mirabilia Mundi. Et Tractatus de Proprii cuiusque nati daemonis inquisitione, Frankfurt am Main: Conrad Eifridus, 1630.*

147 Anonymous, *Ars magica: sive magia naturalis et artificiosa, stupendos et abstrusos effectus, virtutes, & secreta in elementis, gemmis, lapidibus, herbis, & animalibus secundum certas astrorum ac constellationum figuras & sigilla, horasque planetarias exhibens; antehac numquam visa, cognitave; cui praeit Magia superstitiosa de daemonum variis generibus, faunis, satyris, lamiis & spectris* [...]. Frankfurt, Antonius Humm, 1631.

148 Henry Cornelius Agrippa, *His fourth book of Occult Philosophy of Geomancy, Magical Elements of Peter de Abano, Astronomical Geomancy, the Nature of Spirits, Arbatel of Magick, translated into English by Robert Turner*. London: John Harrison, 1655.

149 Various, *Philosophy Reformed & Improved in Four Profound Tractates: The I. Discovering the great and deep Mysteries of Nature by that learned Chymist and Physitian OSW Crollius, The other III. Discovering the Wonderfull Mysteries of the Creation by Paracelsus, being his Philosophy of the Athenians*, translated by Herny Pinnell. London: Lodowick Lloyd, 1657.

150 Anonymous, *Arbatel de Magia veterum*. Wesel: Andreas Luppius, 1686.

151 Anonymous, *Claviculae Salomonis Et Theosophia Pneumatica, Das ist, Die warhafftige Erkänntnüß Gottes, und seiner sichtigen und unsichtigen Geschöpffen, Die Heil. Geist-Kunst genannt*. Wesel: Andreas Luppius, 1686.

Finding our path through this forest of publications does not necessarily require us to study them all. Instead, it does necessitate studying an early 17th century publication that long has become entirely overlooked and forgotten.

Much to my own surprise, I realised that many links in the evolution of the Olympic Spirits from 1620 onwards liberally quoted—and often directly copied long sections without referencing these—from Robert Fludd's epochal *Utriusque Cosmi Historia—Tomi Secundi Tractatus Primi, Sectio Secunda, De technica Microcosmi historia.*[152] Here, in his Latin *Technical History of the Microcosm* Fludd included a thirty-page chapter precisely continuing the exploration on the Olympic Spirits where Oswald Croll's introduction to the *Basilica* had left off. Before we examine it and read it in its first printed English translation in the third appendix of this book, I would like to invite us to step back and learn more about its author. This seems especially appropriate since so little of Robert Fludd (1574–1637) survives in the collective memory of the living Western magical tradition.

> *An English physician, philosopher, and alchemist, Robert Fludd was Welsh in origins. His father, Sir Thomas Fludd, M.P., had been appointed as treasurer to the court of Elizabeth I. Between 1591 and 1598, Robert Fludd was reading for his master's degree at St. John's College, Oxford. In 1598–1604, he traveled on the continent where he was employed as tutor to the children of aristocratic French Catholic families. He also spent a winter in the foothills of the Pyrenees with a group of Jesuit priests, although, as he publically proclaimed, he was always a staunch Anglican. Fludd recorded that the priests taught him various magical practices, not least the art of divination. This contact with the Jesuits probably colored Fludd's magical, as well as his religious, con-*

152 Robert Fludd, *Utriusque Cosmi Historia—Tomi Secundi Tractatus Primi, Sectio Secunda, De technica Microcosmi historia.* Oppenheim: Theodor de Bry, ca. 1620, pp. 85–116. In Fludd's expansive and unfinished magnum opus this section is titled as First Tract, Second Section, Portion Four, Book Three. A digital copy be accessed under: https://mdz-nbn-resolving.de/details:bsb11057773.

cepts to an extent hitherto underestimated by later scholars.[153]

Fludd drew from all the sources available to him—the Bible and the kabbalah, music, astrology, alchemy, as well as technology—to construct his image of the universe. He can be seen as one of the last representatives of the Renaissance homo universalis.[154]

Already from his time as a student at Oxford, we know of Fludd's penchant for "excerpting and compiling encyclopedically", for practical astrology and the magical arts.[155] Early on in his intellectual career he must have devised the plan of an universal attempt to construct a philosophy of the human race.[156] Such high-flying aspiration provides both insights to the lifelong challenges Fludd put to himself, as well as the inflated views he held of his own talent and destiny. The hypersensitivity and vitriolic reactions with which he met all kinds of criticism throughout his career complete the picture of a Welsh nobleman who maintained his own apothecary, conducted extensive alchemical and magical experimentation, and saw himself not only as a pioneer of modernity but also as a restorer of the lost knowledge of an ancient world conceived of in Christian-Hermetic terms.[157]

Fludd worked continuously on his scientific opus magnum, the *Utriusque Cosmi Historia* from at least 1617 to 1625, while in parallel pursuing his ardent interest in and radical defence of the Rosicrucian movement.[158] Both projects make it obvious why Fludd's

153 Urszula Szulakowska, "Fludd, Robert" in: Sgarbi, Marco (ed.), *Encyclopedia of Renaissance Philosophy*. Hamburg: Springer, 2019, https://doi.org/10.1007/978-3-319-02848-4_488-2.

154 Sylvie Edighoffer, "Fludd, Robert", in: Hanegraaff (2006), pp. 371–375.

155 Schmidt-Biggemann 2013, p. 61.

156 Rösche 2008, p. 14.

157 Edighoffer 2006, p. 372, and Schmidt-Biggemann, 2013, pp. 62–63.

158 Ibid. For a most concise assessment of this work, see Schmidt-Biggemann (2013) p. 65: "In this encyclopedia he lucidly presented the motives of the technical and spiritualistic traditions in natural philosophy: qualitative number theory, chemistry, music, Kabbalah, instrument making, meteorology, optics, acoustics, astrology, geomancy, painting, military engineering, fortress construction, automata science. But above all, Fludd's *Utriusque Cosmi Historia* is a key work of early modern medicine. Fludd combined

work was excluded and aggressively rejected by the majority of seventeenth-century academics as backward-looking superstition from the nascent canon of enlightened philosophy and science. In face of such unequivocal rejection by official circles, further dissemination of his work outside academia was additionally prevented by Fludd's Latin prose which is notoriously complex, condensed, and difficult to understand.[159]

Mainly, what has remained in the collective memory of the Western magical tradition of his encyclopaedic endeavour to present the knowledge of a magical cosmos in a new guise are the congenial, strongly evocative engravings which he designed himself and had engraved by the masterful hand of Matthäus Merian the Elder. Derogatorily labelled as *hieroglyphs* by Kepler, it likely was exactly the occult character of Fludd's many engravings that ensured his name survived at least in the sidelines of the history of science.[160]

Fludd travelled the European continent extensively for six years from 1598, during which he established direct contact with the early Paracelsian movement, most notably with Oswald Croll as well as Joachim Morsius (1593–1644), who both became good friends of his.[161] Upon his return to England, he had access to the remains of John Dee's famous library[162] and, despite his prominent position at the College of Physicians in London, never hesitated to put his ideas into practice, as evidenced by his tests of sympathetic cures with *mumia* and parts of corpses upon himself.

> *Last year, when I was with my friend Edmund Stafford at Doctor Robert Fludd's and we talked about these things, Fludd talked about this art, as usual, very astutely and, as it were, covertly; amongst other things, he told me about the magnet miracle, which I had known before but had not yet*

---

classical humoral pathology with hermetic natural philosophy and with elements of the medical theories of Marsilio Ficino and Paracelsus. There is probably no text or pictorial representation in which the analogy of microcosm and macrocosm is documented more clearly in medical terms than in this encyclopedia."

159 Edighoffer (2006) p. 373.

160 Ibid.

161 Rösche (2008) pp. 20–27.

162 Ibid.

tried, namely that it was so strong that when he had put it on the area of the heart, he could not have endured its violent pull for long. But when I asked about the use of this magnet, he remained silent and seemed to regret his words. [...] This magnet is nothing else than dried human flesh, which possesses the greatest attractive power. All of it must be taken as much as possibly from the still warm body of a person who died a violent death.[163]

Locating the Olympic Spirits

The mind walks and passes over feathers and wings of the archangel presiding over it, a divine offshoot who sits on the throne of the rational mind or Empyreum, which is a spiritual cloud that contains the glory of God.[164]

FLUDD's elucidations on the holy daemon, man's mind and soul and the nature and function of the Olympic Spirit are dense, complex, redundant and enwrought with quotes from Porphyry, Iamblichus and of course Scripture. At the same time they are encyclopaedic and elegant, deeply coherent and infused with his personal practice and experience. Here we have one of the brightest minds of the 17th century, himself a practicing theurgist, sharing his *summa* of the heart of the Western Tradition of Magic with us.

We are providing the first English translation of Fludd's chapter on the holy daimon and the Olympic Spirits in the third appendix of this book. A careful study of it—and comparison to Paracelsus' original sources— is highly recommended. Despite the fact that this text has been largely forgotten today, it presents us with perhaps the most important steppingstone of the entry of the Olympic Spirits into Early Modern Western ritual magic. Primarily, it is the explicit comprehensive embedding of the Olympic Spirits in a Christian-tinged cos-

163 Maxwell W., *De Medicina Magnetica*, Libri III, Frankfurt am Main: Zubrodt 1679, in German: *Drei Bücher der magnetischen Heilkunde*, Stuttgart: Scheible 1851 (Reprint: Freiburg im Breisgau: Edition Ambra, 1978) p. 159.

164 Robert Fludd, quoted from Appendix III.

mos of a Hermetic-Neoplatonic nature that lifted them out of their rootedness in authentic Paracelsian practice, and—together with the *Arbatel*—made them known to a much broader (English speaking) audience.

As such, Fludd's elucidations exerted significant influence on later authors and acted as a blueprint or matrix that, in its classical appeal, quickly began to overshadow many of Paracelsus' original teachings of the Olympic Spirits.

Since the scope of Fludd's text is so broad, we will highlight some of its essential aspects here.

The most characteristic aspect of Fludd's text is that it places the Olympic Spirits inside the classical Hermetic-Neoplatonic cosmography, but with a strong Christian overlay: Divinity resides beyond the fiery Empyreum, immerses itself in the garment of archangels and descends through the realm of the fixed stars into the orbits of the celestial planets, from here onwards through the choir of angels into the sublunar realm, through the airy heavens, and into the elemental kingdom of the chthonic daemons. This journey is not understood as a singular event during the creation of the macrocosm, but as an ongoing living reality both at the onset and throughout the life of each microcosm i.e., human.

Towards the end of his elucidations, Fludd gives us the following poetic summary of this process:

> *So the mind enters by a gentle leap down into the region of the stars, where it is served by the Olympic angels who accompany and preside over this mind according to its ruling archangel. And it is received by the subordinates and puts on the robe of the ether, composed of a mixture of the soul belonging to life and the etheric spirit, to which likewise a spirit from the planetary sphere is offered, who acknowledges the archangel who is in front of it as its head and lord. This planetary spirit in any case is appropriately called the spirit of the birth or genius of the child and which tends to have command over the life and all actions that revolve around the life. And by its agency the destiny in every human being is handed over to the consummation.*[165]

165 Third Book, Third Part, Chapter VI.

The Olympic Spirits thus reside below the realm of the archangels and are instructed by the latter; yet above the realm of the sublunar daemons and elemental kingdom. Fludd avoids the question whether they are exactly identical with the classical planetary deities but instead provides detailed description of both.

This awkward ambiguity and seemingly dual terminology for the spirits ruling the planetary sphere stems from the most marked oversight of Fludd's text: despite his life-long reverence for Paracelsus' works, Fludd source-material for the Olympic Spirits in this congenial summary seems to stop with the *Arbatel* and not to include Paracelsus' original writings. Otherwise, he would have highlighted that the Olympic Spirits are referred to by Paracelsus explicitly as the rulers of the *microcosmic* or *inner firmament of man*: They embody the sparks or cells of each planetary spirit-consciousness that come together, embed themselves into and unite themselves with elementary matter in order to form the human mind and body. They are the princeps and rulers of the *Terra Olympi*. This differentiation, between inner and outer worlds, macrocosm and microcosm, of such critical importance to Paracelsus, is reflected nowhere in Fludd's summary.

Alexander von Suchten, Adam Haslmayr, Oswald Croll—the early Paracelsians had gone to extreme lengths, often under risk of their own lives, to ensure the continuation of a living Paracelsian spirituality, at the centre of which stands the microcosmic temple of the Olympic Spirits. yet, the Olympics are not meant to be adored or prayed to in this temple, instead they are the living forces that uphold it: once arranged in balance and harmony within man, the Olympic Spirits come together to open a space for the presence of the divine flame to touch the human mind. And through this flame, from this temple, we look out into the world again. We stride out into the world, without ever leaving the centre of this temple within us.

Rebuilding the Temple Within

The Olympic Spirits thus are critical to uphold the *House of God*[166] within us, but they are not what comes to life in it. Quite the opposite: their colours need to recede, their strength needs to

166 Third Book, Third Part, Chapter II.

part from our minds and flow into the architecture of this temple so that Divinity's spark can be encountered among their midst. Fludd's text alludes to this mystical knowledge, but is nowhere near as explicit or helpful in this regard as, for example, the apocryphal texts of Adam Haslmayr.

Nevertheless, both at the outset as well as the conclusion of his text, Fludd emphasises that according to his experience the only viable path towards communion with one's holy daimon is *divine divination*, that is a *personal encounter*, not mathematical calculations.[167]

As such, he expects people to argue on this subject not from theory but from practical experience. Working with spirits in such a manner, therefore, at least initially is not a matter of objective scientific truth, but of subjective first-hand experience.[168] Fludd stresses that his own approach to the subject will be unapologetically subjective, and "a way which (I say it frankly) is based more on my opinion than secured by any evidence or infallible truth."

Furthermore, in the second chapter of Book III, even before going into much detail, Fludd in passing mentions a practice[169] that acts to replace the governance of a human by one's birth-genius with Divinity itself. His actual words are:

> *He [the birth-genius] controls us so long, until we, who were charged with the leadership of the cult, put the Lord in the place of the daemon. For then the Daemon gives way to God and is therefore either freed from its activity or is conducive to it.*[170]

This opens the vista towards the mystical path the practitioner is guided towards throughout the chapters of Fludd's text:

167 It should be noted that Fludd provides such direct advice despite his own expert knowledge in the field of astrology, which Schmidt-Biggemann even understood to be the key-science (Schlüsselwissenschaft) to all of Fludd's work (Schmidt-Biggemann 2013, p. 76).

168 As with all arts, aiming at mastering the descriptive theory of the underlying methods and techniques is a very different endeavour than aiming to master the practical application of the art itself.

169 Or does he refer to an anonymous cult, i.e., a collective practice?

170 Book Three, Part One, Chapter II.

Upon birth, humans find themselves thrown into a microcosm ruled by the Olympic Spirits and entangled into a fate-line whose consummation is overlooked by their birth-genius.

As such, the first step consists of mastering the Olympic Spirits in the unique constellation in which they present themselves in one's astrological birth chart. Humans have to develop their reason and free will, their faith and their imagination to free themselves from the blind rule of the passionate impulses that flow from the Olympic Spirits as long as they stand in imbalance and isolation.

> *Once the Olympic Spirits within one's inner firmament have been arranged to balance each other and to together form a temple, that is to open and uphold a space free of their passions, man can commence the actual mystical work.*[171] *This is to bring the work of their birth-genius into the light of Divinity: to both fulfill their personal fate-pattern, yet in service to Divinity.*

The prior step guides man from being ruled by the impulses of their birth-genius to come to stand in the light of their holy daemon. These two beings are of distinctly different nature, as Fludd emphasises over and again in his text.[172] The birth-genius stems from the celestial region of the Olympics and is assigned to a single incarnation; the holy daemon is assigned by the Archangels and guides and guards man's soul through many lives.

> *For then, after the purification of the body and the raising of the soul, the mind itself and its angel will be cohabitants, both for the body and for the soul, and the voice, and the whispering of the angel himself will be received by the ears*

171 Book III, Part III, Chapter II: "He merely administers the mind and it all alone with spiritual signs, and in such a way that when the centre of the soul is attached to the mind and neglects the force of thoughts as well as the formal expression of the elements, which has been polluted by the cravings and appetites of the world, the body itself has a taste of the wisdom of the mind."

172 Book III, Part III, Chapter II: "Therefore, admittedly, the [holy] daemon, as Iamblichus rightly says, is both leader of the mind and of a more original intellect and of a higher ancestry and origin than those executors of destiny, who cannot pass over and transgress the orders of God even with regard to (something as minor as) a throwing projectile or a sting."

> *of the body, and he will even sometimes himself emerge into a corporeal form, as can be gleaned from many passages both of the Holy Scriptures and the authorities the ancient writers who deserve credibility.*[173]

According to the tradition Fludd is outlining, the cohabitation of the holy daemon and man's celestial mind can be achieved and maintained in a dual manner. The first of the two paths of theurgy he describes brings us back to his emphasis on *divine divination*, that is "the flowing of the divine spirit into the mind of man." The second works through the astrological calculation of the birth-horoscope, equipped with which the magus "calls the daemon from the cycles" of the planets. This latter path has strong limitations, Fludd points out, as the „holy daemon controls the stars, and in such a way that knowledge of the stars cannot determine it or its nature *a priori*. "The path of divine divination, on the other hand, presents a "universal way beyond the realm of embodied nature."

> *From this it is clear that the true knowledge of astrology and the only way to make friendship with one's holy daemon originates in the divine inspiration, by whose holy breath, indeed, the ancients acquired the knowledge of every thing, even the foundations of the sacrosanct wisdom itself.*[174]

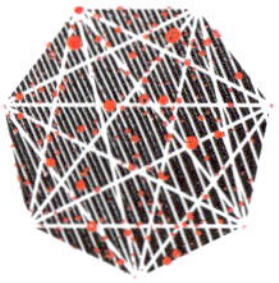

173 Third Book, Third Part, Chapter II.
174 Third Book, Third Part, Chapter VIII.

Understanding the Olympic Spirits

From this broad perspective we can begin to understand the function the Olympic Spirits hold in Fludd's evolved version of an originally Paracelsian cosmography.

Man is born into an ecology of spirits that not only reside in the macrocosm around them, but who weave themselves through their actual body and mind. All of these spirits, however, depend on the Olympic Spirits' ongoing infusion of celestial intelligences into the chthonic realm.[175] Thus, learning to see and engage with the Olympic Spirits opens an initial gate for the aspirant out of this maze of isolated spirit interests and entangled micro-agendas.

Secondly, familiarity with the Olympic Spirits leads the aspirant to the insight that their path will need to be endogenic as well as exogenic at the same time. There is no longer a differentiation between inside and outside, between the world and themselves, because the same spirit forces uphold the world around them as well as the world within them. Pulling a string of the Olympics' power within them creates a resonance in the world and vice versa. Thus, to the practitioner who has begun to understand the Olympics as a first step on their journey, every mundane act is turning into a spiritual act, every passing comment into a prayer, and every poison applied to the world around us into a poison applied to themselves. The Olympic Spirits, once understood in this fashion, are the *one-makers*, the *world-weavers*, the threads that spin the cosmos and on whose strings all life and all information travels. They break the illusion of polarity and weave all worlds and actions back into one.[176]

According to their essential nature in the created cosmos, in the human realm the Olympic Spirits preside over a broad array of func-

175 According to Fludd, the Olympic Spirits are the spirits or daemons who direct the courses of the stars [outside and inside of man]. Their task is to preside over the centre of the soul of man and the souls of the other things that concern life and the meaning of life.

176 *And we say that the daemons who dwell above the stars are good daemons. So too the Olympic daemons and those of the middle world realm are in any case good with regard to themselves and through themselves. But with regard to us, towards whom they act fate-bound, they work sometimes good, sometimes bad and are also called good and bad.* (Third Book, Third Part, Chapter III).

tions. They mediate the influence of the Empyrean Spirits or Archangels into the microcosm, they "are helmsmen of destiny and its course" and from their midst is drawn each human's birth-genius.[177]

They form the cohesive principle that bonds life to both ether and matter, and as "the presider of the soul belonging to life, the Olympic daemon, as best it can, is able to look and pay attention to the beauty and health of the body."

> *Therefore, having really thought this through well, we shall see with our spiritual eyes that there is a [holy] daemon of the mind, a royal and by far principal one, which we have proved above to be an archangel, another for the soul belonging to life, which we call the Olympic spirit, which is always the executor of destiny, and finally a third, which looks after the body and the tasks of the body and its desire.*[178]

Finally, Fludd elucidates that in ancient times it was common practice amongst the magicians to help children turn their birth-genius i.e., the presiding Olympic Spirit or its associated daemon, into a familiar spirit.

> *The magicians used first to ascertain the name and nature of the child's daemon or genius, and then they endeavoured to make the daemon himself familiar and sociable to the child by invocations, incantations, prayers, signs, and other such ceremonies.*[179]

177 *So the mind enters by a gentle leap down into the region of the stars, where it is served by the Olympic angels who accompany and preside over this mind according to its ruling archangel. And it is received by the subordinates and puts on the robe of the ether, composed of a mixture of the soul belonging to life and the etheric spirit, to which likewise a spirit from the planetary sphere is offered, who acknowledges the archangel who is in front of it as its head and lord. This planetary spirit in any case is appropriately called the spirit of the birth or genius of the child and which tends to have command over the life and all actions that revolve around the life. And by its agency the destiny in every human being is handed over to the consummation.* (Third Book, Third Part, Chapter VI).

178 Third Book, Third Part, Chapter V.

179 Third Book, Part Two, Chapter XI.

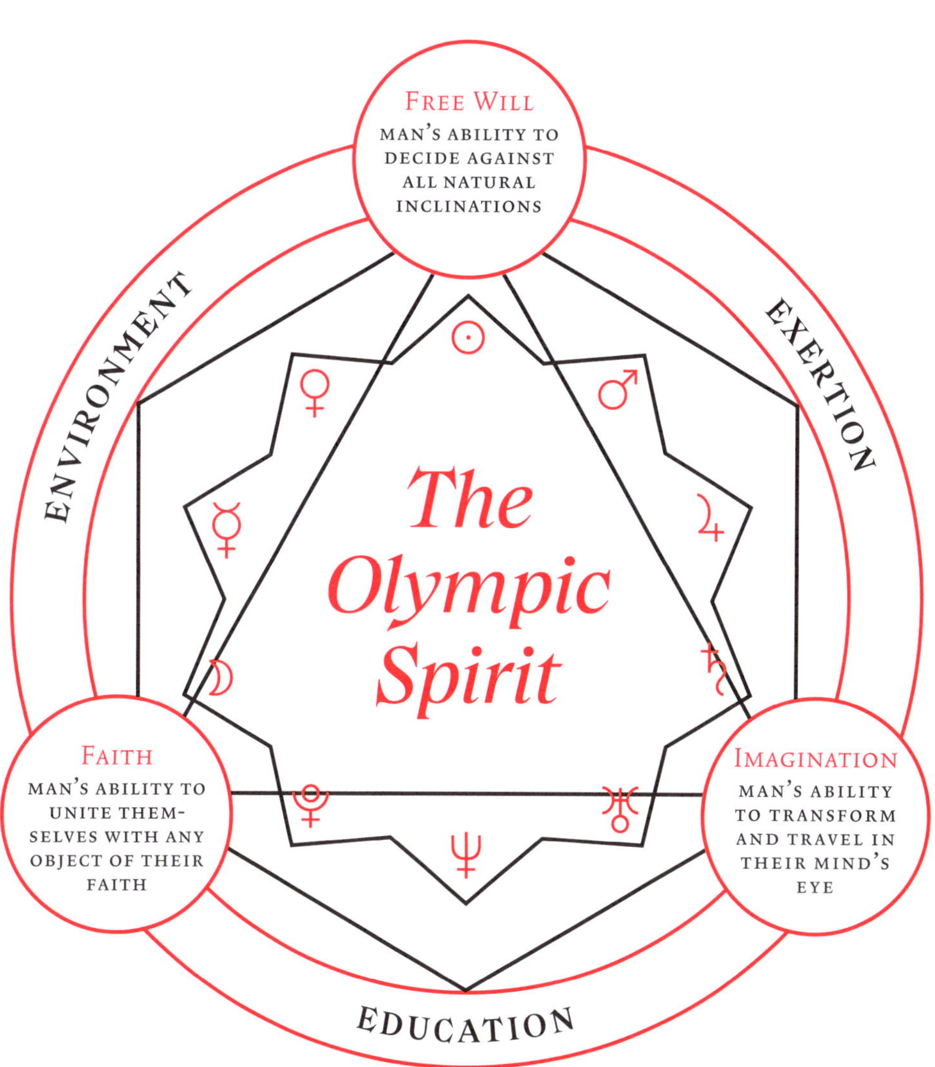
Free Will
man's ability to decide against all natural inclinations
Environment
Exertion
The Olympic Spirit
Faith
man's ability to unite them-selves with any object of their faith
Imagination
man's ability to transform and travel in their mind's eye
Education

The act of making the daemon sociable could be achieved in many different ways. Fludd quotes the practice of engraving the Olympic Spirit seals on metal plates and using these during invocations. Yet, he is quick to add that many of these artificial ways are nothing but "shams." Instead, the following Olympic prayer should be used to create conscious contact:

> *So the pious magicians prescribe to their recruits a speech of the following kind, with which they are to invoke the help of God as the leader of the Daemons, in order to attain knowledge and familiarity with their genius:*
>
> *"Almighty, eternal God, who created every creature for your praise and glory, and for the service of man, I beseech you that my spirit and genius N.N. of solar, Mercurial, Jupiterian, and other order, to form me and teach me what I will ask him with justice and piety, and that he will instil in me those necessary things for my education in the arts and proofs of my ancestors and of the philosophers, or a method of preserving health, or of leading life rightly, or a method of preserving myself from enemies, etc. But not my will be done, but yours through JESUS*
>
> *CHRIST your only Son, our Lord, amen."*[180]

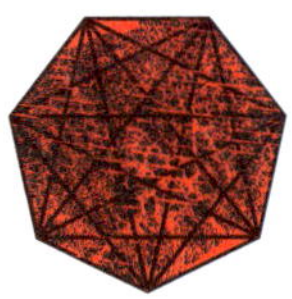

180 Third Book, Part Two, Chapter XII.

BOOK
2

BOOK 2

CHAPTER I

ESSENTIAL PRACTICE

Introduction

THROUGH THE LENS of our own applied practice with the Olympic Spirits, the previous chapters served to carve out an essential insight: the Olympic Spirits are the very medium through which life is woven into the created cosmos, and simultaneously they are the medium through which each created object takes on its unique character. Just like a fingerprint, so the constellation these seven forces adopt within each human is essentially unique. And yet, all of the human race is one in light of the fact that its species holds ties into all of the seven archetypical powers at once. Man is interwoven with the entire world; the entire world is interwoven within man.

All too often, this Hermetic-Neoplatonic foundation has been interpreted through a scientific-enlightened or even psychological lens. As the previous chapters have shown, nothing could be more sharply at odds with Paracelsus' original worldview. To him, everything was inhabited and animated by spirit; and all spirits spoke through bodily encounters.

That is not through abstract, universal and objective encounters, but through deformed, confined and subjectively conditioned experiences.

For Paracelsus, the cosmos within us and around us was *one holy jumble*, a sacred, germinating, blistering, dissolving, coalescing ecology of non-human persons and consciousnesses. It was the magician's work to approach it with a humble plea for understanding, with the patience to untangle the chaos into wisdom, the cacophony into meaningful voices, and to ultimately find their own position in time, place and order from which they could contribute to this living ecosystem.

In this Promethean endeavour the Olympic Spirits do not at all present an aim or goal in themselves, but a most essential *means*. As Paracelsus emphasised often, it is the mastership of the *medium* that defines the range of influence for any medic, mage or human.

So once we have familiarised ourselves with the medium of the Olympic Spirits, the real goal is to begin *working within that medium*: to bring the influences of the seven Olympic Spirits within us into a proper harmony, into an architecture of the temple of our inner self that ensures that their forces support and no longer undermine each other.

This requires that we can express our Jupiter as well as our Saturn, our Moon as well as our Sun, our Venus as well as our Mars gracefully yet emotionally unbound.

No longer identifying with either influence is an essential step in this journey—for we cannot work with what we identify with. Nothing stands more in the way of magical work than the notion of *I*, *Me*, and *Mine* or a person's fear of losing, modifying, or changing a force that they consider an integral part of their being.

Hence our first step must be to turn the tables. It's about moving from the default mode of a child, where the Olympic Spirits have us, to a position of an adult where we have each other.

With this said, let's get to work.

Exercise I
THE OLYMPIC SPIRIT MIRROR

Now look at an example: if nature is to make a fool, it must first put itself into a foolish form, into such a being as that is to become as it wishes to create. As an example: A sculptor wants to carve a fool, he must first put his ingenium into a fool; if he wants to make a hare, he must put his ingenium into a hare. So also

> *nature must do it; so fools make fools, in each case the one [makes] the other.* [1]

Practice Guidance

FIND a quiet place where you will not be disturbed. Face East and sit in a quiet and comfortable position with your back upright.

WITH the help of your preferred meditation exercise, centre yourself in the present moment. Close your eyes.

IN your mind's eye, see yourself sitting in the middle of a circle of approximately three meters (nine feet) in diameter.

SIX smaller circles, in 60° distance from each other, divide the large circle surrounding you into equal parts.

In your mind's eye you gradually walk around the large circle, and behind each of the six empty places you see the respective planet rise on the distant horizon:

FAR ahead of you in the East, the Sun is shining towards you and onto the empty circle directly in front of you.

IN the Southeast, you see Venus rising, illuminating the empty spot half-right in front of you with its light.

FROM a great distance in space, you feel Jupiter shining in the Southwest, reserving its location on the large circle surrounding you.

IN the West, directly behind you, the Moon rises to its place and shines its light over the empty space reserved for it.

IN your Northwest, Mars takes its place on the horizon, sending its light toward the empty space reserved for it on the circle.

AND far out, in your Northeast, Saturn hovers silently in the sky and marks the empty spot on the circle with its presence.

SIT for a moment and allow yourself to fully sense the presence of these seven celestial bodies, far out on the horizon, surrounding you in a perfect circle.

NOW choose one of them and begin your work with it. Perhaps you will start with your Sun; in which case direct your attention to the East, right in front of you.

IN vision, see the light of the Sun intensify. As if directed through a prism, its rays begin to focus on its empty spot on the circle. Grad-

1 Sudhoff (ed.) 1929, Vol. XII, p. 263.

ually, you see its light form a golden, radiating sphere on the perimeter of the circle.

NOW, without any conscious interference from your end, you behold an animal stepping out from this sphere and come to sit on the perimeter of the circle before you. Do not rush this process; it might take a while or even several attempts. Be patient, until the animal of your current Sun is ready to step forward.

NOTE: As you feel the presence of your animal and begin to see it emerge from the light, hold back any of your subjective imaginations and fantasies. Give ample space to your inner Sun to express itself freely. Remember, you are encountering a spirit that has both ontological independence from yourself as well as it forms a part of your human *self*. As such, there is no good or bad in this exercise; instead, we are invited to adopt the position of an attentively focused anthropologist.

WHEN you see your animal before you, the Sun still shining from behind it, take time to sense its unique quality and presence: This animal is the temporary form of a spirit that has been with you from the moment of your birth. your and this spirit's relationship has gone through many iterations already. It is not stable and stagnant, but alive and vibrant. So today, in this very moment, which qualities does this animal evoke? Which emotions does it call into presence? What else comes to the foreground of your experience when sitting face to face with this spirit animal?

WHEN your work is done, bow to the animal and give it a licence to depart. See how it retreats into the sphere of the Sun, then see how the sphere itself begins to fade.

FINALLY, observe how all of the six planets surrounding you on the horizon line begin to withdraw into the depths of the sky again. Each one of them is still present in your inner firmament, but not longer as intense and vivid as before.

SIT for a few more moments, take a deep breath and return to your everyday consciousness. Open your magical diary and write down your experience as detailed as possible.

OVER a period of your own choice, repeat this exercise at least five times to call forth and encounter the other five animal forms of your Olympic Spirits.

Explanatory Notes

The animal form of my Moon likes to appear as a deer, my Sun prefers to take the shape of a snake. Just like you, I had to learn that traditional planetary symbols have no prerogative when we look into the actual mirror of our own firmament. Just like your physical face reflected in a mirror changes under the current of time, place and atmosphere, so do the images we see in the mirror of our Olympic Spirits. Personally, I experienced my animal forms to be stable over relatively long periods (I am speaking of years, sometimes decades); however, the quality of their presence is constantly evolving and inviting me to discover more of their depth and diversity.

Curiously, my Moon-deer was the animal I was most afraid of upon first encounter. Not because its presence was intimidating or domineering, but just the opposite: the moment I first sensed her presence, I immediately realised that many of my most difficult memories as a young boy were based on the very same thread of creation. Like a scent, its presence threw me back into a form of myself that I had begun to hide from myself. The deer did not *symbolise*, it was the essence of my shyness, my vulnerability, my dependence on others, and my inability to care for myself. The deer was a scary space. More than that, the deer was a scary *string* of the world, and I hated the moments when it resonated within myself. If the deer was the medium of the Moon in my own being, I realised that I was deeply afraid of anything it had to say…The deer had to be silent so I could be myself.

Didn't I mention that we cannot work with what we identify with? The opposite is equally true, I learned: we cannot work with what we *cannot* identify with. Devotion and repulsion undermine our work with the Olympic Spirits in equal measure.

It took me a lot of courage to return to my Moon-deer, to accept its presence, and to offer it space and a voice within my current self. To this day, I have a difficult relationship with her, as she interferes with my Saturnian preference for efficiency, order and straightforwardness. Nevertheless, I have come to appreciate the many benefits of the Moon-deer: the caring and gentleness she evokes in me, the calm and gift for quiet observation, the freedom of goals and ideals, the surrender to the moment, and the creative tenderness it takes to watch a seed grow.

My Mars is a bear, my Venus a lynx. At least for now. It all goes to show the zoo we all need to learn to attend to.[2]

But once we form these individual relationships with the Olympic Spirits as they manifest within us, something truly magical can happen in our mundane lives: whether briefly out of the corner of our eye or in full piercing brilliance, we will be able to observe and experience the Olympic animals together with us in the most common life situations.

I still recall what a humbling experience it was when I realised that my foul mood when I'm hungry was nothing more than the untamed roar of my inner Mars-bear. The embarrassingly whiny feeling that swallowed me wholesale when I actually felt like having sex was my wailing Venus-lynx, howling its way through everyday life... The list went on with the rest of the zoo and all their complicated interactions, disputes and love affairs...

From a magical point of view, this is an important stage to pass through. And the most important thing is to remain anchored in our anthropological position of study and observation: there is no good and no bad, there is only wisdom which grows with each day that we learn to escape the blandishments as well as the stranglehold of these spirit-influences.

Because that is what we are experiencing. The animal shapes are only mental interfaces for the purpose of this exercise. What really matters is to develop actual *sensual awareness* for the presence (within us and around us) of a particular Olympic Spirit. We are awakening ourselves to see the very forces of creation at play in every moment of our lives. That is the impact of gazing into the *Mirror of the Olympic Spirits.*

I should stress that we are deliberately not working in this manner with the Olympic Spirit of *Mercury*. This being resides in the centre of the circle with us. By immersing ourselves into the reality of each of the six other celestial spirits, we are actually *polishing* the ingenium that is our inner Mercury. As we will see, the goal at the next stage of this path is to bring the six Olympic Spirits surrounding us to a level of calm correspondence with each other so that our inner

2 And the goal in the work with the Olympic Spirits definitely is to become better zoo-keepers than Julian Barratt and Noel Fielding in the *Mighty Boosh* (BBC, 2004–2007).

ingenium is no longer over-shadowed and absorbed by either of their influences. By going into the conscious relationship with each of the six Olympic Spirits, we aim to free the seventh within us from their voices. When this happens, we can begin to capture the light of Divinity in our ingenium.

Finally, as I am a big friend of *making the serpent bite its tail*, allow me to close the circle and loop this exercise back to the original writings of Paracelsus.

What follows here is one of my favourite sections from Paracelsus' entire body of work. It is such an elegant and yet provocative expression of the idea of *radical immanence*. According to Paracelsus, both virtues and vices among men still belong to the realm of the animals. At the same time, however, they also belong to the celestial realm as their expression is made possible by the respective stars within each being, the Olympic Spirits. Thus, man is not only invited to work through the animal realm and into the celestial realm; man is also invited to recognise that all of these spirits are present and alive within them. We are a but a hive of the entire world; and even the worst in us is travelling on a celestial string that leads back to something divine and beautiful.

Now a 16th century voice will never give us such an explicit visionary exercise as I offered above. Yet, Paracelsus' voice was clear enough to point us directly towards such work. Here is how he expressed the importance of this exercise in his *Foundation of Science and Wisdom*,[3] a writing of unknown date and first published in the ninth volume of Johannes Huser's edition of Paracelsus' collected works:

> *So man is to be seen in his father, and namely in heaven, in the firmament, in the stars, from which he then also became and was made. For in the same way as it [i.e., heaven] becomes and grows and is in the water and from the water, so the firmament of man is a pond, an ocean and a lake. Now know in connection with this that man also takes his animal reason from the same. For the animals are subject to the sky, and man just like an animal. Hence then come the revealed*

3 Sudhoff (ed.) 1931 Vol. XIII 'Fundamentum scientarum et sapientiae', pp. 287–334.

[celestial] signs within which man shows himself just as the animals. Now man must not think otherwise than that his war, his quarrel, his strife is of nothing else than of animal nature and governed by the stars, that is: they are made by the stars. Therefore man is Mars, he is also Mercurius, he is also Saturnus, he is also

Sol, he is also Luna, he is also Jupiter etc. [...]

You see that all animals lie in man. That is all animals lie in man as they appear, without their body, yet otherwise with everything [...].

So it follows also from the sky in this manner that man has in him the manner of the cock. The cock is Mars, as is also the man Mars, which is lured out of this species. In the wolf is Saturn, and just as Saturn is in the wolf so he is in the wolfish man. For man is governed by heaven no differently than an animal. So as the cock is woken up to crow in his time, and heaven wakes him up, so it happens also to the man, because he is a cock. And as heaven provokes the wolf to steal and rob, so also man, who is a wolf.

Now these things are of the animals, so heaven alone is master of the animals and has power over them, and not man. For if heaven makes man mild, kind, patient, so that he is said to be like a sheep and like the sun, then he is like a sheep, wise and reasonable, and so the sun rules him like a beastly sheep and not like a man.

For the animals are [governed] by the stars. And as it stems from the stars, so it is judged out of it and attached to it, and is one and the same thing [i.e., quality] as far as it relates to the manners of the animals. He that is angry is angry as a barking dog, not as a man; he that is murderous is murderous as a bear; he that is thievish is thievish as a fox; he that is adulterous is adulterous as a dog; he that is haughty is haughty as a cock; he that is unfaithful is unfaithful as a dog; he that is a good fellow is a good fellow as a dog. For all this is beastly and of the animal way.

Now pride has its star, murder has its star, adultery has its star, infidelity has its star, and so on and on with all the others. And as in animals are the stars, so you should be aware that they are not different in man. And so whichever

> *man is beastly in his nature, he is afflicted with the virtues of that beast, and the same stars as that beast are in him.*
>
> *And thus one star rules the wolf in the forest and the wolf in man, one star rules the murderer in the forest, that is the bear, and thus also the bear in man. And beastly is the reason, which compares itself to the animals, because it is beastly as well as bodily, like the animal compares itself to another animal. So heaven is the ruler of men, of all men who are animals, and live and dwell animal-like. From this follows the praise that is spoken to him: He is like a lion, he is like a wolf, he is like a fox. These are beastly praises, and die with the beast, and are no more than the beast, worse than the cattle in the pastures. For man shall be human, and not animal.*[4]

I wish you the best of luck in this essential exercise.

May you have the patience not to rush it, the humility and courage to see your Olympic animals in their original form, and the playfulness and forbearance to hear their hearts beating in your own.

Should it all become too much at one point, I invite you to think of my Moon-deer and the many moments I spent in horror of needing to befriend it. We are all together in this work.

I also invite you to listen to Coil's beautiful song *Fire of the Mind*. For their lyrics in the most poetic way bring forth much of the experience we are undergoing when looking into the Mirror of the Olympic Spirits.

> Fire of the Mind[5]
>
> *Does death come alone Or with eager reinforcements?*
> *Does death come alone Or with eager reinforcements?*
> *Death is centrifugal*
> *Solar and logical*
> *Decadent and symmetrical*
> *Angels are mathematical*

4 Ibid., 321–323.

5 John Balance, Fire of the Mind, from: Coil, *Ape of Naples*, Thailand: Threshold House, 2005, with kind permission by Cold Spring Records.

Angels are bestial
Man is the animal
Man is the animal
The blacker the sun
The darker the dawn
Flashes from the axis
Flashes from the axis
On the hummingway
To the stars
Holy holy, holy holy, holy, oh holy
Holy holy, holy holy, holy
Holy holy, holy holy, holy
Man is the animal
The blacker the suns
The darker the dawns

Exercise 2
THE BELL CALL

The pure mind
is the temple.[6]

In the chapter on Paracelsus' spirituality we summarised the goal of our work with the Olympic Spirits as follows: composing the Olympic Spirit (singular) within ourselves is the key operation of the philosophia adepta. When successfully carried out, its effect is very straightforward and simple: it frees the human mind from the chatter of the Olympic Spirits (plural) to be illuminated by the divine light.

Having undertaken the first exercise in its deserved depth and breadth, you have probably come to realise how daunting the above challenge is.[7] As Paracelsus said, most people even praise each other for exhibiting animal virtues, and thus naturally man remains an ani-

6 Adam Haslmayr, *Pura mens ist der Tempel.*, quoted after: Gilly, 1994, p. 194.

7 Again, I like to think of the *Mighty Boosh* and Howard Moon and Vince Noir's many weird encounters in their Zooniverse. I highly recommend (re)watching especially the first series in parallel with our Olympic Spirit work. It provides a powerful antidote against taking ourselves too seriously.

mal and we consciously blacken the sun and darken the dawn, as Coil put it in their song.

With the following exercise we are taking a significant step in the opposite direction—and will move forth from the essential work we have accomplished in the previous exercise.

Rather than zeroing into the individual relationships with the seven Olympic Spirits, we now invite their presence to temporarily liberate our mind from their attachments. For a short ritual moment, we strive to create a void, surrounded by their shielding spirit bodies, that invites the Divine light into our work.

We might want to remember the mentioning of this work in Robert Fludd's text.

> *He [the birth-genius] controls us so long, until we, who were charged with the leadership of the cult, put the Lord in the place of the daemon. For then the Daemon gives way to God and is therefore either freed from its activity or is conducive to it.*[8]

It is a fine line to respect the impact of this operation and yet not to be intimidated by its seeming significance. Just like before, we encourage you to hold onto the mindset of a curious anthropologist, unafraid to immerse themselves into participatory experiences, yet ultimately free from judgement about outcomes. What matters is not what is achieved by the process, but how deeply we are willing to participate in its actual mechanics.

Practice Guidance

EQUIP yourself with a small handbell.

FIND a quiet place where you will not be disturbed. Face East and sit in a quiet and comfortable position with your back upright. Place the bell in a position where you can easily reach it.

WITH the help of your preferred meditation exercise, centre yourself in the present moment. Close your eyes.

IN your mind's eye, see yourself sitting in the middle of a circle of approximately three meters (nine feet) in diameter.

8 Robert Fludd, *Utriusque Cosmi*, Book Three, Part One, Chapter II.

COME to realise the flame that is quietly burning in your heartspace. When you can feel its presence, pull a spark from it in vision and place it before you.

WITNESS how the light of this spark is intensifying and expanding to all sides. The inside of the circle you are sitting in is growing lighter and lighter.

AFTER a while you see yourself sitting inside a brightly glowing sphere of light. Nothing can penetrate this shield that surrounds you. Any disturbing thoughts arising from within you should be handed over to the light around you, then allow them to be burned away.

ENJOY the present experience of being embalmed in light, breathing through all the pores of your body and mind in this sphere of light. you are sitting in the essence of life.

WHEN you are ready, take the bell and ring it once.

IN vision, you see all six Olympic Spirits appear in their assigned positions around your sphere of light. This time, however, they are not stepping forth in their animal-forms, but they appear undiluted in their original spirit forms.

NOTE: Just like when you first encountered the Olympic Spirits in their animal-form, keep all subjective fantasy and imagination out of this work as much as possible. ---Allow the spirits to emerge in whatever kind of presence they choose. They might appear as planets on the horizon, in human form, as geometrical patterns, as sounds, scents or in no sensual form at all other than your awareness of their presence. Again, this work is not here to live up to anyone's expectations of what it might be, but to sharpen your awareness of how it best works *for you*.

WHEN you sense the presence of all six Olympic Spirits, observe how they react to the sphere of light you are sitting within. Gradually you see their own lights form an outer layer around this central sphere. All six of them are coming together, leaning into each other, weaving their presence into one, to shield and uphold the sphere of light you have pulled from your heart-flame. Give them time to complete this process, until you sense your sphere fully protected by the presence of the Olympic Spirits.

YOU are now sitting in your mind's temple. Take your time to sense its quality. Can you feel how easy it has become to uphold the central sphere of light, now that it is shielded by the Olympics? Can you sense the silent harmony vibrating on the outside of the sphere, where it touches the Olympics? Nothing takes effort in this moment. you have unlocked a space that, once established, is almost effortlessly maintaining itself. Give your senses time to attune to it... you might hear things, you might see or taste things. All is welcome, all is possible in this space.

WHEN you are done, ring the handbell again. See the Olympics respond to it, like the tide reacts to the moon; see them dissolving their interwoven shield and slowly withdrawing their presence.

WHEN you are all by yourself again, allow the light of the central sphere to dim. Then pull the remaining spark from the place before you where you had put it, and unite it again with your heart-flame.

FINISH this exercise with the departure-gesture of your preference, whether that is a bow, a prayer or a song.

TAKE a deep breath and return to your everyday consciousness. Open your magical diary and write down your experience as detailed as possible.

REPEAT this exercise as often as you like. But give yourself sufficient time between each operation to observe its impact on your everyday life—both within and around yourself.

Explanatory Notes

THIS exercise will only work when the Moon-deer (or your corresponding counterpart) no longer scares us; and neither any of the other Olympic Spirits in whichever form we might encounter them.

Yet, once this operation works, there is little magical innovation or inventory necessary beyond it. This is not because this operation is any kind of silver bullet or magical remedy. Rather, it is because this exercise all in one can introduce us to the temple, the altar, the working surface and the entire paraphernalia necessary for most other magical work. It truly is the foundation and the beginning.

We discovered the Olympic Spirits as the *one-makers*, the *weavers, the seven mediums* of life and of all creation. The exercise of the bell call allows us to stand face-to-face not only with all six of them, but it also opens our mind (Mercury, the seventh Olympic Spirit, or the human ingenium) to the light of Divinity. In this setting, we hold the potential to arrive in the *House of God* as Robert Fludd put it. Hopefully, at this point we will also understand the responsibility that comes with this experience: the Olympic Spirits are the very beings that come together to form the temple around us. yet, a temple requires indwelling, inhabitance, and incorporation. Thus, it is our choice, a fundamentally human choice of *free will*, *faith* and *imagination*, what we bring forth in the central sphere of light. Which thoughts do we invite into this space? Which beings do we call forward in it? Which pleas do we hold for the cosmos, and which service are we willing to render?

While operating in this temple, you can choose for any one of the Olympic Spirits to step forward and to commune with them. you can also call for any other spirits to appear, either outside the ring of the Olympics or through the gate of your heart-flame from within. Inside this temple the gates of the cosmos are open to all sides.

Maybe you will begin to see now why Paracelsus paid so much emphasis on sharpening the tools of our free will, faith and imagination in our everyday lives. Maybe you will begin to appreciate the importance of ethics and integrity, of knowing how to keep the scales of your life in balance?[9]

To illustrate the versatility and utility of the bell call exercise let me provide a couple of questions for your own research and further inquiry…

1 GO back to the chapter on the *Terra Olympi*; refresh your memory of Adam Haslmayr's elucidations on this very special and yet ubiquitous kind of substance. Then next time you are in the temple of the bell call, bring a purified object with you, be it a glass of earth, a magically cleansed amulet, a bone or a feather. When the Olympics are fully present around you, ask one of them or all of them to touch this object and to lay an echo of its force

9 For the daring among us, I have reconstructed an even more demanding version of this exercise in the second half of my book *Holy Heretics* (2022). Where the present operation opens the altar of choice, the rite presented in *Holy Heretics* is an irreversible choice.

into it. Be careful though what you do with and where you place this object after the rite...

2 FROM the temple of the bell call, ask the Olympic Spirits to help you commune with your holy daimon. See if you can call for her/him together. you might find yourself singing with the Olympics, or in a wise moment of utter silence, inviting in the spirit that comes from beyond their realm...

3 WHEN you are in pain or suffering, return to the temple of the bell call if you can. However, it will require you to still be able to occupy the anthropologist's perspective even on your own pain or sorrow. your pain or harm can be called forth in the light of the central sphere, but they cannot dim its brilliance. If this is a possibility for you, do pursue it. Then invite the Olympics in supporting your journey of healing. Be careful not to invite them to make the pain simply go away, for this could have significant negative ramifications far beyond the suffering you are currently experiencing. Instead, invite them to help you successfully work *through* the pain or injury.

A curious mind might, of course, ask them to speak about why this pain exists in the first place. Saturn's view might differ significantly from the Sun's as to the source of the suffering. However, if you listen to all or several of them in their genuine diagnosis, the magical anthropologist in you will gain valuable insight to exercise your own free will.

As you proceed in this work, it might become less and less important to conjure forth the temple of the bell call in an actual magical operation as we initially have to. Instead, your familiarity with the Olympics within you might grow to a level of awareness where conscious cohabitation with them becomes the norm. your Olympics might become your magical *familiars*.

> *[Austin Osman] Spare spent much of his time alone, and yet not. "I have only to turn my head," he said, "to see the whole gang of familiars, elementals and alter-egos that make up my being."*

> *"Towards the end of his life," says one of his main chroniclers, Kenneth Grant, "when Spare lived more or less reclusively in a Dickensian South London slum, he was asked whether he regretted his lonely existence. 'Lonely!' he exclaimed, and with a sweep of his arm he indicated the host of unseen elementals and familiar spirits that were his constant companions; he had but to turn his head to catch a fleeting glimpse of their subtle presences."*[10]

Exercise 3
I AND THOU

This third exercise is not aiming at a practice centred on the Olympic Spirits. Rather, it is taking a concept developed by Martin Buber in his seminal book *I and Thou* and is applying it to an animistic worldview where we are constantly surrounded by spirits: around us and from within us. It can be helpful in bringing the experience you made in the previous two exercises out into the natural world and into your everyday lived reality. I suppose that Paracelsus would have hated this exercise because it is meant for people who have lost or never had their organic, natural connection to nature. It's meant for all of us who grew up in cities, who were never invited to help our grandparents cut and dry herbs, restore an old well, or drive the sheep in at dusk. It's for all of us who have had too few trees to climb and too little wilderness to get lost in. If this doesn't apply to you, you can safely ignore it and skip to the next chapter.

For the rest of us, allow yourself to be playful with the following instructions. Do them often and not too long. They might read far more complicated than they actually are; which is obviously my fault!

I stumbled across this simple threefold exercise after years of practicing magic, researching the roots of the early Chassidic movement in Lurianic Kabbalah, and never ceasing to follow my childhood habit of speaking to all objects around me. Worst case: this exercise

10 Phil Baker quoting Kenneth Grant on Austin Osman Spare's lived reality of everyday cohabition with familiars. (Phil Baker, *Austin Osman Spare—The Life and Legend of London's Lost Artist*, London: Strange Attractor Press, 2011, p. 150).

will simply do nothing for you. Best case: it will become a utility knife of an exercise to break a narrow sense of identity and open yourself up to a most strange and wonderful world.

I
Arriving

This work is best done outside in nature. Find a quiet space where you will be undisturbed. Sit comfortably and allow your gaze to fall upon a natural, unmanufactured object. When you have found your place and are comfortably seated, observe which object presents itself to you.

When I first did this work, I was looking at a large tree in my neighbour's garden. Equally, it could be a rock surface, an elderbush, the curve of a river, or the slope of a mountain. It is whatever presents itself to you.

Now begin to do your normal meditation practice. Use it to allow yourself to gain calm, presence, and awareness of yourself in the living sphere around you.

Allow yourself to fully arrive, and to come to rest in this place. Once you are settled in, stretch out your awareness in your own body. Can you sense what your body brings to this moment? Stretch yourself out in your breath and feel its presence. Can you do the same with your taste, your smell, your touch? Have all of your senses arrived in this moment yet?

All of your senses have now come to the foreground. They are all sitting here with you right now. And yet, they are all entailed in their own stories and tales. Give them space, give them presence and time, as you sit with them without any expectations.

II
Reaching Out

Now seek for the natural object that naturally presents itself to your gaze. Whatever that is, in this moment it holds the same vibrant depth of aliveness as you do. The only difference is that it is a non-human person. That's why *speaking* to it costs a little effort, like speaking in a new language does. yet, *communing with it* comes at no cost and without any effort at all.

You are already doing it. Let us pull on this communion a little and bring it to the foreground…

All the aliveness you have centred yourself in, open it up to this natural object. Allow yourself to flow forward, beyond the confines of your body, like a scent is carried through the air.

Allow the object to smell your skin, allow it to touch the presence of the myriad cells that establish the presence of "you." Let the tree, let the elder-bush, the river's edge or mountain slope touch your presence. Let it touch the weight of your body, let it taste the shape of your mind, let it see the vibrant, meandering stream of presence that is "you."

Sit in such communion for a while. Maybe you will begin to think of your body as the entrance to a cave of "you", with a light wind that is pushing out of this cave, into this world and towards the natural object of your communion…

Then, lightly, like you would want to be touched while asleep, in your mind begin to repeat the words "I" and "you."

When you speak "I," your awareness is centred on yourself. And when you pronounce "you," your awareness is shifting over to the natural object of your communion. Say "I" and "you." It is as simple as that. For in saying "I" you give all of yourself, and in saying "you" you are receiving all of the other.

Stay with this experience for a while. Do not try to understand or make rational sense of it. Do not look for a *spirit*, anything magical or mundane. Just stay with your shifting awareness between the presence of "I" and "you."

III
Looking Back

Next, and now you will be messing with your own mind, *turn the words around.*

When you say (out loud or mutely in your mind) "I" you centre yourself in the natural object, and when you say "you" you return your awareness to your own body. Now you experience yourself from the viewpoint of the natural object. And you allow the spirit of the object to experience yourself from within.

Stay in the "I" of the object space for a while. you are the elder-bush, the rock face, the river's edge, the mountain slope. What do your senses speak to you now? What is present with you in this moment? And what is absent?

Remain in this communion for a while. you have exchanged the lights of awareness. you have opened a door to learn about a few things at once. you will learn about the *inside experience* of the object of your work. *How does its spirit's presence feel? In which direction does its awareness flow? What matters to this spirit, what does no longer matter from its vantage point?*

At the same time you can look out through this spirit at yourself in your human form. How does this spirit see you? *What are you, what is any human to this being?*

We really are not in a rush when we do magical work.

There is no notion of *performance* or *success* in this operation. In fact, this is the kind of exercise that will always work. Like awakening in the morning, it is best not *performed* but *being allowed to happen*. This exercise is so organic, so ever-present that the only thing that can compromise it is the human desire to force things into a certain shape or experience. *Awakening will happen. Communion is already happening.* "You" is happening, and "I" is happening, both at the same time. Shifting our field of awareness is done as effortlessly as offering a kiss: all it takes is a little reaching out, in full openness, and to trust that a response will come.

IV
I as Otherness

This is how we work with spirits with an empty hand. All it takes is a little "I" and a lot of "you."

We can pass through ourselves like a rotating door, out into the world, and look back at ourselves again. Then when we realise ourselves *as a spirit*.

It's nothing but the narrow thoughts of "I, Me and Mine" that hold our mind back from travelling. Once we walk through the rotating door of "I," we begin to see our mind as a cloud of awareness that can travel with the wind. If only we grant it permission, this *cloud* delights in travelling, in shape-shifting, in playfully and recklessly becoming one with the world. We are no longer *human* then, and neither are we rock or river or mountain. We are *that which experienc-*

es rock, or river or mountain, or human. We are a cloud of curiosity, travelling on the wind of awareness.

Once you have stilled your thirst of tasting, sensing, smelling experiencing the world through the spirits of natural objects, stay away from returning into your *human home* for a little while. Instead, stay in the spirit of the object you are communing with, and look again at how they perceive your human form. What does the river know about the human sitting there? What does the elder-bush see of what it means to be human? What is the human "you" to the "I" of a tree?

Staying with this exploration for a while, you might came to find that *a human is a deeply uncanny thing*. Like a centipede in a cave, or a deep-sea fish. It might reveal itself to you, that we really know nothing about this place that our *cloud of "I"* normally calls its home.

Seeing yourself from the outside in such a way can be an unsettling experience. It distorts into existence what a moment ago you were too close to see. Because you were embalmed in humanness, and now you are no longer. Now you begin to see the form and spirit you yourself are immersed into.

To work with spirits in the way of the empty hand, we must begin our work by beginning to see the spirit that we are ourselves. Stepping into the "I" of a tree, of a river or a rock, and looking back at the "you" of our human form, is the first step of working with an empty hand.

Stopping to think of us as us, is the mind-bending, beautiful, incredible obvious first step on this journey called *magic of the open hand*. Seeing ourselves as a no different from a hive, a fire, a lake, a cave, is the beginning. We then see that all the spirits *are already within us. Communing* is the default state of nature, and yet the illusion of separateness has become the default state of most humans.

Walking the path of the empty hand is a is a walk out into the untamed wilderness of otherness. For when "I" stops feeling like *home*, there is no more home at all and otherness everywhere. Even under our own skin. Then we learn, that all things respond if we only invite them to.

Here is a little prayer that might come handy on your own *familiar* explorations. There is no need to use it as it is. Rather, use it as an inspiration to write your own.

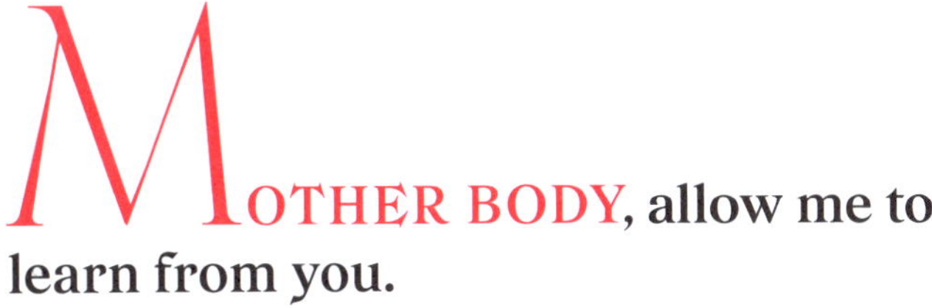

MOTHER BODY, allow me to learn from you.

Tell me your story. Sister heart and brother blood, tell me of the things I have never asked you about.

I am ready now. Ready to see you for what you are: places of spirit(s), just like a river, a rock or a tree, that by chance and for a short period only became the material of Me.

Let's come together, in the presence of your spirits and mine.

BOOK 2

CHAPTER II

WORKING WITH THE *ARBATEL'S SEAL OF SECRETS*

Introduction

IN THE PREVIOUS chapter we jumped straight into the deep end of magical communion with the Olympic Spirits, unimpeded by historical misunderstandings, distorted original texts and man-made orthodoxies. In this chapter we will adopt the opposite approach and aim to show that even on the difficult path laid out by heavily truncated or deliberately obscured source texts we can still arrive at a truly animated and authentic way of working with the Olympic Spirits.

To illustrate this, we choose to single out both one of the most famous and one of the least known source texts on the Olympics: the often-quoted *Arbatel* (Basel, 1575) and the fragmentary manuscript under the signature Cod.Mag.55 from the famous Grimoire Collection of the University Library in Leipzig: *Solomon's Conjuration of the Olympic Spirits.*[1]

1 *Cod.Mag.55* has previously been referenced by Joseph H. Peterson in his online edition of the *Arbatel De magia veterum* as on its final folio the short manuscript contains a full rendering of the *Seal of Secrets*. However, as we will show in the present analysis, the late 17th or early 18th century rendering of this seal seems to be incorrect as far as the source text of the *Arbatel* is concerned.

Cod.Mag.55 presents us with a commingling of the realms of learned and folk magic, of celestial and chthonic beings, of Olympic and animistic spirits. This short manuscript might be nothing more than the scrawled notes of a practicing magician from the late 17th century. Or its hasty assembly of various textual sources might point us to something else, namely to a text in which function outweighed form and pragmatism aesthetics. A *grimoire* in the actual sense of the word, intended exclusively for personal use, and instead of being addressed to a broad audience, giving evidence of one person's lived experience with the spirits.

At the end of this chapter, our path will end at a fully restored ritual for working with the *Seal of Secrets* contained in both documents. Needless to say, our reconstruction offers just one of many possible approaches and holds no claim to singularity or reconstructing the work at hand in exactly the way it was intended by both authors. What it will accomplish, however, is to remain truthful and coherent to its source texts as well as to actual work in applied practice of the present day.

The ritual at the end of this chapter relies upon the skills and experiences described in the earlier chapters. It is not intended nor advised to be performed out of context of the rest of this book. Specifically, it presupposes the practitioner to be able to switch into an animistic spirit paradigm—a worldview in which all levels of being, once awakened, will respond back to us: the plane of stars and angels, the plane of herbs and poisons, the plane of blood and bones, and the plane of stones and shadows.

Equally, I wish to point out that being able to unlock such conscious inter-species dialogue is only the first step for a successful magical rite. Just like humans, so the spirits speak from their own limited perspective, affected by natural bias, and not too rarely with cunning mischief. Working anchored in the light of Divinity has nothing to do with romanticism or even a Trithemian agenda of purging ancient rituals to fit an orthodox Christian paradigm. Instead, working from within the light of Divinity is the time-tested most effective, reliable and smartest way of engaging with the endlessly diverse spirit world around us.

Unfortunately for the lazy practitioner, it is also one of the hardest things to achieve. A simple prayer just won't cut it—that is unless we have indeed walked that far out on the narrow path that a simple prayer *will* actually cut it.

The angels close to Divinity's throne keep their gaze directly directed towards the source of light. Like an angelic mirror, they illuminate the shortest way back to the origin. The position of the mage differs essentially from theirs. Initially, the magician is indeed busy establishing their lives in an unobstructed, direct line that flows back all the way to Divinity. While spanning entire worlds, such line begins and ends in the magician's heart. Where the angels' and mystic's position differs essentially though is with regards to what their are looking at: the magician stands with their back to Divinity, their gaze leading out into creation, God behind them, the light of creation shining over their shoulders into the world. Magicians are tools of successful involution. They partake in the never-ending task of helping the world to maintain balance.

While these introductory remarks may seem convoluted at first sight, they will prove to be essential in light of where we shall be going on the following pages.

I

Source Texts

Cod.Mag.55 and the *Arbatel*

THE MANUSCRIPT WAS sold in 1710 on the clandestine book market as part of a massive private collection of grimoires by one Samuel Schröer, a Leipzig-based medical doctor.[2] The individual texts thus all date to the late 17th century and most of them have been identified as manual copies or excerpts of older source texts within the tradition of Western Learned Magic.

In line with one of the key characteristics of this genre, many of the manuscripts' titles are pseudepigraphic i.e., attributed to a mythical

2 Daniel Bellingradt and Bernd-Christian Otto, *Magical Manuscripts in Early Modern Europe*. Cham: Palgrave Macmillan, 2017; with an open access appendix: THE CATALOGUS RARIORUM MANUSCRIPTORUM https://link.springer.com › bbm:978-3-319-59525-2 › 1.pdf.

name indicating a particular lineage of magical practice or patronage. This also applies to the document at hand which is referred to as *Solomon's Conjuration of the Olympic Spirits*. To ensure there is no doubt about the persona referenced in its title, Solomon is further identified as the Biblical *Son of David*.

Bellingradt and Otto's summary of the document incorrectly identifies it as "an abbreviated German translation of the text *Arbatel de magia veterum*."[3]

Instead, it is precisely the most curious aspect of this document that it actually does not present an excerpt or abbreviated copy of the well known Arbatel but a commingling of its source material with elements of the Solomonic Tradition and German folk magic. Thus, in the present manuscript we find evidence against A. E. Waite's claim that the Olympic Spirits are deemed to have "no connection with the cycle [...] of the Keys of Solomon."[4]

Given that the *Arbatel* has been identified as an expression of a *transcendental*[5] counter-culture against Late Medieval grimoires of demonic nature,[6] coming across such blending of these sub-genres within the tradition of Western Learned Magic is both remarkable as well as expected. It is expected as similar approaches are known from the 19th century onwards, once the publisher Johann Scheible began to flood the mainstream book market with cheap print copies of once scarce magical source text.[7] And yet, it is still remarkable as the present manuscript seems to provide one of the earliest sources of such hybrid magic, mixing elements of *white magic*, the Solomonic tradition as well as folk-magic.

3 Bellingradt, Otto (2017) p. 97.

4 Waite, Arthur Edward, *The Book of Ceremonial Magic*. London, 1913 [1898], p. 27.

5 Waite 1913, p. 24.

6 Gilly 2002, p. 211.

7 Bachter 2005, p. 59.

II

The Olympic Spirits and their Hierarchies

THE TEXT BEGINS abruptly, relating in its first sentence to something that was said earlier but is now lost. Thus, our manuscript presents itself either as a direct excerpt of an older, unknown source text, or, more likely even, as a compilation from multiple sources.

Such notion is further evidenced by the inclusion of the Seal of Secrets on its final folio. Similarly to its abrupt beginning, the image of the seal at its end stands by itself and holds no overt connection to the text. However, this might permit the hypothesis that this compilation was an actual working document of a 17th century mage. For, as we will see, the ritual instructions in the text indeed allow us to make an implicit practical connection to the *Seal of Secrets*; yet it is one that would only be obvious to a practicing magician.

The document then introduces us in subsequent order to the Olympic Spirits: initially to *Aratron*, *Bethor*, *Phaleg*, *Och*, and then collectively to *Hagith*, *Ophiel* and *Phul*. Notably, despite the errors in the Hebrew and Latin renderings, the names of the Olympic Spirits are all spelled correctly. Also, they are given in the correct descending ladder of involution, from Saturn as the outermost planet to the Moon as the closest to Earth. It is notable that the original seals of the Olympic Spirits are not included in our manuscript, yet other characters are given instead for inclusion in the respective magical circles, as we will see later on.

> *Accordingly, certain spirits are required for each thing, such as one for obtaining wealth, another for lifting treasures, yet another for things under the rule of Venus, and so on. So we also have to put different spirits here and teach their invocation.*[8]

8 Cod.Mag. 55, 2 recto.

Already in its first sentence, the manuscript establishes that the key to the art resides in working *with the correct spirit* for each specific concern. A spirit assisting in general matters of wealth is different from a spirit that can help to lift telluric treasures or to bind someone's love to another person. The superficial reader might mistake this advice for simply choosing one of the seven Olympic Spirits. However, after having mentioned all seven, the author emphasis that these merely "are the noblest"[9] but not the only spirits the magician might require for a successful operation. Such notion is further stressed by the introduction of Aratron as "the deliverer of the other spirits";[10] as well as the explanation that the magician is not intended to *work* with the Olympic Spirits, but to ask for their mediation and facilitation to receive access to the correct *operating spirit* for one's specific undertaking.

> *After that, intone your incantation. However, nothing will be felt the first time. Nevertheless, do this incantation again after nine days have passed and ask for the same spirit again, then it will be heard with a great roar and much steam will be around him and he will ask what your desire is. Then you shall tell him your opinion, and after that he will provide you with a spirit as quickly as you ask.*[11]

Thus, the role of the Olympic Spirits has to be differentiated from *performative* spirits and, rather, understood as *gatekeepers of magical agency*. Under their respective patronage, the related magical operation is enabled. However, its actual consummation resides with spirits that remain anonymous in our manuscript.

Such differentiation between named *higher* or gatekeeping spirits as well as nameless lesser or performative ones is a foundational principle among the techniques of Solomonic Magic.[12]

9 Ibid., 4 recto.
10 Ibid., 2 recto.
11 Ibid., 3 recto.
12 Skinner 2015, p. 128—Equally, we are reminded of Robert Fludd's text of 1620 where he emphasises that working within the hierarchy of a spirit-line is an essential technique. It even applies to the nature of a human's holy daemon: "From these things it follows in a most evident manner that not always one of those seven archangels in their very own person tends to preside [as

However, we also find it to be in line with the presentation of the Olympic Spirits in the *Arbatel* itself. Here, in their original source text, we encounter elaboration that, together, the Olympic Spirits rule 196 provinces in descending order from *Aratron* (49 provinces) to *Phul* (7 provinces). More specifically, in Aphorism §27 as part of the explanation of the construction of the *Seal of Secrets*, we learn of the four *Princes* of the cardinal directions, their respective six *Satraps*,[13] and again of the thirty-six *Lower Magistrates* assigned to each of them. Thus, we are given a complete spirit hierarchy of at least 140 operating spirits in total.

The descending hierarchy from *Princes* to *Satraps* (or Lords) to *Lower Magistrates* is emphasised and explained in Aphorisms §30 to §35. The reader is advised to either call for the Prince or one of their Satraps so they can bestow companionship with a particular Lower Magistrate to the operator.

These instructions are further elaborated upon in Aphorisms §17 and §18. Here it is explained that the way of working with the Olympic Spirits depends on the magician's inborn talent and acquired skill: the "true and divine magus is able to use all creatures of God, and the services of the governors of the world [i.e., the seven Olympic Spirits], according to his command". The Olympic Spirits, however, will not appear and work with the "average magician" but "will send some of their spirits, who will obey within certain limits". The risk is highest for "false magi", as these will be thrown into "the jaws of the mocking demons, and [these will] expose them to different dangers, with God's authority."[14]

Aphorism §18 additionally emphasis that the names of the Olympic Spirits are only effective if they are personally given to the operator "by the revealing spirit". While this "*revelatorum Spiritum*"[15] remains nameless in the *Arbatel*, we have seen above that in our

man's holy daemon], but that very often also one of the leaders belonging to them fulfils that protective function on their behalf." (Book Three, Part Three, Chapter v).

13 *Satraps* were the governors of the provinces of the ancient Median and Achaemenid Empires. The satrap served as viceroy to the king, though with considerable autonomy. The term is a Latinised loan-word from an Old Persian term *khshathrapāvan* that literally means *protector of the dominion.* (source: https://www.merriam-webster.com/dictionary/satrap).

14 Peterson 2009, pp. 39–41.

15 Ibid., p. 40.

present document it is identified as no other than the actual Olympic Spirit of *Aratron*, who is signified as "the deliverer of the other spirits."[16]

The risk of such magic is called out, that the desire to "live amongst gods, until the judgement" comes at the peril of turning one's heart "blind" and can easily lead to one's "eternal ruin."[17] The spiritual mechanics behind these risks are explained in Aphorism §35: For it is the soul (*mens humana*) of the operator that is actually joined to the spirit of the operation; a magical process of daring intimacy and rather hard to reverse once successfully accomplished.[18]

> *The human soul is the sole producer of wonders, to the extent that it is joined with the chosen spirit; once joined it will reveal what you desire.*[19]

Now, all of these inner dynamics of the magic at hand remain implicit in our short manuscript.

This could be down to various reasons. Either the manuscript, despite its considerable age for Western grimoires, was already part of the wave of documents specifically created for commerce. In this case, it would not be unlikely that someone extracted and combined key sections of older source works into this new collage. Such an approach would explain the garbled conjurations in Hebrew, Latin and French as well as the co-existence of elements of the Solomonic tradition with elements of angelic and folk-magic.

Alternatively, we have to consider that the manuscript was penned by an expert for either their own use or for secret circulation amongst fellow professionals. In such a case general operating terms and deeper understanding of context—e.g., exact knowledge of the *Arbatel*—would have been considered a given. Implicit references or gaps in in-

16 Cog.Mag 55, 2 recto.

17 Peterson 2009, p. 67.

18 We remind ourselves of the second exercise in the previous chapter, where we established the temple of the bell call. We mentioned the potential of conjuring spirits directly into the central sphere and allowing them to step forth from the flame or heart-space. This is a practical example of the risk alluded to here i.e., the merging of the respective spirit with the spirit of the operator.

19 *Arbatel*, Aphorism §35, Peterson 2009, p. 69.

structions in such a scenario would have not been considered a flaw but expected stylistic devices of brevity and efficiency in an already hazardous text of an illegal and actively persecuted craft.

III

Conjurations and Circles

THE FIRST FIVE pages of the manuscript introduce us to the seven Olympic Spirits. It is an introduction conducted in the shortest possible curtness, or more likely and as mentioned above, in rough excerpts from older material.

Aratron, *Bethor* and *Phaleg* are each given a specific conjuration as well as a customised magical circle design that has to be drawn on the ground. Where the text speaks of the "corners" of these circles, the cardinal points are implied.[20] Where the text instructs us to place certain characters to the *right* or *left*, we can read these as markers on a compass rose. *Right* in this orientation would therefore equal *East*, and so on.

Even with this context, however, the instructions remain fractional at best. The conjurations seem to be a mix of French and Latin; the former possibly giving us a lead as to the provenance of the original source text. We encounter Hebrew divine names (e.g. *Jehova*, *Elohim*) as well as Biblical names (*Lamech* and *Marcus*). Bethor is introduced—incorrectly—as a "protector of venereal things".[21] That is, a ruler over all things related to the realm of Venus, whereas traditionally Bethor aligns to the realm of Jupiter and *Hagith* would have been the correct Olympic Spirit to mention here. *Phaleg's* single-sentence conjuration is equally mutilated. However, it leverages the word *thesaureur* which can be identified as *treasurer*.[22] This suggests the possibility that these abbreviated conjurations were not at all meant to be general keys to the Olympic Spirits, but specialised for a particular operative purpose. *Phaleg* is introduced as the "possessor of

20 Thus, a classical magical circle would indicate up to eight corners: North, East, South, West as well as the midpoints of NE, SE, etc.

21 Cod.Mag.55, 3 recto.

22 *Schatzmeister* in German.

treasures" right before the conjuration is given. The actual rite to work with him for finding treasures is then following further below in the manuscript. The unmotivated gap between the invocation and the rite is another possible indication that the present manuscript is a hastily compiled assemblage.

Och, *Hagith*, *Ophiel* and *Phul* are not given their own conjurations. This means that either they were left out, or the operator indeed made the implicit assumption that these spirits would be introduced to the magician through the help of Aratron, who was called the "deliverer of spirits" earlier on. Their short introduction is followed by a banishing formula of equally succinct and garbled nature:

> *Lamech, Marci, Joannes, dicier se et abicus Laduf salum nac du dasle Lucas sebulda Beelzebub ne Each elenuf quaref ebolabatur.*[23]

While we cannot decipher the meaning of the entire sentence, it is noteworthy to see Beelzebub mentioned in the context of banishing the Olympic Spirits. Unfortunately, we do not know whether Beelzebub was called for as a spirit that rules over these spirits and thus can command them. A more likely scenario would be that his name is listed as a deterrent i.e., exemplifying the fate of banishment into hell that could thwart any unruly spirits.

The three magical circles given for *Aratron*, *Bethor* and *Phaleg* can be codified into the following table if we follow the logic of the cardinal points as outlined above.

23 Cod.Mag.55, 4 recto.

Circles of Cod. Mag. 55

	Aratron	Bethor	Phaleg	
North & Top			אכהר	I will clarify
North East			ומ	and
East & Right	A lamb with a cross on its back	Triangle with dog & magi-cal characters	שכרכח	Who forced
South East			ומ	and
South & Bottom			תבענר	Will burn
South West			ומ	and
West & Left	Magical characters & a mouse	Triangle with Wounds of Christ	אחים	brothers, siblings
North West			ומ	and

While the elements mentioned for *Aratron* and *Bethor* suggest a Christian context (*lamb with a cross* and *wounds of Christ*), they are combined with symbols that refer to a more demonic affiliation (*dog* and *mouse*[24]). Furthermore, *Phaleg*'s circle components switch from German to Hebrew, the latter words being written by an untrained hand.

Finally, the instructions on creating the circles and using the conjurations leave us with another noteworthy hint: in all three cases the operator is advised to create the magical circle and perform the conjuration in a discrete location that is undisturbed and fully reserved to their practice over a longer period. For *Aratron* we find instruction to repeat the conjuration in the circle after nine days, for *Bethor* after seven days, for *Phaleg* it could be either of these two timeframes.

In between these performative moments the circles is meant to remain undisturbed on the ground. This indicates that the author took it for granted that the practitioner would already have established a more permanent secret space for magical operations, whether this would have been indoors or outdoors.

IV

The Olympic Spirits in Folk-Magical Context

AT THE END of page 4 recto, almost halfway into the manuscript, we encounter a distinct break in content and narrative. Up to this point, the author has introduced the seven Olympic Spirits according to their names, qualities, specific conjurations, their customised magical circles as well as a general licence to depart. The professional operator would now have been equipped with the core elements to assemble their own rite. As usual in the Western grimoire tradition, the heart of the matter was not meant to be taught from *human-to-human*, but from *spirit-to-human*. All that was needed to pass on between humans were the raw elements, the *ritual grammar* re-

24 In this context we recall the living mouse offered as a pledge to Lucifer in the *Black Dragon* (Cecchetelli, 2011, p. 20).

quired to create *spirit communion*; everything from here onwards was meant to be learned from the spirits themselves.

Our author alludes to exactly such kind of *spirit-to-human-education* when at the top of 4 recto s/he introduces OCH with the addition that it is this spirit "who gives one wisdom so that one may more quickly understand the books in which this art is described." Further on, the author emphasises again, that Och "teaches all kinds of arts."[25]

What should be highlighted here is the critical combination of direct spirit-tutelage on the one side, and highly sensual folk-magical recipes on the other. The intentional interference of the spirits is not at all an abstract or conceptual undertaking. Rather, the folk-magical recipes listed in our manuscript require the eating and drinking of unusual ingredients; animal body parts are sewn into bags and worn as talismans on human skin, and animal hearts are dried, powdered and sprinkled over a naked lover's chest. In stark contrast to the spiritual elucidations of the *Arbatel*, our manuscript is offering chthonic pathways of embodying spirits. Encountering the Olympic Spirits as tutelary deities over magic drawn from the garden, the hearth and the stables, is a rather new setting for these noblest of spirits.

Specifically, the manuscript lists a rather eclectic choice of folk-magical recipes attributed to *Och*'s governance. In total, the author lists a dozen recipes that instruct the operator how to:

Accelerate mining success.
Keep a woman from courting with other men.
Heal a cough.
Turn clothes incombustible.
Give someone an ulcer.
Drive away an illness by the name Padayra.
Induce fears in enemies.
Make adversaries perish.
Make a lover tell all their secrets.
See things others cannot see.
Understand the voices of birds.
To know the things of the future.

25 Cod.Mag.55, 4 recto.

Emphasising the exemplary nature of this list, the author concludes laconically by affirming again that "these and other things teach the spirits".[26]

The text then abruptly switches to giving further details on the art of magical treasure hunting. As mentioned, this sudden shift in content lends further validity to the notion that the entire manuscript was either copied in haste or assembled from multiple sources by an uneducated hand.

The reader is now given more precise instructions. A specific circle has to be erected over the location where the treasure is supposed to be. To assist with finding such locations it is recommended to use a divining rod. Then the treasure itself is conjured *into the earth below the circle*. After two days, the operator returns to the location and now conjures the Olympic Spirit *Phaleg* to assist (or, as we previously saw, to denote a spirit under their influence to do so) with binding and lifting the treasure. Finally, the treasure hunter needs to dig *one cubit deep into the ground*,[27] then make three crosses on the earth, and repeat the incantation of the treasure.

Implicit in these detailed instructions is the common 17th century idea that treasures are moved around by spirits under the earth. We quote an illustrative summary of this popular belief from Johannes Dillinger's excellent 2011 book *Magical Treasure Hunting in Europe and North America: A History*:[28]

> *The early modern treasure was a magical object. In fact, it was so magical that it can hardly be described as an object in the modern sense. Treasures were supposed to be able to move under their own power. Even if learned demonologists wanted to see the devil at work here, the majority of "common people" seem to have considered the treasures themselves capable of purposeful and independent movement. Thus, treasures occasionally came to the surface of the earth to bask. In 1679, in the Holzgerlinger forest near Tübingen,*

26 Cod.Mag.55, 6 recto.

27 A *cubit* is approximately the length of an arm from the elbow to the tip of the middle finger.

28 Johannes Dillinger, *Auf Schatzsuche—Von Grabräubern, Geisterbeschwörern und anderen Jägern verborgener Reichtümer*, Freiburg: Herder Verlag, 2011.

> *a dig was made at a spot where an old woman claimed to have seen a treasure, "as one says, to bathe in the sun outside". Also near Hohenheim, a treasure was reported to have emerged from a field in thc 1740s to enjoy the sun. Treasures were supposed to be able to wander within a limited radius. In this way, they allegedly kept evading the treasure hunters. They fled from treasure hunters as game fled from hunters. If a mistake had been made in the manifold magical arrangements during the treasure hunt, the treasure escaped: the already discovered find could sink deeper into the earth before the eyes of the treasure diggers and thus elude their grasp again. A 17th century magic book from Transylvania recommended treasure hunters to carry a certain plant, presumably not garlic but chicory, to prevent the treasure from disappearing.*
>
> *[...]*
>
> *To prevent the treasure from escaping, it had to be "banished." This was done simply by throwing an object, usually coins, at it. In fact, it was supposed to be possible to "lure" the treasure by depositing money near it. In a very similar way, hunters pacified game by using a decoy.*[29]

It is only in light of this historic context that the pragmatism of the operation at the end of our manuscript unfolds. The divining rod was leveraged to indicate the general orbit where the treasure was supposed to dwell, then—at the expense of more coercive force—the treasure was approached as a living spirit itself and conjured into the magical circle. Thus, in this text the circle assumes the function of the traditional Solomonic triangle: it is not meant to protect the operator, but to confine the presence of the treasure. Finally, after giving the treasure-spirit two days to arrive in the marked location, the Olympic Spirit *Phaleg* is conjured to seal the deal, as the latter's power clearly was deemed more mighty and thus ruling over any kind of mischievous treasure-spirit.

The last rite, leveraging the active assistance of *Phaleg*, thus is markedly different from the previous twelve recipes. In the prior ex-

29 Dillinger 2011, p. 59–60, translation by author.

amples, *Och* is simply indicated as the general patron of the operations yet does not seem to hold an active role in the enforcing, punishing or healing acts described in traditional folk-magical style.

As we saw above, in the early tradition of the Olympic Spirits the one that is guided by their appearance in the *Arbatel* and Paracelsus' earlier works, we encounter these beings not at all as performative spirits of folk-magical nature. Quite the contrary: they are introduced as the highest rulers, of planetary nature and dignity. In short, they are "the noblest", as our manuscript recalls. To work practical magic through their agency, their function as gates of empowerment is leveraged, and under their aegis related spirits of lower hierarchies and ranks are assigned to and merged with the spirit of the operator.

After introducing the reader to many aspects of what we would thus dub the *original tradition* of the Olympic Spirits, the second half of the present manuscript stands in stark contrast. Here we encounter a derivative tradition that not only seems to take a pragmatic approach to mixing techniques, but is also of decidedly success-orientated nature. Furthermore, the second half is clearly written from an animistic perspective: not only do treasures come alive as travelling spirits in their own rights, but in the same vein all natural substances and ingredients are regarded as genuine carriers of spiritual substance and magical efficacy.

From here it is only a short distance to the *operative appeal* the Olympic Spirits seemed to have held since the early 18th century. Our manuscript might give one of the earliest known examples of such a *remix culture* relating to the Olympic Spirits.

Roughly two decades after the acquisition of the Leipzig grimoire collection, it was a much more popular release that fully cemented the above reputation of the Olympic Spirits. The full title of the anonymous catchpenny release from 1729 was *One Hundred Eight and Thirty Newly Discovered and Perfectly Proven Mysteries, Or all kinds of Magical, Spagyric, Sympathetic and Antipathetic Art Pieces, One of which alone has cost the owner a lot of money.*[30] Given as the 122th secret we hear the following of the Olympic Spirits:

30 Anonymous, *Hundert acht und dreyßig neu-entdeckte und vollkommen bewährte Geheimnüsse, Oder allerhand magische, spagyrische, sympathetische und antipathetische Kunst-Stücke, Derer eines allein den Besitzer viel Geld gekostet hat.* Franckfurt und Leipzig: Carl Christoph Immig, 1729.

Of the Olympic Spirits of Theophrastus.

Theophrastus' book of the Olympic Spirits is a purely nigromantic work, in which it is taught how to summon all sorts of spirits; each spirit has its signature and a certain metal on which the figures are engraved. The characters secretly hold within themselves the hidden pact with Satan and the pledge of the soul with such whimsical incantations and such strange names of the spirits that one can grasp the devil's antics with one's hands. The appearance of these spirits does not mean anything good either. One appears on a goat, another on a pig, the third on a monkey, and so on. These are all signs that no good spirits appear, but only the black angels, who do not do man any favours to serve him and let themselves be seen, except for the robbery of his soul. So there are several examples of how great evil has befallen one and another through such incantations, because the conjured spirit has come, but has twisted the neck of the conjurer. Therefore, the book serves as a warning to everyone to refrain from such works, which are highly detrimental to the soul, straight against God and His word, and not to be seduced by the good prayers mixed in, which are only added to blind people.[31]

The Vinculum SALOMONIS

I command and enjoin you and all your servants
and legions with the infernal fire and by
Laray ✠ Gemay ✠ Naly ✠ Arion ✠ Fateson ✠ fortissimus ✠ Immortalis ✠ potentissimus ✠ Cedoon ✠ Terribilis ✠ Joth, He, Vau He, ✠ Joth ✠ Agla ✠.

31 Anonymous, 1729, pp. 106–7, translation by author.

Dear Lord and God, I have sinned much against you,
but I call upon you as well as these holy names
Agios ✠ *otheos* ✠ *Athanatos* ✠ *Eleison miserere mei* ✠

May you graciously forgive our sinful iniquity,
that the spirits may be the better obedient to me.
Therefore, I quote you quickly, spirit N. together with your servants,
so that you may come without delay!

With humble heart, they shall accomplish my desire, for which you have created them. Come then, come! Visibly and in human form!

This I command all you spirits, in the name of the great and unspeakable torment and chastisement of the damned in hell! That you may accomplish this work for me now![32]

At the end of the manuscript, only followed by the double page design of the *Seal of Secrets*, we find a short version of the traditional *Vinculum of Solomon.*

Vinculum is the Latin word for a *bond* or for *that with which anything is bound*. It is derived from the verb *vincire*, to bind. The title *Bond of Solomon* is a standing term in Western Ritual Magic at least since the 14th century to identify a textual section that offers precisely that: the authority to call for, bind, and often release the respective spirit of one's operation.

> *In fact, the Vinculum is well attested in the magical tradition under the title Vinculum spirituum or Vinculum Salomonis.*[33]

Johannes Trithemius mentions it as a discrete book in the famous list of necromantic texts in his *Antipalus Maleficiorum.*

32 Cod.Mag.55, 7 recto–8 verso. *(See page 382 for full page setting of prayer).*

33 Florence Chave-Mahir and Julien Véronèse (ed.) 2015, p. 118, translation by author.

> *There is also a book, called vinculum spirituum [the bond of spirits], containing many prayers and conjurations, through which vain men and lost daemons trust that they can bind each other to every kind of obedience. This book begins as follows: We must not be silent about the bond of spirits.*[34]

As Julien Véronèse and Florence Chave-Mahir observed in their masterful analysis of a late 14th century ritual compendium,[35] the *Vinculum* exists in many variants, most of them not preserved as stand-alone manuscripts but as elements of larger magical or exorcist literature. Its length, content and structure, therefore, can vary significantly. Some variants contain full prologues, historiolae, conjurations, as well as exorcisms or licence to depart.

The assumption is obvious that the *Vinculum of Solomon* is not only closely related to the *Key of Solomon*, but that the latter text served as its direct model.[36] In this case, the *Vinculum* would have to be seen as a pragmatic abbreviation and condensation of the ritual instructions, prayers and conjurations of the Key of *Solomon* into a single, easily transferable and applicable text. Thus, in the *Vinculum* we might encounter the attempt to extract from the Solomonic Tradition a portable general key which could be used (especially by laymen) uncompromisingly and without context as a ritual matrix for any magical operation.

We close our brief exposition on the *Vinculum* with the concluding observations given by Véronèse and Chave-Mahir in their excellent study. While we encountered the *Vinculum* in an explicitly magical manuscript, their significantly older text from the late 14th-

34 *Est quoque liber, dictus vinculum spirituum, multas continens orationes et conjurationes, per quas vanissimi homines et perditi daemonas se posse constringere ad omnimodam obedientiam confidunt. Hic liber sic incipit: De vinculo spirituum non est silendum.* Johannes Trithemius, Antipalus Maleficiorum, Mainz: Balthasar Lippium, written 1508, published 1605, Book I, Chapter III, p. 300.

35 Julien Véronèse and Florence Chave-Mahir (eds.), *Ritual d'exorcisme ou manuel de magie? Le manuscrit Clm 10085 de la Bayrische Staatsbibliothek de Munich (début du XVe siècle)*, Florence: SISMEL Edizioni del Galluzzo, 2015.
Access of the digital manuscript version: https://www. digitale-sammlungen.de/en/view/bsb00048180?page=,1

36 Véronèse 2015, p. 121.

century (Clm 10085) presents a fascinating hybrid between heretical grimoire and orthodox exorcism.

> *The Vinculum spirituum makes the coercion of demons its primary function [...]: more than expelling demons, it always aims at commanding and dominating them by "binding" them. This coercion is made possible by the divine names revealed to the ancients (Adam, Noah, Aaron, Moses, David, Solomon, etc.), jealously guarded and preserved by the sages over the generations, and which take effect on the demons due to their highly sacred character, like so many implacable vincula.*
>
> *The principle of the revelation of these names to divinely inspired authorities is not strictly coincidental on the onomastic level. [...] In the Vinculum, however, the time of revelation also includes the New Testament and thus Christian history, as the numerous implicit references to Revelation [...] show. Moreover, the distribution of these names in the Vinculum, whatever the version, is not random; on the contrary, it rigorously follows the order of biblical history, which is also that of Revelation (and thus of the revelation of the names), [...] which is proof, if proof were needed, of an elaboration in a clerical milieu.*
>
> *Some of the names listed in this text are recognised as canonical by Christian tradition (El, Adonay, Sabaoth, On, etc.), but many are not. Their massive presence in magical contexts, which establishes the art of conjuration as a divine art, contrasts with their near absence in the canonical exorcism formulae in use in the West, where their strange form makes them suspect [...]*
>
> *The true exorcist does not normally act by virtue of these mysterious names, but only by virtue of God, Christ, the Virgin, the saints, and all the elements that recall Christian history, dogma, and customs. Their presence in this Ritual of Exorcism is therefore surprising and shows that, for some clerics, the supposed impermeability between the two domains—one legitimate, the other illicit—was neither self-ev-*

ident nor an insurmountable barrier, contrary to the wishes expressed by theologians.[37]

VI

Restoring the Seal of Secrets

IN APHORISM §27 the Arbatel provides detailed instructions for the design of a *Seal of Secrets* (*Sigillum Secretorum*). While not illustrated in the original *Arbatel*, our manuscript on pages 9 verso and recto contains an alleged rendering of this seal. Unfortunately, the design of Cod.Mag.55 has little to do with the instructions given in the *Arbatel*. As such, it either represents a misinterpreted version of the seal, or a personal innovation of the anonymous operator of our manuscript.

In 2019 Joseph H. Peterson provided a clean rendering of the seal,[38] another version of which, according to him, is included in the collection of magical treatises from the 14th to the 17th century *Tractatus et experimenta magica*.[39] While Peterson's rendering renders a clean and slightly corrected version of the one included in Cod.Mag.55, he does not call out the misrepresentation of the actual instructions of the *Arbatel*. These read as follows:

> *Make a Circle with a center A, which is B. C. D. E. At the East let there be B. C. a square. At the North, C. D. At the West, D. E. And at the South, E. D. [E. B.] Divide the Several quadrants into seven parts, that there may be in the whole 28 parts: and let them be again divided into four parts, that there may be 112 parts of the Circle: and so many are the true secrets to be revealed. And this Circle in this manner divided, is the seal of the secrets of the world, which they draw from the onely center A, that is, from the invisible God, unto the whole creature. The Prince of the Oriental secrets is resident*

37 Ibid., pp. 125–127, translation by author.

38 Not included in his 2009 print edition of the *Arbatel*, but accessible in his online version under: http://www.esotericarchives.com/solomon/arbatel.htm

39 MSS Sloane 3851, fol. 10r–29v.

> *in the middle, and hath three Nobles on either side, every one whereof hath four under him, and the Prince himself hath four appertaining unto him. And in this manner the other Princes and Nobles have their quadrants of secrets, with their four secrets.*
>
> *But the Oriental [Eastern] secret is the study of all wisdom; The West, of strength; The South, of tillage; The North, of more rigid life. So that the Eastern secrets are commended to be the best; the Meridian [Southern] to be mean; and the West and North to be lesser.*[40]

It seems what led the author of Cod.Mag.55 astray, is the numeric unison between the number of the seven Olympic Spirits and the division of each quadrant into seven and 28 in total. Thus, they assigned tutelage of the Olympic Spirits over the seven parts within each quadrant in a cyclical manner.

Such design is obviously reminiscent of a classical *tabula lunarium*, depicting the 28 mansions of the Moon with their assigned angels.[41] However, it has nothing to do with the instructions provided to us by the *Arbatel*.

The above illustration is a graphical transcription of the instructions given in the *Arbatel* on the *Seal of Secrets*, as exact and unbiased as I was able to render it. The only liberty I took was the sequential numbering of the satraps for better readability. The important point here is that each Prince in each cardinal direction is surrounded by six satraps.

The garbled design of the *Seal of Secrets* in our document is another example of Western magicians' dysfunctional obsession with the orthodoxy of spirit names and seals. The desire to have a constant catalogue of pinned-down spirit identities strangles the necessary insight that spirit communion is first and foremost a *natural and organic process*. Like all processes in nature, it is highly sensitive and subjected to the tides of time and place as well as to the spirit of the

40 *Arbatel*, §Aphorism 27, in: Peterson 2009, pp. 57–59.

41 A beautiful modern rendition of such circular tables was created in 2009 by Joseph Uccello and released by Ouroboros Press in partnership with Viatorium Press. Details of its creation process can still be found here: http://bibliomancer.blogspot.com/2010/03/tabula-lunarium.html

operator themselves. Thus, spirit names and seals are entrusted personally and individually to each magician once contact has been created. They are *seals* in the most literal sense: textual and graphical *imprints left behind* by the spirit contact we were able to facilitate and uphold.

The origination of personalised spirit names and seals therefore always flows out of individual spirit contact and does not precede it.

What magicians anchor themselves in to create first-time contact with a spirit is their *office*, that is, their *function in nature*. Such act could not be simpler, and generations of magicians have been guilty of making this overly complex since the emergence of the *Arbatel* in 1575: the spirit of the wind is called *wind*, the spirit of an Eastern wind is called *East wind*. The spirit of a lake or river is called precisely that: the spirit that enlivens and guards *this* lake or *that* river.

Ironically, despite all the misunderstanding in subsequent centuries, the *Arbatel* is most explicit about this point. It emphasises that "the characters and names of stars have not power by reason of their figure or pronunciation, but by reason of the virtue or office which God hath ordained by nature."[42] Even more directly, it advises in Aphorism §13 that the magician's "GOAL therefore must be that you master the names of the spirits, that is their office and powers". Before giving the names and descriptions of the Olympic Spirits, it repeats again:

> *Magically the Princes of the seven Governments are called simply, in that time, day and hour wherein they rule visibly or invisibly, by their Names and Offices which God hath given unto them; and by proposing their Character which they have given or confirmed.*[43]

Logically, in our first conjuration of a spirit we go by their function in nature (i.e., *office*) alone. Once this has successfully been accomplished, contact will be facilitated through the personal name and seal or character this spirit might have offered us.

42 *Arbatel*, Aphorism §8, in: Peterson 2009, p. 17.
43 *Arbatel*, Aphorism §17, in: Peterson 2009, p. 31.

> *All evocation of spirits is of one kind and form, and this is the method used in former times by the Sibyls and high priests. In our time this is totally lost, due to ignorance and impiety.*[44]

Just like Franz Bardon in *The Practice of Magical Evocation*[45] over 150 pages shares the personal seals and names of the *Ur-intelligences of the Earthbelt-zone*, so the *Arbatel* almost four hundred years earlier shared the seals and names of the seven Olympic Spirits with us: precisely not to use them as carbon copies for our own practice, but as possible traps for the lazy practitioner.

At best, these individual names and seals can offer organic starting points for our own exploration. At worst, they congeal into venerated artefacts of man-made orthodoxy.

VII

The *Seal of Secrets* as a BOOK OF SPIRITS

BUT IF NAMES and seals should not be leveraged as anchor points to create first-time spirit contact, what could a *book of spirits* look like? The *Arbatel*'s answer is given in the *Seal of Secrets*.

The seal divides the circle of the Nature into four quarters. Each quarter is governed by a Prince whose kingdom represents one of the four essential realms of human life:

THE axis of Wisdom (i.e., knowing what not to will and what to will) and Strength (i.e., the ability to do what we will) running East to West;

THE axis of Rigid Life (i.e. respecting the necessities of Nature) to Tillage (i.e., making human life prosperous) running North to South.

44 *Arbatel*, Aphorism §34, in: Peterson 2009, p. 69.

45 Franz Bardon, *Die Praxis der magischen Evokation. Anleitung zur Anrufung von Wesen uns umgebender Sphären*. Freiburg im Breisgau: Bauer Verlag, 1956.

These four kingdoms then open up into an array of possible spirit relationships with four Lower Magistrates under each Satrap and the respective Prince.

Faced with this *book of spirits in the form of a single seal*, the preeminent question for the mage no longer is whether they have cryptically extracted an individual's spirit seal or name from the work of their human predecessors. The question that matters most is, rather, whether the mage truly knows the nature of their desire and where the fulfilling agent of this desire *is located in the map of Nature.*

Allow me to provide a few mundane examples.

THE desire to grow one's business would reside under the celestial tutelage of *Bethor* and under the telluric governance of the Prince of the South, who resides over the kingdom of *tillage* i.e., of making human life prosperous.

THE desire to win a court case would reside under the celestial tutelage of *Ophiel*. However, the decision under which Prince's governance to place one's inquiry could lead it into very different directions and thus attract very different spirits for companionship:

IF I want support to repel and defeat an unfair attack from my opponent's solicitor I might place my request under the Prince of the North (*rigid life*). But then I have to accept that I am invoking the merciless spirits who work to uphold Nature's own laws. Could this backfire on my own position?

IF I want to boost the smartness and tactical agility of my own legal counsel, I might place my request under the Prince of the East (*wisdom*). That looks good at first glance. But what might be wise in the eyes of the spirit evoked might not be helpful in terms of my mundane intentions. Again, careful alignment as well as mutual understanding between spirit and human operator are of the essence.

IF I simply want to assert my position and dominion in the case, I'd go with the Prince of the West (*strength*). But is being perceived as strong really the same as coming out of the court case successfully in the end? And if I invoke the spirits of strength, might I inadvertently increase the price at stake?

FINALLY, if I want to go straight to the ultimate outcome of the court case, I could turn to the Prince of the South (*tillage*). Now I am focused on the gain derived from winning the case as such. This could look like a smart choice, as it skips over the dynamics of the process as such and remains anchored in the ultimate goal alone.

As we can see, the work with the *Seal of Secrets* requires careful consideration on the operator's side. Just like with most divination techniques or in applied sigil-magic, identifying the essential nature of our question is one of the most difficult and yet most critical parts of any magical operation.

With *heart, head* and *hand*, we need to master the art of bringing the compass rose of our inner intention in harmony with the compass rose of the spirits surrounding us.

Once we have locked into a specific intention, the work becomes relatively straightforward. Now it is a matter of holding onto this clear purpose, of calling upon the tutelage of the respective Olympic Spirit, and asking the responding spirit to step forward from the kingdom of the associated Prince.

> *When he perceives incorporeal agents around himself, with either the outer or the inner senses, then he should govern himself in accordance with the following seven laws for the work of magic.*[46]

Once the spirit is present with us, the *Arbatel* in Aphorism §40 instructs us to observe seven simple rules, or "laws" as it terms them. I am rephrasing these seven principles here in order to make them more accessible and tangible to modern practitioners.

1 UNDERSTAND that any act of magic is an act of stepping closer to the scales of Justice and Fate.[47] Thus, whatever we do now, we need to be ready to accept the full consequences of it.

2 ENSURE we are not guided by our human desires and ego, but by our "Holy Spirit".[48] That is, the power to resist our own temptations and to decipher lies from truth.

46 *Arbatel*, Aphorism §40, in: Peterson 2009, p. 81.

47 To learn more about this magical concept and the essential dynamics of creation, I recommend the careful study of the respective Apprentice section in the *Quareia* curriculum: https://www.quareia.com/apprentice-module-3

48 *Arbatel*, Aphorism §40, in: Perterson 2009, p. 83.

3 TEST the spirit(s) that appeared with us according to their own nature and intent. Are these truly the right spirit companions for the work at hand? Can we trust them?

4 GUARD our own emotions and fantasies, and stay fully anchored in the pragmatics of the magical operation at hand.

5 AVOID turning the spirit allies who present themselves into idols. We are all here to do good work together, not to romanticise or idolise what happened or will happen next.

6 UNDERSTAND the motives of the spirit(s) we work with. They also have an agenda, a will and a desire on their side. In order not to give them an incentive to deceive us, what consideration do we offer them?

7 CENTER ourselves in communion with our holy daimon i.e. the personal spirit directly involved in guarding our personal fate-pattern. While performative success magic always is an option, the question we might want to ask ourselves is: are we still on a path that will "improve our whole heart"?

All MAGIC is the revelation of that class of spirit, of which nature the magic is.[49]

The highest teaching of magic is to understand what should be accepted from an attending spirit, and what should be rejected.[50]

49 *Arbatel*, Aphorism §48, in: Peterson 2009, p. 97
50 *Arbatel*, Aphorism §45, in: Peterson 2009, p. 91.

VIII

A Ritual of the *Seal of Secrets*

I AM DELIBERATELY presenting the following summary as *an* operative framework and by no means *the* definite version of it. The intention is to consolidate the above findings—both from the analysis of Cod.Mag.55 as well as the original *Arbatel*—into a framework of action which reveals a possible approach the anonymous operator of our manuscript might have taken in practice. Or one we might choose to practice today.

The tension we won't be able to bridge, however, is the essential difference in tone of the two source texts at hand. The *Arbatel*'s goals for magic are remarkably "transcendent" as A. E. Waite, or "lofty" as Joseph H. Peterson called them.[51] *The Conjuration of the Olympic Spirits*, on the other hand, does not shy away from getting its hands dirty and drawing the Olympic Spirits alongside with it.

Instead of attempting to resolve this tension, I invite everyone to embrace it. As many of us will have found, *evolution* and *involution* can be practiced in a mutually enriching way as part of one's magical path. Where we will all need to make our own wise choices is with regards to the kinds of spirits we are willing to affiliate with. As the *Arbatel* says, the spirits we decide to commune with hold access to our soul. Summoning demons according to the flavour of one's day, coercing them to become the Swiss Army knife of one's life in terms of ubiquitous utility, simply doesn't seem to be a smart or sustainable choice within such a paradigm.

> *The HUMAN SOUL is the SOLE producer of wonders, to the extent that it is joined with the chosen spirit; once joined it will reveal what you desire. Therefore we must proceed CAUTIOUSLY in acts of MAGIC, lest we be cheated by sirens and monsters. Who are also attracted to the HUMAN SOUL.*[52]

51 Peterson 2009, XVIII.

52 *Arbatel*, Aphorism §35, in: Peterson 2009, pp. 69–71.

Whatever you will have learned, repeat it often, and fix it in your mind, and learn much, but not many things, because the human mind cannot be equally capable in all things [...][53]

With this in mind, we can sketch out the following reconstructed ritual to work with the Seal of Secrets. We will do this in two different versions. First a classical one, in tune with the Late Medieval magic referenced in Cod.Mag.55. Following this, we will offer a second version more aligned to the Olympic Spirit work we presented in the previous chapter of this book.

Version 1
THE RITUAL OF THE *SEAL OF SECRETS*

PRELIMINARY NOTE: This is a ritual for the advanced practitioner. We will not repeat here the usual introductions and prerequisites for successful ritual magic. Instead, we rely on your basic practice and your ability to integrate the following suggestions and hints in a useful manner.[54]

START with attuning your life to the principles defined in the first two septenaries of the *Arbatel*. Einstein is quoted as having said: "If I had an hour to solve a problem I'd spend 55 minutes thinking about the problem and five minutes thinking about solutions." The same principle applies here. Everything given in the first 14 aphorisms of the *Arbatel* contains the foundations and essence of how to lead a magical life, both in theory and practice.

53 *Arbatel*, Aphorism §35, in: Peterson 2009, p. 15.

54 In case you are not yet at this stage and have to build stronger practical foundations first, I recommend the following titles: Josephine McCarthy, *The Magical Knowledge Trilogy*, Exeter: TaDehent Books, 2020. Frater U∴D∴, *High Magic: Theory & Practice*, St. Paul: Llewellyn Publications, 2005. Frater U∴D∴, *High Magic II: Expanded Theory and Practice*, St.Paul: Llewellyn Publications, 2008. Jake Stratton-Kent, *The True Grimoire*, London: Scarlet Imprint, 2022.

Examples of the *Seal of Secrets* as a Book of Spirits

		East ***WISDOM*** *Greatest Secrets*	South ***CULTURE*** *Medium Secrets*	West ***STRENGTH*** *Lesser Secrets*	North ***A RIGID LIFE*** *Lesser Secrets*
ARATRON Saturn	¶ All things naturally created ¶ Turning things to Stone ¶ Treasures into coal and vice versa ¶ Granting familiars ¶ Teaches alchemy, healing and magic ¶ Unites pygmies to people ¶ Rendering one invisible ¶ Fertility & longevity	ANGEL OF *Wisdom*	ANGEL OF *Healing*	ANGEL OF *Endurance*	ANGEL OF *Fortification*
BETHOR Jupiter	¶ Achieving dignities ¶ Finding treasures ¶ Cooperation of aerial spirits (to provide precious stones or miraculous medicines) ¶ Familiars of the firmament ¶ Prolongs life to 700 years	ANGEL OF *Treasures*	ANGEL OF *Wealth*	ANGEL OF *Nobility*	ANGEL OF *Eternity*
OCH Sun	¶ Achieving wisdom ¶ Grants excellent spirits ¶ Teaches perfect medicine ¶ Achieves alchemical transmutation ¶ Provides honour of other rulers	ANGEL OF *Philosophy*	ANGEL OF *Alchemy*	ANGEL OF *Honour*	ANGEL OF *Domination*
PHALEG Mars	¶ Achieving peace ¶ Ascending to highest military dignities	ANGEL OF *Artfulness*	ANGEL OF *Embodiment*	ANGEL OF *Victory*	ANGEL OF *Attack*
HAGITH Venus	¶ Becoming Beautiful and Attractive ¶ Turning copper to gold and vice versa ¶ Grants spirits who will serve faithfully	ANGEL OF *Beauty*	ANGEL OF *Love*	ANGEL OF *Desire*	ANGEL OF *Servitude*
OPHIEL Mercury	¶ Grants familiar spirits readily ¶ Teaches all arts and provides dignity ¶ Turns Mercury into Philosopher's Stone	ANGEL OF *Mathematics*	ANGEL OF *Speediness*	ANGEL OF *Memory*	ANGEL OF *Prudence*
PHUL Moon	¶ Changes all metals into Silver ¶ Governs all Lunar matters and things ¶ Cures edema (dropsy) ¶ Grants spirits of the water that serve physical and invisible form. ¶ Prolongs life to 300 years	ANGEL OF *Divination*	ANGEL OF *Seasons*	ANGEL OF *Resilience*	ANGEL OF *Fear*

AS you are preparing for this rite, sketch the *Seal of Secrets* on a sheet of paper by hand. The diameter and text should be large enough that you can easily read it in the conditions under which you will perform this rite. So consider how bright or dim the light will be, the available space on your altar etc.

WHEN the moment to perform your operation has come, ensure you are working under a good star. A proficient astrologer will know which calculations to perform. A lay-astrologer will avoid dominant and obtrusive positions of Mars and Saturn in particular. Of course, choosing a day and hour when the associated planet of the respective Olympic Spirit is in elevation will be helpful as well.

SEARCH out a quiet place where your work will neither be observed nor disturbed for the duration of the operation. This can be outdoors in a remote location, or indoors in a locked room.

DRAW out the circle as given in the text. Or, if you consider its given version as incomplete or garbled, design a circle that is in tune with your magical paradigm. In doing so, always ensure to follow the logic of spirits, not the logic of humans.

RECITE the *Vinculum Salomonis*. Or, if you consider its given version as incomplete or garbled, design your own prayer, conjuration and licence to depart that is in tune with the operation at hand. Pay specific attention under whose protection you are planning to perform this act. Meticulously avoid including any divine, daemonic or traditional names who you are not intentionally calling up to oversee and partake in your work. For example, do not call upon the Biblical *El*, *Sadai*, *IHVH*, *Aaron*, *David*, *Enoch* etc. unless you know exactly who they are and how this will affect your rite.

CONJURE the respective Olympic Spirit associated with your operation. Or, if this is your first act, consider summoning *Aratron* initially and asking for their permission to associate with the spirits under their general dominion. If you have observed the first step well enough, this step should not pose significant problems. The conjuration of the Olympic Spirit is as much a call from your heart-space as it is one from your lips. Consider placing the seal of the respective Olympic Spirit into the centre of the *Seal of Secrets* and to focus your entire presence on this point.

ONCE the tutelage and presence of the Olympic Spirit is established, use the *Seal of Secrets* to call forth the performative spirit relevant to your specific operation. This can be done e.g., by turning in the adequate cardinal direction, calling for the Prince, stating your desired goal and asking them for their permission to work with one of their spirits. Then, observe how they respond or who will approach you.

ALTERNATIVELY, you could work with the table below or develop your own version of it. It is based upon the seven Olympic Spirits and the four cardinal directions with their essential qualities according to the *Arbatel*. Which quality therefore do you see reside under which Olympic Spirit in each quarter? The below is my own attempt of a map. I recommend creating your own, and then validate it in practice.

YOU can consider asking the appearing spirit to identify themselves on the *Seal of Secrets*. I.e., are they one of the Princes, Satraps or Lower Magistrates? Asking the spirit to identify their precise location on the *Seal of Secrets* will allow you to validate their nature and remember their position for future communions.

NOW work with the respective spirit to fulfil the purpose of this rite. Ideally, under first-time conditions, this should include getting to know the spirit, possibly receiving their personalised names and seals, negotiating what you are willing to afford each other, by when your request might be fulfilled and what you will do in return etc.

Allow the spirit to depart.

FROM here onwards, holding the personalised name and seal of the spirit in your hands should be sufficient for your mind to reconnect with the conscious of the respective spirit. Because remember, this spirit now holds access to your soul.

Version 2
THE RITE OF THE SEAL OF SECRETS

PRELIMINARY NOTE: This is a ritual for the advanced practitioner. We will not repeat here the usual introductions and prerequisites for successful visionary magic. Instead, we rely on your basic practice and your ability to integrate the following suggestions and hints in a useful way.[55]

55 In case you are not yet at this stage and have to build stronger practical foun-

START with attuning your life to the principles defined in the first two septenaries of the *Arbatel*. Einstein is quoted as having said: "If I had an hour to solve a problem I'd spend 55 minutes thinking about the problem and five minutes thinking about solutions." The same principle applies here. Everything given in the first 14 aphorisms of the *Arbatel* contains the foundations and essence of how to lead a magical life, both in theory and practice.

AS you are preparing for this rite, sketch the *Seal of Secrets* on a sheet of paper by hand. The diameter and text should be large enough that you can easily read it in the conditions under which you will perform this rite. So consider how bright or dim the light will be, the available space on your altar etc. Also, equip yourself with a small handbell. Finally, make sure to know which of the seven Olympic Spirits you will be conjuring: whether you will start with *Aratron* as the general mediator of the other spirits, or whether you want to go directly to one of the other six Olympic Spirits. It all depends on your experience in these things as well as the nature of your intent for this rite. According to this, you should also know the cardinal direction associated with your intent.

FIND a quiet place where you will not be disturbed. Face whichever cardinal direction according to the description of the *Arbatel* is broadly associated with your intent. Sit or stand in a comfortable position with your back upright. Place the bell in a position where you can easily reach it.

TAKE a few deep breaths to centre yourself. Then close your eyes.

IN your mind's eye, see yourself in the middle of a circle of approximately two to three meters (six to nine feet) in diameter.

COME to realise the flame that is quietly burning in your heartspace. When you can feel its presence, pull a spark from it in vision and place it before you. (Note: If you are working with an altar, the spark is now hovering over the centre of the altar.)

WITNESS how the light of this spark is intensifying, growing into a flame and expanding to all sides. The inside of the circle you are sitting in is growing lighter and lighter.

AFTER a while, you should see yourself inside a brightly glowing sphere of light. Nothing can penetrate this shield that surrounds you. Hand over any disturbing thoughts arising from within you to

---

dations first, please see the literature recommended in the prior footnote.

the light around you and allow them to be burned away. Enjoy the present experience of being embalmed, breathing through all the pores of your body and mind in this sphere of light. you are sitting in the essence of life.

WHEN you are ready, take the bell, ring it once, then intone your conjuration of the Olympic Spirit under whose patronage you have come to work.[56] Repeat the conjuration as often as required, but do not ring the bell more than once.

DIFFERENT to our work in the preceding chapter, the Olympic Spirit will not appear in any of the "corners" of the circle that surrounds you. Instead, you shall see it form a second sphere above your own. Observe the colour, texture and dynamic of this sphere, and see if you can perceive the Olympic Spirit's form within it. Remember that these celestial beings do not have *one form* just like they do not have *one name* or *seal*. What you are looking for is to see *your-and-their form*, that is the form in this present moment, in which the Olympic Spirit and you create a bond in vision.[57]

WHEN the Olympic Spirit is fully present and the sphere above you as solid as the one you are protected by, state the intention of your rite. Ask the Olympic Spirit to show you the spirit with whom you should be working to accomplish this operation.

NOW remain open and unbiased in your mind's vision. Do not force any images to appear, in order not to mix human fantasies with the realities your imagination is able to capture in vision. Unless

56 Yes, intentionally there is no template for this conjuration. You will need to write your own during the time of preparation for this rite. As mentioned earlier, pay particular attention that it does not include any divine, daemonic or traditional names you are not intentionally calling to oversee and partake in your work. For example, do not call upon the Biblical *El, Sadai, IHVH, Aaron, David, Enoch* etc. unless you know exactly who they are and how this will affect your rite. You will find plenty of guidance in the *Arbatel* itself for this work, but also some false leads.

57 From personal experience I recommend to ensure that the sphere of light you are standing or sitting in at all times remains *strictly separate* from the sphere of the Olympic Spirit. Keep them distinct, like pearls on a string, as tempting as it might be to *draw down* the presence and power of an Olympic Spirit into your own sphere. Our human bodies are not made to endure the unmediated presence of the Olympic Spirits. You might pay for a moment of high endorphins and the *inside view* of an Olympic Spirit with chronic mental and/or physical illnesses afterwards. The beauty and tragedy of all magic is that at all times we are truly free to choose.

the Olympic Spirit is offering to work with you directly, you will see a performative spirit step forward from any point of the circle around you. Obviously you are now standing in the middle of the *Seal of Secrets* yourself: the spirit could appear from the cardinal point you are facing; but it could also appear from anywhere else if the Olympic Spirit sees a different logic of how to best support your intent. Remain entirely open until you see the spirit appearing in a particular section of the circle surrounding you.

THEN ask the spirit to identify itself on the *Seal of Secrets*. I.e., is it one of the Princes, Satraps or Lower Magistrates? Asking the spirit to identify its precise location on the *Seal of Secrets* will allow you to validate its nature and remember its position for future communions.

NOW work with the spirit to fulfil the purpose of this rite. Ideally, under first-time conditions, this should include getting to know the spirit, possibly receiving itsr personalised name and seal, negotiating what you are willing to afford each other, by when your request might be fulfilled, and what you will do in return etc.

WHEN you are done, allow the spirit to depart.

FROM here onwards, holding the personalised name and seal of the spirit in your hands should be sufficient for your mind to reconnect with the conscious of the respective spirit. Because remember: this spirit now holds access to your soul.

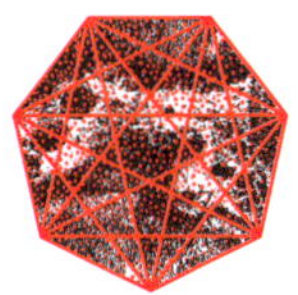

BOOK 2

CHAPTER III

THE OLYMPIC SPIRITS AS FAMILIARS

Introduction

YOU HAVE ARRIVED at the shortest chapter in the present book. Fortunately, though, brevity does not equate with superficiality. Taken on its own, the succinct excerpt at the end of this chapter is marked by a casualness that contrasts sharply with its significance when read in the context of the preceding chapters. We established that Paracelsus first coined the term OLYMPIC SPIRIT(S) in 1531/1532, when he wrote *De causis morborum invisibilium*, which was printed posthumously in 1564. He expanded on the nature of these spirit(s) in many of his other works and especially in his magnum opus, the *Philosophia Sagax*, written in 1537 and first printed in 1571. Four years later, in 1575, the Olympic Spirits received the *grimoire treatment* with the original publication of the *Arbatel*. With the help of the *Arbatel* and Cod.Mag.55, we have taken the liberty of translating the *Arbatel*'s hints into the construction and practice of the *Seal of Secrets* into two ritual variants which are now open for your own validation.

What we want to illustrate now is how deeply and firmly the Olympic Spirits became embedded in the (German) folk magic of the 17th century. Whether this in turn should inspire similar modern practices, we want to leave to every reader's personal discretion.

From a purely historic perspective the following example may illustrate how complete and radical the uprooting of the Olympic Spirits from their Paracelsian soil had been effected even before the onset of the 18th century. At first glance, any echo of man's inner firmament or their role as celestial mediums of creation seems to have evaporated. Simultaneously, what is left of them looks to have been forced to fit the general mould of folk-grimoires. Not surprisingly, their trace in (literary) history is no longer marked by their embeddedness in a broader animistic cosmos but by the imprints that were meant to be recreated by each practitioner in their own time and place: their spirit seals and purported names according to the *Arbatel*. However, from a practical magical perspective, as always, things are much more ambiguous and open to interpretation. At least theoretically, the truncation of the Olympic Spirits in the present example does not make any absolute statement on the absence of a deeper understanding of their nature by the respective practitioner.

Placing your kitchen under the aegis of *Aratron* and your bedchamber under the guardianship of *Hagith* displays a level of folk magical attitude and pragmatism that many rituals of learned magic never will achieve. In fact, in a possibly accidental expansion, working with the Olympic Spirits as *lares* or *household deities* echoes their original function as celestial spirits within the body of man, only that the realm of the microcosm was expanded to include one's entire hearth and house. As such, I am sharing the following example as more than a historic footnote. Rather, I like to read it as an expressly modern reminder to never allow one's practice to become constrained by orthodoxy.

I

The Manuscript Cod.Mag.66

THE FOLLOWING PASSAGE is taken from the manuscript titled *Magia de Furto* (*Magic of Theft*) and registered as Cod.mag.66[1] in the *Leipzig Collection of Grimoires*.[2] As mentioned in the preceding

1 https://histbest.ub.uni-leipzig.de/receive/UBLHistBestCBU_cbu_00000089

2 https://www.ub.uni-leipzig.de/aktuelle-ausstellungen/zauber-buecher-die-

chapter, the entire collection was acquired by the Leipzig University in 1710. Cod.mag.66 was identified as a translation from an earlier Latin text. Thus, it should be dated to the late 17th century or earlier.

The text was first spotted by Adolf Spamer (1883–1953) to contain a reference to the Olympic Spirits. Still a figure overlooked in English-speaking countries, Spamer was a preeminent scholar in establishing both the field of German V*olkskunde* (folklore) as well as specifically the academic research on the grimoire tradition. His 23,000-item strong slip box collection *Corpus der Segen und Beschwörungsformeln* (*Corpus of Benedictions and Conjurations*) contains an unparalleled number of transcripts of benedictions, conjurations, charms, amulets, celestial letters, and letters of protection dating from the Middle Ages to the 1960s.[3] The current excerpt forms part of the collection under the keyword *Confronting Thieves* (*Diebesstellung*—III C1).[4]

A full translation of the *Magia de Furto* is still outstanding. From an initial overview, though, it keeps the promise made by its full title: *MAGIA DE FURTO that is various secrets to keep one's things from thieves, to banish thieves so that they have to bring back the stolen goods, also to torment and damage such* [*people*] *in various manners.*[5]

Accordingly, Bellingradt and Otto in their survey of the Leipzig grimoire collection give us the following summary:

> *Cod.mag.66 is all about protecting one's goods from thieves, regaining stolen goods, and punishing or torturing thieves by different procedures. These include the use of protective prayers, sigils and charactêres, various types of divination, and the construction of a sophisticated figurine of the thief. The technical terminology used throughout the text reveals*

leipziger-magica-sammlung-im-schatten-der-frue-haufklaerung/—for an indexed list of the grimoire manuscripts included see: http://studies-vartejaru.blogspot.com/2013/08/complete-list-of-leipzig-university.html

3 Available for digital access in German: https://www.isgv.de/projekte/volkskunde/erschli

4 Accessed on 01/07/2022: http://digital.slub-dresden.de/idDE-611-BF-67803

5 In the original: *MAGIA DE FURTO das ist Unterschiedene Geheimnüße, Seine Sachen vor dieben zu verwahren, diebe zu bannen, daß sie den diebstabl müßen wiederbringen, auch solche auf unterschiedene art zu peinigen und zu lædiren.*

that the text has been translated from Latin, and a Latin reader has indeed amended lengthy commentaries—which include alternative recipes—in the margins of some pages. Some of the recipes in this book resemble prescriptions in the nineteenth century German compilation Romanus-büchlein.[6]

II

The Olympic Spirits as *Lares*

WHAT MAKES THIS example stand out from the broad array of appearances of the Olympic Spirits in 17th to 19th century folk magic is their explicit use as *household deities*, or *lares* in their original Latin term.

As we can see from the below translation, their application is both innovative as well as eclectic. Three of the seven Olympic Spirits are assigned to specific rooms or spaces in and around a house. Following common practice, known already from Archaic Greek and Jewish traditions, their names and brief conjurations could have been written directly on the crossbeam of the respective door or on a paper-note which then was fixed there or slipped into the wall.[7]

IN a seeming act of apotropaic magic *Aratron*, the Olympic Spirit assigned to *Saturn*, is asked to guard the domestic places that otherwise would be considered most vulnerable to the negative impact of Saturnian forces i.e. loss, hunger and poverty. Thus, *Aratron* is requested to protect the kitchen, larder and all other locations

6 D. Bellingradt and B. C. Otto, Magical Manuscripts in Early Modern Europe, Cham: Palgrave Macmillan, 2017, with an open access appendix: *THE CATALOGUS RARIORUM MANUSCRIPTORUM* https://link.springer.com › bbm:978-3-319-59525-2 › 1.pdf

7 For further reference on the magical use of doors see for example: (1) Hanns Bächtold-Stäubli (ed.), *Handwörterbuch des deutschen Aberglaubens*, Augsburg: Weltbild, Vol. 8, 2000, columns 1185–1209, (2) Heinrich Cornelius Agrippa, *Three Books of Occult Philosophy*, Book 1, Chapter 42, Rochester: Inner Traditions, pp. 140–1, (3) Pliny the Elder, *Natural History*, Book 28, Chapter 27 (4) Aletta Seifert, *Der Sakrale Schutz von Grenzen im Antiken Griechenland—Formen und Ikonographie*, Freiburg 2006.

where food for animals are stored.

Bethor, the Olympic Spirit associated with Jupiter, finds a more traditional application and is asked to guard the study—the traditional place of domestic learning, writing and reading.

Finally, *Hagith*, the Olympic Spirit associated with Venus, is asked to protect the domestic locations of rest, renewal, intimacy, as well as—if ever practiced—of incubation and dream-magic.

The short excerpt below refers to this practice as given by an anonymous *theologus* at an unspecified time in the past. While it is positioned as a practice explicitly against thievery, the text also recognises the three Olympic Spirits as general "laribus domesticis."[8] Therefore, it does not seem unlikely that this magical practice was originally intended to establish general dominion and protection of the respective Olympic Spirits over the targeted locations. However, the practice found inclusion in the current manuscript through a distinctly utilitarian perspective—that is, the classical lens of all folk magic—and was narrowed down to the pragmatic use of warding off thieves.

As such, the excerpt can be read as a typical example of ritual folk magic. It still shows echoes and outlines of a formerly more coherent creative process of spirit partnership. yet, in its present form, it places the accessibility of the practice, the immediacy of the effect and the utilitarianism to the layman above anything all else.

Further studies should examine how Olympic Spirits in Western folk magic came to displace traditional household guardians such as goblins or brownies from their ancestral positions. What exactly conditioned the belief in the higher efficacy of these relatively unknown spirits who had only recently been introduced into the pantheon of German folk magic?

8 The Latin term can be translated as *domestic spirits*, *household deities*, or *hearth gods/goddesses*.

III
EXCERPT OF COD.MAG.66

German/Latin Transcript

Cap.1

Wie man seine Sachen soll vor den Dieben verwahren, dass sie nichts können stehlen, noch von dem gestohlenen Gute fortbringen.

1.

Ein gewisser Theologus hat vor [...] ein bewährtes Mittel rekommandiert, seine Sachen vor den Dieben zu verwahren, denen laribus domesticis anzubefehlen. Deswegen er in Ostern denen Choris Angelicis sein Vermögen auf folgenden Art und Weise anvertraute. E.g.

Über die Küche pflegte er zu schreiben wie auch über den Keller, Speisekammer, Kornhaber und Heuboden folgendes:

Aratron, S. Aratron, hoc sacrum est ne atlingite fures, mit diesem Character:

Über die Studierstube pflegte er zu schreiben: Bethor, S. Bethor, hic locus sacer est, heu fugite fures, mit diesem Character:

Über die Schlafkammer und Bett schrieb er:

Hagith, S. Hagith, hic locus sacer est heu fugtet fures mit diesem Character

English Translation

Chapter 1

How one should keep his things from thieves, so that they cannot steal anything, nor carry away the stolen goods.

1.

A certain theologian has [missing] ago recommended a proven means to keep one's things from the thieves, to command the laribus domesticis [i.e., domestic spirits/household deities/hearth gods/goddesses]. Therefore, during Easter he entrusted his property to those angelic choirs in the following manner. E.g.

Over the kitchen he used to write as well as over the cellar, pantry, granary and hayloft the following:

Aratron, S. Aratron, hoc sacrum est ne atlingite fures [this place is sacred, lest thieves snatch away], with this character: [SEAL OF ARATRON]

He used to write over the study room: *Bethor, S. Bethor, hic locus sacer est, heu fugite fures* (this is a sacred place, yea it will drive away the thieves), with this character: [SEAL OF BETHOR]

Over the bedchamber and bed he wrote:

Hagith, S. Hagith, hic locus sacer est heu fugtet fures (this is a sacred place, yea it will drive away the thieves) with this character: [SEAL OF HAGITH]

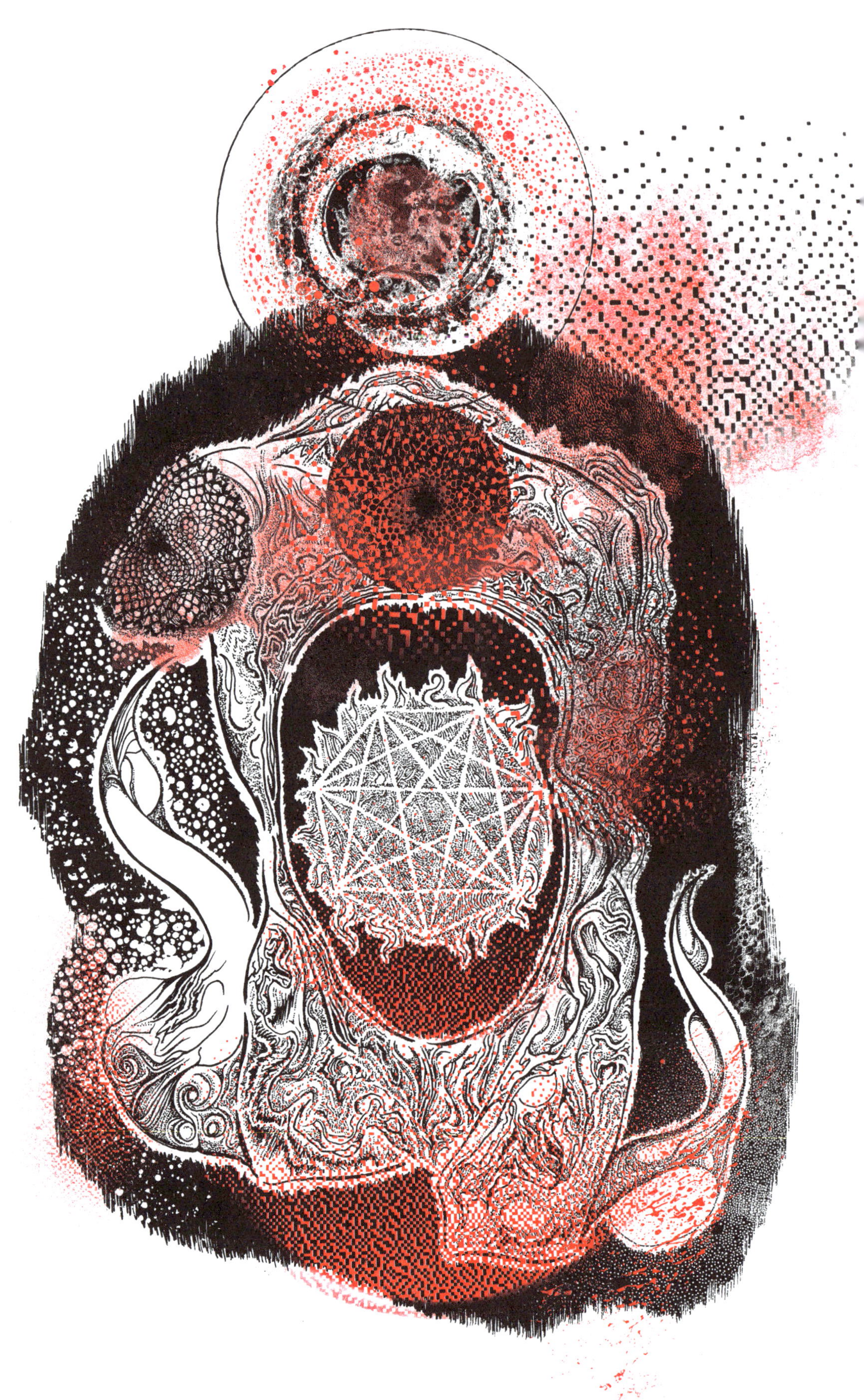

BOOK 2

CHAPTER IV

IN LEAGUE WITH SPIRITS!

Introduction

WE CONCLUDE OUR reflections on the practice of Olympic Spirits with a curious case from the time of our great-grandparents. Almost still within reach of our living memory, we discover in the year 1928 in a newspaper completely fallen to oblivion a long report which contains a folk magical invocation of the Olympic spirits.

How wonderful would it be, leaning over an old pub table, between empty beer mugs and worn-out card games, to peruse this article together with Paracelsus? What would his ghost make of it—the ghost of the man for whom nothing could be down-to-earth and honest enough, and yet who detested nothing more than the stupidity of the lazy and presumptuous?

On the one hand, an interplay of essential set pieces of lived Western magic shines from the lines of this text: the setting around an act of dream incubation, the calling of spirits not in an instance but over an extended period of time, the foundational intention of attracting a familiar spirit, and, especially, the explicit indication that only the manifesting spirit itself can reveal its name and seal.

On the other hand, the tendrils of archaic folk superstition protrude deeply into what is read: the intermingling of Olympic Spirits and Lucifer, the lashing of a written conjuration with freshly cut thorny branches in the sympathetic belief of tormenting those meant by it in the same manner,[1] the carrying of a daemonic seal only in one's left hand as that which had long been assigned to the sinister side...Finally, this version of the text appears to us in a wonderful hermaphrodite form: half folk magical grimoire, half romanticising newspaper article.

On our long journey from the Paracelsian emergence of the Olympic Spirits in the 16th century, we have almost arrived in the outer periphery of our living present memory: the Olympic Spirits still surround us, though they appear interwoven with ghost stories, attic treasures and the lost narratives of German folklore.

The article originally was printed in the *Upper Lusatia Homelands Newspaper*, in their 17th issue of the 9th volume on 19th of August 1928.[2] It is titled *In League with Spirits! A contribution to the old Ebersbacher belief in spirits*[3] and ran over three full pages. Let's read the English translation in relevant excerpts.

WERNER ANDERT, 1928

In League with Spirits!

The spells listed are all taken from old manuscripts and are reproduced in the old spelling. Spelling errors are not taken into account. Only the vowel v is replaced by the u.

If we were still in the Middle Ages, in the age of the Inquisition, I would have long since been made to walk the path through the air as a sorcerer at the stake. However, since we live in the enlightened modern age, I can

1 See also: Albrecht Dieterich, *Kleine Schriften*. Berlin: B.G. Teubner, 1911, pp 199–200.

2 Otto Marx (ed.), *Oberlausitzer Heimatzeitung—Blätter für Geschichte, Heimatkunde, Kunst, Literatur*, Nr.17, Jahrgang 9, Reichenau: Alwin Marr, 1928.

3 Werner Andert, *Mit Geistern im Bunde! Ein Beitrag zum alten Ebersbacher Geisterglauben.*, in: Marx (ed.), 1928, pp. 259–262; reprinted in excerpt in: Andert, *Ebersbach—Ein Heimat- und Wanderbuch*. Ebersbach: Adolf Israel, 1929, pp. 58–66.

calmly confess that I deal with spirits and rummage in attics and in old junk rooms for long-forgotten spells.

When I then read in deep night by the dull glow of the lamp in the foxed papers, I am often embraced by a rare creepiness. In uncanny wildness supernatural, demonic faces appear. People rise from the torn papers gnawed by mice. People I don't know come to life again. People of whom nothing remains but a few characters on yellowed sheets of paper. People who lived like flowers in the world, blossomed, withered and crumbled to dust. People who resisted this natural course of nature with all their might. People who believed in spirits and uncanny creatures—in defiance of science. Not professional magicians and dark sorcerers—but simple people who firmly trusted in the effectiveness of their means. Even if such a belief could not be logically justified, it was and still is irrevocable to the people. […]

A SECRET TO ATTAIN A SPIRITUS ASTRALEM IN A SHORT AND EASY WAY.

Hang the characters described below written by your own hand cum emox tuo[4] *the u. 1 ma hora in front of the window of your bedroom and pray the 7 penitential psalms*[5] *then say the following:*

I N.N. adjure you Olympic Spirits by the God of Abraham, Isaac and Jacob, per a [read: alpha] w [read: omega] by the power of the infinite ineffable name ______ (symbol. sign) jod he van he Zebaoth the Creator of heaven and earth whose name fear and honour all that is in heaven on earth and

4 Possibly can be restored from other sources as: *on a Sunday while the Moon is waxing.*

5 Psalm 6: *Domine, ne in furore.* Prayer in Distress.
Psalm 32: *Beati quorum remissae.* Remission of Sin.
Psalm 38: *Domine, ne in furore.* Prayer of an Afflicted Sinner.
Psalm 51: *Miserere mei, Deus.* The Miserere: Prayer of Repentance.
Psalm 102: *Domine, exaudi.* Prayer in time of Distress.
Psalm 130: *De profundis.* Prayer for Pardon and Mercy.
Psalm 143: *Domine, exaudi.* A Prayer in Distress.

under the earth, by the Great Prince standing before God's throne ______ (symbol. sign) Michael that one of you will come to me and pray to me. Michael, that one of you may appear to me this night, without rumour and terror, in a pleasing form, answering my desire through Jesus Christ the Sehilo,[6] *who has conquered death and hell.*

Here you can demand [printed libra sign, read: spirit] whichever one you want, go to sleep and let the characters hang in the air outside the window, as long as follow [read: these] hang, the spirits even Lucifer himself have no rest and incessant torment.

Cut a branch of blackthorn in nomine Dei P.F. u. GS.[7] *one morning before sunrise in the new moon. With an unused knife make the Characteres*

✠ ✠ ✠ *quis ut Deus*[8]

thereupon, whip the characters hanging in the air in front of the window 7 times a day and say with each blow: Micoel;[9] *after some days you will hear a strong commotion in the midnight, be courageous and summon them thus:*

In the name of Adonai Elohim who created me and you, I, N.N. summon you that one of you may answer!

As soon as you have spoken this, they will ask you to remove the characters from the air in front of the window and will promise to do your will for all. Then ask for the spirit with his sigil, and he will immediately follow you [and] bring [it] drawn on a special piece of paper; ask for his name as well,

6 Read: *Messias.*

7 The abreviated Latin insert should probably be translated as "in the name of God the Father, the Son and the Holy Spirit". However, in the original what should read "S. S." for *Sanctus Spiritus* (Holy Spirit) was abreviated as "G. S." which stands for *Gottes Sohn* (Son of God) in German.

8 Latin, translates as: *Who [are you] to God?*

9 Read: *Michael.*

so that you can call him, and be assured that he will come by day and by night without refusing; ask him for science or money, and he will satisfy all your wishes; but do not let him come without asking something from him, for then you are done for. Do not keep him for more than an hour; if you want to be rid of him, bid her or him farewell as follows.[10]

In the name of God t[...]
Praise and glory are due, [...]
the place of [...]
with me [...]
to come [...][11]

Give thanks to God for his mysteries, and you have been granted such grace, and use it for his glory.

10 The following license to depart is redacted as deliberately cut up in the original, just as the actual spirit's seal.

11 This deliberately destroyed section most likely gave the licence to depart as we still find it in alternative versions of this rite: *By the power of Almighty God, return now to your God-ordained place and kingdom until I call you again, and that without harm to me, either to my soul or to my body. In the name of God the Father, the Son and the Holy Spirit. Amen.* (Anonymous, 1910, p. 379)—Theoretically, however, it could have also contained a blessing of the place, as we find it in relatively intact Latin in the *Arcanum Arcanorum Maximum Anonymous*—This is the Jesuit's *Venus Booklet or True Coercion of all Spirits* which also begins with an invocation of the Olympic Spirits. It is part of another folk magical compendium of the same time, best known under its title *Sammlung der grössten Geheimnisse ausserordentlicher Menschen in alter Zeit*, Koeln am Rhein: Peter Hammer, 1725 [Stuttgart: Johann Scheible, 1857], pp. 219-242.
—Here is the English translation of the Latin blessing of the place:

Blessing of the place.
S[peaker]: [I call on] *our Helper in the name of the Lord.*
S[peaker]. *R*[espondents]: *Who made heaven and earth.*
S[peaker]: *The Lord be with you.*
R[espondents]: *And with your spirit.*
Let us pray.
Bless, O Lord God Almighty, this place, that in it may be health, constancy, victory, virtue, humility, goodness, and thanksgiving to God the Father, the Son, and the Holy Spirit, and may this blessing rest on this place and on those who dwell in it, now and forever.
R[espondents]: *Amen.*

NB: Keep well the name and sigil of the spirit. If you want your spirit, go to a place alone, hold the sigil in your left hand, call its name and it will come and serve you.

Take care that you do not get involved with them and lose your happiness; if you are wise and secretive, you will be happier than a king.

Again the paper is cut [into pieces]. What a shame! Here was the "Sigill." A signature still testifies to it.

"I have cut the 'Sigill' [for] it shall not be made. If he wants to do magic, he must be connected with the spirits, then he can perform the supernatural arts with the recipes. The sigil is the main thing and that is why I cut it." [...]

NB. Apply it well.

Yet, enough now! For ______ the church clock strikes at the witching hour, the electric light is out, the ink is spent, the quill is sprained, and the paper is painted upon. The "raven-beast" of a puss knocks over the empty caraway bottle by a vile saltomortale. ______ Tree [sic]—the last chime of the bell dies away, and again there is silence. —There, the spirits are calling me.

"I greet you creatures,
of the nightly times."

✠ ✠ ✠

Explanatory Notes

The author of this article was Werner Andert (1907–1983), an elementary school teacher, local historian, folklorist, chemist and publicist from Upper Lusetia who was just twenty-one at the time of its publication. He was also the son of the local historian and geologist Hermann Andert (1879–1945) and throughout his life focused on continuing the research and work initiated by his father. With the exception of his time in the Second World War and English captivity, he spent his entire life in a small village between Leipzig and Dresden, originally called *Ebersbach*, today *Ebersbach-Neugersdorf*.[12]

His relative youth in 1928 and the desire to gain recognition with the continuation of his father's legacy may explain the romantic framework in which he embedded the transcripts of the magical documents he held access to.

Next to the operation to attain a familiar spirit with the help of the Olympic Spirits, his essay includes folk magical aids as diverse as a Christian fire protection spell, a spell for remote killing over five miles, the instructions for the Paracelsus-inspired construction of a magical bell, though now devoted to "the judges of the infernal kingdom,"[13] a Thieves' Blessing, as well as a spell for becoming invisible, "for a witcher must be able to make himself invisible."[14]

If we focus on the section on the familiar spirit mediated by the Olympic Spirits, we can quickly identify it as a common German folk magical operation.

It is usually given under the title *Arcanum Experientia praetiosum*[15] and assumed to stem from the monastery in *Salmansweiler*.[16] To this day, the text itself cannot be assigned an exact origin

12 Brigitte Emmrich and Werner Andert in: *Sächsische Biografie*, Institut für Sächsische Geschichte und Volkskunde e.V. (ed.), online-edition: http://www.isgv.de/saebi/ (12.7.2022).

13 In the original: Judices Regne Infernalis (Andert, 1928, p. 261).

14 Andert 1928, p. 262.

15 Read: *A Secret Precious Experience.*

16 The Imperial Abbey of Salem was a monastery of the Cistercian Order and one of the wealthiest and most important abbeys in the Lake Constance area. It was founded in 1137/1138. Beset by wars in the 17th century and almost completely destroyed by fire, it experienced its second high period in the 18th century as a center of southwest German Rococo. The attribution of

nor date; however, it was the infamous and obsessive distribution of grimoires by the publishing house of Johann Scheible that first made it appear in print in 1853.[17] In the early 20th century it was reprinted anonymously by Eugen Bartels around 1910, this time included in a compendium titled *The Book of Jezira, Eighth and Ninth Book of Moses or the Egyptian House Treasure with the 101 Mysteries of All Mysteries.*[18]

Using this late publication of the *Book of Jezira*, Adolf Spamer gave a comprehensive assessment of the nature of these folk magic reprints in his seminal 1955 article on the German grimoire tradition, *Grimoire and Spell:*[19]

> *The writings summarised in the Book of Jezira give us deep insights into a magical-medieval and post-medieval world which was formed from the flowing-together and intermingling of ideas of many ages and peoples, of what has grown historically and what is elemental beyond history. Strangely interlinked and boundary-free, they show us the coexistence of ecclesiastically approved elements in Bible verse and commandment with anti-dogmatic, diabolical conjurations, the conflation of only theoretically separate "white" and "black" magic. Spells and religious-philosophical doctrines, sigils, characters, talismans and other arcana, largely immigrated to us from the Egyptian and Hebrew habitats across the melting pot of Hellenistic culture, modified and enriched with the rediscovery of the Kabbalah in the 13th century, walk hand in hand here and—misunderstood*

---

the present ritual to this abbey could possibly point to an origin in the 18th century, or at least to a "cover story" designed during this period.

17 Anonymous, Handschriftliche *Schätze aus Klosterbibliotheken umfassend sämtliche vierzig Hauptwerke ueber Magie, verborgene Kräfte, Offenbarungen und geheime Wissenschaften.* Köln am Rhein: [Stuttgart: Johann Scheible], [around 1853].

18 Anonymous, *Das Buch Jezira. Achtes und neuntes Buch Moses oder der egyptische Hausschatz mit den 101 Geheimnissen aller Geheimnisse. Nach einer alten Handschrift, mit hoechst sonderbaren und originellen Abbildungen.* [Berlin-Weißensee: E. Bartels], [appr. 1910].

19 Adolf Spamer, *Zauberbuch und Zauberspruch, in: Deutsches Jahrbuch für Volkskunde, Bd. 1, pp. 109-126; reprinted in: Spamer, Adolf, Romanusbuechlein—Historisch-philologischer Kommentar zu einem deutschen Zauberbuch.* Berlin: Akademie Verlag, 1958, pp. 5–23.

> *or carelessly—mutilate themselves progressively through the ages in copies and prints. Demonological talismanology stands next to angelology fed from Jewish-Pauline sources, the 16th—18th centuries donate new secret symbols to astrology, pharmacology, natural magical chemistry and alchemy, recipes for preparing the philosopher's stoneetc. And all this ends up in the folk magical grimoire of the 20th century, after having passed through the hands of* PARACELSUS, TRITHEMIUS, AGRIPPA VON NETTESHEIM *and many other brooders on magic powers and their adepts. Until the publisher BARTELS, untroubled by historical-philological scruples, replaces the old sigils (already largely mutilated) with the stocks of his ornamental types and random print-clichés, so that now the coat-of-arms stamp of the "Republica de Colombia" becomes the "Character of Compulsion and Obedience" and we are offered the "Scutum Mosis"*[20] *in a "Registered Trademark" of the Dresden ink factory of one August Leonhardi. It hardly needs saying that such circumstances, combined with the fragmentary nature of the surviving documents and the obscurity of magical cryptography, which was intended from the very beginning, often present textual genetic research with difficult tasks.*[21]

What we have before us in young Werner Andert's newspaper article is thus indeed an echo of medieval grimoire practices. At the same time, we recognise it as a modular system of folk magical framework plots—in this case an act of dream incubation, facilitated by the hanging of a magical conjuration from one's bedstead window into the night sky—and the arbitrary insertion of daemonic names, rather randomly chosen from the living memory of the Western magical tradition, or simply made up altogether.

How random the appearance of the Olympics in this operation truly is, becomes obvious when we compare our version of this nightly rite with the alternative surviving versions. In Scheible's print edition of the *Arcanum Experientia praetiosum* from 1853 we are advised to conjure one *Neli*, a "prince by this name has two legions

20 Read: *Shield of Moses.*

21 Spamer 1958, pp. 16–17. Translation by author.

of servant spirits and is very willing to serve and help".[22] And while Scheible's edition still includes Neli's seal, the youngest edition of 1910 by Bartels has already lost these characters.

Still, Scheible's compendium of more than 600 pages is full of surprises and entirely lacking of critical editing. Thus it contains another version of the same rite at a later point in its convoluted text. Here the operation is simply called *Experimentum*; Neli's name has disappeared altogether, yet the spirit's now anonymous seal is given out of logical sequence on the last page of its instructions as a seal for finding treasures. Similarly surprising, the same text still gives us the alleged master-seal that has to be written on the conjuration which is then hung outside one's window, and which was cut up in Andert's attic discovery...Of course, Scheible's *Experimentum* does not fail to call out that the character has "to be written with the blood of an all-white dove or an all-white baby lamb on virgin parchment".[23]

So here we are at the end of our long investigation into the history of the Olympic Spirits and their passage through time. We realise that the closer we get to our own present day, the more their names seem to degenerate into gap-fillers, offsets and placeholders. No longer do we encounter echoes of a true knowledge or even a personal communion with these spirits. Rather, we see their names only two steps away from village fairs and stalls, from tricksters and illusionists. Their *magic* has long since fallen by the wayside.

22 Anonymous, 1853, p. 312.
23 Anonymous, 1853, p. 550.

But why should we deliberately conclude this book on such a sad note? More importantly, you might ask, why should we even include Werner Andert's example in the *practical* part of this book?

And my answer is: we close with this disillusioning chapter in order to nip in the bud any feelings of reverence towards an alleged magical line of tradition. Printed paper is as much a product as are bread, shoes or cars. For all these products there is only one feature that is usually even more important than their *actual use* and that is their *market value*. Before all these products want to be used, they want to be sold. And it is the same with books.

So whatever a book tells us—and I encourage you to include the book in your hands here as well—has to be unravelled. Its sentences must be split open: into those that serve to create market value, and those that serve to create practical utility.

Our hunt for the Olympic Spirits in old archives and libraries could go on endlessly. Countless are the examples of their appearance that have not been mentioned here; especially with regards to the past three hundred years. And yet all these *treasures* on printed pages and between the covers of books fade away when confronted with *the work of your own hands*.

I tip my hat to anyone putting the *Arcanum Experientia praetiosum* into practice in their own time and day. Equally, I bow to anyone entering the *temple of the bell call* and greeting the Olympic Spirits—may that be in their animal or angelic forms.

We opened this book with two short quotes; now it is time to return to them. One was Paracelsus' famous saying *Alterius non sit, qui suus esse potest.*[24] The other was the alleged quote of the famous magician and artist Austin Osman Spare: *Rather stray than follow.*[25] I conclude this book with a tribute to all those of us who still *have the courage to stray*. To those amongst us who still know how to wander about, to roam, and drift, and run loose—not guided by obsession for achievement or external gratification, but quietly guided by the stars of their inner firmament. By the light in the temple of the Olympic Spirits, and their heart-flame in its centre.

24 Read: Let them not be another's [servant] who can be their own [master].

25 Kenneth & Steffi Grant (eds.), *ZOS SPEAKS—Encounters with Austin Osman Spare*, London: Fulgur Limited, 1998, p 16.

I remember an old scouting trick that a friend once told me about when I was still a schoolboy. If you want to see an object in the twilight of the night, it is best *not* to look directly at it, but slightly to its side. It is the *gaze past* it that achieves sharpness in the periphery of our view…

Today I know, it is the same with *straying*: as soon as we lose sight of our goals, as soon as we are willing to lose ourselves, we open a space within ourselves. It is a magical space. And it is a necessary space if we aim to hear the voices of our familiars, and to recognise the many faces of our own Olympic Spirits. Then, maybe slowly, if we continue to walk and wander, they will step forward—like animals in the night—and become accustomed to the presence of our human mind.

I greet you creatures,
of the nightly times.[26]

26 Werner Andert, see above.

BOOK 2

CHAPTER V

Closing

ALEXANDER VON SUCHTEN, one of the great Paracelsians we did not have occasion to highlight sufficiently here, emphasised the importance to understand Paracelsus' books as written in a "stylo magico."[1] That is, they were *magical tools* to help us decipher the two Books that could never be lost, whatever happened to the world: the *Book of God* and the *Book of Nature*.

The one who chose to anchor their work in the Book of God, according to Paracelsus, would become a *Sanctum*; the one who grew the roots of their work in the Book of Nature would become a *Magum*.[2] Both of them were united, though, in the practice of the art he called *Gabalia*.[3]

1 Alexander von Suchten, quoted in Gilly 1998, p. 159.

2 *For there are saints in God to blessedness who are called Magi. God is wonderful in his saints, both in the realm of God and Nature, which is not possible for others to do except those to whom it will be given in particular. Thus the distinction between Sanctum and Magum is that the Sanctus works from God, the Magus from Nature.* Sudhoff (ed.) 1929, p. 130.

3 Michael Toxites (1514–1581), one of the earliest Paracelsists who equally should have received more space on these pages, gives us a wonderful description of the art *Gabalia*, which clearly has little to do with Hebrew Kabbala here, but follows a decidedly Paracelsian current: *Cabala, Cabalia or the Cabalistica is a divine knowledge [scientia] that opens to us the meaning of the divine teaching about the Saviour and that establishes friendship between its followers and the angels. It also gives us the knowledge of all natural things, and with its divine light it dispels darkness and enlightens our minds. The word is Hebrew, it means "reception"*. Toxites after Brandl 2021, p. 324.

Learning or even mastering the art of *Gabalia* required every aspirant to do a simple and yet most challenging thing: to turn over the pages of these two magical books *with their feet.*[4] That is, the pages of the Book of God and Nature had to be turned over by firsthand experience, by plunging ourselves fully into their joys, agonies and raw realities. To Paracelsus, the master key to unlocking such divinely inspired, magical experience was offered in Matthew 7:7[5] and its threefold approach of *asking, seeking* and *knocking.*

With this simple modus operandi, Paracelsus walked out into the world. Different to the modern misperception on Paracelsus, we showed that to the man himself first and foremost this was not a medical nor a chemical or theological world. To Paracelsus it was an *animist's world*, where each being—once properly addressed through *gabalistic art*—would awaken and speak back to us: the plane of the stars, the plane of the poisons, the plane of the human constitution, the plane of the angelic beings and the chthonic ones with their "infernal pharmacy."[6] All these beings were waiting to be addressed; they were all holding their words waiting for our minds to open. As we have seen, generating such living contact, to Paracelsus, was not at all a romantic ideal but a gritty, grizzled everyday reality. Just like humans, these spirits spoke from their own natural bias, motivated by subjective passions, with limited perspective and often cunning mischief. Whether we approached them as a *Sanctum* or as a *Magum,* the underlying language we had to decipher was that of the Olympic Spirits. For it was the entire mesmerising beauty and the agonising terror of creation that unfolded from their sevenfold influences, orbiting powerfully within the inner firmament of each being.

My hope is that this book will inspire you to walk out into this world, just as Paracelsus did before us. Proudly, as no one's servant but his own master, and yet with an open hand, an open heart and

4 *For this I will testify of Nature: He who wants to explore her, must tread her books with his feet. The Scripture is examined by her letters, the Nature however by country to country. As often a country, as often a page. Thus is the Codex Naturae, thus one must turn its pages.* Paracelsus after Goldammer (ed.), 1955, p. 50.

5 Matthew 7:7: Ask, and it shall be given you; seek, and ye shall find; knock, and it shall be opened unto you.

6 Sudhoff (ed.) 1929, Vol. XII, p. 272.

an open mind, to listen to all and everyone: the rich and the poor, the hurting and the healed, the human and the non-human.

My humble hope is this book helped you *hear*, *taste*, and *smell* a little of the Paracelsian spirit as it lives on in his ancient words and as it inspired my contemporary ones. Just like for me writing it, I hope this book turned into a *sensual experience* for you. Because it is not through mental speculation, but through sensual engagement that we *ask, seek and knock* onto the many of doors of this world.

Because once this works, *practice* becomes a curious thing. Once your senses are imbued with the *Olympic Spirit* you can no longer *not* practice. Of course, you can chose implicit or explicit ways of performing, you can follow endogenic or exogenic forces, you can sit silently or circle around an altar at night. yet, even taking a spoonful of soup from a bowl can turn into a sensual, into an animistic and atavistic adventure.

This is the *great work* that lies ahead of us: to arrive again at the magically animated world of our ancestors, yet not to draw the spirit that animates it from fantasy and fairy tales, but from lived communion with the living spirits around us.

No more Tolkien and Disney, but pure, raw embodiment: breathing upon a skull and hearing a spirit's words return to us. Standing under Olympic patronage, when a daemon steps forward from the compass rose of the Seal of Secrets. Sensing the pulse of our blood below our skin, and within it, the beating rhythm of our daimon.

We have come to live in a world that marvels more about the possibility of independent consciousness in *algorithms* than in the spirit-world around us. In our relentless desire to pin down the shortest route between 0 and 1, A and B, Today and Tomorrow, we have mistaken the straight line for sound travel advice. Nature, however, does not do straight lines, nature curves and bends and mixes and stains. Nature *strays*, and so should we.

Here is one last quote for us. It is taken from Adolf Spamer's abovementioned essay *Grimoire and Spell*. At its very end, Spamer evokes back to life the world many of us have lost. I encourage you to make this cosmos entirely your own again—and yet to heed fragrant romance just as much as the stainless-steel shimmer of enlightenment. What will guide you safely is the Paracelsian triple star of *free will*, *faith* and *imagination*.

It is the animistic world of spirits, in which humans, gods, demons, animals, trees, plants, stones, waters, agents of destruction and agents of healing lead their equal and coequal lives, in which Odin the helper can become just as much a spirit of harm as the Virgin Mary [...]. A world in which the elves do not go overland without the elf-women, the gout not without the gout-woman, in which balm and balm-woman and our Lord Jesus Christ sit at the same table, the willow tree enters into battle with the lichen, the remedy becomes the demon and vice versa, in which the sufferer greets the sun with the words: "Welcome to God, Sunshine, where did you ride in from?" and addresses the helping elder-bush and the spruce in the same friendly manner as the demon of illness from which he wants to free himself.[7]

Have a good trip, my friend.
Vale.

7 Spamer 1958, p. 22.

Appendices

I–IV

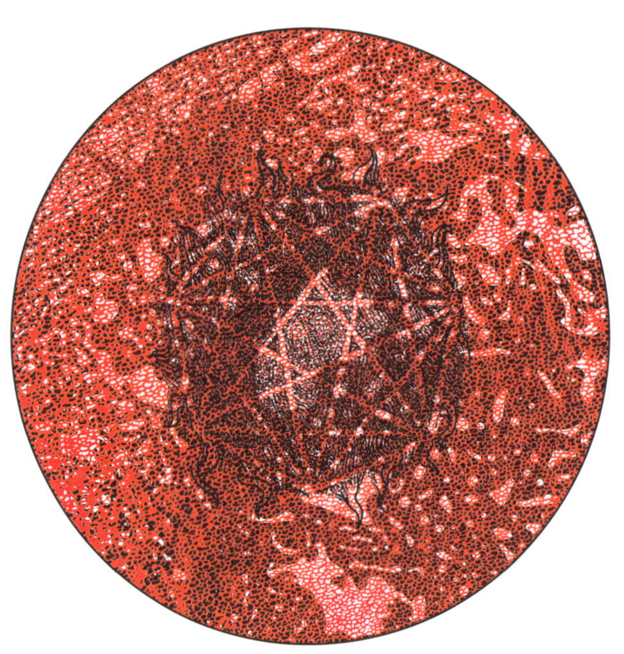

APPENDIX I

Adam Haslmayr
EXTRACT AND INTRODUCTION
to
THE THEOPHRASTIC CABALA[1]

Preliminary remark: The following text is the first complete transcription and English translation of a unique early Paracelsian manuscript now in the Herzogin Anna Amalia Library in Weimar. Written in three parts, it was authored by Adam Haslmayr and offers one of the most insightful and authentic summaries of the Theophrastic Cabala, i.e., the mysteries of the human microcosm according to the original Paracelsian teachings.

It summarizes in sharp and condensed form, and even more explicitly than Paracelsus' own theological writings, central aspects of his heretical Christian-Animistic cosmology, and sets forth how the contact between man and spirit arises organically from within man. Referring to "the soul [as the] one house and seat of the spirits, good and evil," he lays the groundwork for the Olympic Spirits as inner agents and active forces within every human being and teaches the reader the essential principles for establishing a positive relationship with them.

In this current edition I am providing ample explanatory footnotes, especially with regards to its many biblical references as well as Paracelsian neologisms.

1 Source: Paracelsus [Adam Haslmayr], *Theophrastica Cabalistica—Extractus & Theophrastiae Cabalisticae Isagogen,* MS Q.286/20, s.l., [early 17th century], Herzogin Anna Amalia Bibliothek; with kind permission of the Klassik Stiftung Weimar and the Herzogin Anna Amalia Bibliothek. Transcription from Manuscript: Anne Hila, Translation into English: Frater Acher; for further reference see: Sudhoff 1899, Vol. II, pp. 636–8.

For more context on this important text of early mago-mystical Paracelsianism, please refer to the section on Adam Haslmayr in Book I, Chapter III: The Birth of the Olympic Spirits.

Extract and Introduction to the Theophrastic Cabala[2]

This is the Introduction of the
Holy, Secret Art and Wisdom of the Prophets.
Without Which Art and Grace No One can Understand
Or Thoroughly Explain the Holy Scriptures.
Here Follows the Interpretation
Of the Mysteries of the Theophrastic Cabala.[3]

THE CABALA is the Olympic Spirit, or the Sacramental Body of the inner spiritually deified man in *Anyadei*:[4] seeing with bodily eyes of the mind into the Godhead and its throne. *The Holy Cabala* gives us to understand that we humans are angels and equal to the spirits, and like them we can know all things. However, nothing in the animal body may hinder or prevent us from doing so.

Anyadum[5] we call a true Christ-believer and cabalist, which means a spiritual, heavenly glorified body, one burning in Christ's

2 In the original Latin: *Extractus & Theophrastiae Cabalisticae Isagogen.*

3 In the original Latin: *Sic definit. Cabala Theophrastus Mysteriarcha.*

4 The following three magical terms are central for a proper understanding of the present manuscript. We are providing their explanation here in a single footnote for easier reference. Their explanation is taken from an anonymous, late 16th century manuscript in 97 pages which explains many of the most occult Paracelsian terms: Aniadey *means in Hebrew the "shine", a new world, a new earth realm or the paradise, which is full and full of angelic people.* Aniadus *is a spiritual blessed man, or a heavenly body, an eternal body, of an eternal life, a Clarified body, or a new creature from Christ.* Aniadum *is a heavenly body which is implanted in us Christians by the Holy Spirit in the sacraments of the body and blood of Christ.* (Anonymous, *ONOMASTICON—Das ist eine gründliche Erklärung und Offenbarung heimlich verborgener Paracelsischer Wörter und Namen*, in: *Codex Vossianus Chymicus* No. 35, manuscript, University Library Leiden, between 1582–1600. Quoted after: Sudhoff 1899, Vol. II, S. 698–699. See also: Franz Hartmann, *The Life and the Doctrines of Philippus Theophrastus Bombast of Hohenheim : Known by the name of Paracelsus.* United States Book Company, 1891, p. 40.

5 See previous footnote.

body and doctrine, and living according to the reason of the New Creature.

Of these, we find two in particular named in the Old Testament: As there are Enoch and (as the written theology tells us) Elijah. As their successors in wisdom and mysteries of the spirit (besides John the Evangelist and Paul) we know four: Hermes Trismegistus, Alphonsus Magnus, Solomon Israelita and Theophrastus the Germanic Hermit. These have recognised their mind i.e. themselves in Christo Magicae. Therefore, they have become immortal, and have become God's principals, to whom God has shown and revealed His holy mysteries and dominion over miracles as the chosen ones. These cannot err, whose writings we must believe.

Those in the old Cabala, as well as all the other holy prophets and men of God, have revealed and shown us the Messiah under the veil and shadow or figurative appearance. Which Messiah is Christ, who rose from the heart of the Master (that is Mary) to redeem the people fallen from the holy Cabala from their curse.

Messiah is the Word, Fiat, which the Creator had as instrument, together with Mary in the creation of the world. As the German Cabalist teaches us in the first chapter, *Super Johannem*,[6] the Word is everything, and in everything it is the life, the power and the soul. The Tabernacle of Moses, and also the Temple of Solomon in Jerusalem, is divided into three parts: as into the forecourt or *Vestibulum*, following it the sanctuary, and thirdly into the Holy of Holies, so the *Mehsiae Cabalam* proves it to us.

This Cabala has not been explained by any mortal amongst the children of men since the time of the apostles, except for the most noble wise man and German Trismegistus Philippus Theophrastus. That is why he is also called a *stella signata*[7] from Germania, and

6 Haslmayr is most likely referring to a lost manuscript mentioned by Benedictus Figulus and possibly written by Basilius Valentinus, which in its full title was called *Opus praeclarum ad Utrumque Magistri Valentini, Super Johannem Azoth.* Carlos Gilly identified that Figulus had suggested to the famous publisher and printer Lazarus Zetzner (1551–1616) for this text to be included in the Chrysotheatrum novellum. (Gilly, 2002, pp. 461–462). Of course, in principle Haslmayr could also be referring to Johannes Chrysostomus' (349–407) famous *Homiliae super Johannem*; however, this seems unlikely given his reference to the author as the "German Cabalist."

7 The German term *Signatstern* took on an important meaning in masonic writings, especially from 1803 onwards after the publication of the same ti-

as *Monarcha perpetuus*[8] sent by God into this last world, his like the earth has not yet born, therefore all reason outside of his Cabala is to be regarded for nothing but for error, ambition and deceit of the devil.

Apart from these German Cabalist writings, there is no reason to seek nor to find the divine, celestial *Thesaurinellae*[9] and *Philosophiae Sagacis*.[10] Whoever lies outside this ground and now supposes himself to be a Theosophist, will find himself entirely to be an erroneous Cacosophista in himself. Therefore, only the sacred Cabala interprets the Biblical Scriptures correctly, and no other science.

Because the Cabala has made by her *Necromantia* the *Turbam magnam*, the *Trarames*, the *Euestra* (these are the prophetic spirits by which Moses performed his miracles).[11] She has inspired God to

tle: Anonymous, *Der Signatstern oder die enthüllten sämmtlichen sieben Grade und Geheimnisse der mystischen Freimaurerei nebst dem Orden der Ritter des Lichts, für Maurer und die es nicht sind*, Two Volumes, Berlin: E. G. Schöne, 1803.

8 Read: *eternal monarch.*

9 *Thesaurinella* is a sub-category of the *Coelestis Nectromantia* (see Book 1, Chapter II) and in Paracelsian language refers to the living magico-mystical forces hidden in the Scripture. Knowing how to enliven and partake in these divine forces is one of the highest secrets of the adepts. Or in Paracelsus' own words: *The heavenly Thesaurinella teaches to search the treasure of the scripture, what is hidden in it, and to understand, know and recognise the same. Not only the scripture, but the heart of God towards man, his will, understanding and opinion. It learns to understand these things the word [ungrammatical], the teaching that God hides, not wanting man to know. As one who buries a treasure does not want another to have it, as with the same treasure he would abuse his opulence. […] But he who knows the same is thesaurinella coelestis.* —Sudhoff 1929 (ed.), Vol. XII, p. 337.

10 Refers to Paracelsus' magnum opus *Philosophia Sagax*, also called *Astronomia Magna.*

11 These three terms are essential to Paracelsus' work *Philosophia ad Athenienses* (published 1564) which clearly left a strong impression on Adam Haslmayr as the author of our current manuscript. Here we attempt to explain the three terms in short form and encourage further research in the original source: Evestrum is a complex Paracelsian term that can be summarised to express the embodied and dynamic celestial spirit. Accordingly, whoever understand the *Evestrum* of a being understands its essence as well as its predestination. Thus it is not corporeal itself but more like a shadow that originates in the Light of Nature, and in its specific appearance is tied to any creature across the four elemental realms. For easier understanding, we recommend to consider the *Evestrum* as the collective dynamics of the seven Olympic Spirits within each created being. Or as Paracelsus says: *The Evestrum is a thing like a shadow on the wall. The shadow that grows*

turn stone into water and water into blood. This Cabala explains to us thoroughly why the New People, that is, the present New People in the New Testament, is a holy people, and a Royal Priesthood. And gods and sons of the most high God they all may be, if they have the word of Christ in their hearts, and keep his four gospels, and believe in simplicity, and keep one word with them.

This doctrine Theophrastia or Cabala *Sancta* reveals to us that there is no greater and holier wisdom that has been amongst the children of men from the beginning of the world than it is now, where it is sought and loved from the heart: that Christ is the eternal wisdom. For it not only shows us the angels of God for the holy knowledge of heavenly and natural things, but it also gives us a complete understanding of how the holy Trinity wants to make the eternal inseparable Godhead dwell in us.

Therefore, it appears to us from the clear, visible light of the Gospels, which suffer no world-wit,[12] but the pure, simple love of God

---

and comes with the body and remains with the same until its matter decays. Evestrum takes its beginning with the birth of any thing. [...] For Evestrum gives the prophecy, [...]. Then to prophesy what will come in the future to man, animal, wood or other from shines from the Evestrum [...]. Therefore the Evestro are at the same time initial and uninitial. —Sudhoff (ed.) 1931, Vol. XIII, pp. 413–4. Trarames according to Paracelsus is an invisible shadow-like being that comes into existence with the awakening of the senses within animals and humans. Its office in nature is to take the impulses of the natural senses and to make them accessible to the mind, thus it functions as a bridge between sensing and reasoning, or in Paracelsus' words: *Trarames gives the sharpening [...]. What is the reason [comes] from the trarames. The uninitial [i.e. the senses] has the initial [i.e. the ideas contained in the Light of Nature, the above Evestrum] to traranium, that is to sharpen within the mind.* —Sudhoff (ed.) 1931, Vol. XIII, p. 414. Turban magna [sic] is a cosmic medium that Paracelsus thought of as containing individual consciousness i.e. to hold independent spirit-nature as well as an embedded ecological function in nature: The prophets and sages of all times used the turban magna to gain access to the Evestrum across all four elemental worlds and thus to gain knowledge of the eternal things that lie beyond the sublunar realm. As Paracelsus says: *And it is necessary for the prophet to recognise the great turban, for it is of great reason and unites with reason. Therefore it is possible for a mortal to recognise the great turban until his last destruction. From within it all the prophets have spoken, for within it are all the signs of the world.* —Sudhoff (ed.) 1931, Vol. XIII, p. 415.

12 In the original *Weltwitz* i.e., scholarly knowledge orientated towards the world.

and neighbour, which love has made a Paul out of a Saul, and comes from a shepherd. Not according to the worldly synagogue, doctrine, schools and pagan documents, but according to the school of the holy day of Pentecost,[13] in this way it is opened to us. As the three Cabalistic principles give: that is, if we desire to be taught by the Holy Spirit, and must ask, seek and knock not for long life, nor for riches, but for divine wisdom (not of the world).

In time, then, everything is revealed to us in an instant, not only in the *Vestibulum*, which is in the mind of man's body, but also in the sanctuary, which is to be known in the mind of the soul, and finally in the holy of holies, which is in the holy Godhead. *Jeremiah 4:9.*[14]

Sapientiae:7.9.15.[15] Therefore, the human body or limbo is synonymous with the forecourt of the temple of God, the sanctuary is the soul, the holy of holies is the Holy Spirit who wants to be our inhabitant and teacher, if we do not make a dive out of his temple with fornication, eating, drinking, gambling, strutting, usury, cutting, scraping, buying and selling.

To us[16] [taught][17] this Theophrastic *Cabalia* that the human body is a house of the soul and the soul a house of spirits, good and evil. Therefore, if our hearts are set on God, and on His Four Gospels to send them into the work of mercy, holiness, and wisdom, we think and speak nothing but godly and heavenly things: but if our hearts are set on base and corruptible things, our hearts and souls are possessed with evil spirits. Then one hears nothing of holiness and wisdom, but only of murders, wars, robberies, stealing, usury, adultery. That is then the hellish fire. There is false teaching and sophistry, jugglery of the high schools and monasteries.

13 This school is a metaphor for the individual practitioner's personal experience of the direct inner inspiration by the Holy Spirit. For further reference read: Acts 2:1–13.

14 Jeremiah 4:9: *And it shall come to pass at that day, saith the Lord, that the heart of the king shall perish, and the heart of the princes; and the priests shall be astonished, and the prophets shall wonder.*

15 See *Book of Wisdom*, chapters 7, 9 and 15. Two critical sections read: *Because all gold, in view of her, is a bit of sand, and before her, silver is to be accounted mire.* [...] 7:15: *Now God grant I speak suitably and value these endowments at their worth: For he is the guide of Wisdom and the director of the wise.*

16 Word is crossed out in the original manuscript.

17 Verb is missing in the original text.

Therefore the foundation of the holy wisdom is the breath of God,[18] that is the spirit of God (who of course wanted to stay 120 years in his temple). *Genesis:6.*[19] *Sapientiae:7.*[20] That man should know God and himself, to be so attached to the mighty Lord Jesus Christ that he becomes spiritually one with Him. Not with the Tartaric gods,[21] that is with the princes of this world, or with the children of darkness and hellish fire: for this purpose the three points registered above: As there be *ask*, *seek* and *knock*.

If we do this diligently, we must not let our holy thoughts be led into Evangelical philosophy and heavenly *Magia*, but cheer ourselves up with all the Wise and holy men of God, and follow Christ. This following is not a path we tread with our feet, but with the holy feeling of mercy toward our poor and neighbouring people, and in which we despise all the honour of this vile world, abandon temporal goods, and love our enemies, converting them to us with holy wisdom, and not forcing them with murderous sword. Then the spirits, the creatures will talk with us and reveal to us the *Arcana Philosophorum* and *Mysteria Cabalistarum*, for they are first commanded to us for

18 In the original: *Vaporis Die.*

19 Genesis 6: *My Spirit will not contend with humans forever, for they are mortal; their days will be a hundred and twenty years.*

20 Book of Wisdom 7:20–30: *For wisdom, which is the worker of all things, taught me: for in her is an understanding spirit holy, one only, manifold, subtil, lively, clear, undefiled, plain, not subject to hurt, loving the thing that is good quick, which cannot be letted, ready to do good, Kind to man, steadfast, sure, free from care, having all power, overseeing all things, and going through all understanding, pure, and most subtil, spirits. For wisdom is more moving than any motion: she passeth and goeth through all things by reason of her pureness. For sheis the breath of the power of God, and a pure influence flowing from the glory of the Almighty: therefore can no defiled thing fall into her. For she is the brightness of the everlasting light, the unspotted mirror of the power of God, and the image of his goodness. And being but one, she can do all things: and remaining in herself, she maketh all things new: and in all ages entering into holy souls, she maketh them friends of God, and prophets. For God loveth none but him that dwelleth with wisdom. For she is more beautiful than the sun, and above all the order of stars: being compared with the light, she is found before it. For after this cometh night: but vice shall not prevail against wisdom.*

21 In the original: *Tartarischen Göttern.*

knowledge and for seeking, as the kingdom of God and subjected to our feet. *Psalm 8*[22] and *110.*[23]

I tell you then, whoever knows, understands and preaches more of the mysteries of the works of the realm of God, will be more and more constant in faith, consequently in blessedness. But an

Ignorant will be cast out into the outer darkness with the ignorant empty lamp-bearing virgins. The poor in spirit are already provided for by God. But we must not seek such a realm of God on their side of the wall, there or thereabouts in the perishable walled temples, but in ourselves. For Christ has come to seek and to find, that is, in his temple, which the holy Cabala reveals to us, that is the man who calls upon God in spirit and in truth, in the wasteland.

Therefore, the more the children of men have fallen from the Cabala, that is, from the *Nosce te ipsum,*[24] the more the [external] temples, the synagogues, the sects and religions have been built up, which have killed the temple of God because of this little word (faith), and have thought they were doing God a favour.

O insanity of Nero, Titus and Vespansianus. O tyranny of Herod, Caiaphas and Annas. O disheartened judgment of Pontius Pilate, O Sodom and Gomorrah, you all shall suffer more unbearably than these wicked bloodthirsty men who condemn the treasure greater than heaven and earth. *Revelat Cabala Sancta haec. Finis.*[25]

Summa Cabala Communis.[26] Where God is to be seen. *Hermes in Pymandro.* God is all in one by nature, indeed he is nature itself in all things. Alpha and Omega. *August: Super John: Psalm 19.*[27] God is completely all things to you. If you hunger, he is your food and

22 Psalm 8: [...] *what is mankind that you are mindful of them, human beings that you care for them? You have made them*[d] *a little lower than the angels and crowned them*[f] *with glory and honour. You made them rulers over the works of your hands; you put everything under their*[g] *feet* [...]

23 Psalm 110: [...] *Sit at my right hand until I make your enemies a footstool for your feet.*

24 Latin: *Know thyself.*

25 Latin: *The holy Cabala reveals these things. End.*

26 What follows is a summary of important references for further study.

27 Psalm 19: *The heavens declare the glory of God; the skies proclaim the work of his hands. Day after day they pour forth speech; night after night they reveal knowledge. They have no speech, they use no words; no sound is heard from them. Yet their voice goes out into all the earth, their words to the ends of the world.*

bread; if you thirst, he is your water; if you are in darkness, he is your light. In your nakedness he is unto you an immortal garment. *Nosce igitur te ipsum.*[28] S. Paul in Acts:17. *In Christ we are, in Christ we move, in Christ we live.*[29] See also 2 Corinthians:13.[30] Finis.

The Other Part of the Theophrastic Cabala

Of the Highest Good
And the Blessed Holy Life,
Which Concerns the Philosophy
Of the Natural Elementary Body.
This is an Insurmountable Blessed Wisdom,
Which has Never Been Heard as So Holy,
Thorough and Simple, as Long as the World Stands.

S*uper nosce te ipsum.*[31] Preamble. Now that we have told you, dear reader, with a brief, simple mind, what man is in spirit, understand also what his office and calling is in this world. From this we take first of all that we men cannot do a more pleasant service in eternity to God's Son, whose dominion is in heaven and on earth, who was given by his heavenly Father to suffer and die, than to follow his inspiration, his spirit, his mandate (on which all trimmings and planets hang).

And to renounce completely all heathen writings, schools and teachings, and to study only the book of the Eternal Wisdom Teaching, which is *Know Thyself*,[32] of which there is no number nor end, so that we may all become like Solomon in wisdom, in which wisdom God wants us to be as perfect as He is, as His prophets, apostles and

28 Latin: *Therefore know thyself.*

29 In the original: *In Christo sumus, in Christo movemur, in Christo vivimus.*

30 2 Corinthians 13: [...] *Examine yourselves to see whether you are in the faith; test yourselves. Do you not realise that Christ Jesus is in you—unless, of course, you fail the test? 6 And I trust that you will discover that we have not failed the test.* [...]

31 Latin: *Beyond knowing thyself.*

32 In the original: *Nosce te ipsum.*

Old Fathers are. For God has no pleasure in fools, jesters, worldly wits and meddlesome world-children.

For such fools cannot know God, much less praise, honour, and glorify Him, who do not recognise, humble, hold in low regard, nor deny themselves. And follow Christ in the poor spirit, not in the wealthy spirit of the ancients. Therefore, to acquire such personal knowledge also hear the elementary body, or the *Corpus Physicum* thoroughly, not paganly. *Vale.*[33]

I
PARAGRAPH PROEMIUM

BECAUSE GOD wants His works and their mysteries to be revealed amongst the children of men (for His glory alone, and for the benefit of men as His image and temple), every man in his time, place and person, as Job 35 also reports, is marked in their hand by God. The works of God (which in this way are known to man and are to be wondered at, as the Psalmist says) he should recognise and examine as living letters, according to the Cabalistic Biblical Doctrine, when they are as it were thrown as a light under our feet, to give us therein unfit for all heathen writings, according to the royal prophet David's teaching, as he says: *Et meditabor in omnibus operibus tuis, et in adinuentionibus tuis exercebor.*[34]

Thus it follows that the man who understands, knows and teaches more about the works of God is also firmer, greater and more in faith, and therefore also the more in blessedness. For the works or creatures of God are the Word. And the book of the Eternal Wisdom of God [was given] to all to philosophize from it and to give his talent to his neighbor not to usurp for self-interest.

Diuitiae salutis, sapientia et scientia,[35] Isaiah says. This book is free to study to the emperor and the beggar, publicly it is placed in the whole nature.

33 Latin: *Be well.*

34 From Psalm 76 in the Vulgate Latin Bible: [...] *and I will ponder over all your works and with your inventions I will occupy myself. For further reference see: Fieger, Michael, Ehlers, Widu-Wolfgang, Beriger, Andreas (eds.), Psalmi—Proverbi—Ecclesiastes—Canticum canticorum—Sapientia—Iesus Sirach.* Berlin, Boston: De Gruyter, 2018, S. 394.

35 Isaiah 33:6: [...] *a rich store of salvation and wisdom and knowledge.*

Os igitur iusti meditabitur sapientiam,[36] David says.
Item. Eccl: *Effudi sapientiam super omnem Carnem.*[37]

This wisdom is given only to those who seek it, ask and knock at God, there it is to whom it is due. Thus says the apostle Jacobus, the one who goes to God with him it abounds, but not in the synagogues or colleges, whose wisdom is only foolishness. *Sapientia 9.*[38]

Where it does not emerge from the Cabala, that is, from the holy

36 Psalm 36:30: *The mouth of the just shall meditate wisdom* [and his tongue shall speak judgement].

37 *I have poured out wisdom on all flesh*; most likely Haslmayr is quoting an adopted sentence from Vulgate: Jesus Sirach 1:10: *et effudit illam super omnia opera sua / et super omnem carnem secundum datum suum = and he has poured it out on all his works and on all flesh according to his gift.* (Fieger (eds.), 2018, p. 1028)

38 Book of Wisdom 9: *Solomon's Prayer for Wisdom: O God of my ancestors and Lord of mercy, who have made all things by your word, and by your wisdom have formed humankind to have dominion over the creatures you have made, and rule the world in holiness and righteousness, and pronounce judgment in uprightness of soul, give me the wisdom that sits by your throne, and do not reject me from among your servants. For I am your servant*[a] *the son of your serving girl, a man who is weak and short-lived, with little understanding of judgment and laws; for even one who is perfect among human beings will be regarded as nothing without the wisdom that comes from you. You have chosen me to be king of your people and to be judge over your sons and daughters. You have given command to build a temple on your holy mountain, and an altar in the city of your habitation, a copy of the holy tent that you prepared from the beginning. With you is wisdom, she who knows your works and was present when you made the world; she understands what is pleasing in your sight and what is right according to your commandments. Send her forth from the holy heavens, and from the throne of your glory send her, that she may labor at my side, and that I may learn what is pleasing to you. For she knows and understands all things, and she will guide me wisely in my actions and guard me with her glory. Then my works will be acceptable, and I shall judge your people justly, and shall be worthy of the throne*[b] *of my father. For who can learn the counsel of God? Or who can discern what the Lord wills? For the reasoning of mortals is worthless, and our designs are likely to fail; for a perishable body weighs down the soul, and this earthy tent burdens the thoughtful*[c] *mind. We can hardly guess at what is on earth, and what is at hand we find with labor; but who has traced out what is in the heavens? Who has learned your counsel, unless you have given wisdom and sent your holy spirit from on high? And thus the paths of those on earth were set right, and people were taught what pleases you, and were saved by wisdom.*

Thesaurinella and Biblical or Theological *Arcanis*, all that it lectures and instructs is in vain. *Sapientia 4.6.7.13.* This wisdom, together with its proud worldly wise men, disapproves and rejects God the Eternal: for it teaches nothing but usury, interest, taxes, benefices, endowments, self-interest, and *Geotiam*[39] and *Gastrimargiam.*[40]

But the eternal wisdom does not seek what you are,[41] she gives to her needy poor people more than herself, she does not beg, *id est*[42] she does not complain about anyone, she sees, knows and has everything, she lacks nothing, she also does not have and yet possesses everything from the graces of God, *id est*, she cures all lepers who fall down and all who are sick. These wise men of God[43] know themselves and therefore they are humble and believe and follow Christ, in simplicity of their hearts, not twisting around his holy word, but letting it remain as it is in Himself, sweet and lovely, without all lavish doctors and mere doctrines and interpretations, easy to understand.

II
PARAGRAPH PROEMY

ALL THE writings of the Christians, I tell you, are falsified, where their reason does not come from the Bible or Theological *Arcanis* (which the Apostle calls *profunda Dei*[44]) and which do not understand the *Trarames*, the *Euestra*, the *Turbam magnam*, the *Durdales*,[45]

39 Read: *goêtia* or daemonic magic; probably a deliberate distortion of the term.

40 Read: *gastromancy* or divination from the belly; probably a deliberate distortion of the term. A likely source of the time for both terms would have been Georg Pictorius' *Pantopōlion—Continens Omnivm fermè quadrupedum* [...] *Quibus accedit Eivsdem De Speciebvs Magiae Ceremonialis*, Basel: Petrus, 1563.

41 The address is now referring to the *worldly wise men* from the previous paragraph.

42 Latin: *that means*

43 Now *wise men of God* is read in opposition to the *worldly wise men* from above.

44 Read: *the depths of God*

45 Possibly a Paracelsian neologism derived from the Greek *Dryades*. As far as I am aware, *Durdales* are only mentioned twice in Paracelsus' entire work. However in his *Philosophia Athenienses* he goes into great detail to explain how the various species of spirits were generated during creation. Air was born as the first and most subtle element from the original fire or chaos, and thus after the separation of the four elements each of them took on their own

which are the angels or spirits of the prophets, by which they performed their miracles, which turn water into blood, like Moses, who struck water from a hard rock and turned a staff into a snake. *Item.*[46] Or also Samson who could slay 1000 Philistines with one donkey, and other prophetic signs more, of which the holy Bible is full, according to the omnipotence of God and the will of His wisdom. Now we find none in our kingdom who understands or has opened and described such mysteries, according to divine honour and understanding; one who actually wills that we all should know and prophesy well and thoroughly (not only a little or supposedly or when drunk) from all his works. *Joel 2*[47] *Item. 1 Corinthians 14.*[48]

For in Christ we have all been taught one mind[49] in every word and wisdom by Christ's future, teaching, walk, life, deeds, and miracles, which He has publicly, personally, and mercifully displayed in this world: where we will not believe His words, yet shall we believe His

---

and pure dynamics and were populated by the respective elemental spirits. Accordingly, *Durdales* are the spirits who enliven the flora and plant-realm; thus of particular importance to the medic and spagyric. Or in Paracelsus words: *And after such separation [of the elements], each [spirit] is assigned its own pre-registered seat and its essence is pre-conditioned. Therefore they are invisible but we can sense them: for no element is more subtly created by the highest Arcane than air. Diemeae dwell in the hard stones, therefore, as soon as they are divorced from the air in the void. Durdales dwell in the trees as soon as their divorce into that substance has taken place. Neufareni dwell in the air of the earth, thus in the pores of the earth. Melosiniae come into the human blood after their divorce from the air in the bodies and in the flesh. The spirits are separated in the air which is in chaos.* Sudhoff (ed.) 1931 Vol. XIII, p 395.

46 Read: *Likewise.*

47 Joel 2: *Blow the trumpet in Zion; sound the alarm on my holy hill. Let all who live in the land tremble, for the day of the Lord is coming. It is close at hand—a day of darkness and gloom, a day of clouds and blackness. Like dawn spreading across the mountains a large and mighty army comes, such as never was in ancient times nor ever will be in ages to come.*

48 1 Corinthians 14: *Follow the way of love and eagerly desire gifts of the Spirit, especially prophecy. For anyone who speaks in a tongue does not speak to people but to God. Indeed, no one understands them; they utter mysteries by the Spirit. But the one who prophesies speaks to people for their strengthening, encouraging and comfort.*

49 The German *Verstand* can also be translated as *reason.*

works, to follow Him therein. *John 14.15.*[50] To create more equity than existed in the Old Testament.

And therefore more shall be possible for believers in Christ than was possible for the peoples in the Old Testament, especially since we[51] are the holy elect people and royal priesthood, as St. Peter tells us. *1 Peter 2.*[52] But where we will not follow Christ in his holy works, there will be no faith, no love, no understanding, no wisdom. There will be no virtues, no mercy, but only the bloody sword, murdering, robbing, lying, cheating, adultery, fornication, wantonness, eating, drinking, gambling. From such fruits the true believers will be known, from the child to the prophet. And then Sodom and Gomorrah will be dealt with more tolerable than such Mouth-Christians, who lead their work only in the empty mouth, who hate others much, and even attack in the smallest cause in cowardly manner.

III
PARAGRAPH PROEM

Now we have found until our time[53] no Cabalistic or *Aniadean* writers at all who would not have borrowed their writings and views from the pagan writings and the sidereal urge.[54] Therefore, the feather has been given to us from above, from the hand of God, which marked me as Theophrastus and anointed and embalmed me for writing. So that from the beginning of the world no greater wisdom shall have been heard to instruct the *sons of the sacred doctrine*,[55] to shame the bastards and pretended wise men, with their heathen confusions and seductions. Therefore, we see all the writings to be

50 John 14: *Do not let your hearts be troubled. You believe in God; believe also in me* [...]. *John 15: I am the true vine, and my Father is the gardener. He cuts off every branch in me that bears no fruit, while every branch that does bear fruit he prunes so that it will be even more fruitful. You are already clean because of the word I have spoken to you.*

51 I.e., the Christians in opposition to the ancient peoples.

52 1 Peter 2: *Therefore, rid yourselves of all malice and all deceit, hypocrisy, envy, and slander of every kind. Like newborn babies, crave pure spiritual milk, so that by it you may grow up in your salvation, now that you have tasted that the Lord is good.*

53 In the original the Paracelsian term: *Monarchei.*

54 The German *syderische Trieb* is here most likely referring to astrology.

55 In the original, *filios doctrinae sanctae* is meant as a derisive appellation of the ecclesiastical scholars.

falsified. For none knew after *Electione Dei*[56] to stimulate the chosen spirits according to Esdra the holy prophet. *4 Esdras 8.9.13.14.* nor to explain or understand the fire. *Nehemiah.*[57] Which fire was shut up in a well until the time of the redemption of the children of Israel.

He who does not have spiritual inspiration from God, let him be silent about theology or the teaching from the school of Pentecost,[58] and do not speak of synagogue or worldly wisdom, Claudicants and Miserants. For we are commanded to know the mysteries of the kingdom of God, and to seek them there first. Therefore, we consider entirely reasonable and seeing those who are grounded in the *Mysteris Dei et Naturae*[59] from above, especially since this is true to the testimony of God, to give the little [people] invocations, seeking wisdom or mysteries, according to the gift of the Holy Spirit and not through the raven, which is now invoked by the opulence of the world instead of the Holy Spirit.

But such mysteries are not to be understood by us in any other way than now to be described: in the same way as with the sealing and sequestration[60] by Nehemiah the Prophet, that no one should find them nor understand them but the true *Aniadus* or believer and follower of Jesus Christ. Therefore, from our writing, the reasonable, wise, believing man can easily understand that no one can interpret and translate the theology and the Bible thoroughly and wisely, truly according to the mind of the evangelists, unless there are the mysteries within him.

56 Latin: *by the election of God.*

57 As is often the case in the manuscript, this word stands alone in the text, not tied into a complete sentence, but as a textual reference for independent further study of the topic at hand. *Nehemiah* is the central figure of the *Book of Nehemiah*, which describes his work in rebuilding Jerusalem during the Second Temple period. Thus, he exemplifies a man (possibly a eunuch) of humble position who still achieved greatness in rebuilding especially the defence-walls around Jerusalem i.e. to defend the genuine faith from its enemies. Just like with the other Bible references in this text, the careful study of the *Book of Nehemiah* is highly recommended to fully understand its relevance and many hints to the present manuscript.

58 See earlier footnote; also compare Acts 2:1–13.

59 Read: *the Mysteries of God and Nature* i.e., the mysteries hidden and revealed in the Divine and Natural Light.

60 *Sequestration* today is used as a legal term to refer to the seizure of property; in context of the Book of Nehemiah it refers to the repossession of Jerusalem i.e. the true faith.

That is why almost all scribes have written according to the pagan and random sect only in the quest of their own honour, glory, praise, ambition and cake [sic!]. The longer, the more. And thus the leadership has come from one to another and has been understood as if heaven hung on only such dead scribes.

IV
PARAGRAPH INCHOATIO

SINCE NOTHING was yet in the whole nature, God created a corpus or *mam*,[61] to which He gave a spirit to govern the corpus and to operate the corpus through a spirit. From such *ma*[62] then by the divine Azot or word *fiat* was made and created the whole *Machina Mundi*[63] and all its notions. [It came forth] From the mouth of God the Father, whose word is a vapour or power and a warm spirit of God's omnipotence and wisdom, which sustains and favours all things with its validity forever. Although the wisdom of God has no number, why then do you many scribes make a number of your pagan Aristotelian wisdom and philosophy which the prophets did not accept. Such a [prophet] would not have finished your *Cursum Philosophicum Narristotelis*[64] or judged according to your worldly wisdom, [understanding] that such a one is not to be a friend of the emperor nor of his school. For it was in vain for the heathen to stand up before your light, Christo, to write [in this light], because they had no understanding nor reason of the word *Fiat* without the prophets and evangelists. Therefore the pen is given to us now to write without all the books of the Gentiles, only from the book of the Word of the Father, which is Christ, the eternal Wisdom, consisting without number in the holy Trinity, poured out for testimony over all nature in heaven and on earth, according to which three are testimony-giving over na-

61 Indicated as abbreviation in text. Read: *materiam* i.e., matter.

62 Abbreviated word again; read: *matter.*

63 Read: *world machine*, yet note the different meaning and connotation of the term *machine* in the early 17th century. [This reference would merit at least a short, succinct explanation for the uninformed reader.]

64 The three words refer to the philosophical course of Aristotle; yet Haslmayr plays a derisive pun on the name Aristotle, calling him *Narristotelis*, which is a hybrid between the German word for fool (*Narr*) and Aristotle. A direct translation would be *Foolistoteles*.

ture, as Father, Spiritus Sanctus in nature [⊖ ☿ ♁]. For equal for him does not appear as unequal; whoever seeks and describes more or less than three in the united number is a liar.

V
PARAGRAPH

ARISTOTLE AND his disciples taught only two principles and described them as the *prima materiam* of all creatures. These are ♁ and ☿; a third no one before me has thought that there is a mother of minerals, which is the ⊖. Now whoever has not understood these principles in the nature of their Trinity, how could anyone write without falsehood and lies about the Trinity, which is without beginning and end, was and will be forever.

If then all (except Hermes) have not known of the Eternal Trinity, why then do you Mouth-Christians set up their writings in your synagogues: they are not your gods, for shall we not all be taught by Christ alone in the natural and supernatural things, who says to us all, *Discite a me quia mitis sum et humilis corde.*[65] Is not he alone the Eternal Wisdom, and the Word *fiat*, wherein is comprehended all things that comprehend the nature of the whole world, in the Holy Spirit, *Spiritus Domini replenit orben terrarum.*[66]

O how sweet is thy spirit O Lord in all things: Is not this speech of the Holy Ghost better unto you than your father's Narristotle the Blue Philosopher,[67] who hath caused a woman to bridle and to ride

65 Matthew 11:29: *Take my yoke upon you, and learn from me, for I am gentle and lowly in heart, and you will find rest for your souls.*

66 From the liturgic introduction to the Sunday of Pentecost: *The Spirit of the Lord fills the circle of the earth.*

67 The colour *blue* has to be read as a symbol for *fantasy*. The derisive term of being a *blue philosopher* is used by Paracelsus in his *Book of the Natural Things* (Sudhoff [ed.] 1930, Vol. II, p. 163). The term also appears again in the Pseudo-Paracelsian compendium *Philosophia Mystica*, published in 1618, large parts of which Carlos Gilly identified to be authored by Adam Haslmayr as well. Here our scribe explains the same idea in greater depth: *Everything comes about through great lot of talking without any thorough inner sensing. Neither the professor, nor the student, nor the disciple, realise: it is just an opinion, a persuasion, a phantasy, a blue vapour, their whole philosophia patched up from the blue philosopher Aristotle. And they cannot be persuaded otherwise, both the professor and the discipulus, for that knowledge flows from the books, yet it is not true; it is*

him?[68] How shall you not be his children and pupils, and become great fools, and fall away from Christ's Eternal Wisdom? If you have Christ in an empty mouth, and Narristotle in your hearts, and in the hearts of your children, and if you esteem him: but whosoever shall be able to put away Narristotle and Plato out of his sermons, let him be a mighty man, and a wise man.

VI
PARAGRAPH

WHO THEN are ever your logicians or philosophers of Christendom, who possess Eternal Peace in wisdom and in a contrite, unpenitent heart in Christ? They want to catch and master Christ in his holy speech as pompous scribes after a proud Pharisaic manner. As if His word required your father Narristotle for the proof of his miracles and holy wisdom, which is only to be found in the little unnoticed [things] after the holy manner of *Magica*, that is, of theology and astronomy, and of *Medicine*, of which you know nothing, [as revealed in] the three evangelical magicians, who were graced by God, that they recognised and sought their Centre and Inspiration in themselves, and lived according to it, in the command, as it were, of the mighty penetrating word *fiat*. So that in all things they have seen and known and attended to physical and metaphysical agents in their material embodiment. As the sacramental body and power of [direct, divine] inspiration, without which nothing can live that lives and strives in heaven and on earth. So that they sought in their own living person the God and the Man, out of themselves, not out of the Narristoteles, in Bethlehem, not in the cushions.

Therefore, we say and teach in our Archidoxical and Philosophical Christian writings that there is no greater wisdom than to know one-

---

absurd, for man is before all books, and the books are of man and man is not of the books. But they never get to that point, that they could think about it, where the reason must be […]. They believe Aristotle, who only recognised the light of nature and only wrote from it. (Adam Haslmayr in *Philosophia Mystica*, 1618, quoted in Peter Peterson, *Geschichte der Aristotelischen Philosophie im protestantischen Deutschland*, Leipzig: Felix Meiner, 1921, p. 272).

68 This is a reference to the story of Aristotle and his lover Phyllis. For a vivid illustration see the woodcut *Weibermacht* (Women-Power) from 1513 by Hans Baldung Grien.

self. And we also say that no man shall see God his Redeemer for ever (except the poor in spirit), unless he understands himself as the New Creature, and learns to realise himself in Christ. After all, [we live] in this transient and destructible body, and understand why man is the image and temple of God, as we teach in the first treatise of this booklet.

VII
PARAGRAPH

THEREFORE, IN this we give you to understand physically and from the Natural Light, that the body, that is the Red Earth of Adam and now all mankind, is an artificial extract from the hand of God, that is a *Quinta Essentia* from the four elements of the great world, from this comes to man the noble name of the small world, that is Microcosm. In this small world, the Son, God wants to put his tabernacle. In this temple's walls Christ wants to be the altar. In this house's walls the Holy Spirit wants to have his dwelling. Now let man examine himself, that he may be found pure and clean at all times, to give lodging to the inhabitant according to his worthiness. From this the reasonable man can easily understand that a mighty king does not take the worst *anima* for his building and house or temple, in which he wants to dwell, but [he takes] the noblest and most virtuous. Strong are those whom he may find in all the world. To this temple rock, the prophet Esaias points out to us in the 51st chapter not in vain, namely that we should have respect for it. This is the stone or rock of true wisdom. A garden of the Eternal Delights of God the Lord. On Abraham is built his castle and in Sarah, who gave birth to us, blessed and multiplied in eternity in *Christo Ihesu et Matrae eius Maria Alma Virgine*[69] in whose lap, in the pleasure garden, the unicorn alone may be caught.

69 Read: *Christ Jesus and his Mother Mary the nourishing Virgin.*

VIII
PARAGRAPH

ON THIS rock now we call all philosophers *Veros et Sanctos*,[70] that they search the great-powerful, virtuous Red Earth, from which the highest medicine extract (in the vegetabile realm, all herbs roots and flowers, also the animal realm, as unicorn, deer, snake, and all metals and minerals, as sun, moon, pearls, adamant,[71] emerald, sapphire, antimony, sulfur, dripsulfur[72] may and shall be drawn from the essences. Therefore we tell you that from this garden of secret power and virtue (which God showed us, not your blasphemers Galen and Aristotle) we can heal again the greatest wounds, even an arm or foot cut off in 24 hours; also have cured dropsy, leprosy, consumption, *podagram*, *caducum*, and all desperate diseases. And where the *Lapis philosophorum* [failed] us, this rock or *Microcosmus* and Adam did not [fail] us. Therefore, we teach you from our philosophy, which comes from the Holy Spirit, not from the spirit of nature alone, and say *Universaliter: Ex quibus sumus, ex eiusdem pascimur, et Nutrimur, et medemur.*[73]

Where man has his infirmity and disease, there he also has his medicine and remedy, [which stands] above all unicorn, gold, and balm, and antimony. Now this is the sacred book of the prophet wrapped together: *Ezekiel 1.*[74] In it all mysteries are read, and the balm of eternity is found, by which miracles are wrought. In which everything is arranged in order, measure, weight and number, as in a great machine. This is John's measurement in the *Apocalypse: 10.*[75]

70 Read: *true and holy.*

71 *Adamant, adamas, adamantite, adamantium* and similar words denote fictitious, very hard metals, minerals, crystals or (semi) precious stones.

72 Note: The final three substances are indicated by their alchemical symbols only.

73 Latin: Universally: *From what we are, from what we feed and are fed and with that we heal.*

74 It's highly recommended to read Ezekiel 1 in full, in order to understand the current metaphor of the book of the prophet wrapped together. Such a wrapped-up book (in German: *zusammengewickeltes Buch*) here refers to the spiritual constitution of man i.e., the divine teachings contained within man and mediated by the inspiration of the Holy Spirit.

75 Apocalypse 10: *Then I saw another mighty angel coming down from heaven. He was robed in a cloud, with a rainbow above his head; his face was*

For this holy temple God suffered on the cross, so that it did not occur to him and he did not regret to have built and created the temple,[76] and not to have it fall to the outcast angels.

As this book is only one, and can only be read by a magician, that is by a true theologian, astronomer and physician, so also the Christian law is only one from Christ, not from Bartholomew nor Baldo.[77] He who can only read this book, judges rightly the blood.

Dixi, in te est, quare, pete, pulsa.[78]

FINIS.

SUMMUM BONUM SIVE VITA SANCTA ET BEATA PHILOSOPHI CHRISTIANI INCOMPARABILIS. D. THEOPHRASTI AB HOHENHAIM.

THIS IS:

The Blessed Life of the Incomparable Christian Doctor
THEOPHRAST OF HOHEHEIM.

WRITTEN IN SHORT RULES,
And Given to All Christ-Zealous,
Holy Fellow Men as a Holy Guideline.
Sursum Corda.[79]

---

like the sun, and his legs were like fiery pillars. He was holding a little scroll, which lay open in his hand. He planted his right foot on the sea and his left foot on the land, and he gave a loud shout like the roar of a lion. When he shouted, the voices of the seven thunders spoke. And when the seven thunders spoke, I was about to write; but I heard a voice from heaven say, "Seal up what the seven thunders have said and do not write it down."

76 Read: *mankind.*

77 Baldo d'Albona (1502–1556) was a Venetian Franciscan and Lutheran martyr.

78 Latin: *I said, it is in you, ask, search, knock.*

79 Latin: *Lift thy hearts.* Liturgical expression.

PREFACE

SINCE THERE are many shouters and writers in the world, we find that they have all written without Cabala and therefore have not recognised what man is, much less what God is. Where there is such ignorance, the people will inevitably be destroyed and not the smallest of the mysteries of God and nature will be revealed, about this, dear reader, trust the scribe who speaks with a fiery tongue and know thyself. Vale.

Nosce te ipsum.[80]

Man should first of all know why he is on earth: what his office is; namely, to do nothing else than to live according to the holy *inspiration*[81] of God, to know himself. For the holy *inspiration* is the breath or spirit and image of God blown into us all; this *inspiration* or spirit of God is the right man, not the body in us men, not Adam's blood.

Sursum Corda.[82]
Ad Sacramentum non Elementale Corpus.[83]

This *inspiration* is the cause of man's being here on earth and taking from it all that he should be. From *inspiration* arise three wisdoms of man, as the animal, the sidereal and the eternal. The first two wisdoms are transient and mortal, but the third is eternal, according to the Gospels.

The fall of Lucifer brought the fall of Adam to depart from the Eternal wisdom and inspiration to the mortal. Therefore, Adam fell from the *inspiration* and Sacramental Body, *id est*, from the *inspiration* of the Eternal Wisdom, and let himself be persuaded to the animal [realm] by the serpent. Therefore, God repents for having blown His Spirit into the body and made man.

80 Latin: *Know thyself.*
81 The term *inspiration* appears in italics in the manuscript from here onwards. It is meant as a decidedly spiritual term indicating a lifestyle and habitus which enables direct personal communion with the Holy Spirit.
82 Latin: *Lift thy hearts.* Liturgical expression.
83 Latin (in this context): *For the Sacramental and not the Elemental Body.*

The body and *limbus* was blood and flesh, which now broke and left the *inspiration* behind. From it had followed that many holy arts, miracles and gifts have vanished and are no longer revealed. So the flesh and blood blinded [man], so that man took care of his flesh alone and not of the *inspiration*. That is, man no longer perceived why he was placed on earth and in paradise, or what he himself was. That is why he became like the animals. And God was afraid that he had blown into man that which is heavenly. From this it can be understood that the *inspiration* was the Holy Spirit, who was with man from the beginning. That is in the flesh and in the blood was the Spirit of God, which was flesh and blood from the earth, [and] was the *Quinta Essentia*. This spirit has therefore departed from the whole world at once. It remained only in seven people. That is: in the ark of Noah, likewise in Sodom and Gomorrah, only in Lot and his [kin] the spirit remained.

At that time, the blood and flesh was turned against the Spirit of God, that is, against the Holy Spirit, against the third person of the Trinity, and believed the wiles of the devil more. Thus it took its origin that the deceiver's head should be crushed, and that God caused His Son to be born, the other Person of the Trinity, whereby He brought and made us into a New Creature, that the flesh and blood also might be of heaven, and [not only] of the earth, and no more against the Holy Spirit, but with Him, in all our walk. This, then, is how it is to be understood. Just as the Holy Spirit comes down from above, so now also our blood and flesh is from Christ, as [it was] then from Adam (which flesh, however, shall be no more). It has come to us, according to the flesh and blood, from the earth below, just as from above.

The other person of the Godhead, that is Christ, makes a whole man. The flesh is to be like the flesh and blood of Christ, we are accordingly born anew every moment now, and regenerated and baptised in the water and spirit of the Body of Mercy (that is bread, wine and other nutriments). They are equal[84] to Jews or Gentiles. *1.Corinthians 12.*[85]

84 Read: *equally accessible* to all people through the act of baptism.

85 1 Corinthians 12: *Now about the gifts of the Spirit, brothers and sisters, I do not want you to be uninformed. You know that when you were pagans, somehow or other you were influenced and led astray to mute idols. Therefore I want you to know that no one who is speaking by the Spirit of God says, "Jesus be cursed," and no one can say, "Jesus is Lord," except by the Holy Spirit. There are different kinds of gifts, but the same Spir-*

Signate mysteria naturae.[86] The mystery of nature is man's baptism, which we should better understand in our book Azoth. In it we teach according to our philosophy, how all creatures, heaven and earth, sun and moon, are the word of God, in which is read what man is, according to theology and Bible, and not according to Plato and Aristotle, who despise the prophets.

Understandably, therefore, we regard as nothing all that philosophy, wisdom, and reason which does not take its ground from theology and is not founded on its mysteries. That is, which does not understand that the Spirit of God is the right man, and that the *mysteria naturae* is the life of man, and that the Spirit of God is the sweetness in all things, and is the life, virtue, and power of all things, which live and float, without which the spirit or word cannot live. *Ecclesiastes: 1.*[87] *Sapientiae: 12.*[88] Hereupon we understand that the old must give way to the new, therefore we believers in Christ now have to use a holy twofold body, that is a heavenly and an earthly one. If we use [only] the earthly one (as is happening now in all Christianity, as well as in the times of Noah and Lot), we lose the heavenly one, which is the highest good in heaven and on earth. Jesus Christ. *Notate Ver-*

---

it distributes them. There are different kinds of service, but the same Lord. There are different kinds of working, but in all of them and in everyone it is the same God at work. Now to each one the manifestation of the Spirit is given for the common good. To one there is given through the Spirit a message of wisdom, to another a message of knowledge by means of the same Spirit, to another faith by the same Spirit, to another gifts of healing by that one Spirit, to another miraculous powers, to another prophecy, to another distinguishing between spirits, to another speaking in different kinds of tongues, and to still another the interpretation of tongues. All these are the work of one and the same Spirit, and he distributes them to each one, just as he determines. Just as a body, though one, has many parts, but all its many parts form one body, so it is with Christ. For we were all baptised by one Spirit so as to form one body—whether Jews or Gentiles, slave or free—and we were all given the one Spirit to drink. Even so the body is not made up of one part but of many.

86 Latin: *Signifies the mysteries of nature.*

87 Ecclesiastes 1: *For with much wisdom comes much sorrow; the more knowledge, the more grief.*

88 Book of Wisdom 12: *For thy immortal spirit is in all things. Therefore thou dost correct little by little those who trespass, and dost remind and warn them of the things wherein they sin, that they may be freed from wickedness and put their trust in thee, O Lord.*

ba.[89] Of this you Epicureans, you Bacchants, you gluttons and drunkards, you buyers and sellers, fornicators and gamblers and dancers have to take good heed. And better than the peoples of Noah and Lot. *Luke:17.*[90]

Three elements also eradicate. Accordingly, we must put off the old leaven, that we may be an unmixed bread, that is, a pure body of Christ, born of the pure virgin, to the new nature, to the new Adam and Eve, that is [drawn out] from the other [old] Adam. Such [born-again] flesh does not resist the Spirit of God, but only the earthly Adamic [flesh], in which it is impossible to look at God our Saviour or to perform miracles.

Now it is to be heard that it is up to us from here on whether we want to let the clay and the earth remain with the Holy Spirit, although they can be so much more [as well as] so much less. Just as Mercury can remain with the Sun and be gilded, so the sun should shine. The pagans are not able to do it. They have to tame their earthly body very much before the true gift, which is given to them and to all men, comes out of them.[91] So one says of Aristotle and the same of many others, but what is in them all that would be found without lies, what does it do: the flesh, which resists the gift of the Holy Spirit, and is distorted to idolatry, in its own madness. Whether they would come on the right track, so it goes wobbly, like a pipe in the water, without stability.

What have the Jews had amongst them that may be found without falsehood: nothing at all. But what was in Abraham, Isaac, Jacob, in Moses, David, Solomon, in Isaiah, Jeremiah, and the like many others, in all of them, however many there may be, amongst them were [many] with a divine, holy voice, and with *inspiration*, and they were guided higher. But this has not happened from *inspiration*, so

89 Latin: *Note the words.*

90 Luke 17: Jesus said to his disciples: "Things that cause people to stumble are bound to come, but woe to anyone through whom they come. It would be better for them to be thrown into the sea with a millstone tied around their neck than to cause one of these little ones to stumble. So watch yourselves."

91 Note the ambiguity of the text here and in later passages. While pagans of all other creeds are condemned as diluters of the original teaching of Christ, they are still included in having received the same divine gifts as Christians in principle. However, it is their pagan lifestyle, their alien morals and idols that prevent them from materialising this gift i.e., the communion with the Holy Spirit.

that they would have acted from it [voluntarily], but God has given it directly so. From intended cause [it has happened], because God caused it so.[92]

But we Christians are those who, without all flesh, may use and open the Spirit of God, so that we put away that body which the Jews, pagans, and [worshippers of] idols have, and walk in that body which we have received from Christ. So the flesh and blood no longer resist the Spirit, but are with the Spirit. For they are both [given] from above. But if we let the First Adam, *id est*, the old blood and flesh walk in us, and do not look to Christ's command and order, according to the holy gospels, the same error is now also with us, as with the Jews, Pharisees, Sadducees, Hypocrites, Gentiles, Tartars, Mamluks and the like.[93]

And not only the same error of the flesh, but also the fancies of evil spirits and devils will possess them, so that they will completely take in the usurers, gamblers, whoremongers, gluttons, and drinkers, the proud, the buyers, and the sellers, the rich, the selfish, and the miserly, and inspire them with such vices, saying that it is not sin, but only a pastime.

But the true believers in Christ have no pleasure and seek to learn from Christ and to do his work as gentle teachers. Once there is no one who praises himself of Christ, but does not pray and perform his works perfectly, without constraints and without fiction, then everything is possible for a believer. *John:14.* And the true believers are to be recognised only by the works of Christ, not by the works of the unholy ceremonialists and sacramenters of this last world, who cause the bloody sword and the mighty hand and wrath of God in the elements, with earthquakes, thunder and lightning, water fountains,

92 Again, our author attempts to resolve the seeming paradox of the wisdom found among pagan ancient authors. Thus, he condemns the foreign gods, habits and lifestyles of their people in general, but admits that particular individuals amongst them had been chosen by God to reveal true wisdom. This, according to our author, did not happen because they held communion with the Holy Spirit, but through a direct intervention of God.

93 As harsh and generalising as the condemnation of non-Christian peoples may be, this paragraph does limit the priority of the Christian claim to salvation: it is not baptism alone that draws forth the divine spirit out of the old, Adamic flesh, but it requires everyday action in daily life to realise this spirit in life. According to our author, therefore, a baptised Christian who performs nothing good is no better than a pagan.

storm winds.[94]

For conversion, we teach from these set paragraphs to all Christians that reason in us is an authority from God, inspired and blown in, because it is the Spirit of the Lord. To it we must perfectly prove obedience in the place of God. It seeks nothing but love and mercy: whatever means or instructs something else, it sees a raven for the Holy Spirit.

The blessed reason asks no one for advice, because it knows everything. Through it we must come close to the Most High Eternal God. *In Vitam beatam et aeternam,*[95] that is to Christ Jesus in *Novum Olympum et Aneyadei.*[96]

Who actually knows Christ, it is enough for him that he knows nothing else. For to know Christ means to understand and know everything, and to want, do and leave nothing else than what Christ wants, does and leaves. This is the Eternal Life. Those who know and believe this stand against thousands and a single pound weighs them on the scales. In these last times of ours, everyone still thinks he is right, that he has and teaches the right, true, saving faith, when he has not yet learned and understood what the spirit and the water of generation are. For the old Adamic flesh, in which no miracles can take place, blinds the light of the Holy Spirit, which is hidden in nature. Thus, there is no more faith in the world when everyone thinks that he is in the world for lust and free will, no matter whether he may walk in the way of God or not. O blasphemy of God and contempt of the commandments of the Holy Spirit. Instead of such an angry teacher, a rope or a millstone around the neck would be better.[97]

Therefore God has ordained from the beginning that all things should be within us, that they should come by *inspiration* from the mouth of the Father, and further that the body should be of the Son and not of the earth: as then the apostle says, *Know ye not that ye are the temple of God, the body of Christ, and an habitation of the Holy Ghost? 1 Corinthians: 3:6.*[98]

94 We note the acknowledged efficacy of pagan ceremonial magic in this text. As in many early Christian texts, ancient magic is not depicted as ineffective or illusionary, but more importantly as morally and spiritually wrong.

95 Read: *in the good and eternal life*

96 Latin: *Christ Jesus in the New Olympus and* the *Anyadei.*

97 Reference to Luke:17, see earlier footnote.

98 1 Corinthians 3: *Brothers and sisters, I could not address you as people*

In this way, the gifts of God that God the Father has inspired us with, that is, through the Holy Spirit, are blown into us without hindrance of the blood and flesh of the earth. That the great works and wonders of God may be inaugurated and brought forth from us, which are in us through God the Father, and through the Body of God the Son. Now the Holy Spirit is in His temple, now the works and miracles of Christ are performed by such a spiritual, wise man, there the lepers are cleansed, there the blind are made to see, the lame are made straight, there the devils are cast out, there the poor are taken in, fed, watered, clothed, the prisoners are released, the enemies are loved, the temporal goods are left behind, the perishable honour is destroyed. There the golden chains, rings and precious stones are not worn on the neck, but given to the poor, the natural miracle medicine is extracted, the *Arcana* are learned, the pagan scribes and books are considered a folly against the Christian wisdom. There nothing is acted but alone the holy work, the mindfulness of the virtues of blessedness, according to the teaching of the four evangelists, and not according to Bartholomew nor Baldo. Not Cicero but Christ.

Therefore, we must know that the Holy Spirit is so inspired in us, through God the Father, without whom the body acts nothing. That is, He does not make the body act what He [the Holy Spirit] wills, but what the Eternal Word *Fiat* wills, and in which He Himself is. *2 Corinthians: 2. John: 1.*[99]

Therefore we write here, through the heart know yourselves. Read yourselves, O all ye believers in Christ. For we know no nobler, higher, holier, and more beautiful art, wisdom, and understanding in this na-

---

who live by the Spirit but as people who are still worldly—mere infants in Christ. I gave you milk, not solid food, for you were not yet ready for it. Indeed, you are still not ready. You are still worldly. For since there is jealousy and quarrelling among you, are you not worldly? Are you not acting like mere humans? For when one says, "I follow Paul," and another, "I follow Apollos," are you not mere human beings? What, after all, is Apollos? And what is Paul? Only servants, through whom you came to believe—as the Lord has assigned to each his task. I planted the seed, Apollos watered it, but God has been making it grow. So neither the one who plants nor the one who waters is anything, but only God, who makes things grow. The one who plants and the one who waters have one purpose, and they will each be rewarded according to their own labor. For we are co-workers in God's service; you are God's field, God's building.

99 Both relevant passages extend over several lengthy paragraphs and are best read in their entirety.

ture of the whole world, than to know, read, and study, and understand ourselves. To be the kingdom of God in and with ourselves. To seek from Christ the Word, the power and the wisdom of God, which we ourselves are all commanded to seek first of all.

The prophet Esais says this explicitly in chapter 51: *Attendite ad Petram.*[100] Pay attention to the rock, and you are water made from it. From this rock and the red earth came the book wrapped together. *Ezekiel: 1.* And the true temple of God, which was built without the hand of man. *Acts: 17.*[101] The temple which John measures. *Apocalypse: 10.*[102]

Know yourselves therefore now, from this writing of ours, since this art was wholly confounded by the heathen arts and logics, and was never so truly and thoroughly described, even unto our days.

Therefore all arts have been taught wrongly, therefore the common good and the eternal religion of the highest good, to the eternal, blessed, heavenly life has been destroyed and the selfish, Jewish,[103] devilish benefit has been raised in all kinds of sects. And therefore hardly one has become a righteous man, even out of 10,000 hardly one has become blessed, and all prayer has been in vain. For all the children of men have forgotten their hearts, as the eyes of the inner, rational man. It is in vain for those to look to God who have not yet learned, who are not yet fit, to see themselves, to humble themselves, to deny themselves, and to follow Christ and the Word of God completely according to the teaching of the four Gospels and their works.

100 Isaiah 51: *Look to the rock from which you were cut and to the quarry from which you were hewn.*

101 Acts 17:25: *The God who made the world and everything in it is the Lord of heaven and earth and does not live in temples built by human hands. And he is not served by human hands, as if he needed anything. Rather, he himself gives everyone life and breath and everything else.*

102 This section actually refers to Apocalypse:11: *I was given a reed like a measuring rod and was told, "Go and measure the temple of God and the altar, with its worshipers."*

103 A clearly antisemitic term, unfortunately common for the time, equating Jewishness with usury. For a more detailed view on antisemitism in Europe in the Late Middle Ages we recommend: Jonathan Adams & Cordelia Heß (eds.), *The Medieval Roots of Antisemitism—Continuities and Discontinuities from the Middle Ages to the Present Day*, Abingdon-on-Thames: Routledge, 2020; as well as: Joshua Trachtenberg, *The Devil and the Jews: The Medieval Conception of the Jew and Its Relation to Modern Anti-Semitism*, Philadelphia: Jewish Publication Society, 1983.

Therefore, not this one is a good Christian who makes a well-ornamented cross on his forehead or wears it on his body, but who performs the holy works of love or mercy of Christ, against friends and enemies, and receives his wisdom from above, from the heavenly *Anyadic* school of the apostles, the prophets (not the synagogues and logicians), who is sustained only by the three Cabalistic principles of *praying, seeking* and *knocking* in spirit and in truth from God, in *Adech.*[104] For if we are all to be taught by God, as the prophet and also Christ say, it must be God Himself and not our supposed earthly schoolmaster or pedagogue, who teaches us about all the creatures and works of God, which are our living books full of mysteries. *Job: 12.35.37.*[105] *Sapentiae: 7.9.*[106] Just as the Theologia teaches, not Plato. Not Galen. Not Cato nor Cicero. Nor other dead letters of the

104 The term *Adech* is another neologism coined by Paracelsus and of critical importance. He used it to specifically refer to the inner man, that is the spirit within humans by means of which they can affect and work with the Olympic Spirits and their inner firmament. In Paracelsus' own words from his Buch der Grossen Wunderarznei: *Who would blame me for reporting that man also works inwardly in the small world, just as in the outer, also inwardly he transmutes nature over nature, [from within] he changes and creates the other beings. For more is in the inward than in the outward [man]. So man is twofold. As his person is a worker in the large world, so in him is also the small world and in the same he has his spirit, which is the other man. [...] And whether I call the same spirit adech because of the difference, who would deny it? So understand that man works in two places, through his [outer] person and through his [inner] laboratory assistant adech.* (Sudhoff (ed.) 1928, Vol. x, p 320).

105 Job 12: *But ask the animals, and they will teach you, or the birds in the sky, and they will tell you; or speak to the earth, and it will teach you, or let the fish in the sea inform you.; Job 35: People cry out under a load of oppression; they plead for relief from the arm of the powerful. But no one says, "Where is God my Maker, who gives songs in the night, who teaches us more than he teaches the beasts of the earth and makes us wiser than[c] the birds in the sky?"*; Job 37: *At this my heart pounds and leaps from its place. Listen! Listen to the roar of his voice, to the rumbling that comes from his mouth.*

106 Book of Wisdom 7: *Therefore I prayed, and understanding was given me; I called on God, and the spirit of wisdom came to me.*; Wisdom of Solomon 9: *O God of my ancestors and Lord of mercy, who have made all things by your word and by your wisdom have formed humankind to have dominion over the creatures you have made and rule the world in holiness and righteousness and pronounce judgment in uprightness of soul, give me the wisdom that sits by your throne, and do not reject me from among your children.*

idolatry Tartars.

So we conclude this little book of ours on the highest good to eternal life. For after work and talent are done, we rejoice heartily, and hope for rest in eternity.

Therefore, we say in a short summary, for our own knowledge: as the human body and the heart are one house and seat of the soul, so also the soul is one house and seat of the spirits, good and evil. Therefore, if our hearts are not at all times aligned beyond themselves, but rather to the pomp, splendour, and folly of the world, then our hearts are possessed with evil spirits and our consciences forget the *inspiration* of God our Creator, through Christ, according to the nature of the mind of the New Creature. Then also the [Holy] Spirit and His virtues are forgotten forever, and His mercy is sinned against. This is the *Lamentatio Jeremiae.*[107]

From this we now teach that man has only to look well to himself, what and who he is, and how the soul springs from the word of God, and how it is the word of God and his breath or *spiraculum vitae.*[108] From the mouth of God made flesh by nature, into mortal flesh, which is created by faith into the living flesh of the new birth. He who now overlooks it, we say, has overlooked it for eternity. *Cognoscite Vosmetipsos,*[109] according to the holy church of St. Peter's humility and doctrine, and not according to Aaron or Solomon nor Constantine.

Now if we let our hearts go to heaven beyond ourselves, *id est*, in ourselves we shall direct it, God sets out to come down towards us. Now this is the circle of man, which is to turn and turn, from man to heaven. Such is the ladder which the Forefather Jacob saw in his sleep,[110] by which the angels ascended and descended: where such climbing shall not be in all points and moments in all our work, art, and wisdom, which the angels teach us daily, and where we carry not our light again towards God, that is, in all our drudgery on earth, and in the works which shall follow us unto Eternal Life, we shall not be found righteous according to the words of Christ *Sequere*

107 This refers to the lamentations of Jeremiah the Prophet that describe the destruction of Jerusalem. See Jeremiah: 33.

108 Read: *the light breath of life.*

109 Read: *know thyself.*

110 Genesis 28:10–17

me, relinque omnia.[111] There is then nothing good about us. Even the Lord's Prayer is then only a poison in our mouth, and a roaring weeping.

Therefore, all true believers in Christ put away pagan concerns, reason and philosophy and follow Christ as obedient children in the simplicity of their hearts. Not in footsteps, but only in the two highest beatific jewels or churches of St. Peter. This is the worship of Christ and all His true followers and faithful Christians and Mary, the Eternal Wisdom and the Holy Trinity, and all the holy elect of God, to whom all men are called.

Pereat igitur multitudo, quae sine causa nata est.[112]

4.Ezra:9.[113]

FINIS.[114]

111 This section refers to Matthew 19:21: Jesus said to him, "If you would be perfect, go, sell what you possess and give to the poor, and you will have treasure in heaven; and come, follow me."

112 Read: *Therefore, let the multitude perish that was born without a cause.*

113 4. Ezra 9:22–25: *So let the multitude perish which has been born in vain, but let my grape and my plant be saved, because with much labor I have perfected them. But if you will let seven days more pass—do not fast during them, however; but go into a field of flowers where no house has been built, and eat only of the flowers of the field, and taste no meat and drink no wine, but eat only flowers, and pray to the Most High continually—then I will come and talk with you.*

114 Read: *The End.*

APPENDIX II

ADAM HASLMAYR
ERGON AND PARERGON
of the
BROTHERS OF THE ROSYCROSS[1]

PRELIMINARY REMARK: The following is a transcription and English translation of a letter today kept in the library of the University of Kassel. It stems from the collected chemical correspondences of the Landgrave Moritz of Kassel and was authored by Adam Haslmayr as personal instructions to the former.

It is of particular relevance to understand the intersection of physical matter and the Olympic Spirits or the Terra Olympi.—For further context and the accompanying diagram given by Haslmayr, please refer to the section on Adam Haslmayr in Book I, Chapter III: On the Birth of the Olympic Spirits.

WORK [ERGON] AND BY-WORK [PARERGON] OF THE BROTHERS OF THE ROSYCROSS

Which is the Cabalistic Descent
of the Earth from Olympus,
Through Whom Nature, Whose
Doctrine is Preferably Hidden in the Earth,
Refers Back to Its Creator
By Drenching and Transposing the Metals.
FATHER, SON, HOLY SPIRIT,

1 source: Chemische Korrespondenz des Landgrafen Moritz, 2° Ms. chem. 19[5], Kassel, 1604-1631, Universität Kassel, https://orka.bibliothek.uni-kassel.de/viewer/image/1380890069017/1/

MIND, SOUL, BODY,
FIRE, WATER, EARTH,
SULFUR, MERCURY, SALT.

1. *God was since eternity imperishable fire, eternal light, full of the spirit and eternal clarity, without beginning and without end.*[2]

2. *This spirit is stronger in God than in his body, because it was made alive by the fire, but in this life it is the soul of the Creator.*[3]

3. *The same spirit, united with itself and consolidated in Divinity, produces a third, of course, the soul that has been in the spirit since eternity, of course, the Word itself. And in the word and through the word is the spirit of fire.*[4]

4. *Such a spirit of the fire of love remains in God without end and is the divine commanding spirit, and who, while He spoke—as everything is created by the word—was in the word the spirit floating above the water.*[5]

5. *This eternal wisdom of God, the Father, and the word causes everything invisibly in itself, as the spirit and soul of God. But in order that the supreme mysteries of the fire and the spirit of God in God might become visible, the fire and the*

2 As we will see, this statement can be read in a dual manner. The appearance of Divinity as pure fire makes both a statement about the quality in which it expresses itself outwardly into creation, as well as about its location in this cosmos. In the Ancient Greek worldview such heavenly fire refers to the realm of the Empyreum which is located beyond the fixed stars.

3 This paragraph refers to the all-penetrating two sides of creation: its inner and outer or spirit and body aspects. It emphasises that the essence of Divinity is indeed present within the outer substances of creation (i.e., the body), but more pure and undiluted in its inner form as fire or spirit, which enlivens the elements.

4 Here we encounter the transcendent ontology of the divine trinity. The fiery spirit sent forth by Divinity, still anchored in the transcended Divinity beyond the realms of creation, brings forth the soul or the *word*. Equally, the last sentence emphasises the mutually dependent nature between *spirit* and *soul/word*: the one cannot be without the other.

5 Now the text is weaving its Neoplatonic narrative into the process of cosmic creation as encountered in the biblical book Genesis. Again, it stresses the simultaneous paradoxical distinctness as well as union of (1) Divinity beyond creation, (2) its expression as divine fire, and (3) its coming into form and individual beings through the souls i.e., the Divine words.

spirit of God in itself came down [as a spirit] to be poured out of itself into the untouched human body, and thus what had been hidden was made visible, and the fire and the spirit of God out of God were glorified through the whole of nature.[6]

6. *Through the spirit floating above the sea, the Creator carried out a division of the divine eternal fire and the outer bodies of creation.*

7. *After such a division had been carried out in the essence of the Creator, God ordered the four elements.*[7]

8. *Finally, the spirit and the fire of the Creator plunged downwards to the stars and the firmament. But in all these individual [beings] was hidden that most holy and blessed essence of the Creator, as the soul in the spirit, which later comes out through all his wondrous creations just like the bodies. Therefore, the divine knowledge of the things was given to this hidden inner and mysterious creation, which drew the lower to the higher. And after the enrichment [of the inner creation] with this divine soul they advanced in their order and multiplied.*[8]

9. *After the fire of the spirit or also the divine essence was given to the creation by the blessing and the [macrocosmic] work was thus completed, it advanced to a beautiful, pure and clear body, namely on the earth and on the water, and the creator took what was pure, clear and beautiful from the*

6 The world of the visible creation is here described as a deliberately anti-gnostic vantage point. The material world is a place of divine revelation enclothed in organic and unorganic matter. All beings, all objects and elements are infused with and expressions of the Divine. The human body is the pinnacle of such creative, divine emergence and a chalice filled with divine fire.

7 In the preceding two paragraphs we see point 5 relativised and brought back into the relation, which was already underlined above: Not everything in the macrocosm has the same share in the divine fire, but there runs a narrow line between inside and outside, between soul and shell, spirit and body.

8 This single paragraph provides a condensed version of the Neoplatonic doctrine of emanation. The divine fire descends from the Empyreum into the realm of the firmament, the stars, and from these into the sublunar world of the elements. It emphasises that throughout this process the integrity of Divinity itself is maintained, however small the spark of its fire might be in any one being, object or element. Thus unmediated God's presence is preserved all the way from the Empyrian realm of fire to grain of sand at the bottom of an ocean.

earth, and drew it out of the hidden [creations] and made it visible, forming an image similar to himself, of course, [this was] man, whom he formed from the fifth essence of the Earth of Olympus, which consisted of the spirit and soul, through the spirit and soul of the Creator, whereby in the earths occurs salt, sulfur and mercury.[9]

10. *If one looks at the metals and other minerals, they are found nowhere else than in the [river] mouths and under the earth [which] consists of salt, sulfur and mercury. These earths are not by themselves and not unmixed, but are mixed by nature with mineral water. While these thus combine and grow, the root of all metals is formed. This is the first substance of all wise men, whom God endows with the knowledge of the highest doctrine of nature. The power of which is in the body, [thus] in the salt, because the body or also the salt maintains with itself sulfur and mercury or also [differently expressed] the spirit and the soul. And one finds such a substance of the highest teaching in the fire and in the water or in [something mixed with] added water, which is not liquid water and does not wetten the fingers. Everything is one thing united. This water cannot exist without earth, which sustains the fire and the air by the spirit of the Creator drifting [around it]. For the connection of the divine essence with the created bodies is perpetual. The divine essence continues in the fire and in the air, as in the spirit and in the soul. But the created continues and becomes visible in the earth and in the water, as in the bodies.*[10]

9 Here we encounter the creation of mankind as the concluding act of divine creation. It is described as the pinnacle of the entire process and derived from the most *pure, clear and beautiful* components of the macrocosm. What emerged from this final act of divine creation was the *fifth element*, the Terra Olympi or the microcosm.

10 In the last section, the narrative switches from the process of cosmic creation to the way of the sage to attain to the revelation of the mysteries of the cosmos. Interestingly, the seeker is directed to the chthonic realm, the sphere of minerals and earth, to begin this journey. In particular, it is the root of the metals that forms the first substance of all sages, which God endows with the knowledge of the highest teachings of nature. The seven classical metals obviously belong to the purest expression of the seven Olympic Spirits in the realm of the macrocosm. Thus, the aspirant is directed to seek at the very place and moment where the metals begin to take form and em-

And this is the secret and mystery of the linkage of the highest knowledge of the philosophical work with the harmony of the inviolable divine Trinity, as the work [Ergon] with the by-work [Parergon].[11]

And this is the work [Ergon] and the by-work [Parergon] of the Brothers of the Rosycross. To God alone the honour.

bed themselves in matter. This coincides perfectly with our discussion of the Terra Olympi in previous chapters, as a term denoting the physical immanence of the Olympic Spirits in actual matter. So in this final section, the aspirant is instructed to reverse the process of creation, to dissolve the metals again, and to explore their roots, where spirit and generative forces are still fluidly intermingled.

11 The text concludes by stressing the linkage of Ergon and Parergon, work and by-work. In other words, to the reader who was able to decipher the hints provided in the prior paragraphs, it emphasises the connectedness and interwoven nature of divine spirit and material matter. It also points the aspirant to inquire carefully into and meditate deeply on the exact nature of *the connection of the divine essence with the created bodies*, which is the mysterious interface of Divinity and created substance, called *Terra Olympi*.

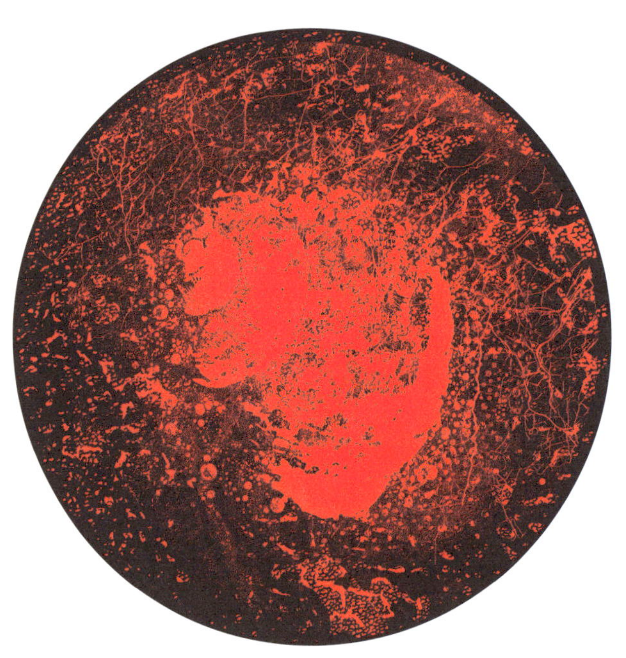

APPENDIX III

Robert Fludd
On the Olympic Spirits
And their relation to Man's Holy Daimon[1]

Preliminary remark: The following is the first full English translation of this critical section by Robert Fludd on the Olympic Spirits and their relation to man's holy daimon. It establishes a critical link in the literary evolution of the Olympic Spirits from 1620 onwards, is liberally quoted by many other authors, and often so in long sections without referencing these. In this thirty-page chapter, Fludd continues the exploration on the Olympic Spirits where Oswald Croll's introduction to the Basilica had left off. Fludd's elucidations exerted significant influence on later authors and acted as a blueprint that, in its classical appeal, quickly began to overshadow many of Paracelsus' original teachings of the Olympic Spirits. Reading this appendix is especially recommended in connection with the section on Robert Fludd in Book I, Chapter III: The Birth of the Olympic Spirits. Additional context as well as the central passages of this text are explained in further detail there.

Third Book. Part One.
Of the Genius of Birth of Each Man

1 Source: Fludd, Robert; Utriusque Cosmi, Tomi Secundi Tractatus Primi, Sectio Secunda, De technica Microcosmi historia: in Portiones VII. divisa, [Oppenheim]: [de Bry], ca. 1620, accessible under: https://www.digitale-sammlungen.de/en/view/bsb11057773?page=86,87

First Chapter
On the Different Opinions of the Authors on The Genius Particular to Each

Porphyrius was of the opinion that for everyone from the ruler of the birth i.e., from the stars an individual daemon or genius comes forth and descends into the human being. This, however, apparently contradicts the opinion of Iamblichus who says that to everyone an individual daemon descends from the form of conception,[2] but, he says, it itself flows out of an even older origin than the stars or the guides of the stars are.

So he [Porphyrius] will have it that each individual Daemon does not proceed from any part of heaven or the elements, but rather from the whole world, the multiform life that is in it, and from the multiform bodies through which the soul passes at its descent into the procreation; and Iamblichus recognises that that Daemon would have been in the *exemplari*,[3] before it had slipped into the conception of the soul. As soon as the soul accepts this as its directing instance,[4] the daemon stands at one's side as fulfiller of the lives[5] immediately after.

C. Maternus,[6] on the other hand, a man versed in astrology who adheres rather to the opinion of Porphyrius than to that of Iamblichus, seems to insist that acquisition and origin of the individual Daemon proceed from the heavens and stars. And yet he seems equally to disagree with Porphyrius on the point that, while the latter, as has been said, seeks to fathom the genius of conception from the star, the former says that it flows forth either from the planets, which show more evidence of dignity and strength in time or space of that of nativity, or from that planet whose (astrological) house the moon entered after that which it possessed at the birth of man.

2 In the original: *figura generationis.*

3 I.e., the sphere of the Platonic ideal.

4 In the original: *dux*, literally leader.

5 [sic!] The original actually gives the plural, *lives*, not life. This is likely to refer to the general function of the daemon in the cosmos, i.e., this process is happening for all human lives.

6 Probably referring to Julius Firmicus Maternus, a native of Sicily, who was a Roman lawyer of the senatorial class. He lived in the first half of the fourth century AD (c. 280–c. 360). His work *Mathesis* is one of the lengthiest astrological treatises that have come down to us from the classical period.

Similarly, the Chaldeans deviate from Iamblichus. Partly they agree with Porphyrius and Maternus apparently in this point; however, partly they also separate themselves with a different opinion from them and say thus that an individual Daemon and/or Genius would come to a child exclusively from Sun and Moon. Therefore they examine it also from these (two planets alone). Others again (to this belong the vast majority of the Hebrews) opine that this must be aspired from some axis of the heavens or even from all of those.

But those again who are versed in popular and folk-astrology, usually strive for the good daemon from the eleventh house of the celestial body (from where also the designation of that house as good daemon comes). Conversely, according to some others, they seek the evil genius of the nativity from the sixth house which is responsible for the blows against the body and the diseases. Or we can rather, according to our opinion, attract the disposition of the genius from that of the twelfth house, insofar as that is the place of the enemies of the child. What is more villainous to the human race, what is more hostile to it, than a cacodaemon? From this it comes also that according to some this domicile is called cacodaemon or evil daemon.

From this it follows that although a certain manner and method are applied to recognise one's own personal genius with the help of astrological rules and observations, these are nevertheless so remote and buried under the impression of wrong opinions and by obscurities in such a way that sometimes it is even considered more impossible to find out the truth of this mystery with the help of the stars' orbits[7] than to produce gold with the help of the teaching and writings of the alchemists.

But as we see that in tracing and searching for God and the true nature we make the most progress with our conceptions *a posteriori*.[8] So it is beyond doubt that although the truth of this matter must be declared by means of a proof *a posteriori*, because according to the possibilities of our imagination we only show the thing itself (i.e., its abstract idea), we cannot in truth say or assert that it behaves in

7 In the original: *per viam syderum.*

8 *A posteriori* knowledge is about inductive logic which derives from observational evidence. It stands in contrast to *a priori* knowledge which can be deduced from pure reason and logic alone. Fludd therefore affirms that what is needed here is practice and personal experience, not mathematical and astrological calculations alone.

such and such a manner unless the very test of our thought proves the result in a plausible way. This is what Porphyrius also seems to agree with when he says: *If someone knew the figure of birth, he would also find as lord of this figure his Daemon, and with its help he would be cured of the fate of birth. But it is impossible to know the former and to find the latter, because the rules of astrology cannot be understood and are uncertain and because around those (rules) many contradictory opinions tumble and are disputed by many etc.* With this he seems to admit that although in astrology a certain method for finding the Daemon or Genius is applied, it is nevertheless almost impossible because of the plenitude of rules and their contradictions.

But we will explain below that there is nevertheless a certain way of finding one's own Daemon by an astrological method, a fashion which (I say it frankly) is based more on my opinion than secured by any evidence or infallible truth. For we confess together with Iamblichus and others, who are extremely versed in the most sacred investigation of this matter, that one's own daemon and guardian originates or derives to each from an older, higher and more metaphysical source or beginning than from the stars and their guides.

Therefore, it will be necessary for us to return to exalted divination in order to obtain through it a rock-solid truth; for divination, to use the words of Iamblichus, will be able to teach us the nature and influence of the stars without artifice. May it be difficult through astrology alone, yet it is easy for the genius to be found through exalted divination—but more on that later.

Chapter Two
About the term Genius, How it Descends with the Child's Soul, And About its Task in the Child's Life

The personal daemon of a child is therefore called genius, because, as it were the daemon of birth[9] i.e., it glides down from the disposition of the world[10] and the stars' orbits, which are present at the procreation, it descends to the origin and procreation.

9 In the original: *daemon genituræ.*

10 In the original: *mundi dispositio.*

The way of this descent seems to be described by Iamblichus as follows. The personal daemon to each one, he says, is not distributed from a particular part of the structure of the heavens or the elements, but from the entire world structure, which, as soon as the soul descends, governs and adapts to it a personal daemon, which the soul has chosen as the executor of life. But what refers to his function in the disposition of the child, the daemon himself, this testifies Iamblichus, connects the soul with the body of the conceived and provides him a combined life (of body and soul) and assigns to the soul a life making power. He teaches to the constant thinking his principles,[11] and after the person is born (and the child is forced), he is forced to do such as what the daemon itself introduces into the mind. He controls us so long until we, who were charged with the leadership of the cult, put the Lord in the place of the daemon.[12] For then the daemon gives way to God and is therefore either freed from its activity or is conducive to it.[13]

But the personal destiny of anybody is assigned to their soul while it descends from the entire body and life of the world,[14] according to how the destiny will behave towards the soul; and such destiny is led and fulfilled by a certain daemon. From this Iamblichus concludes that it is impossible to state constellations of causes with certainty, because we cannot comprehend the interaction of all causes, unless we achieve this by divine inspiration. But our perspective on this we will explain below.

Chapter Three
Whether the Daemon or Genius Is a Part of the Child's Soul or

11 I.e., the personal daemon imprints his nature into the consciousness of the newborn human.

12 Fludd seems to refer to a ritual act as part of an 'inner church' where one's personal daimon is replaced with a direct contact to Divinity.

13 I.e., conducive to divine guidance.

14 In the original: *a toto mundi corpore et vita*

Not and Whether We can Escape Our Destiny with the Help of The Knowledge of the Daemon of Our Conception[15]

PORPHYRIUS ASSUMED that the personal daemon represents a certain part of the soul, obviously the intellect. But Iamblichus tries to refute such opinion with the following words: *If this were so, there would be no other order more exalted than man and superior to man, but amongst the parts of the soul the superior dominated the inferior; but where all are related, none, as it were, absolutely dominates over the inferior. Porphyrius adds furthermore: If the figure of nativity*[16] *and its daemonium could be recognised and pinned down, such Daemon would redeem the child from the fate of its birth.*

To him Iamblichus seems to reply that we are redeemed from our fate not so much by the Daemon as by the worship of the divine power, and adds that the Daemon of nativity proceeds from an older origin than the stars, apparently from the exalted gods. From this he seems to conclude that with the help of the cognition of the figure of nativity[17] we are not freed from destiny, adding at the same time that if the daemon of birth was recognised, the one who recognised the daemon of conception would not necessarily be happy.

And who then accepts this guide to escape from the fates? What we think again of these views, we will state in the last part of this booklet.

Chapter Four

Whether Several Daemons will be Assigned to Each

PORPHYRIUS THOUGHT that a daemon directed the body, another the soul, and yet another the mind. But Iamblichus rejected his opinion and argued that all this is controlled by one and the same dae-

15 Fludd seems to use the terms *daemon of one's birth* as well as *daemon of conception* interchangeably. Thus, at least in the current chapter of the text, he does not differentiate the astrological hour of conception of a child from the hour of its birth approximately 10 months later.

16 In the original Fludd uses the term *figurae nativitatis*. What is meant is the exact astrological horoscope of the moment of birth.

17 *Cognitio figurae nativitatis*.

mon. For it is absurd, he says, to think that one and the same living being is preceded by something multiform.

Furthermore, Porphyrius seems to insist also in another place that each one is given several daemons, each of which controls something else in man. So it occurs apparently in such a fashion that one oversees the health of the child, another its beauty, again another for its particular bodily shape, and in the same manner another one precedes all of these. This Iamblichus denies and responds to it: a single daemon does not merely preside over any part of us, but it stands by the whole all at the same time, it guides everything, as it was assigned by all orders which exist in the world.

Porphyrius, in turn, introduces the contrariety of the daemons which, as it were, govern us; for some he makes good, others evil; whereas nevertheless, this is testified by Iamblichus, nowhere do evil spirits hold strong leadership, nor are they distributed with equal authority and number in comparison with the good.

The magicians, however, who rebel against the Iamblichian unity, assign three guardians or daemons to each person at birth. The first of these they call "holy", which, according to the doctrine of the Egyptians, is attributed to the rational soul not by fixed stars nor by convertible stars, but by the upper heaven, apparently by the Empyreum through God himself, a close confidant of the daemons.

They also say that it is this daemon's task to assign life to the soul and to always provide good thoughts to the mind and to constantly work with enlightenment in us, although we do not always notice it. But as soon as we are purified and live serenely, then it is grasped by us and virtually speaks to us and unceasingly strives to lead us to holy perfection.

The second one is called "genius" insofar as it is the daemon of conception, who descends from the world structure and the star orbits that are present at our conception.

They have it that, however, the third daemon of the child is responsible for its profession and education, of which they convey that it was given by the stars and provided the character traits of the soul and guides the way to worldly dignities and honours.

And in any case they add the following, which was gained from experience, that when our profession is in accordance with our nature, there is a daemon similar to us and in harmony with the genius, and our life becomes more serene, happy and productive. But if we are on the path in a profession which is contrary or dissimilar to the nature of the genius, this will be paid back to us with a laborious life confused by unruly actions, and so on.

Chapter 5
Whether an Evil and Infernal Spirit is Given to Every Single Human Being and Whether The Souls of the Unbelievers After their Separation From the Body will be Granted to These

As every single human being is given a good genius or spirit, so also a bad and infernal one was attributed to him. Each of these strives for a union with our spirit, and its tries with the highest effort to lure and draw it to itself; and just as wine is mixed with water, it tries to bring it into its power at every attempt.

The human being is consequently in the middle between these two antagonists and has free choice there in such a fashion that he usually chooses the one of both as the winner whom he desires. This is because the good spirit or daemon makes us like himself through good works that conform to him, and transforms us into angels by uniting us with himself.

That is why it is also said in Malachi 4:6[18] about John the Baptist, *Behold, I send my angel before your face.* About this transformation and union was written elsewhere: *He who adheres to God becomes one spirit with Him.* But also the bad daemons try to make us conform and unite with bad actions. This is what we can also read from the words of Christ that he said about Judas: *Did I not choose you as twelve and one of you turns out to be a devil?* The same thing seems to be asserted by Trismegistus: *When a daemon flows into the human soul, it scatters seeds of its own knowledge.*

Therefore, having been sown with such seeds, the soul, pregnant with delusion, produces wondrous things and that which is within the daemon's purview. For as soon as the good daemon has flowed into the holy soul, it lifts it up to the light of wisdom. The evil dae-

18 Malachi 4:6: *He will turn the hearts of the parents to their children, and the hearts of the children to their parents; or else I will come and strike the land with total destruction.*

mon, on the other hand, after having been poured into the unformed soul, incites it to theft, murder and lusts, and whatever else is within the scope of the evil daemons. For the good daemons—my witness is Iamblichus—purify the souls extremely thoroughly and by their own presence they lend health to the body, virtue to the spirit, security to the mind. They destroy what is deadly and promote the temperament and make it more effective for life and always render light to the mind in perceptible harmony. Furthermore, amongst the philosophers it seems that a significant division gradually arises, whether daemons will join the human soul after its separation from the body.

In any case, the opinion of the magicians is, this testifies Porphyrius, that the souls take the nature of daemons and become harmful, as those are. Indeed, their opinion seems to be confirmed by Christ's words about Judas Iscariot, appended above.

Mercurius Trismegistus also seems to agree with it explicitly and completely when he says: *A wholly unformed soul, when it becomes a daemon, assumes a body of fire in obedience to God. From there it is poured over into a criminal soul and plagues it with the lashes of sinners etc. But the souls of the good ones are transformed into angels by the virtuous administration of the good daemons.*

Third Book. Part Two.

Of the Genius of Birth of Each Man

First Chapter
About Some Principles to Understand Before We come to the Practice

Before proceeding to the practical part of the Daemon of conception, it will be necessary to understand first the things that lead to such practice, without which it is as impossible to arrive at the perfection of this art, just as it is impossible to arrive at a comprehensive knowledge in geometry without points, lines, planes and solids.

In the first place one must understand that as a point in the geometry is origin and beginning of this art, also in this investigation as in every other matter God is sole unity and beginning, from which the most worthy, very first and strongest creatures have flowed out abruptly.

These behave according to the number of the Trinity, which are simple in the highest measure and rest within themselves; like the numbers one to ten when compared to the fingers, which all are derived directly from the fingers.

The creatures of the number ten[19] are therefore more powerful, because they come closer to the number of pure formality.[20] But as these necessary numbers,[21] by exerting influence and ordering, behave in their scope towards the creatures of the number ten, so also the creatures of the number ten are placed before the number hundred in the announcement of the disposition of the First Ruler. Moreover, also those creatures themselves still further in the things ordered by God the highest by his secret and hidden plan, according to the announcement and exhortation of the spirits respectively creatures of the number ten, complete the will of the King of Kings, assigning to the inferior spirits belonging to the number thousand their part, which is also owed to them and necessary, and dividing equally amongst themselves according to each one's dignity, because it is established to them by the one Creator and made known to those through the creatures closest to him.[22] By means of the creatures of the number ten, then, we understand the hierarchies of the angels, one of whom communicates to the other from above downward, whispering after their manner, the will of their indispensable king. And finally, the archangels and the angels of the lower ranks proclaim that, what they have received from the seraphim and cherubim, and these, finally, communicate the will of their spiritual leader to the lower ones, always appearing as sacred and supra-celestial leaders of the minds which float further downward to the origin of men, as we shall elaborate more broadly below. By means of the creatures of the number hundred, however, we understand the spirits or daemons who direct the courses of the stars. Their task is to preside over the center of

19 *Creaturae numeri denarii.*

20 *Numerus merae formalitatis*, i.e. the Holy Trinity.

21 I.e. the Trinity

22 A slightly convoluted section. Essentially Fludd is using the logical sequential emanation of numbers from the original Trinity to the first decade, century, millennium etc. to illustrate the descending hierarchies of spirits. Through this "ladder of numbers" they all remain inherently connected to Divinity, yet extend in increasingly large and diverse numbers out into creation.

the soul of man and the souls of the other things that concern life and the meaning of life.

From these things is obtained the genius of each individual man, which Porphyrius strove and wished to find with a broad attempt without losing any thought on a supra-celestial daemon who is leading this genius in return. In a learned man, at any rate, this is the greatest mistake and sign of highest negligence, as also Iamblichus seems to recognise with his very frank words. By the spirit, finally, we designate the daemons of the number thousand, who preside over the winds, elements, and earth zones, and who exercise a recognisable power over flesh and body, and who create and prepare a path by which the mind is introduced into the realm of the highest heaven, and the soul or spirit from the middle realm through the air into a lower realm. But what we intend with the simple Trinity, the tens, the hundreds, and the thousands numbers in the book of this treatise, we demonstrate most profitably with the divine numbers: via the simple numbers we have described the simplest nature of the indispensable essence and the harmony or Single Point and, as it were, the unity. From there we have described via the tens the radiant or linear structure of the empyrean i.e., the proportion of the light and the spirit of the same. Via the number hundred the square or surface-shaped composition of the ether in the light and in the spirit. And finally via the number thousand we have shown the body- or cube-shaped structure of the lower heaven.

Consequently, it is said that from the Empyreum these angels or daemons looked upon the bodies of the seven planets; just as also the spirits of the number one hundred, called Olympic, could do nothing without a nod, command and consent of those who show the orders of God to the daemons of the middle region of the world and see to it that they execute correctly and according to divine will what has been ordered and decided by God.

Chapter Two
The Angels of the Empyreum, Guides of the Mind And Protectors of the Child, Who have Power of the Planets And the Daemons of the Same

According to the Fathers of the Hebrews, also the magicians in more recent times and especially Trithemius Abbas, that man blessed with an admirable wisdom, seems to attribute to Saturn an angel named Orisiel, who is also called by others Zabkiel, to Jupiter he attributes Zacharias, or as others want, Zadkiel, to Mars Samael or according to others Gamael, to the Sun Michael, may others also attribute to it Raphael, although this—as seems to me at least—is less correct.

For as it is said of Michael in the Apocalypse that he is, as it were, the leader of the heavenly hosts who has driven back the devil with his posse from above and freed the Empyreum from its belligerence and conflict and from all impurity, so also the heavenly Sun has the power of life, of purification, of multiplication, and is of the highest strength and splendour in the visible world—all the more so precisely because God has pitched His tent in it.

Venus is presided over by the angel Ariel, Mercury by Raphael and the moon by Gabriel. This is also what Trithemius Abbas seems to insist on with the following words: *The opinion of most of the ancients was that this lower world was controlled by the ordering power of the first intellect, which is God, by means of the second intelligences.*

The *Conciliator Medicorum*[23] agrees with their opinion and says: *The seven planets are preceded by seven spirits from the origin of the heavens and the earth for guidance, and so on.*

These seven angels, then, are those most powerful by whose command not only the wandering stars, but especially also the Olympic Daemons, to whom since the creation of the planets the immediate presidency over these very planets has been given, derive their movement. For as the One God looks at the angels of the Empyreum, so also those look at those of the ether and these finally at those of the elementary heaven.[24]

23 The 13th century Italian scholar, Petrus de Abano, translated Hippocrates, Galen and many other Classical Greek medical texts into Latin. His *Conciliator differentiarum philosophorum et medicorum* represents the attempt to create a synthesis of Greek, Arabic, Jewish and Latin authorities on medical questions.

24 In the original: *coeli elementaris.*

Third Chapter
About the Olympic Spirits and First of All About Those Who are Subject To the Regulations of the Empyrean Angels, From Which the Genius of Birth Emerges

The magicians call those spirits "Olympic" who inhabit the firmament and the stars of the firmament. Their task is to determine the destinies and to administer the turns of fate, insofar as God has granted, ordered and permitted this. For neither an evil daemon nor an evil fate can do harm beyond the command of God Most High.

No matter who of the Olympic Spirits teaches this or brings about what the star to which it is attributed will prophesy, without the divine permission they can nevertheless all set nothing in motion. Because it is God alone who gives it to them to be able or to bring about something. And therefore, when they bring a bad fate from a superior angel to someone in whom there is nothing bad, they are corrected by the divine will.

Consequently, God, the Creator of all things, is obeyed by the supra-celestial and the celestial, as well as by those who are under the moon and the hell-dwellers.

Chapter Four
About the Olympic Spirits, Who Have a Direct Power of Command Over the Planets, Together with their Characters

Aratron is the spirit of Saturn, which enables the child to have strength of character and thoughtfulness, and he teaches alchemy, magic and physics.

His character looks like this:

Nota bene: the planetary imprints were turned from right to left due to the carelessness of the scribe.

BETHOR controls what is attributed to Jupiter and leads it to the highest dignities, he brings forth treasures, he unites the spirits belonging to the air that give true answers, he guarantees miraculous remedies in his impulses and he usually promises a long life.

Its character, in turn, looks like this:

PHULEG[25] presides over Mars and his attributes, which leads the one conceived under its domination to the highest dignities in warfare.

His character is this:

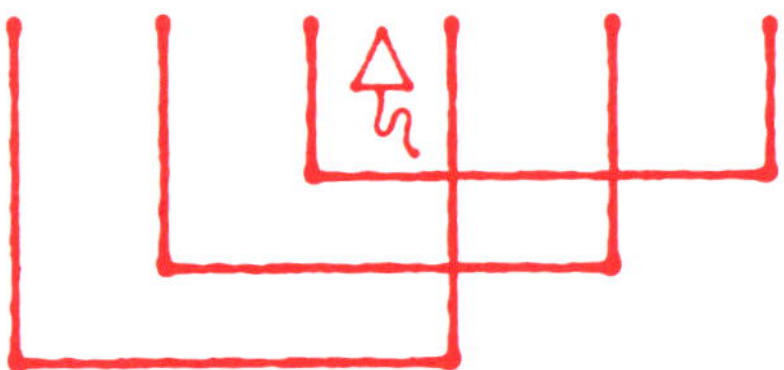

THE SUN[26] offers truly outstanding spirits that teach accomplished medicine. He transforms everything into extremely valuable gold and precious gems, he gives gold and a purse bursting with gold.

Its character, however, looks like this:

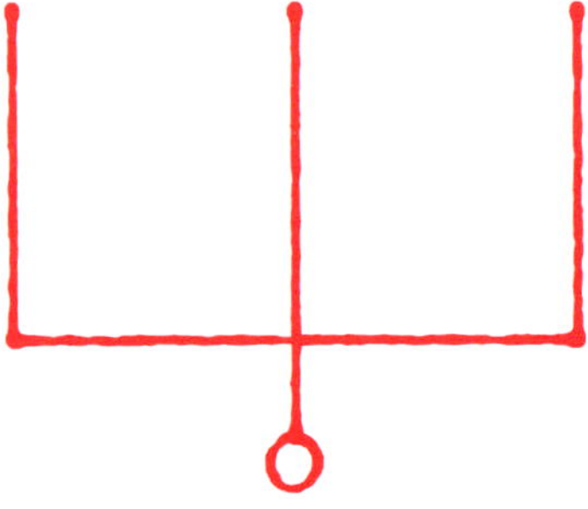

25 [sic], i.e., misspelling of Phaleg as Phuleg.

26 The Olympic spirit name OCH is left out in Fludd's manuscript and replaced with the plain title *the Sun*.

HAGITH, the spirit of Venus, controls the love affairs. The one whom he finds worthy of his imprint, he makes affable and adorns him with every honour. He turns copper into gold in an instant and vice versa gold into copper. His character looks like this:

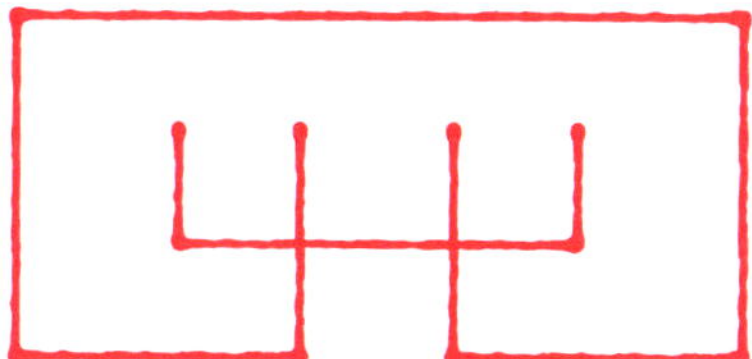

OPHIEL is the spirit of Mercury and helmsman of the merchants.

His character, in turn, looks like this:

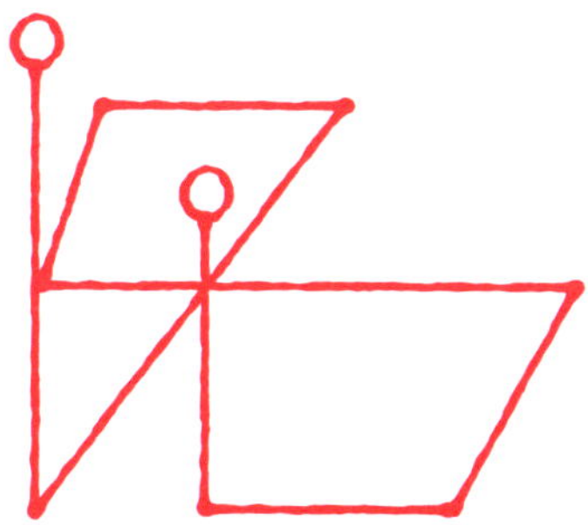

THE MOON[27] bestows the familiar spirits, which teach all arts quite easily. And to the one whom he finds worthy of his imprint, he gives the ability to transform natural ("living") silver into the philosopher's stone in an instant.

His character, in turn, is as follows:

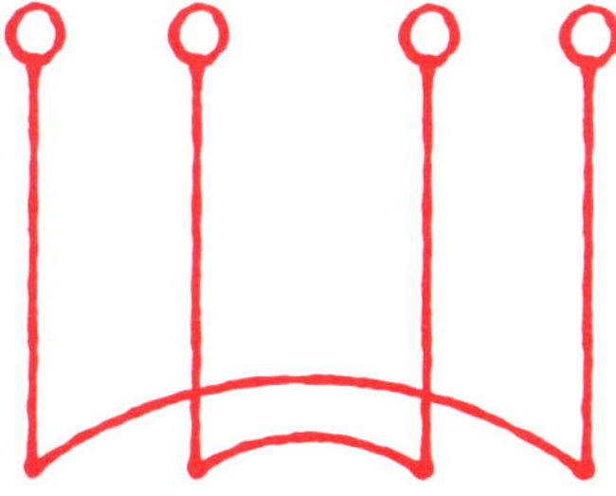

27 The Olympic Spirit name PHUL is left out in Fludd's manuscript and replaced with the plain title *the Moon.*

Chapter Five
About the Olympic Spirits or Angels that Govern the Lunar Houses

THERE ARE even 28 daemons presiding over any lunar house. They begin, of course, with the first lunar house: Geniel, Enediel, Amixiel, Azariel, Gabriel, Darachiel, Seheliel, Amnediel, Barbiel, Ardes(/f)iel, Neciel, Abdiznel, Jazeriel, Ergediel, Ataliel, Azeruel, Adriel, Egibiel, Amutiel, Kyrjel, Bethnael, Geliel, Requiel, Abrinael, Aziel, Tagriel, Atheniel and Amnixiel.

These spirits, then, coincide with the nature of the lunar houses we wrote about in our book on astrology.

Chapter Six
About the Olympic Daemons Who Rule the Signs of the Zodiac

FURTHERMORE, AN animal daemon also presides over each of the twelve signs e.g. Aries is presided over by Malchidael, Taurus by Asmodel, Gemini by Ambriel, Cancer by Mariel, Leo by Verchiel, Virgo by Hamael, Libra by Zuriel, Scorpio by Barchiel, Sagittarius by Adrachiel, Capricorn by Hanael, Aquarius by Cambiel and Pisces by Barchiel.

About these, according to the magicians, it was written in the Apocal, where it is said that in the twelve gates of the New City twelve angels were posted, etc.[28]

Chapter Seven
About the Elemental Spirits And those Who Preside Over the Regions of the Earth

IT IS also necessary to know that in the lowest region of the world, spirits or daemons can be found with many tasks, while others are

28 Fludd refers to the Apocalypse as described in final chapter of the Gospel of John in the New Testament; specifically Revelation 21:12: *It had a great, high wall with twelve gates, and with twelve angels at the gates. On the gates were written the names of the twelve tribes of Israel.*

in charge of the four winds and have been assigned the leadership over the four parts of the earth.

But because the winds are spirits that take their origin from God, the powers of command over them are therefore assigned to the angels of the uppermost region. Therefore Michael was charged with the direction of the east wind, Raphael with that of the west wind, Gabriel with the north wind, and Nariel or Uriel with the south wind. In the same way Cherub leads the element air, the water Tharsis, the earth Ariel and the fire Seruph or according to Philon's opinion Nathaniel. But each one of these spirits is an exalted leader[29] and has the power of great liberty in the dominion of his planets and signs, and in their tides, years, months, days, and hours, and in their elements and the earths and the winds, and in particular each one of them commands several legions.

These are conducive to the disposition of the human body and other creatures at conception.

Chapter Eight
About the Angels Assigned To the Hours of Each Day

To each planet is assigned some supra-celestial leader, as explained above, obviously so: to the Sun Michael, to Venus Anael, to Mercury Raphael, to the Moon Gabriel, to Saturn Orif(/s) iel, to Jupiter Zachariel, and so on.

Therefore, if we want to find the angel that has influence in the corresponding hour of each week and day, we must proceed as it was explained in our book on *Astrologia* in finding the planet that has influence in each hour of the day of the week.

For example: The first hour of Sunday, beginning at sunrise, is claimed by the Sun, the second hour by Venus, the third by Mercury, the fourth by the Moon, the fifth by Saturn, and so also with the rest, as it has been explained accordingly in the previously cited place.

So also we say that the first hour of Sunday will possess Michael, who is the spirit of the Sun, the second Anael, who is the spirit of Venus, the third Raphael, who is the spirit or angel of Mercury, and so on.

29 In the original: *princep.*

Chapter Nine
How the Signs and Planets,
And Consequently the Daemons Presiding over Them,
Will be More Likely to Descend
To a Certain Place on the Earth
Than to Another,
And Therefore, on the Face of it,
Will be able to Exercise and Direct their Powers
There More than Elsewhere

WE GATHER from cosmography that the planets each claim their own region[30] for themselves; thus Saturn is assigned the first region, Jupiter the second, and so on.

We have also learned from the Chaldean writings that other regions are also subjected to a particular sign of the Zodiac. For example: Aries presides over Germania, Britain, Gaul, Syria, Palestine, Poland, Burgundy, Sweden and over the cities of Naples, Florence, Capua, Verona, Bergamo, Padua, Marseilles, Saragossa and others of this kind. Taurus presides over Media, Persia, Cyprus, Poland, Russia, Campania, Rhaetia, Switzerland, Lorraine, Britain, Ireland, and over the cities of Bologna, Mantua, Taranto, Pavia, Palermo, Zurich, Breslau, Leipzig etc. See so also to the other signs according to the order handed down by us in our book on *Astrologia*. There we have explained which Zodiac sign rules over which regions and cities.

After we have recognised this, it will be extremely easy to find the very familiar places of these spirits here on earth. And therefore we must carefully observe the region, the city and the small town or place and which are the houses and the sign in which the lord of a good place is found to be of a daemon or genius of birth.

Chapter Ten
For What Reason the Magicians
Used to Look for the Individual Genius
Of Birth Naturally

THE MAGICIANS, who were versed in cosmology, used to look for the genius in order to be able to avert the fate by his knowledge, familiar

30 In the original: *clima*.

contact and presidency, and so that by his nod the works of life would be successful, happy and favourable.

Therefrom Porphyrius says: *If someone recognised the constellation of the nativity and the originator of such figure, he would find his daemon and would be redeemed by him from his fate and would be able to escape the course of fate and would be happy.*

Chapter Eleven
On the Fashion of Finding The Individual Genius Of Each Human

The magicians used first to ascertain the name and nature of the child's daemon or genius, and then they endeavoured to make the daemon himself familiar and sociable to the child by invocations, incantations, prayers, signs, and other such ceremonies.

Because we want to trace him now, we want to primarily look for the Lord of the eleventh house in the hour of birth. In a second step we want to see which Olympic spirit is assigned to that planet and further which Daemon is entrusted to the sign in which the Lord is found. From that we will see how these two spirits harmonise with each other. Moreover, the spirit of the sign of the eleventh dwelling must also be considered.

So, according to whether the planetary spirits harmonise or disharmonise with the others, the life status of the child will also be determined: either more constant or less constant. Some understand—and this is quite witty—the spirit of the lord of the first dwelling as genius, in so far as he moves above all in the context of the life. Then also the spirit of that lunar house, in which the conception takes place, must be observed. Furthermore, one must pay attention to which wind actually blows more strongly from a region or angle of the world and which element has more influence over the others in that time in which the conception occurs, obviously it depends on whether it is a warm and hot annual time or whether it is windy and rainy or whether it tends to frost and cold. For it is by this that we shall grasp the dominant element, and consequently we shall elicit the more powerful spirit, which also has the strongest influence on the elements.

After these thorough considerations it will be quite possible to gather together the circumstances favourable or obstructive to the birth genius, and we shall all at once recognise which planet's dominion, which house and sign's entry, which wind's blowing, which element's command, which place i.e., which region's existence can be more or less useful to the birth genius.

And by this way and reasoning we will undoubtedly be able to bring about great things, considering and contemplating those things which have been said beforehand with great care.

Chapter Twelve
How to Make One's Mind Familiar And Sociable After Finding Out Its Planet and Nature and Name

Iamblichus states that there are two kinds of treatments for the daemon of each person: a holy or God-made one, which calls the daemon from above with chants[31]. And this one, in any case, does not make use of the research of the conception of each individual, but cherishes and cares for the Daemon in a more comprehensive way beyond nature.

And there is another artificial one which calls the daemon from astrological cycles and this one deals with the conception, researches the conception of each person and nurtures the daemon according to nature in a more specific way.

The former treatment, then, looks to the divine, supernatural, and first leader of the mind, and deals with the angels and archangels, the chief guardians of men. The latter, however, deals with the Olympic Spirits or governors of the centre of the soul, who are subordinated to the angels and archangels. And these Olympic Spirits are those whom those who work artfully around nature, habitually call from the decans, that is, from the shape of the signs and the balances of their influence, from the celestial bodies, from the stars, also from the sun and moon, and likewise from the poles and all the elements and from the world—that is, in the way we said it above—from the structure of the grades of the dwelling of the genius, of the spirit of the same sign and of the Daemon, who is master of the dwelling of the good Daemon or of the eleventh dwelling, and of the Daemon who dominates in the corresponding area of the world and of the Daemon of that element,

31 In the original: *cantis*.

which has stronger influence on the world at the time of the birth etc.

But the way of invoking each daemon is suggested by Iamblichus in the following words: *The invocation takes place with the help of God, the one Lord of the Daemons, who also has determined to each (man) his own Daemon from the beginning and reveals to each man by sacrifice according to his own will.*

For always in the orderly institution of sacred acts by higher deities, lower ones are called. Therefore, amongst the Daemons, a single leader of them, who holds the first rank in conception matters, sends a personal Daemon to each man.

So, after each one has received their Daemon, he extends the way of life consistent with himself and reveals his name and the way of invocation peculiar to him. Now such daemons are the higher ones and they are always benevolent in so far as their seat is above the zone of influence of destiny.

Another order, though related to those previously mentioned, is that of those whom we have called "Olympic." These, in their capacity as executors of destiny, bring to the child either good or bad, and yet they are sometimes hindered in their actions by the divine willpower of the higher-ranking leaders, who are the most powerful messengers of the divine will.

For example: The spirits of the sun and the solar activities of the celestial body itself are hindered by the virtue of the archangel Michael, because God willed it so, and in such a way that the sun at the time of Joshua, as it seemed, came to a standstill for the period of one day.[32]

I say therefore "by the virtue of Michael" because he himself is the supra-celestial overseer and steward of the celestial spirits that inhabit the sun and because he is always ready to carry out the will of his God as much in the demand of an consummation as in the control of the activities at the solar sphere.

But to return to the subject. If we want to have familiar intercourse with the genius or Olympic Spirit of birth, we have to particularly observe that time when the lord of the celestial constellations has a familiar intercourse and a good attitude towards the lord of the eleventh house of the moment of conception. And they should be located, if at all possible, to be found in those houses in which they were

32 Joshua 10:13–14.

at the time of conception. Moreover, if possible, the time should be chosen when the same wind blows that blew at the birth, and there should also be such a mixture of elements as at the birth, and likewise the lunar houses and the arrangement of the sun should harmonise with those, if it is possible.

Under this constellation the character of the planets, which were the lords of the ascendant and the eleventh house, shall be stamped and carved on metal plates according to the nature of the planets. And those characters must be carved even at the times of exaltation and fortitude of both aforesaid planets at the exact hour and day over which these planets have the strongest influence. Then, the person should hold these plates and at the appropriate time, or slightly earlier, but especially at the exact hour and on the exact day the invocation should take place.

Also, the magicians say that Olympus and its inhabitants, in the form of spirits, voluntarily expose themselves to people and perform their duties to those, even if they do not wish to. So how much more will they assist you if you ask for them!

The sages, however, admonish us not to think that the divine invocations of the spirits are similar to human ones, or that, although inexpressible, they can be made more expressible, or that what exceeds every limit and limited measure can be compared to human commands and orders, whether these are finite or infinite. Therefore the inventions of men are stupid and simple-minded and in the end shams when it comes to overpowering daemons and to subjecting to their own command those whom no mortal is able to force against their will. Thus at least this work must be carried out only with the permission of God alone and his invocation, who alone has power and influence over the Daemons.

This also Baconus[33] seems to recognise with these words: *Therein lies the error of those who, disregarding the laws of both theology and philosophy, believe that they can subdue the spirits and that the spirits are coerced by human will. For this is impossible, since human power is far inferior to that of the spirits, or because they err most in the point of believing that by any natural things which they use bad spirits could be summoned or given form, and they err even when men endeavour to appease them by invocations,*

33 Fludd seems to be referring to Roger Bacon (1219–1292).

prayers, and sacrifices, or to make them be useful to men. For whatever man must consider useful would be disproportionately easier to accomplish by God than by good spirits.

God, then, is primarily and solely to be petitioned by prayers, so that the begotten may be permitted to take notice of and gain familiar intercourse with his Daemon, because to him alone and to no one else do the angels of the first rank obey, or those of the region of the Empyrean, and the Daemons or spirits of the middle heavens, called Olympic, render obedience first to God and then to the superior angels. And finally, the lower ranks are subordinate to God first, then to the archangels and angels, and last but not least, they also obey the Olympic Spirits and in such a way that each lower rank of angels honours the higher one. And from this it is said that the higher ones had authority to act over the lower ones and governed and directed them with a certain recognisable power.

So the pious magicians prescribe to their recruits a speech of the following kind, with which they are to invoke the help of God as the leader of the Daemons, in order to attain knowledge and familiarity with their genius:

> *Almighty, eternal God, who created every creature for your praise and glory, and for the service of man, I beseech you that my spirit and genius N.N. of solar, Mercurial, Jupiterian, and other order, to form me and teach me what I will ask him with justice and piety, and that he will instill in me those necessary things for my education in the arts and proofs of my ancestors and of the philosophers, or a method of preserving health, or of leading life rightly, or a method of preserving myself from enemies, etc. But not my will be done, but yours through JESUS CHRIST your only Son, our Lord, amen.*

Therefore, when you have thought through what has been said before in the best way, it is necessary that you also, for the fulfilment of your prayers, prepared in this way, humbly pour out this speech before God from the deepest motion of your heart.

Chapter Thirteen
How, After Knowing the Two Figures of Nativity,[34] We Can Most Easily Recognise in Which of the Two Genius is Stronger, So that, Starting from This, We Can Distinguish Which of Those Two Is More Powerful in Any Zealous Action

After knowing the two people amongst whom there is a familiar intercourse or who have to eke out their life together, a good artist can find out the birth of one or the other, and in both cases he elicits the lord of the eleventh house and the genius of the same, and from that he can very easily deduct which of these has a power over the other, whether in terms of prosperity or in battle or in a position of honour.

Yes, when you have found out which is the lord of the eleventh house in the one and which is his good daemon, but that in the other there is a cacodaemon or spirit of the twelfth house, and that this cacodaemon of the second is stronger, more powerful, and happier in heaven than the good one of the former, amongst these companions or allies, the nature of the one will be highly threatening, dangerous and hostile to that of the other, and what is much more important, this wickedness of the second will always prevail over that of the former.

Thus we read that Marcus Antonius and Octavian Augustus were bound together by a unique friendship and therefore often used to play with each other. But when Augustus always came away victorious, some magician admonished Antony with the following sentence: *What do you want with this young fellow, Antony? Get out of his way and stay away from him! For although you are older and more outstanding by your life experience and also more famous by your ancestors and have endured many wars as a commander of still several people, your genius nevertheless recoils from the genius of this fellow and your fate flatters his fate a little bit; if you don't avoid him, your fate seems to overflow completely to his.*

The genii of Pompey and Caesar, Alexander and Darius were undoubtedly of this kind, too, and although the armies of Caesar and

34 In the original: *geniturarum figurae*. What is meant is one's natal chart.

likewise of Alexander the Great had the size of only a maniple[35] and were not large compared to those troops which Pompey and Darius led, yet the genius of the one was stronger than the genius of the other, and the legions of the one and of the other fought with each other, in a visible and spiritual struggle, and therefore the weaker spirit was defeated and finally lost.

This opinion of ours does not even deviate from the holy scripture, because first we read in Isaiah the following: *There visited the Lord of the hosts of heaven, and in heaven, and above the kings of the earth, and upon the earth etc.* About this fight of the spirits and leaders we read also in Daniel 10—apparently about the ruler of the Persian Empire and the ruler of the Greeks and the ruler of the people of Israel and about the feud of these amongst themselves. And exactly this seems to be recognised also by the poet Homer with this poem:

Such a loud rumbling went through the heavenly court,
When the divines broke out in furious battles against each other.
Phoebus Apollo fought against Neptune,
Pallas Athena fought against Mars,
Juno was opposed to the war by Diana's quiver,
The winged Kyllenian[36] *harassed Latona with firearms.*

But it also happens sometimes that the genii of two conceptions are positioned by nature opposite to each other and the one is nevertheless not more powerful than the other, but that the wickedness of the one equals the wickedness of the other. It may even occur that the genius of one is the cacodaemon of the other and vice versa. For we see in astrology that there are greatest friendships and enmities amongst the planets, for example, amongst Saturn and Venus, as we have shown in our *Astrologia*.

Of this kind were undoubtedly also the genii of the two brothers Eteocles and Polyneikes, whose wickedness as well as power were equal. Therefore, both boasted of victory, both were killed by the hand of the other and what is more important: their spirits did not cease after death to war with each other in a spiritual struggle, in such a

35 Fludd uses an old term to indicate the third of a military cohort.

36 Read: *Mercury.*

way that it was observed that even the funeral pyre on which they had been burned together after their deaths, according to the usual custom, divided, split and were separated, as it were, by mutual hatred.

Apologetic Epilogue

Do not think, dear reader, that I deserve the name of a godless magician because I have lost words about the names of the spirits and about some of their characteres. For I want you to know that I have merely spoken through the mouths of others, and have entrusted to paper those things which I say must not be followed, or at any rate which must not be safely believed.

Nevertheless, I wanted to deal with them in this place, partly for the sake of method and partly from the consideration with which logicians usually taught their fallacies—apparently not to deceive people, but so that they would beware of fallacies and be forewarned.

In fact, in this place we have also traced the empty or rather uncertain void of the ancients, so that you, instructed in a more reliable way, may follow the true, simple and pious path with greater hope and confidence, and so that you may find the genuine daemon of each man and also recognise the hidden truth of the remote astrology.

So, we have done it in the part preceding this book as painters usually do when they spread inferior colours on the edge of some well-known portrait so that the beauty in the inner part of the drawing looks more brilliant. Take care, then, good reader! And when you have carefully thought things through, according to how they behave, perhaps you will not disdain these toils of ours that we have endured, and will by no means expend your effort in vain!

Take care.

Third Book. Third Part

On the True Discovery of the Genius

First Chapter

The Author's Opinion about the Finding of the Genius

Or Daemon of Birth, Individual to Each One. And First about the Angel Proper to the Human Mind.

IAMBLICHUS SAID not quite inappropriately, with which he rejected the unwise opinion of Porphyrius: The consistently personal daemon is conferred from an older origin than from the stars or the constellation of the conception.

For if we think the matter through correctly, we will understand well with the eyes of the intellect that any daemon proper to any of the stars, which we have called above "the Olympic", is the executor and not the corrector of the destiny itself ordered by the divine principal. For whatever God orders the stars and His angels to execute, is necessarily done entirely by them, and is either for good or ill, and is necessarily entrusted to consummation, since everything moves at His nod and obeys His command.

But the angels of the upper heaven, considering that from the moment of their creation they are outside and above the limits of destiny and have been set up accordingly, they do not use to do anything malefic to man or to the world, except in so far as they charge to each one according to his merits the good or the bad, that is, they either assist with their presence the one who is pious and good, or they leave someone in the power of the avenger also for his impiety.

Therefore, Porphyrius very often meant that man would be redeemed from the fate of his birth via the knowledge of his birth figure and the finding of his genius or that he would wander through his life happily. Therefore, admittedly, the Daemon, as Iamblichus rightly says, is both leader of the mind and of a more original intellect and of a higher ancestry and origin than those executors of destiny who cannot pass over and transgress the orders of God even with regard to (something as minor as) a throwing projectile or sting.

Rather, there is a greater power in the angels of the Empyreum to loosen the fate in view of the fact that they are more worthy, more righteous, and closer and more intimate to God than those of middle or lower rank. Hence, because of their outstanding righteousness, they are accorded greater power, not only over men, but also over the lower angels themselves. For as it has been explained in the foregoing that the mind is something divine and not at the mercy of suffering, and not subject to fate, and that consequently the man who adheres to it would command over the stars, in so far as the virtue of his mind is unimpaired, and therefore also over fate, so it follows all the more, that the angels of higher rank, having a most careful care of him, can do much in ordering and directing the mind in man, so that, in the form of a navigator, they may safely guide his way against the stormy dangers of the world, and the cold and rough tempests, into the craved-for harbour of bliss.

But in order to come nearer to my previously stated opinion, and to prepare myself for the breaking up of the dispute of the old philosophers—at least in this case—I want you to remember, provided you have read through the foregoing with careful attention, that I have spoken about three regions of the world, which we have called heavens, and about as many parts of the human soul which derive from those. I have explained that their first and supreme part, obviously the mind, is carried in the spirit of the Empyreum, or the rational and belonging to the intellect, as if it were a vehicle or chariot.

The middle part, however, admittedly the soul's centre,[37] is pulled down into the elementary region in between the spirit of the middle-aether, the one that belongs to life, with its leader and the supra-celestial spirit of the Empyreum. From the forms of the elements—and above all from the fire—these are taken up as kings and are drawn finally through the air down to the earth and originate probably as shadow-bodies.[38]

After these things have been recognised, it will be right and just to believe that the interior of man contains within itself three spiritual parts of the three regions of the world, and that therefore without doubt each one of these parts possesses its own daemon or angel, which takes its nature and seat according to the dignity of the spiritual part of man.

Hence it comes to pass that the mind itself, the divine ray of God, immediately expired by the celestial essence, is received by the first and supreme hierarchy, where one is inflamed with the most flaming love for the Seraphim, and one overflows with the fullness of the knowledge of the Cherub, and likewise one is full of the righteousness

37 In the original: *media anima.*

38 With regards to the particular idea of spirits descending into the elementary realm as shadow-bodies we will want to recall what we discovered in Paracelsus' writings about the power of the Olympic spirits that "tears off the shadow from all the works of the body". See Sudhoff (ed.) 1925, Vol. IX, p 297.

and plentiful in the balance of the Throne. These three[39], I say, from whatever order of epiphany they were chosen, to the glory of the Trinity from which the mind flowed forth, with wings of fire kindling from love, wisdom, and justice, uphold the mind itself, and while closely surrounding it on all sides, they lead it down to the second hierarchy of the Empyreum, and finally leave it in the care of the angels of that hierarchy, having enriched and adorned it with their gifts.

Here, then, the mind is received into a spiritual intellect as into an active vehicle, which is likewise maintained by an angel from any rank of the middle hierarchy or belonging to the epiphany. Thereby, apparently, an angel from the rank of *Dominationes* teaches as a leader in spiritual battles and another angel from the rank of *Principatus* naturally teaches the shunning of the rulers and the way of return to God, while a third from the rank of *Potestates* is entirely in command of the evil spirits. Supported by their brilliance, that spirit in a descent over the west wind in its vehicle belonging to the intellect, draws the mind, adorned with the flames of the light created on the first day from all sides, down to the lowest hierarchy, admittedly to the Ephionia,[40] and is concentrated there.

And with this procedure these angels adorn that mind with its flashing chariot before they disperse with their duties and virtues, and thus the mind is already caught up with the intellect by the rational spirit,[41] the brightest, purest and supra-human spirit, which seems to rejoice and exult extraordinarily in their presence.

In this hierarchy, then, the mind with the intellectual light[42] is similarly received by the three angels, each of whom seems to belong separately to some class of the three ranks of the hierarchy. Therefore, one angel belongs to the rank of those of *Virtues*. To this one it is given from its origin to work miracles; for it is said that in this one the virtue of God shines forth. The second belongs to the rank of the *Archangels*, who is one of the highest messengers of God or the leader of the messengers of God, who represent as it were kings, chiefs and leaders amongst the other angels. But the third belongs to the rank of the Angels. These, I say, receive the mind in its twofold vehicle

39 I.e., the angelic orders of Seraphim, Cherubim and Thrones.
40 I.e., its manifestation or appearance.
41 In the original: *spiritus rationalis*.
42 In the original: *lux intellectualis*.

from the Empyreum with love and respect. To this angel is assigned one of the seven archangels, who (according to Job 12:15) stand at the side of God, like an image of his parents in the place of a leader under the command of God.

From these things it is clear that the mind has in itself the indivisibility, the eternity, the immutability, the lovelessness and majesty of the *Divine Essence*, from which it sprang from the beginning and whose action comes forth. From the *Seraphim* the mind accepted the gift of fire and godly love, from the *Cherubim* the fullness of knowledge and insight, from the Throne the balance and justice, from the *Dominationes* he has it, that he emerges victorious from the spiritual battle and that he has strong influence on stars and destiny and when he is on the carnal earth, he is taught by the *Principatus* to worship their God and to behave decently towards the superiors, from the *Potestates* he has command and power towards the bad spirits of the world. From the *Virtues* it has the ability to work miracles before the world and divine illumination, from the Archangels the gift of prophecy.

Yea, it is even by nature susceptible to all these things, inasmuch as it is a godly ray. But because it is nevertheless per se and in its nature above all angelic ranks and in consequence it is a continuation of God, therefore it could not enter the lower realm step by step without the garb of the virtues of the lower ranks nor think about worldly or earthly things. And because now this divine essence, adorned with his robe from the Empyreum, immersed in a shadow-body, through the wickedness of his hostel, the heaviness, the gloom and the manifold darkness cannot exercise this his virtue or hand it over to the consummation, therefore God attributed to him a good angel as a guide and tenant, so that by his assistance the hostel respectively palace may be protected from the malice and rottenness of the worst spirits, both corporeal and incorporeal, and in such a way that the centre of the soul can remain safe and unharmed from the hostilities and violence of the devils.

Yes, sometimes even an archangel enters the inn of the mind and unites with soul and mind. Indeed, this is how we read it in Zechariah 2:3: *And behold, the angel who had spoken in me left me etc.* The literature, at any rate, bristles with examples of this kind, as will be better seen from the following elucidations.

This error of Porphyrius must be obvious, who groundlessly and voidly asserts that if someone recognised the figure of birth, he could quite easily find out as its commander an angel or daemon, through whom he could be freed from the fate of birth and become happy. For it follows from those said things that this Daemon, who has power over the workings of the stars, holds his place and primary and foremost zone of influence outside the region of the stars and above the firmament in the supra-celestial kingdom, so much so, at any rate, that it is impossible to draw out his nature either from the stars or the nature of his character or his lord, since indeed the power of such a Daemon is exalted above the nature of the heavens on infinite levels.

Yes, he rules even the stars themselves and not do the stars rule him, and all the more we cannot determine his remote structure by means of the investigation of the stars.

More correctly, therefore, Iamblichus asserted that the beginning of the Daemon who averts destiny is older than that it could come from the stars, and he says that he cannot be recognised from the figure of nativity, and he also says that even if the figure of nativity or the Lord or his Daemon were recognised, the child would not be happy. And he says: *Who would accept this leader to escape the fate?* Therefore, he concludes that this overpowering spirit in man cannot be recognised except by divination. But how this is to be done, we will say below.

So it is evident that Porphyrius looked only at the heavenly daemon or the Olympic one, the one belonging to the centre of the soul or to the soul belonging to life, of which we will explain below that it is called *genius* i.e., the daemon of the conception or of the life of the child, and not that holy and supernatural one, which was attributed to the mind, of which the former dwells around the nature and the life of the child and performs there its function and duty destined by fate and by necessity. But the latter equally precedes the mind, the body and the life, and presides even over the middle daemon or genius of birth itself like a ruler, and also over the stars and sometimes over fate, exerting influence by divine will.

Iamblichus says that this holy daemon *therefore unites the soul with the body and takes care of the life shared with the body, that it directs the life of the soul and gives principles to the constant consciousness and we do what that one gives to our mind; he rules in so far until we preside over the holy acts and then we put God into the place of the Daemon.*

And in this fashion we find that holy daemon who, according to the teaching of the Egyptians, is attributed to the mind neither from the stars nor from the planets, but from the upper kingdom, that is, from the ruler over daemons and angels himself, before the latter descends into the midst of his chariot, and we shall show below that this in turn is an angel from the choir of the archangels.

Chapter Two
Some Examples, Taken from the Holy Scriptures and Other Passages, About the Daemons of This Supreme Rank, Who Serve the Pious People

Because of the fall of Adam, according to Sapientia 9,[43] the body weighs down the spirit and the earth-bound dwelling suppresses the thinking power that thinks through many things, therefore we hold that the things that are on earth are difficult and we find the things that open up in our field of vision with trouble. But who will fathom what is in heaven? For who can know the thoughts of God except for the one whom God has given wisdom and sent His holy spirit from on high?

Therefore, the leader of our mind, of whom we have already explained above that he is from the number of the archangels, and which we shall prove below, has no common or intimate intercourse with our body because of the impurity of the flesh. Rather, he is a stranger to it, as it were, and neither does he set up the mind nor control it in such a way that it is received in the body or that its mystery is understood. He merely administers the mind all alone with spiritual signs, and in such a way that when the centre of the soul is attached to the mind and neglects the force of thoughts as well as the formal expression of the elements, which has been polluted by the cravings and appetites of the world, the body itself has a taste of the wisdom of the mind.

And though the angel himself, the chief tenant of the mind, may be ignored by the body of such a person, the angel is nevertheless

43 Fludd is referring to the latest textual addition to the Old Testament, the *Sapientia Salomonis*, most likely written in its current form during the 1st-century CE.

glimpsed by the eyes of the obedient soul centre (through the virtue and beneficence of the mind), and he has some common intercourse with it through a spiritual whisper, though this is not perceived by the shadow-body.

On the other hand now, as soon as the soul, rejecting the control of the mind, is devoted and inclined to the lusts of the flesh and the appetites of the senses, the mind seems to stand empty in the body, not noticing that the body and its soul centre is absorbed in the world of the senses. But the mind continuous to have a communion with its good angel; they have a conversation among themselves according to their custom about the matters of the supra-celestial kingdom and forget the lower things, with the restriction that they are led around by their house, the body.

And a soul of such kind, which has been abandoned by the intellect, I say, is then subjected to fate and has the spirit of fate, which we have called *genius*, as the supreme leader and in such a manner that such a man can just as little avoid his fate and its course as a foolish man. For he does not control the stars, because he cannot be wise nor direct his destiny, because he lacks the helmsman who has power over everything evil that is obviously the mind and its tenant.

Therefore—according to that saying of Mercurius Trismegistus in Pimander XII[44]—*it was determined by fate that he who has committed something shameful shall suffer, and it was determined by fate that some shall be adulterers, some religious abusers etc.* And may it even be that, according to Pimander, everything is the work of fate and nothing corporeal comes without it and nothing good or bad can happen without, that we still say that evil can be averted from the soul if it obeys those superior to it, by the virtue of the good angel and the astute testimony of the intellect.

For Adam, before the Fall, lived in the meadow with the virtue of his super-heavenly guides, that he never for a moment acquired a taste of evil. For who, according to that passage from Sapientia IX included before, can ever avoid that cup of destiny, oh inviolable Founder and Creator of things, if you had not given us wisdom, if you had not sent us your holy spirit from on high? Under the presence of the

44 Fludd is referring to the first tract of the Corpus Hermeticum, Poimandres (Greek: Ποιμάνδρης) also known as Poemandres, Poemander or Pimander; and specifically to section XII: 5–7 which deals with fate.

holy spirit we will be filled with wisdom again and we will overflow and we will be full of all understanding up to the brim, so that we will be free from the impurity of the parents and we fools will turn into wise, and we will rule over the stars and subjugate the wickedness of the destiny and we will acquire the grace of the Son of the living God [...].[45]

For then, after the purification of the body and the raising of the soul, the mind itself and its angel will be cohabitants, both for the body and for the soul, and the voice and the whispering of the angel himself will be received by the ears of the body, and he will even sometimes himself emerge into a corporeal form, as can be gleaned from many passages both of the Holy Scriptures and the authorities of the ancient writers who deserve credence.

From these things it is evident that the divining spirits, after thorough purification of souls and preparation of bodies, will make themselves visible and offer themselves as companions. For example: In the Holy Scriptures we read that an angel appeared to Abraham, further to Hagar, to Jacob and Gideon, to Solomon, to Moses, Joshua, Manoah's wife, David, Elijah, Daniel, Tobias, Joseph and Mary, the mother of Christ, to Peter, John and others. These angels were undoubtedly the very ones who appeared as the first leaders of the minds of those to whom they appeared, as if these angels had been entrusted from their birth with the care of such people as their first leaders.

That is why the magicians and ancient sages assigned to each diviner of the patriarchs and prophets their own divining spirit. They wrote, in fact, that Adam had a familiar communion with the angel Raziel. The name of this angel seems to mean *secret* or *mystery* in the Hebrew language and also the will of God. This, in fact, because Raziel had the best relationship with Adam, in so far as Adam was the first vessel and, as it were, a sanctuary or ointment phial in which God had placed the mystery of humanity, which is His image, and because through this angel He also gave for the first time a revelation of His divine majesty.

In any case, Shem, the son of Noah, had Jophiel as his angel, whose name means *beauty of God*. To Abraham they attribute Zabkiel or Zabdiel, which means *gift* or *gift of God*, who is an archangel and has

45 Three missing words here as text is illegible.

command over the star Jupiter, which others call Zachariel, which means *remembrance of God.*

And surely Zabdiel does not bring the gift of God without reason, because this is also due to Jupiter. It is handed down that he presides over the highest God of the pagans, because where the gift of God is, there is also his valour and prosperity.

From hence also Jehovah Himself and His angel appeared so often to Abraham, made him so rich and clothed him with such great prosperity, and granted him such a fulfilled age of 175 years, in such a way that it is written of him that he departed from life in a good old age, of advanced age, highly aged i.e., he fulfilled the root of the fourfold seven,[46] of which we spoke above in connection with the divine numbers, with the number of his age. Hence it is, obviously under the beneficence and sphere of influence of this angel, that Jupiter is such a favourable star of human life, for which reason those versed in astrology called him *greater fortune.*[47]

Furthermore, they attributed to Jacob the angel Pelle, as if someone said *Pelaia*, that is, *mystery of God* and *miracle of God.* For by the virtue of this angel, Jacob in his vision perceived the angels ascending and descending the stairs, and had the mystery of God, as is evident from the following words of Genesis 28:6: *When Jacob had awakened from the dream, he said, "Truly, God is in this place, and I did not know it." and trembling he said, "How awful is this place; it is nothing but the house of God and the gate of heaven!" So Jacob got up in the morning and carried the stone he had placed under his head, set it up as a memorial, and poured oil on it etc.*

Thus they dedicated Gabriel, the Lord of the Moon, to Joseph, Joshua and Daniel; the hidden meaning of this name is *strength of God, man of God* and *strong is my God.* Moses claimed for himself the angel Metatron, as if someone said *gift of God*, by whose virtue he showed so many miraculous things in Egypt and elsewhere.

Elias had Meltiel, meaning *deliverance of God*, as his servant. Tobias was preceded by Raphael, meaning *remedy of God*, who is the first leader of the star Mercury, or, as some would have it, of the Sun. To David they give Cerviel. To Ezekiel they attribute Hasmael, to Ezra Uriel, which means *light* or *fire of God.* So they attribute to Solomon

46 In the original: *radix quadrati septenarii.*

47 In the original: *maius fortunium.*

Michael, who gives the following explanation of his name: *Who is like God* and likewise *blow of God*. In any case, this angel is the leader and helmsman of the Sun. From this arose the glory of Solomon, from this arose his dignity, his wisdom, and his command, and in such a way that here on earth people used to exclaim: *Who is like Solomon?* yea, there was even, as it were, the stroke of Solomon, that is, fear and terror amongst all nations. This is not surprising, since the archangel Michael is a leader under Jehovah, under whose rulership and virtue Satan with his angels was defeated and cast into the Abyss.

And with all these, it happened in such a way that it is probable that the angels who had familiar intercourse with those mentioned usually appeared to them with a natural bond and affection, and delivered to them the divine commissions rather than the angels who were strangers to their natures.

For thus we see that the nature of Mars is opposed to the disposition of Saturn and the Moon, and likewise the nature of Saturn is fatal to the peculiarity of Jupiter and Venus. And thus we will notice that the disposition of the angels are also opposed and recalcitrant amongdt themselves in a certain manner, if we appreciate Daniel 10 with a careful reading, where we see it written as follows:

The angel said, "*The leader of the Persians opposed me for 21 days, and behold: Michael, one of the first leaders, came to my aid and I remained there beside the king of the Persians*" etc.

On this it is revealed that different angels preside over both different kings and men, and that an angel presiding over a man fights against the angel of the other in war and other disputes. So also the angel of one kingdom fights against the angel of another. And this is also the reason of the transformation or affirmation of a kingdom in a monarchy, and this in turn is the reason of the dissolution and passing of the same monarchy into the controlling hand of another.

But if we already may descend from the sacred to the narratives of the pagans, we find that many more were breathed upon and inspired besides those treated in the Holy Scriptures. Thus we read that Socrates was directed and controlled by his Daemon, whose exhortations he eagerly obeyed, and he often heard his voice and then even saw him constantly in the form of the Daemon. It is said that Socrates with the help of his holy Daemon escaped the malice of fate. For, having been diagnosed by an expert in physiognomy, who had previously looked thoroughly at the face of Socrates, as being highly devoted to all faults and to every vice of indolence, he himself honestly confessed that he had an inclination to all those faults which his physiognomy exhibited, but that under the control of a celestial power he had subdued his own fate and bad inclination, and thenceforth had walked in the paths of justice and probity. Mercurius Trismegistus also did not hesitate to affirm that he had drawn a true and infallible knowledge from his Daemon. His elucidation in Pimander XII is the following: *I heard the good Daemon speak repeatedly, who, if he had written down some exhortations, would have brought some benefit to the human race day after day; that one alone, as if I myself had been born instead of myself as a god, overlooks everything and thus gives us divine oracles.* With a daemon of this kind Plato was undoubtedly also endowed, since he himself expressly affirms that we would be helped by him, turning away evil from us sometimes in dreams, sometimes by signs, and preserving good in greater numbers.

Third Chapter

On the Archangels and Their Duties with Men, Considering the Mind Over Which They Preside, And that the Rest of The Angels Are subject to Them Like a Kind of Slave, And in Consequence all Evil Angels Are subjected to their Will and Power

An archangel is, as it were, the leader and head of the rest of the angels who submit themselves. What is called angel in Greek is called *malach* in Hebrew and *nuncio*[48] in Latin.

The archangels have more dignity than the other angels, because due to their perfection they are perceived and revealed earlier than the others to the [divine] messages, and because through their diligence the lower angels are informed about the divine mysteries.

Their duties to men both according to the Scriptures and according to the treatises of the Platonists and Egyptian sages we shall briefly review.

Isidore says in Book VII, Chapter V: *Among the duties of the archangels is to teach and instruct in those things which are conducive to faith, such as the coming of the Son of God etc.* Indeed, we have it

48 All terms can be translated as *messenger.*

from Genesis 24:7 that *Jehovah sends angels of this kind before the righteous in their undertakings.* And according to Psalm 91:10: *The angels of the Lord will take care of the righteous.* This is what is also evident in the words of the royal prophet in Psalm 91:10, which is this: *No evil shall befall you, and no whip shall come near your tent, because he has charged his angels for you, that they may protect you in all your ways. They will carry you on their hands so that you will not strike your foot against a stone. You will walk over vipers and basilisks and tread down lions and dragons.*

This is the sermon, Jerome testifies, that the prophet intended not only in reference to Christ, but also in reference to every other pious person.[49]

Similarly, according to Kings 3:9, *they spur us on to good and rouse us from the sleep of faults and sins and provide us with spiritual rest so that we do not collapse under the burden.*

In this manner they also drive away evil daemons, as we read in Tobias 8. In situations of doubt, they endow us with sure resolve and make doubtful things clear to us. According to Daniel 11:10, they benefit us on our way and journey. From there, in Exodus 23:20, we read this: *Behold, I send my angel before thee to protect thee in this way, and to bring thee to that place etc.*

We also have such an example in Exodus 32. According to 3 Kings 19, they bring comfort to people struck by grief and melancholy. In Luke 23 and Genesis 16 they move with sympathy and compassion towards us sinners and do not allow or permit us to fall into despair; in Isaiah 24 and Judges 2 they stand by people so that they do not fall, in Isaiah 24 they help the righteous against their enemies so that they are not defeated. In Genesis 32 Machab. penult. they offer medicine to the wounded so that they do not die, in Tobias 11 they bring food and drink to the hungry so that they do not perish in the midst of hunger. In 2 Kings 19 they present our sins to us and set them before us so that we may see them and be filled with shame and remorse on their account. In Joshua 2, they open up the will of God to us and teach us what to do. In Luke 2 they lift up obstacles and impasses so that we

49 We recall Paracelsus' view that the apostolic time was still with us in the present moment and open to everyone as a first-hand experience. That is, the Christian apostles should not be revered, but understood as personal role models for people's own way of life and of perfecting their own faith.

may serve God, according to Exodus 23 they often visit us and during the visits they admonish us not to transgress the divine will. In Isaiah 40 they are always in the presence of God to behold Him. According to Luke 1 and Daniel 7, they bring the prayers of the people before God and worship God ceaselessly. In Isaiah 6 and Apocalypse 5, they behold God face to face without veiling; according to Matthew 18, they teach people and reveal to them the future. Hence the archangel Gabriel says to David, whom he had preceded as a guard, "*I have come to teach you what will come to pass for your people on the last day,*" Daniel 10:14.

So they teach prophecies and make prophets, they expel cacodaemons that have power over people, as we read exactly in the story that this was performed by the archangel Raphael. So the archangels repel evil spirits from men, as the [spirits of the rank of the] *Potestates* repel undertakings of evil daemons against the divine majesty, as narrated by Dionysius, who even seems to affirm that intelligences of this kind raised, inspired and brought men to the knowledge of God, and that they taught and instructed them to live piously.

And so we could go through infinite other duties of the archangels and their servants, secured by the testimony of the Holy Scriptures, but it would be too lengthy to describe all this here. —Let us hear, then, what the pagans imagined about these daemons and what duties they assigned to them.

Iamblichus was the first to point out that the intelligences amongst themselves do not differ or harmonise according to their nature or differences therein (for they are unmixed in the highest degree), but they are distinguished by how they behave for whatever reason towards the First; and they are distributed on the highest, others on the following and still others on the lowest levels of perfection.

Taking into account therefore the difference in the perfection of these stages, he separates elsewhere the intelligences into gods, daemons, heroes and pure spirits. Above all these he recognises the highest Good or the one God, on whom the created gods follow. The souls he makes the last and lowest level of the intelligences, between which and the gods he has placed two links, apparently the daemons and the heroes, just as between fire and earth are located air and water.

The daemons, which are superior to the heroes, have more share in the nature of the gods, but the heroes have more share in the nature of the soul. Therefore it comes that two middle parts have share and are composed of the peculiarities of the two extremes.

Therefore, since the peculiarity of the soul is to incline to the multitude, it follows that also the heroes, who participate in those, incline and turn more to the parts and the movable things than the daemons do. Since the peculiarity of the gods consists, as it were, in unity, their abiding in themselves, in the immovable ground of movements, of outstanding foresight, it follows from this, in a similar way, to the contrary, that the daemons, in so far as they adhere to them, contain within themselves the gifts of the gods and incline to unity.

Duty and task of the daemons is to circle around the worldly natures, the perfection/completion of things and the attachment of the soul to the body. Duty of the heroes, however, is to animate, to guard the souls and to detach them from the body.

From this it is clear that the duty of the daemons extends further than that of the heroes, since the former work more around the totality, while the latter work more around the souls. The archangels and angels, however, the philosopher seems to place instead under the higher daemons; or rather he seems to ascribe to them elsewhere a rank of their own between gods and daemons.

His words are the following: *The images or figures of the gods are obviously completely unchangeable etc. Those of the archangels and angels are gradually less unchangeable, but still close to the gods. Those of the daemons are changeable etc. Those of the heroes are almost alike those of the daemons. Those of the souls finally are by far more changeable than those of the daemons.*

Here he apparently separates archangels and angels from the daemons. But in the place quoted before he mixes them with the daemons. In the latter distinction, however, he seems to perceive those intelligences which are placed next under the Empyreum to be placed above the daemons. Apparently these are the twelve zodiac signs of the daemons, which also possess the starry heavens; and above the heroes he seems to perceive the Olympic Daemons, or those spirits which preside over the planets.

Therefore, he says that it is the duty of the daemons to carry out their work on the worldly natures down to the detail, and at the same time to complete it, and to bind the souls to the bodies.

The duty of the heroes, he says, is to enliven and to guard the souls. And as the duty of zodiac extends further than that of the planets, inasmuch as it acts first upon the planets and the elements, so it revolves more around the totality. So also the duty of the daemons extends further than that of the heroes, because the latter revolve more around the totality, the former rather around the souls.

Still, we gather from the testimony of the sages that all intelligences, whether they are called "created gods", or "archangels and angels", or "spirits, daemons, and heroes", are often subsumed under the appellation of "daemons", as different species are subordinated to the same genus.

And we say that the daemons who dwell above the stars are good daemons. So also the Olympic daemons and those of the middle world realm are in any case good with regard to themselves and through themselves. But with regard to us, towards whom they act fate-bound, they work sometimes good, sometimes bad and are also called good and bad.

Thus the daemons of Saturn are called "bad misfortunes"[50] and Saturn itself is called "bad star" or "greater misfortune".[51] Similarly, the daemons of Mars are called "minor misfortunes",[52] whereas the peculiarities of the daemons of Jupiter and Venus are sometimes opposite.

The Chaldeans and the Egyptians, therefore, seem to divide them into sacred daemons, star daemons or hosts of procreation or birth or birth constellation, and elemental daemons, which are judged to be the worst of all. They claim that the sacred daemons are those attributed by the god of daemons supreme to the descending rational soul, all of whom are elevated above mundane nature.

They say that it is their duty or assignment to direct the life of the soul, to always instil good thoughts in the mind and to work towards constant awareness within us, even if we do not always notice this activity in our soul. But as soon as we are purified and live serenely, then the daemon itself is registered by us and, as it were, talks to us and lets us participate in its voice, where before it was present in silence, and it constantly strives to lead us to the holy completion.

They also pass on that with the help of this daemon we could avoid the malice of fate and we read that Socrates did it in this fashion. And the Platonists believe that this daemon helps people in a miraculous

50 In the original: *mala infortunia.*

51 In the original: *maius infortunium.*

52 In the original: *minora infortunia.*

way, averting bad things sometimes by dreams, sometimes by signs, and preserving good things in greater numbers.

And this also seems to be affirmed by Iamblichus in the following words: *This one unites the soul with the body and takes care of the life shared with the body, that it directs the life of the soul and gives principles to the constant consciousness and we do what that one gives to our mind; he rules in so far until we preside over the holy acts and then we put God into the place of the daemon. Then the Daemon gives way to God or desists from his work or benefits Him.*

And in another place he says: *The daemon had been in the likeness before he slipped into the begetting of the soul, whom the soul at that time first assumed as leader. This daemon from then on stands by our side as the fulfiller of the lives, it binds the descending soul to the body and as their common being it takes care of them, directs the life proper to the soul. Whatever we compute, he gives us the rules of computation, and we do what he puts into our minds, and he directs us until, purified by holy works, we approach God instead of the daemon as leader, to whom the daemon so yields after these things that he is idle or contributes benefit under God's presence.*

Porphyrius also says that by the help of this holy daemon we avoided the malice of fate. But we conclude that this daemon is the supreme of these three daemons of the body, the guardian of the intellect, leader and tenant who subdues to the mind what is best for the intellect and repels from it what is shameful, steersman of discursive reason in the case of the righteous and the good, who fills the interior of the intellect with wisdom.

Thus he has the helm and power over the whole man and in the consequence also over the daemons, which precede man, himself — not differently to the intellect of the wise man compared to the living, air-like or feeling soul.

For inasmuch as the mind is descended from supra-celestial generators, on its way down it seeks a supra-celestial leader and tenant within itself, who, together with its friends—the intellect of course and reason—leads it into the light or mid-heaven soul and its spirit. And at the same time, in addition to all this, he connects them with the body under mediation of the more fluid elements, as we will elaborate more broadly below.

From this it becomes evident that archangels of such kind, while serving them as their leaders, have command not only over the Olympic Spirits, who are helmsmen of destiny and its course, but also over the elemental spirits and the cacodaemons, who possess the lowest region of the world and want to strike men with evil. As we can read in the book of Tobias that the archangel Raphael seized a daemonium named *Asmodeus* and bound him in the desert of Upper Egypt etc. Through these things we are taught that everything that is good has command and power over evil from the time when the supreme good with its angels expelled the supreme evil and contentious from heaven to earth. Therefore, the divine foresight has positioned anterior or more powerful daemons of this kind near us and entrusted them with leadership, to whom it has entrusted us, as it were, as our shepherds and guides, to help us daily and to keep evil daemons off, in check and in fetters, so that they do not harm us at will, as it is also explained in the attached story.

Chapter Four
About the Seven Angels Who Stand in the Presence of God And that Each of Them is the Leader Of Several Thousand of the Leading Angels, The Ordinary Angels and Those of the Lower Species

We gather both from the teaching of the Holy Scriptures, but also from the order of the nature belonging to the destiny, that the highest heads of the archangels were set up in the number seven by God, because indeed this number is that principal and virgin one, from which and in which and through which God—in His form unmixed, whole and with regard to his nature indispensable—mixes Himself with the unformed matter, so that He leads it down from the power to lead the water or the wet nature.

In quite similar view also the heads of the archangels are chosen in such a number by their creator, so that they behave in the number three in analogy to the sacrosanct Trinity, the one God and their Lord, and fulfil and accomplish in the number four the orders and His will in the material mass.

This, at any rate, seems to be recognized by the royal psalmist in an unequivocal utterance in Psalm 103:20: *Praise Jehovah, ye his angels, who are exceedingly strong with your power, who perform his word, and listen to the voice of his word. Praise Jehovah, all you his armies, you his servants who follow his will.* But to demonstrate the number seven of these first archangels with a weightier testimony from Scripture, we read Tobias 12:15: *I am Raphael, an angel of the seven who stand by Jehovah.* And Luke 1:19: *I am Gabriel, who stands on the side of God and was sent to speak to you.* And Daniel 10:13: *The angel Gabriel said to Daniel, "See, Michael, one of the chiefs, came to my aid etc."*

Now these three are the chiefs from that group of seven, which Raphael also mentioned in the place quoted before, and each of these has power over any of the seven planets, clearly in light of the fact that they always stand at the side of God and hear the voice of His word, and yet in between accomplish and execute His word, as well through themselves as through servants, armies and virtues set up amongst them and subjected to them, who are in the middle and lower heavens, as we understand from the words of the psalmist mentioned before.

Hence it comes that even though the aforementioned seven archangels are in the presence of God, they nevertheless exercise command over the seven planets and the daemons that are theirs and likewise over the fixed stars that are related to them in terms of their nature and disposition.

Thus we see that one and the same emperor remained in Rome, while Africa, Asia and Europe nevertheless obeyed him. And again, the helmsmen of Africa, Asia and Europe could stand by the side of the emperor who stayed in Rome, while those kings who were used to preside over each region of these continents could nevertheless not execute or order anything except what was permitted and ordered by the helmsmen, who nevertheless dared to distinguish themselves by nothing against the will and order of the supreme and greatest emperor. Therefore, in a similar fashion, it is allowed to compare the highest and greatest as well as best[53] God with the first emperor, to whom one after another, in the direction of his kingdom, one rank of angels is subordinated step by step.

Thus the archangels hear the voice of the divine word, the second rank of angels carries out that word, and the third rank is that of the servants who carry out the divine decree shown to them by the upper

53 In the original: *optimus maximus.*

ranks from unity. So the angels in the middle receive from the upper ones the enlightenments and clarifications that they reveal and give to the lower angels in such a manner that the will of God is done on earth as in heaven.

To these archangels the sages have given such names: Oriphiel, Zachariel, Samael, Michael, Anael, Raphael, and Gabriel, who, according to this order, are assigned to each planet as they descend, evidently as Trithemius Abbas, who in this does not differ from the opinions of the magicians, says, namely, that Oriphiel presides over Saturn, Zachariel over Jupiter, Samael over Mars, Michael over the Sun, Anael over Venus, Raphael over Mercury, and Gabriel over the Moon. He also relates that the helm was attributed to each of them for 354 years and according to the order for a period of four months each. This position was agreed to by most highly learned men so far. His words are as follows: *The opinion of most of the ancients is, wisest Caesar, that this lower world is controlled by the ordering power of the first intellect, which is God, over the following intelligences, and so on.*

These seven angels are undoubtedly those who measure the time of the world, which John mentions in his revelation, reporting that each one of them consecutively blew into their horn and poured out the bowl of tribulation, in such a way that amongst the former judges of England, whenever any impossibility in the law or in the court was encountered by them, it used to be said therefore in the proverb: *This will come to pass in any case when Gabriel will sound or sound with his horn.*

From there it is clear that amongst the ancients it was certainly believed that the name of this best angel, to whom it is given by God to sound the horn on the Day of Judgement, is Gabriel, who presides over the last and lowest of the planets and therefore will have the last rank also at the end of the world.

To these ideals of the seven archangels, all the lower good angels are subordinated and obey them and wage spiritual warfare under them as their leaders, according to Apocalypse 12:7: *And there arose a great battle in heaven, Michael and his angels fought with the dragon, and the dragon fought and also his angels etc.*

Similarly, we gather from the following words of Zechariah 2:3 that the lower angels take the role of servants for the upper ones and render obedience: And behold, the angel who spoke in me went out.

And another angel stood in his way, and said unto him, "Run, and speak unto this lad, saying, Jerusalem shall be inhabited without walls." etc. From these things it is evident that one angel presides over another, and that an angel with a higher office commands one with a lower office. Having considered these things, we see that there are seven chief angels, or archangels, who stand by the side of God and undoubtedly exercise command over the lower ranks and those of lower office who are in the multitude, as we gather from Matthew 26:53: *Or do you think, said Christ, that I cannot ask my Father to send me more than twelve legions of angels?* So also Luke 2:13: *And suddenly there was with the angel the multitude of the heavenly host praising God and saying, "Honour to God in the height."* And elsewhere, *One million etc.*

So it is evident that there are an infinite number of angels other than these seven who are the heads and the angels, to use the words of the prophet, who listen to the voice of God. And they are all servants and slaves to these first angels. Therefore also below the archangels the good angels have the first place and receive their illuminations from the archangels not differently than the archangels from the upper hierarchies and God Himself. Furthermore, the Olympic Spirits also receive their illuminations directly from the angels who occupy the lower rank in the last hierarchy of the Empyreum.

Having recognised these things, it must be known that each of these angels, by a certain natural disposition, has a certain period of dominion over its own star or planet which is subject to it, and in the same way, above the specific sign of the Zodiac, possesses the more powerful angel of the whole heavens.

Hence it comes that at the time when an angel thus holds his dominion, the daemons both of the zodiac sign and of the planet over which he rules are also stronger, freer and more active than the other daemons of the rest of the stars, which are indeed subjected to him for this period. But this period of supremacy lasts as long as that planet over which any one of the aforementioned seven angels rules has a more exalted expression of its strength throughout the heavens.

Thus, if someone is born in the time when, for example, Gabriel becomes head of the whole heaven and the world, then either he himself or one of his supra-celestial angels will become helmsman of the child's mind and one of the daemons from the lunar region will preside over the life of the native, and likewise a spirit of the element of water, which is most subordinate to the moon by its nature and disposition, will control its air-like soul, which has arisen from a formative merging of the elements. And similarly in the other cases—and in such a manner that the spirits of the legions, which are devoted to each of the aforementioned angels, in the time when their masters become stronger, will dominate the other daemons of the world, as it has been plausibly un folded in the formation of the meteors, in the change of the world and in the change of the seasons.

Chapter Five
About that One of the Seven Angels or One of Their Leaders, Who are very close to Them In Authority, has power over The Human Mind. And about the Fact that Several Angels keep Watch over a Human Being. Also A Refutation of the Opinion of Iamblichus, who assigns a Single Daemon over the Inner Realm of the Human Being

I know, there are many who will say or—if I am not mistaken—even now say that not every man has his individual angel, who presides over him, as a controller of his mind.

To these we will answer with a single saying from the words of Joseph, that every man has a holy daemon that presides over him. The words, according to Genesis 48:15, are as follows: *The angel who keeps me from all evil blesses me and these boys etc.* From this it clearly appears that Joseph himself confesses that he was saved in his life by a daemon and his holy angel and was preserved from every danger and sin. Similarly, we gather the same from the words of our Savior: "*See that you do not condemn one of these lowly ones. For I tell you that their angels in heaven always see the face of my Father who is in heaven.*" Matthew 18:10.

Therefore it is that the magicians never tire of saying that Adam consorted with the angel Raziel out of familiar habit. Shem, the son of Noah, with Jophiel. Abraham with Zadkiel; Jacob with Peliel and Joseph with Gabriel. Therefore it is clear that also that angel, whom Joseph mentions with the words indicated before, was the angel Gabriel. It is said that the same one also presided over Joshua, Daniel and even Mary. So Moses was on intimate terms with Metatron, Elijah with Maltiel, Tobias with Raphael, David with Cerviel, Ezra with Uriel, Solomon with Michael, and so also with the rest, as was said before.

From these things it follows in a most evident manner that not always one of those seven archangels in their very own person tends to preside, but that very often also one of the leaders belonging to them fulfils that protective function on their behalf. Thus, on the basis of what was said before, we see that Abraham had in the place of his angel Zadkiel or Zacharias, the head of the star Jupiter. Daniel had Gabriel, helmsman of the Moon; Tobias had Raphael, presiding over Jupiter. Solomon had Michael, head of the solar sphere.

Hence it must be observed that each one at birth is granted one of these leaders, who shall preside over the mind of the child, and shall make it admirable to man, and fit for him to know the mysteries and secrets of God, and to possess the revelation of the sacrosanct majesty. Similarly, the rest of the angels also have a tremendous and remarkable power from those guides, with whose help they thus constantly endow the child with much happiness and knowledge.

Hence, Jophiel is, as it were, the beauty of God, Raziel the secret or mystery of God, Uriel the fire or light of God, Peliel, as it were, the mystery and wonder of the Lord, Phadael the salvation of God etc. They derive directly from the other heads both as to their power and as to their authority.

Yea, it even sometimes comes to pass that these holy angels claim for themselves the name of the child; thus we read in Ezra that the name of the archangel Jeremiel comes from the prophet Jeremiah, so also Zachariel from Zacharias, and Uriel from the prophet Uriah, whom Joachim slew. In the same way, Samael and Samuel, Ezekiel and Daniel are names of prophets and angels in the same way etc.

Yea, even several angels are guardians of the microcosm[54], as was said before: of them, one looks after and cares for the mind, intellect and reason as a leader, another looks after life, and a third after the condition of the body and its desires.

But because this opinion of ours will seem to some to be harsh and too far from the truth, we maintain that it is explained and proven by

54 I.e., a human being.

the words of the prophet David, who says in Psalm 91:10, *No evil shall befall thee, neither shall any whip come nigh thy tent, because he hath commanded his angels to watch over thee in all thy ways. They shall bear thee up in their hands, lest thou dash thy foot against a stone; thou shalt walk upon the adder and the basilisk, and tread down the lion and the dragon.* This is what, according to Jerome's testimony, applies not only to Christ, but to every human being.

Therefore, all men are directed by the service of different spirits, contrary to that opinion of Iamblichus, who says that a single daemon assists not only any part of us, but the whole man, and guides him as a whole, and he delivers that it is also better that body, soul, and intellect be controlled by one and the same daemon, and concludes with the following words: *Do not make this division, that one daemon belongs to the body and another to the soul, still another to the intellect; for it is absurd, that while there is one living being, at the same time to think that the daemonium, which is charged with the direction of living beings, is multiform, and so on.* With these words he tries to reject the views of Porphyrius, who affirms that each man is presided over by several daemons, one of which bears concern for health, another for beauty, and yet another for a certain bodily form, and who also makes the assertion that one daemon governs the body, one the soul, and another the mind. On this point, then, I am Porphyrius' advocate, and will therefore equip myself well to wipe away the disgrace with which he has been smeared by Iamblichus, with the following considerations.

First: If only one daemon, be it supernatural, presided over the body and soul as well as the mind, then every man, through the virtue and assistance of this daemon, would escape his fate and would avoid all blows of fate, and in consequence neither fate nor stars would have any power over man, which Iamblichus himself seems to deny, contradicting himself, who, indeed, recognises in one place, that there is fate to which men are subjected, and yet he says that fate can be avoided by virtue and the presence of the daemon who presides over man. And in such a manner that—if this were so—all men could indiscriminately avoid their fate, in so far as they participated in such a daemon and only one daemon, and from this consideration would be entirely free of fate daemons.

Further, he says that it is better that body, soul and intellect be controlled by one and the same daemon, whereas all authorities in both theology and philosophy recognise that between soul and body there is a huge discrepancy and antagonism, so that one wonders how and through what mediator these two should be linked.

Besides, it is a peculiarity of the archangels, as Iamblichus himself testifies, to be opposed to darkness. Therefore, they do not rejoice and delight in the body, because it is the prison of the divine mind, but with the greatest effort they train the mind and direct it to escape from the temptations of the body and carefully guide and persistently strive to free the mind and the imprisoned soul from the dark body with the help of their perfected virtue.

And likewise, if a single and solitary archangel or daemon were head and helmsman of both the body and the mind, it followed that it directed both the body and the mind, which can never err. Nevertheless, we see that body and flesh is inclined to every vice and kind of lust, and therefore there can be no doubt that the latter is controlled by an inferior daemon, which is of lower constitution than the archangel. The former, however, becomes subject to the archangel, as does an inferior to the superior, when the centre of the soul is constantly and faithfully attached to the mind.

By a similar reasoning, the soul belonging to life, if it had no other daemon distinct from the two external ones—i.e., one separate from the daemon of the mind and from the daemon of the body—would not be so inconstant and changeable as to adhere sometimes to the mind, sometimes to the aerial soul, which is a more formal part of the corporeal composition.

Further: If only one daemon directed the whole substance, both inner and outer, it would be strange that the mind would be so alien to the soul and the body, and likewise the body to the soul, and both mind and soul to the body, as we perceive it to be in human beings.

From this it is evident that there are more daemons than one, which have power over the whole man. Therefore the last consideration of Iamblichus is as void as the previous ones, when he says the following: *Do not make this division, that one daemon belongs to the body and another to the soul, still another to the intellect; for it is absurd that there should be one living being, but that the daemonium charged with the direction of the living being should be multiform.* For I answer that it is more absurd to believe that a single living being has only one daemon, than if someone said that the world, which is one, has only one daemon, which controls all and each of its parts. But who doubts that on the one hand there are daemons of the Empyreum, on the other hand there are Olympic and etheric and elementary daemons, by which those regions of the world are controlled?

Who, since the human body is composed of the four elements, will hesitate with a similar consideration in the question whether one of the elemental angels has command in the body? Rather, one must believe that each partial spirit of each element has power of command in its part of the body.

As far as the interior of man is concerned, however, it is impossible to believe that the bond of life with the ether can be maintained without the guidance and protection of the Olympic daemon, or that the blows of fate which befall man would be imposed without regard to the celestial spirits.

But on the point that Iamblichus says that a living being seeks one leader and not a multiform one, we add that both macrocosm and microcosm have both a single and a multiform presider. I say that they have *one* in so far as they are looked at by the supreme and one God, and they have a multiform leader in so far as they are controlled by servants or intelligences according to the will of God. For man is called microcosm because he has in his composition a share in a certain region of the macrocosm and in consequence also seeks the worldly daemons and angels of the same to control those aforementioned parts.

But to return at last also to the error of Porphyrius, by which he thinks that several daemons existed according to the number of our parts, and that further also in the body itself there are different daemons, of which he lets some be responsible for beauty, others for health, and still others look to the form in these, I answer that what is possible by fewer is done in vain by many. Therefore, if one daemon, charged with the direction of the body, can look and pay attention to all the parts of the body, one looks for several daemons in vain. Since, then, as the leader of the soul belonging to life, the Olympic daemon, as best it can, is able to look and pay attention to the beauty and health of the body, why seek several daemons for such a task? Therefore, having really thought this through well, we shall see with our spiritual eyes that there is a daemon of the mind, a royal and by far principal one, which we have proved above to be an archangel, another for the soul belonging to life, which we call the Olympic spirit, which is always the executor of destiny, and finally a third, which looks after the body and the tasks of the body and its desire. But about these we will share more in another place.

Chapter Six
On the Descent of the Mind into Soul And the Middle Spirit, Where it Connects with Material Life And Where Its Dark Harborage[55] Lives, Moves, and Makes its Capacity Flexible

Apuleius, in his most appealing story of Cupid and Psyche, relates that Psyche, via the wings of the west wind, spread her splendour from the top of a cliff down into a most respectable valley, and then, equipped with all things necessary, she descended. And he relates that there, surrounded by invisible servants, she received all that was essential. What, then, must we make of this descent of the supra-celestial psyche into the heavenly valley, which was assigned to Cupid or the heavenly light?

Of course in Psalm 104,4 it is said: *You who walk on the wings of the wind, you who make your angels spirits or winds and your servants burning fire.* In particular, therefore, does not the divine mind also tend to descend over the wings of the winds or angels, over the divine breath of God, its unformed agency, and over the ray springing forth directly from God? And does it not tend to descend from above, in the form of its maker, into the middle region of the world?

According to those words of the aforesaid prophet *(He who uses a cloud for his ascent, he who walks on the wings of the winds etc.),* thus also the mind walks and passes over feathers and wings of the archangel presiding over it, a divine offshoot who sits on the throne of the rational mind or Empyreum, which is a spiritual cloud that contains the glory of God etc.

This is also evident from the Psalmist's saying in Psalm 91:11, cited above: *He charged his angels that they should guard thee in all thy ways; they shall bear thee up in their hands, that thou put not thy foot etc.* This must also be so heard in reference to the leader of the inner man, the word of God, and the mind, which is a breath of God

55 In the original: *diversorium obscurum.*

and proceeds immediately with the word from the mouth of Jehovah.

The mind, then, is that divine ray or breath of God which has been prepared for its journey into the visible and material world, so that after leaving the supra-celestial realms it may traverse the kingdoms of nature, both heavenly and elemental. From there it emerges, equipped and adorned with all the figures of the hierarchies, and secured and protected against the evils and sufferings of the world by the presence of the archangel destined and associated with it, seated on the wing of his servant. So the mind enters by a gentle leap down into the region of the stars, where it is served by the Olympic angels who accompany and preside over this mind according to its ruling archangel. And it is received by the subordinates and puts on the robe of the ether, composed of a mixture of the soul belonging to life and the etheric spirit, to which likewise a spirit from the planetary sphere is offered, who acknowledges the archangel who is in front of it as its head and lord. This planetary spirit in any case is appropriately called the spirit of the nativity or genius of the child which tends to have command over the life and all actions that revolve around the life. And by its agency the destiny in every human being is handed over to the consummation.

Nevertheless, this spirit is not subjected to the leader of the mind differently than the king to the emperor or a slave to his master, as is established on the basis of the previously quoted passage from Zacharias 2:3, where indeed an angel, as it were, as the master of the other, gives orders to this one and says to him as to a slave: Run, speak to this boy.

From these things it is clear that it is in the power of the archangel or first or ruling angel to change destiny and to control and command the angel of destiny who is subordinate to them, so that it does not do this or that.

In the same way, the daemons of the twelve Zodiac signs, who, called "protectors" by Mercurius Trismegistus, are assisting the planetary spirits in the execution and the consummation of destiny's course to be delivered, have no power to oppose the archangels proper to them, but are, as it were, obedient and compliant to them as their chief lords and leaders.

And therefore, when the centre of the soul harmonises with the mind and adheres to it obediently and as to its head, neither the stars nor their daemons have any power or authority over it. Hence comes the following proverb: *The wise man will rule over the stars etc.* That is, he who controls the mind and its head, whose virtues are known to be preferred to the qualities of the stars and the daemons of the same, this one will avoid the action and influence of the stars and their daemons.

Chapter Seven
On the Descent of the Mind with the Soul and the Middle Spirit into the Lowest Region of the World

The divine mind, armed by the power of the archangel and clothed in the garment of the soul belonging to life, guarded also by its own genius, rich in all the virtues of the ether necessary for the preservation of life, glides (after, of course, the will has been received from the first mover and the first action from the firmament or the eighth sphere, steadfastness from Saturn, natural power from Jupiter, might of anger from Mars, life force from the Sun, desire from Venus, imagination from Mercury, and life force from the Moon,) down into the region of the elements, where it braces itself against the injustice of the chilling cold and assumes a fire- and air-like nature, shrouding its older garments of the ether with a simple yet shapely covering of the elements.

There, then, all the daemons belonging to the rank and constitution of the archangel influencing the mind, run to meet it[56] and, while it sits on its etheric vehicle, receive it with cheerfulness and surround it against the plagues of the daemons of opposite disposition. But already here the question can arise how these elementary daemons can be put in relation to each of the seven planets, when there are only four elements in which the lower daemons participate?

To this doubt we want to answer briefly, that even if one counts only four elements, these four can nevertheless easily be related to the dispositions of the seven planets, taking into account their nature, and that in consequence they also fit to the daemons of each of the planets. For example: Saturn has a connection with the earth, but Jupiter and Venus with the air, Mars with the fire, and the Sun with the air and the fire i.e. with the last section of the air inflamed by fire.

56 I.e., the now fully-embodied divine mind.

The Moon has a connection with the water and Mercury with all these and in addition with the winds. From this it will be quite easy to find out which elemental daemon had power, care and authority over the body of the child at birth.

This daemon, however, is commanded and governed by the presider of the mind, not unlike a slave by his master, and is established in a right and holy way when the centre of the soul and its daemon look more to the mind than to the element.

Hence we see that the mind has its leader, who is an archangel, and likewise the soul centre has its leader, who is a genius and Olympic spirit, and that finally also the airy or emotional soul, which is composed of a formative part of the elements, also has its leader, which is hostile to the rest and especially to the mind, in so far as it is more immersed in the substance of matter.

And in this fashion the inner realm of man is forged, and each of his three parts, derived from the natures of the three heavens of the world, has its own individual daemon, and as God exercises power over the angels, and the angels over the stars, and the stars finally over the elements, so it follows that the angels of the Empyreum exercise power and authority—both over the stars and over the elements and their angels.

Chapter Eight
On the Way to Seek Knowledge and Familiarity of the Sacred and Supernal Daemon Assigned to the Mind of Everyone

Iamblichus has set up a double way of trafficking with the daemons. A natural one, sacred and godlike, which he knows to derive from the celestial heights, and this one, in any case, does not care about the research on the procreation of man, but cherishes the daemon in a more universal way beyond the realm of embodied nature. The other one he knows to be artificial, which calls the daemon from the cycles and focusses on the moment of procreation and this one explores the nativity of each man etc., as it has been examined.

From this he understood, as it seems to me, the first mode of treatment from the good and super-celestial daemon, which is assigned to the mind and which he elsewhere calls holy; and the second he understood from the angel or daemon which is called Genius or Olympic

Spirit. This one, at any rate, Porphyrius wanted to trace or find with all his effort, because he believed that if someone recognised their figure of nativity and its natal ruler, they would find their daemon, through whom they could be redeemed from the fate of birth. Against this, Iamblichus argues and affirms that the holy daemon of a man is not granted by one's birth chart, but by an older and higher origin—manifestly the upper gods. From this he seems to recognise that the daemon as the head of man flows forth from a higher and more prominent place than the region of the stars, and that it is therefore impossible for us to come to the true knowledge and familiarity of this archdaemon, or that we can know him by the virtue of astrology or the science of the stars. But the same thing seems to be ultimately recognised by Porphyrius, after long and intense nocturnal studies, when he speaks words of this kind: *It is impossible, he says, to know the figure of birth and to recognise the daemon of birth, because, after all, the rules of astrology are incomprehensible and uncertain.*

And we say that even if the rules of astrology were intelligible and unambiguous, we still could not, under this presupposition, recognise or comprehend the holy daemon of procreation, or obtain familiar intercourse with it, because, after all, such a holy daemon controls the stars, and in such a way that knowledge of the stars cannot determine it or its nature *a priori*.

In what way, then, must we acquire the knowledge and familiarity of this daemon, since the sky and even the stars cannot explain to us its nature, name and property?

If we now descend into lower regions, we will not find there the way of knowing one's holy daemon amongst the elements, as they are more incomplete than the celestial ones. For the impurity of the elements in the human composition is the primary reason why we do not know the upper, middle and lower daemons. What, then, will have to be done in order that we may attain to the knowledge, familiarity, presence, assistance and enlightenment of that holy creature and of our most excellent progenitor?

To this question Iamblichus seems to answer thusly: *The daemon,* he says, *is difficult to find by astrology, but simple by divine divination.* And elsewhere: *Not by human art, but divine we can find the personal daemon.*

Moreover, he also says, *that exalted divination can teach the nature and influence of the stars without mediation of the arts and can pinpoint the individual daemon of anyone who exerts the strongest influence over the child.*

However, what divination is, we will explain broadly below, but it is obvious that it is *the flowing of the divine spirit into the mind of man.* For only receiving the breath of divine power can lead to attaining the true knowledge of the stars, the communion and familiarity with one's own individual spirit.

Yea, that portion of the spirit which was granted to man at his birth is, it seems to me at any rate, itself, as it were, a holy daemon by which the human mind is directed, controlled, and inspired. For see Job 33:4: *The strong spirit of God made man.* Proverbs 16:3: *And he searcheth out all his ways. Wisdom 1:7: He has knowledge of the voice;* Wisdom 7:14: *And it is a treasure for men that never runs dry. Those who make use of it make friends with God. Wisdom 7:17.*

This spirit of wisdom grants reliable knowledge and causes man to understand the constitution of the world, the power of the elements, the beginning, middle and end of time, the course of the years, the positions of the stars, the nature of living creatures, the minds or anger of the wild animals, the forces of the winds and spirits and thoughts of the people, to know and understand above all also what is hidden and what is revealed. According to Wisdom 7,21 he is the creator of all things, who teaches the wise, according to Numbers 11,25 he also makes the prophets, according to Exodus 28,3;31,2;35,30 he is the one from whom all knowledge comes. For according to Kohelet 1:17, this spirit pours out the knowledge of wisdom and the knowledge of intelligence like rain, and increases the glory of those who hold those. Indeed, according to Proverbs 30:1, he is the knowledge of the saints; according to Wisdom 8:4, he is the one who teaches the knowledge of God and chooses his works; according to Wisdom 7:2, he is the spirit of intelligence.[57]

This spirit of wisdom is holy, unique, one, manifold, tender, moderate, eloquent, agile, tainted [sic], clear, distinct, sweet, loving good, innocent, and free from harm, not forbidding to do any good, foreseeing all things, and comprehending all understanding spirits etc. Because of his purity he reaches everywhere. For he is the vapour of God's virtue and power. And he is virtually the stream and pure river of the clarity of the Almighty God and no pollution comes to him. He is

57 In the original: *spiritus intelligentiae.*

the gleam and shine of the eternal light and a mirror of God's majesty without blemish and image of his goodness, and although he is one, he still can do everything and persists in himself and yet makes everything new and brings himself over the peoples into holy souls and determines the friends and prophets of God.

For God loves only the one who dwells with the spirit of wisdom. For this one is more beautiful than the sun and above every disposition of the stars. If one compares him with the light, then the first place is to be granted to him, because the night follows that. This therefore is that holy spirit by whose inflow and enjoyment a prophecy can be acquired.

According to Numbers 11:25, he is that spirit of Jehovah who created man and who acts within man as the divine mind, which, according to Job 33:4, searches out all his ways. According to Proverbs 16:3, he is the spirit with which Jehovah also adorned his heaven in the beginning, see also Job 26:13.

Therefore, it is clear that either a greater or lesser portion of this spirit can be in one man versus another, according to the gift granted by God to them.

This portion of the spirit, then, because it has been left to us only in pitiful quantity since and because of Adam's fall, therefore, because of the tremendous complication of the shadowy and corrupt body, obviously cannot guide man in his manner, according to that oft used verse in Wisdom 9:15: *The body being corrupt weighs down the soul, and the earth-bound dwelling oppresses the mind which thinks through many things, and we consider that which is on earth to be difficult, and find that which is in our sight with difficulty etc.*

From hence arises the necessity that that spark of the divine spirit which is given to us by nature at birth should be enlightened from on high by the grace and mercy of Jehovah according to the following sentence from Wisdom, which reads thusly: *But who shall fathom what is in heaven except thou hast bestowed wisdom, and hast sent thine Holy Spirit from on high etc.?*

For by the breath of the Spirit of Jehovah's nostrils wonderful works are wrought, all hidden wonders come to light, things led below are wrought and accomplished, and the knowledge of any thing is acquired, see 2 Samuel 22:16. For from this spirit nothing and no one can hide, see Psalm 139:7 and Wisdom 1.

But let us now consider how that spark of the divine spirit, which has been left in us since the fall of Adam, can be enlarged and enlightened by his like.[58] And let us consider whether God, out of His grace, is willing to pour upon men the spirit of discipline by which they establish the knowledge of God, because they suffer from poverty and are oppressed by the burden of their unclean bodies.

The wise man in Wisdom 9,10 says: *God sends his wisdom from the holy heaven, from his throne, I say, he sends it to man for God's glory, so that it may be with him and be together with him in hardship and he may know what is good with him; for by it he knows and understands everything. Moreover Wisdom 9:17: If God had not given his wisdom and sent his holy spirit from the highest places, who amongst the men would have known God's plan?* For so are the paths of men righteous, who walk upon the earth, and who have been taught the things that please God. For so it is in Wisdom 10: *Men were saved by wisdom. For this preserved Adam, and gave him power to rule all things etc.*

Finally, it is certain (see Wisdom 9:17) that Jehovah sent his Holy Spirit from the highest places to give wisdom to men, that by it they might know His purpose. And therefore, having considered those things, it is certain that God can so illuminate the sparks of understanding left in man by His spirit sent from on high that this divine light, which is as it were inactive in the shadow-body and sunk in darkness, can be illuminated by the spirit that is like it or can be enlightened. And it is certain that the Lord, after this consideration, steps over the errors and darknesses—and in such a way that what was previously unrecognised and hidden to man, burdened by his ignorance, afterwards becomes recognisable and clear to him through the virtue of this holy light flowing in and gliding in. By the breath of this supra-celestial spirit, Elizaeus turned from a peasant into an admirable prophet and led all the astounding miracles to their summit and goal. Through its illumination and inflow into the minds of the patriarchs and prophets and the rest who were inspired by divine breath, they themselves saw their holy daemon and the archangel presiding over their minds face to face, and even recognised his name and quality, and took part of friendship and assistance in every work.

58 What seems to be implied is the question if a way of life attuned to the divine spirit within man will enlarge its presence within.

For the angels, whom the royal prophet calls "children of God," take great delight and pleasure in the company of an inspired man, and strive fiercely for the presence of the holy light that dwells in him, for whom, indeed, the holy spirit of intelligence is life, illumination, and activity. And this happens in such a manner that wherever this holy spirit shows itself in fullness and clarity in man, his holy angel also stands forth and is ready for the protection of both body and soul, as is shown in many passages of the Holy Scriptures. From this it is clear that the true knowledge of astrology and the only way to make friendship with one's holy daemon originates in the divine inspiration, by whose holy breath, indeed, the ancients acquired the knowledge of every thing, even the foundations of the sacrosanct wisdom itself.

Therefore, we conclude our booklet with the opinion of Iamblichus, obviously with the one that the holy daemon of each man must be known from an older and higher origin than from the stars and the natal chart, and that soon the nature of this daemon, its name and its peculiarity, soon also the most reliable truth about the stars can be possessed and recovered with the help of exalted divination, which alone comes about and succeeds from the sending and the infusion of the Holy Spirit into the people.

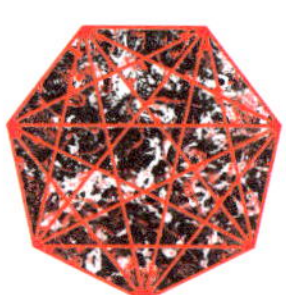

APPENDIX IV

Cod.Mag.55
The Conjuration Of the Olympic Spirits According to Solomon, Son of David[1]

Preliminary remark: This appendix provides the first full transcription and English translation of the manuscript with the shelfmark Cod.Mag.55 from the famous Grimoire Collection of the University Library in Leipzig: *Solomon's Conjuration of the Olympic Spirits*. It presents the reader with a mix of learned and folk magic, of celestial and chthonic beings, of Olympic and animistic spirits. While it would be easy to dismiss the document as e.g., the working notes of a practicing folk-magician of the late 17th or early 18th century, the document provides essential practical clues if read in parallel with the Arbatel. For an in-depth analysis of its content and a practical restoration of some of its underlying working methods, please see Book II, Chapter II: Working with the *Arbatel*'s *Seal of Secrets*.

Num. 37

[1] Accordingly, certain spirits are required for each thing, such as one for obtaining wealth, another for lifting treasures, yet another for things under the rule of Venus, and so on. So we also have to put different spirits here and teach their invocation. Accordingly, the most distinguished amongst the Olympic Spirits is ARATRON. He is a deliverer of the other spirits, for which reason it is necessary to summon him first. This is done now with the following words:

1 Source: Anonymous, *Salomonis filii David Beschwerungen der Olympischen Geister*. Leipzig University, Cod.mag.55, s.l., ca. 1750. Transcription from manuscript: Anne Hila. Translation into English: Frater Acher.

Eli Jehova, Elohim habab damali colling, esease milee conna se bub damani duc banavuur kaj ebascha.

But first draw a circle around you with the following figure: make around the circle the following figures and signs, as namely on the right side a lamb with [2] a cross on its back, then the wounds of Christ; but on the other side these signs and a mouse:

After that, intone your incantation. However, nothing will be felt the first time. Nevertheless, do this incantation again after nine days have passed and ask for the same spirit again, then it will be heard with a great roar and much steam will be around him and he will ask what your desire is. Then you shall tell him your inclination, and after that he will provide you with a spirit as quickly as you ask. But take care that you can recite the above conjuration word for word, otherwise it will go badly for you. This is all for the first spirit. [3] Bethor is a protector of the venereal things; therefore you shall use the following conjuration for this spirit:

Langusch Charusch lami lanolsata curi embouit caoroirse Venus sediel ac dura.

The spirit will appear as soon as you repeat this incantation a second time after seven days. But make the following circle, namely that at the two corners there be a triangle with the following characters and letters: on the right side a dog with these characters and the wounds of Christ. And state your desire, and he shall be obedient unto you in this matter.

[4] The third spirit is Phaleg. He is a possessor of treasures, and use the following words with him:

Thesaureur en le trout duc lour mon thea seurunc, che manlu empour Eloim.

However, first enclose yourself in a circle that has four corners, and on the side write this word [ומ, i.e. *and from*] and further these words written in Hebrew:

שכרכח	WHO FORCED
הרענר	THE REFRESHER
אהומ	AHUM?
אכהר	AKHAR?

After that, act as already described above. We have dealt with treasure digging; now let us deal with the other spirits.

[5] The fourth spirit is called Och, who gives wisdom so that one may more quickly understand the books in which this art is described.

The fifth, sixth and seventh spirits are called *Hagith*, *Ophiel* and *Phul*. These are the noblest; but if you want to banish them again, speak:

Lamech, Marci, Joannes, dicier se et abicus
Laduf salum nac du dasle
Lucas sebulda Beelzebub ne Each
elenuf quaref ebolabatur.

Then the spirits will be gone. As for the spirit Och, he teaches all kinds of arts, for example, if you want a mine [6] to give quick booty, let the miners drink from the Urim and then attach these letters, so there will be no danger [באβα, i.e. ABA, *father*].

Or if you want a woman not to courtesy with other men, take the tail of a wolf, the hairs of your eyebrows and those under your beard, burn these to a powder along with a note on which are written the words Futuc cheche. In this way she will not hold another. Och also teaches to cure diseases. If you want to drive away a cough, let that stone which is found in a sponge hang around the neck with these signs, so it will change comfortably.

Also, if you want a fire [7] not to burn the cloth or anything else, take the white of an egg and alum, smear the cloth with it, wash it off again with salt water, let it dry so that fire cannot burn it.

If you want to give someone an ulcer, make a ring of myrtle wood, engrave the following letters into it. Pretend that you want to give him a ring of rare wood and let him put it on his finger. As soon as he wears the ring, he will get an ulcer on his armpit. These are the words to engrave into the ring: **δε λανεγα**. And he will not get rid of the ulcer until he puts the ring away and gives it back to you.

If you want to drive away the Padayra, take the right foot of a snail and hang it over the sick person, and a note on it these words: εζαλμον ἐπα, so it will soon pass away.

[8] Moreover, if you would that another should be afraid of you, and that you should be mighty and fresh, and that your adversary should perish, let a wolf's eye be sewed into a little bag for you, and these words with it: הדלא, and none shall overtake you.

Moreover, if you want your beloved to tell you all that she has done, take the heart of a dove and the head of a frog, make them both dry, and while she sleeps sprinkle the powder on her breast, and she will tell you all that she has done.

Or if you want to see what others cannot see, take the gall of a cat and the fat of a white hen and smear it on your eyes. That way you will see everything.

If you would understand the voices of birds, take two birds with you as when you go to hunt, and the first game which you [9] catch take home with you, and prepare it with a fox's heart; so shall you understand all birds, so take it and kiss him[2] with it, straightway it shall be done. If you want to know future things, eat the heart of a weasel while it is still warm, and write these letters on it [תחת], so you will know what is to happen in the future. These and other things teach the spirits. It is also to be reported that the good things must happen under a good planet, but the bad things under an evil planet i.e. Sat-

2 Unclear in the original who or what is referred to here.

urn or Mars; so I want to assure that everything comes true what is written above, that I have seen and tried it myself. From this it follows for the lifting of treasures, who shall succeed, he must not dawdle and not hurry, so that in the end all effort will not be in vain [10]. So let us come to the explanation of the same and how such a work should be started.

At night, at eleven or twelve o'clock, go to the place where you think the treasure should be. Make a circle there four cubits wide, and around it write the names Aaron, Moses and Elisha. Then make the following signs around the circle

Then begin the invocation of the treasures, which reads thus:

> *Sebub Baal zeda Beezebub, lusor Elisa, Marcus et Lucas Semour, Leandae, Heautria mount a trate le curlande respurmande penetrav.*

Do this for the first time. After two days have passed, go again to the same place, and after quoting the spirit Phaleg with the above incantation [11], dig about a cubit deep into the earth. Then make three crosses on it and repeat the incantation. But you have to let a divining rod strike before, so that you can see whether something is there or not.

Vinculum Salomonis

I command and enjoin you and all your servants and legions with the infernal fire and by Laray ✠ Gemay ✠ Naly ✠ Arion ✠ Fateson ✠ fortissimus ✠ Immortalis ✠ potentissimus ✠ Cedoon ✠ Terribilis ✠ Joth, He, Vau He, ✠ Joth ✠ Agla ✠. Dear Lord and God, I have sinned much against You, but I call upon You as well as these holy names Agios ✠ otheos ✠ Athanatos ✠ Eleison miserere mei ✠ May You graciously forgive our sinful iniquity, that the spirits may be the better obedient to me. Therefore, I quote you quickly, spirit N. together with your servants, so that you may come without delay [12]! With humble heart, they shall accomplish my desire, for which you have created them.

Come then, come! Visibly and in human form! This I command all you spirits, in the name of the great and unspeakable torment and chastisement of the damned in hell! That you may accomplish this work for me now!

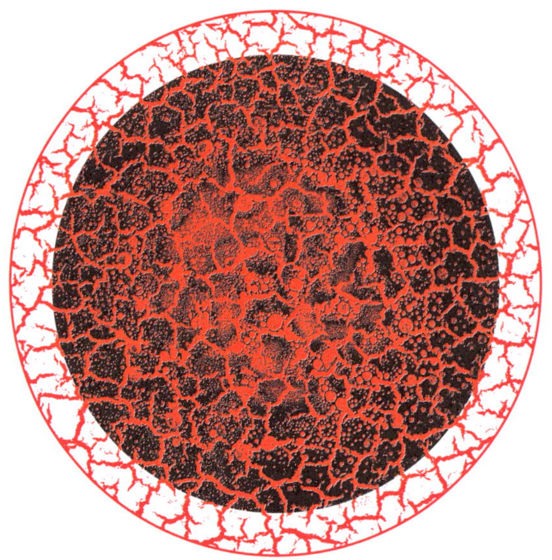

Bibliography

Adams, Jonathan, and Cordelia Heß (eds.). *The Medieval Roots of Antisemitism—Continuities and Discontinuities from the Middle Ages to the Present Day*. Abingdon-on-Thames: Routledge, 2020.

Andert, Werner. "Mit Geistern im Bunde! Ein Beitrag zum alten Ebersbacher Geisterglauben," in: Otto Marx (ed.), *Oberlausitzer Heimatzeitung—Blätter für Geschichte, Heimatkunde, Kunst, Literatur.* Nr. 17, Jahrgang 9, Reichenau: Alwin Marr, 1928. Reprinted in excerpt in: Andert, Werner Ebersbach—*Ebersbach. Ein Heimat- und Wanderbuch*: Adolf Israel, 1929.

Anonymous. *Das Buch Jezira. Achtes und neuntes Buch Moses oder der egyptische Hausschatz mit den 101 Geheimnissen alles Geheimnisse. Nach einer alten Handschrift, mit hoechst sonderbaren und originellen Abbildungen.* Berlin-Weißensee: E. Bartels, ca. 1910.

Anonymous. *Handschriftliche Schätze aus Klosterbibliotheken umfassend sämtliche vierzig Hauptwerke ueber Magie, verborgene Kräfte, Offenbarungen und geheime Wissenschaften.* Köln am Rhein: [Stuttgart: Johann Scheible], [around 1853].

Anonymous. *Hundert acht und dreyßig neu-entdeckte und vollkommen bewährte Geheimnüsse, Oder allerhand magische, spagyrische, sympathetische und antipathetische Kunst-Stücke, Derer eines allein den Besitzer viel Geld gekostet hat.* Frankfurt und Leipzig: Carl Christoph Immig, 1729.

Anonymous. *Magia de furto, das ist unterschiedene Geheimnüsse, seine Sachen vor Dieben zu verwahren, Diebe zu bannen, dass sie den Diebstahl müssen wiederbringen, auch solche auf unterschiedene Art zu peinigen und zu lädiren.* Leipzig University, Cod.mag.66, s.l., ca. 1750.

Anonymous. *Nigromantisches Kunst-Buch, handelnd von der GlücksRuthe, dem Ring und der Krone Salomonis, den Fürsten-Geheimnissen, den dienstbaren Krystall- und Schatz-Geistern und andern wunderbaren Arcanen.* Köln am Rhein: Peter Hammer's Erben [Stuttgart: Johann Scheible], allegedly 1743.

Anonymous. *Nodus Sophicus enodatus, d.i. Erläuterung etlicher vornehmer Philosophen Schrifften vom Stein der Weisen.* s.i.: Friedrich Gruner seel. Erben, 1639.

Anonymous. *Salomonis filii David Beschwerungen der Olympischen Geister*. Leipzig University, Cod.mag.55, s.l., ca. 1750.

Anonymous. *Sammlung der grössten Geheimnisse ausserordentlicher Menschen in alter Zeit.* Köln am Rhein: Peter Hammer, 1725 [Stuttgart: Johann Scheible], [around 1857].

Arnold, Klaus. *Johannes Trithemius (1462–1516)*. Würzburg: Kommissionsverlag Ferdinand Schöningh, 1971.

Arnold, Klaus, and Franz Fuchs (eds.), *Johannes Trithemius (1462–1516)*. Würzburg: Königshausen & Neumann, 2019.

Bachter, Stephan. *Anleitung zum Aberglauben—Zauberbücher und die Verbreitung magischen "Wissens" seit dem 18. Jahrhundert*. Hamburg: n.p., 2005. https://ediss.sub.uni-hamburg.de/bitstream/ ediss/1653/1/Diss-Bachter.pdf

Baker, Phil. *Austin Osman Spare—The Life and Legend of London's Lost Artist*. London: Strange Attractor Press, 2011.

Bardon, Franz. *Die Praxis der magischen Evokation. Anleitung zur Anrufung von Wesen uns umgebender Sphären.* Freiburg im Breisgau: Bauer Verlag, 1956.

Beck, Paul. *Die Bibliothek eines Hexenmeisters.* In Bolte, Johannes (ed.), *Zeitschrift des Vereins für Volkskunde, 16. Jahrgang Heft 4, 1905*. Berlin: A. Asher & Co, 1905.

Bellingradt, Daniel, Otto, Bernd-Christian (eds.), Magical Manuscripts in Early Modern Europe, Cham: Palgrave Macmillan, 2017.

Bowen, Willis Herbert. *JACQUES GOHORY (1520–1576)*. Dissertation submitted in partial fulfillment of the requirements for the degree of Doctor of Philosophy in Harvard University, Cambridge: (typewriter manuscript), 1935.

Borggrefe, Heiner, with Vera Lüpkes, and Hans Ottomeyer (eds.), *Moritz der Gelehrte—Ein Renaissancefürst in Europa, München*. Edition Minerva, 1997.

Brooks, Jeanice. "Music as Erotic Magic in a Renaissance Romance". *Renaissance Quarterly*, Vol. 60, Number 4, Winter 2007.

Buber, Martin. "Ich und Du", in: *Werke, Erster Band: Schriften zur Philosophie*. München: Kösel Verlag, 1962.

Cecchetelli, Michael. *Crossed Keys*. London: Scarlet Imprint, 2011.

Craven, James Brown. *Count Michael Maier—Doctor of Philosophy and of Medicine Alchemist, Rosicrucian, Mystic, 1568–1622, Life and Writings*. London: Dawson of Pall Mall, 1968 (1910).

Debus, Allen G. *The Chemical Philosophy—Paracelsian Science and Medicine in the Sixteenth and Seventeenth Century*, 2 Volumes, New York: Neale Watson Academic Publishing, 1977.

Dieterich, Albrecht. *Kleine Schriften*. Berlin: B.G. Teubner, 1911.

Dillinger, Johannes. *Auf Schatzsuche—Von Grabräubern, Geisterbeschwörern und anderen Jägern verborgener Reichtümer*. Freiburg: Herder Verlag, 2011.

Dörrer, Anton. "Die Tragödie des Bozner Tondichters Adam Haslmair", in: *Der Schlern 20. Jahrgang*, 2. Heft (1946) , Bozen: Athesia, 1946.

Fieger, Michael, with Widu-Wolfgang Ehlers, and Andreas Beriger, (eds.). *Psalmi—Proverbi—Ecclesiastes—Canticum canticorum—Sapientia—Iesus Sirach*. Berlin, Boston: De Gruyter, 2018.

Figulus, Benedictus (ed.), *Thesaurinella Olympica aurea tripartita. Das ist: Ein himmlisch güldenes Schatzkämmerlein, von vielen außerlesenen Clenodien zugerüstet* [...]. Frankfurt am Main: Stainius, 1608.

————, *Rosarivm Novvm Olympicvm Et Benedictvm, Das ist: Ein newer Gebenedeyter Philosophischer Rosengart: Darinnen vom aller weisesten König Salomone, H. Salomone Trismosino, H. Trithemio, D. Theophrasto, &c. gewiesen wirdt, wie der Gebenedeyte Guldene Zweig, vnnd Tincturschatz, vom vnverwelcklichen Orientalischen Baum der Hesperidum, vormittels Göttlicher Gnaden, abzubrechen vnd zu erlangen sey; Allen vnd jeden Filiis doctrinae Hermeticae, vnd D. Theophrasticae Liebhabern zu gutem trewlich eröffnet in zwen Theilen*. Basel: in *Verlegung des Autoris*, 1608.

Fludd, Robert. *Utriusque Cosmi, Tomi Secundi Tractatus Primi, Sectio Secunda, De technica Microcosmi historia.* In *Portiones VII. divisa.* [Oppenheim]: [de Bry], ca. 1620.

Forshaw, J. Peter. "Oratorium—Auditorium—Laboratorium: Early Modern Improvisations on Cabala, Music, and Alchemy". In: *ARIES* 10.2. Leiden: Brill, 2010.

Frater Acher. *Holy Daimon.* London: Scarlet Imprint, 2018.

————, *Holy Heretics.* London: Scarlet Imprint, 2022.

————, *INGENIUM.* Exeter: TaDehent Books, 2022.

Frater U.·.D.·.. *High Magic: Theory & Practice.* St. Paul: Llewellyn Publications, 2005.

————, *High Magic II: Expanded Theory and Practice.* St. Paul: Llewellyn Publications, 2008.

Frietsch, Ute. *Häresie und Wissenschaft—Eine Genealogie der paracelsischen Alchemie.* München: Wilhelm Fink, 2013.

Gehr, Damaris. *Magie und Alchemie in der paracelsistischen Schrift* לאתעברא *Arbatel De magia veterum* (Basel, 1575). In: Feuerstein-Herz, Petra, Frietsch, Ute (eds.), *Alchemie—Genealogie und Terminologie, Bilder, Techniken und Artefakte, Forschungen aus der Herzog August Bibliothek.* Wolfenbüttel: Harrassowitz Verlag, 2021.

Gilly, Carlos. *Adam Haslmayr—Der erste Verkünder der Manifeste der Rosenkreuzer. Amsterdam: Bibliotheca Philosophica Hermetica*, 1994.

————, "Theophrastia Sancta: Oder Paracelsismus als Religion im Streit mit den offiziellen Kirchen," in: Telle, Joachim (ed.), *Analecta Paracelsica—Studien zum Nachleben Theophrast von Hohenheims im deutschen Kulturgebiet der frühen Neuzeit.* Stuttgart: Franz Steiner Verlag, 1994.

————, "On the Genesis of L. Zetzner's Theatrum Chemicum in Strasbourg." *Magia, alchimia, scienza dal '400 al '700*, Vol. I, Amsterdam: Bibliotheca Philosophica Hermetica, 2002.

————, "Theophrastia Sancta: Paracelsianism as a Religion, in Conflict with the Established Churches." In: Grell, Ole Peter. *Paracelsus—The Man and his Reputation, his Ideas and their Transformation.* Leiden: Brill, 1998.

———, "ARBATEL De magia veterum. Il primo prontuario di magia bianca in Germania—The first book of white magic in Germany". *Magia, alchimia, scienza dal '400 al '700*, Vol. I, Amsterdam: Bibliotheca Philosophica Hermetica, 2002.

Grafton, Anthony. *Worlds Made by Words—Scholarship and Community in the Modern West*. Cambridge: Harvard University Press, 2011.

Gohory, Jacques, aka Leone Suavio. *Theophrasti Paracelsi Philosophiae Et Medicinae Utriusque Universae, Compendium: Ex optimis quibusque eius libris; Cum scholiis in libros IIII. eiusde[m] De Vita Longa, Plenos mysteriorum, parabolarum, aenigmatum*. Paris: Rovillius, 1567.

Goldammer, Kurt. *Paracelsus Studien*. Klagenfurt: Verlag des Geschichtsvereins für Kärnten, 1954.

———, *Theophrastus von Hohenheim, genannt Paracelsus, Die Kärntner Schriften*. Klagenfurt: Amt der Kärntner Landesregierung, 1955.

———, *Theophrastus von Hohenheim, genannt Paracelsus, Sämtliche Werke—Theologische und Religionsphilosophische Schriften, Vol. IV*. Wiesbaden: Franz Steiner Verlag, 1955.

———, *Theophrastus von Hohenheim, genannt Paracelsus, Sämtliche Werke—Theologische und Religionsphilosophische Schriften, Vol. VII*. Wiesbaden: Franz Steiner Verlag, 1961.

———, *Theophrastus von Hohenheim, genannt Paracelsus, Sämtliche Werke—Theologische und Religionsphilosophische Schriften, Vol. II*. Wiesbaden: Franz Steiner Verlag, 1965.

Grant, Kenneth & Steffi (eds.). *ZOS SPEAKS—Encounters with Austin Osman Spare*. London: Fulgur Limited, 1998.

Han, Byung-Chul. *The Disappearance of Rituals: A Topology of the Present*. Cambridge: Polity, 2019.

Hanegraaff, Wouter J. (ed.), *Dictionary of Gnosis & Western Esotericism*. Leiden: Brill, 2006.

Hargrave, John G., *The Life and Soul of Paracelsus*. London: Victor Gollancz, 1951.

———,"Paracelsus," in: *Encyclopedia Britannica*, 20 Sep. 2021. https://www.britannica.com/biography/Paracelsus. Accessed 1 February 2022

Hartmann, Franz. *The Life and the Doctrines of Philippus Theophrastus Bombast of Hohenheim: known by the name of Paracelsus.* United States Book Company, 1891.

Huser, Johannes (ed.). *Theil I–X Der Bücher und Schrifften, des Edlen, Hochgelehrten und Bewehrten Philosophi und Medici, Philippi Theophrasti Bombast von Hohenheim, Paracelsi genannt.* Basel, 1589–1591.

Jevons, F. R., "Paracelsus' Two-Way Astrology. I: What Paracelsus Meant by 'Stars,'" in: *The British Journal for the History of Science*, Vol. 2, No. 2, Cambridge University Press, 1964.

———,"Paracelsus' Two-Way Astrology, II: Man's Relation to the Stars", in: *The British Journal for the History of Science*, Vol. 2, No. 2, Cambridge University Press, 1964.

John, Johann Friedrich: *Handwörterbuch der allgemeinen Chemie*, 4,2: T–Z, Leipzig [u.a.] : Brockhaus, 1819.

Kazhdan, Alexander P. (ed.), *The Oxford Dictionary of Byzantium*, Vol. 3, New York, Oxford: Oxford University Press, 1991.

Khunrath, Heinrich. *Amphitheatrum Sapientiæ Æternæ—Schauplatz der ewigen allein wahren Weisheit,* in *Clavis Pansophiæ 6*, Stuttgart-Bad Cannstatt: frommann-holzboog, 2014.

Kühlmann, Wilhelm, and Joachim Telle (eds.). *Oswald Crollius, De signaturis internis rerum.* Stuttgart: Franz Steiner Verlag, 1996.

Lehmann, Paul. "Nachrichten von der Sponheimer Bibliothek des Abtes Johannes Trithemius," in: Jansen, Max (ed.), *Festgabe zum 7. September 1910—Hermann Grauert zur Vollendung des 60. Lebensjahres gewidmet.* Freiburg im Breisgau: Herdersche Verlagshandlung, 1910.

Lehmann, Paul. *Merkwürdigkeiten des Abtes Johannes Trithemius.* München: Verlag der Bayrischen Akademie der Wissenschaften, 1961.

Lippomano, Luigi. *La Catena in Genesim.* Paris: C. Guillard, 1546.

Maier, Michael. *Tractatus Posthumus, sive Ulysses; hoc est: Sapientia Seu Intelligentia, Tanquam Coelestis Scintilla beatitudinis, quod si in fortunae et corporis bonis naufragium faciat, ad portum meditationis et patientiae remigio feliciter se expediat.* Frankfurt: Lucas Jennis, 1624.

Malter, Heinrich, and Alexander Marx (eds.). *Gesammelte Schriften von Moritz Steinschneider, Bd. 1: Gelehrten-Geschichte*. Berlin: M. Poppelauer, 1925.

Maxwell, W. *De Medicina Magnetica, Libri III*. Frankfurt am Main: Zubrodt 1679. In German: *Drei Bücher der magnetischen Heilkunde*. Stuttgart: Scheible 1851. Reprint: Freiburg im Breisgau: Edition Ambra, 1978.

McCarthy, Josephine. *The Magical Knowledge Trilogy*. Exeter: TaDehent Books, 2020.

Moran, Bruce T. "Moritz von Hessen und die Alchemie," in: *Borggrefe, Heiner (et al.), Moritz der Gelehrte—ein Renaissancefürst in Europa*. Eurasberg: Minerva, 1997.

Müller-Sternberg, Robert. *Die Dämonen—Wesen und Wirkung eines Urphänomens*. Bremen: Carl Schünemann Verlag, 1964.

Paracelsus. *Astronomia magna: oder Die gantze Philosophia sagax der grossen und kleinen Welt des von Gott hocherleuchten erfahrnen und bewerten teutschen Philosophi und Medici Philippi Theophrasti Bombast, genannt Paracelsi magni: Darinn er lehrt des gantzen natürlichen Liechts vermögen (...) Vor nie in Truck außgangen*. Frankfurt 1571. http://mdz-nbn-resolving.de/urn:nbn:de:bvb:12-bsb10196224-9

Paracelsus. *Sammelband mit Werken des Theophrastus Paracelsus*. München: Bayrische Staatsbibliothek, Code: BSB Cgm 9544. https://www.digitale-sammlungen.de/en/view/bsb00105878?page=8,9

NOTE: FOR OTHER WORKS OF PARACELSUS, *SEE* SUDHOFF.

Pagel, Walter. *The Smiling Spleen—Paracelsianism in Storm and Stress*. New York: Karger, 1984.

Paulus, Julian. "Alchemie und Paracelsismus um 1600. Siebzig Porträts," in: Telle, Joachim (ed.), *Analecta Paracelsica—Studien zum Nachleben Theophrast von Hohenheims im deutschen Kulturgebiet der frühen Neuzeit*, Stuttgart: Franz Steiner Verlag, 1994.

Peterson, Joseph H., *Arbatel De magia veterum* (*Arbatel: Of the Magic of the Ancients*), n.l.: Twilit Grotto: Archives of Western Esoterica, 1997–2022. http://www.esotericarchives.com/solomon/arbatel.htm

———, *Arbatel: Concerning the Magic of Ancients, Original Sourcebook of Angel Magic, Newly translated from the original Latin, edited & annotated by Joseph Peterson*. Lake Worth, FL: Ibis Press, 2009.

———, "Arbatel: Concerning the Magic of Ancients," in: *Watkins Review*, Aug 15, London: Watkins Books, 2009.

———, *Elucidation of Necromancy Lucidarium Artis Nigromantice*. Lake Worth, FL: Ibis Press, 2021.

Peuckert, Will-Erich. *Theophrastus Paracelsus*. Stuttgart, Berlin: W. Kohlhammer Verlag, 1941.

———, *Pansophie—Ein Versuch zur Geschichte der weissen und schwarzen Magie*. Berlin: Erich Schmidt Verlag, 1956.

———, *GABALIA—Ein Versuch zur Geschichte des Magia naturalis im 16. bis 18. Jahrhundert*. Berlin: Erich Schmidt Verlag, 1967

———, *Paracelsus Werke, Vol. 1–5*. Basel: Schwabe reflexe 4, 2010.

Rampton, Martha. *Trafficking with Demons—Magic, Ritual and Gender from Late Antiquity to 1000*. London: Cornell University Press, 2021.

Rösche, Johannes. *Robert Fludd—Der Versuch einer hermetischen Alternative zur neuzeitlichen Naturwissenschaft*. Göttingen: V&R unipress, 2008

Saif, Liana. *The Arabic Influences on Early Modern Occult Philosophy*. London: Palgrave Macmillian, 2015.

Schmidt-Biggemann, Wilhelm. "Geschichte der Christlichen Kabbala, Vol. 2: 1600–1660." *Clavis Pansophiae* 10,2, Stuttgart-Bad Cannstatt: frommann-holzboog, 2013.

Schneider, Wolfgang. Paracelsus—"Autor der Archidoxis Magica?" *Veröffentlichungen aus dem pharmaziegeschichtlichen Seminar der Technischen Universität Braunschweig*, Vol. 23, Stuttgart: Deutscher Apotheker Verlag, 1982.

Schröder, Gerald. "Croll, Oswald," in: *Neue Deutsche Biographie*, Vol. 3, Berlin: Duncker & Humblot, 1957.

Skinner, Stephen and David Rankine. *The Complete Magician's Tables*. Singapore: Golden Hoard Press, 2006.

———, *The Veritable Key of Solomon*. Sourceworks of Ceremonial Magic, Volume IV, Woodbury: Llewellyn Publications, 2008.

——————, *Techniques of Solomonic Magic: The origin and methods of the Solomonic grimoires.* Singapore: Golden Hoard Press, 2015.

Spamer, Adolf. *Zauberbuch und Zauberspruch,* in: *Deutsches Jahrbuch für Volkskunde, Bd. 1.* Berlin Ost: Institut fuer deutsche Volkskunde, 1955.

——————, *Romanusbuechlein—Historisch-philologischer Kommentar zu einem deutschen Zauberbuch.* Berlin: Akademie Verlag, 1958.

Steinschneider, Moritz. *Zur pseudepigraphischen Literatur insbesondere der geheimen Wissenschaften des Mittelalters aus hebräischen und arabischen Quellen.* Berlin, 1862.

——————, *Die arabischen Übersetzungen aus dem Griechischen.* Leipzig: Otto Harrassowitz, 1897.

Steinschneider, Moritz. "Zum Speculum astronomicum des Albertus Magnus, über die darin angeführten Schriftsteller und Schriften." In: Cantor, M. (ed.), *Zeitschrift für Mathematik und Physik,* 16. Jahrgang, Heft 5, Leipzig: Verlag B.G. Teubner, 1871, pp. 357–396.

Stillman, John Maxson. *Theophrastus Bombastus von Hohenheim, called Paracelsus, his Personality and Influence as Physician, Chemist and Reformer.* Chicago & London: The Open Court Publishing, 1920.

Stratton-Kent, Jake. *The True Grimoire.* London: Scarlet Imprint, 2022.

Sudhoff, Karl. *Bibliographia Paracelsica.* Berlin: Verlag Georg Reimer, 1894 [Reprint by Martino Publishing, 2000].

Sudhoff, Karl (ed.), *Theophrast von Hohenheim, gen. Paracelsus, Sämtliche Werke, Vol. I–XIV.* München / Berlin: R. Oldenbourg, 1922–1933.

Telle, Joachim. "Benedictus Figulus: Zu Leben und Werk eines deutschen Paracelsisten." *Medizinhistorisches Journal,* 1987, Bd. 22, H. 4 (1987).

Telle, Joachim (ed.). *Analecta Paracelsica—Studien zum Nachleben Theophrast von Hohenheims im deutschen Kulturgebiet der frühen Neuzeit, Stuttgart.* Franz Steiner Verlag, 1994.

Trachtenberg, Joshua. *The Devil and the Jews: The Medieval Conception of the Jew and Its Relation to Modern Anti-Semitism.* Philadelphia: Jewish Publication Society, 1983.

Trithemius, Johannes. *Antipalus Maleficiorum*. Mainz: Balthasar Lippium, 1605.

Various. *Chemische Korrespondenz des Landgrafen Moritz, 2° Ms. chem. 19*[5]. Kassel, 1604–1631.

Véronèse, Julien, Chave-Mahir, Florence (eds.). *Ritual d'exorcisme ou manuel de magie? Le manuscrit Clm 10085 de la Bayrische Staatsbibliothek de Munich (début du XVe siècle)*. Florence: SISMEL Edizioni del Galluzzo, 2015.

Waite, Arthur Edward (ed.): *A Golden and Blessed Casket of Nature's Marvels by Benedictus Figulus, now first done into English from the German original published at Strasburg in the year 1608*. London: James Elliot & Co, 1893.

Waite, Arthur Edward. *The Book of Ceremonial Magic*. London, 1913 [1898].

Wels, Volkhard. *Magie und (Al)Chemie im 16. Jahrhundert. Thesen zu ihrer Begründung im Neuplatonismus, bei Paracelsus im Paracelsismus, in: Emine, Jutta, Wels, Volkhard (ed.), Der Begriff der Magie in Mittelalter und Früher Neuzeit*. Wiesbaden: Harrassowitz Verlag, 2020.

Zambelli, Paola. *The* Speculum Astronomiae *and Its Enigma: Astrology, Theology and Science in Albertus Magnus and his Contemporaries*. Berlin: Springer, 1992.

———, *White Magic, Black Magic in the European Renaissance*. Leiden: Brill 2007.

Zosimos of Panopolis. *The Book of the Keys of the Work, Kitāb Mafātīh as-san'a*. Theodor Abt, Wilferd Madelung (eds.), *Corpus Alchemicum Arabicum*, Vol. II, Zurich: Living Human Heritage Publications, 2016.

List of Illustrations

VINCULUM SALOMONIS

I COMMAND AND ENJOIN you and all your servants and legions with the infernal fire and by Laray ✠ Gemay ✠ Naly ✠ Arion ✠ Fateson ✠ Fortissimus ✠ Immortalis ✠ Potentissimus ✠ Cedoon ✠ Terribilis ✠ Joth, He, Vau He ✠ Joth ✠ Agla ✠.

Dear Lord and God, I have sinned much against you, but I call upon you as well as these holy names Agios ✠ Otheos ✠ Athanatos ✠ Eleison Miserere Mei ✠.

May you graciously forgive our sinful iniquity, that the spirits may be the better obedient to me. Therefore, I quote you quickly, spirit N. together with your servants, so that you may come without delay!

With humble heart, they shall accomplish my desire, for which you have created them. Come then, come! Visibly and in human form!

This I command all you spirits, in the name of the great and unspeakable torment and chastisement of the damned in hell! That you may accomplish this work for me now!

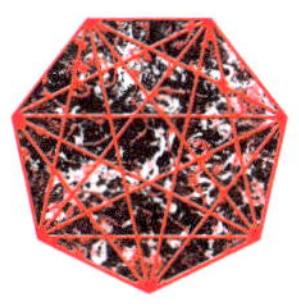

THIS FIRST EDITION of *The Olympic Spirits* was published at Winter Solstice, 2025 by Three Hands Press. Of this are 1,500 standard hardcover copies bound in red cloth with color wraps; 49 deluxe slipcased copies with marbled endpapers quarter bound in crimson goatskin; 28 special slipcased copies bound in full white goatskin with marbled endpapers & signed by the author, and a privately-distributed *Terra Olympi* edition of 7 copies in black goatskin, each of which is devoted a separate Olympic Spirit. A softcover edition was also released in an edition of 2,000 copies.

SCRIBÆ QVO MYSTERIVM FAMVLATVR